United Government and
Foreign Policy in Russia
1900–1914

# United Government and Foreign Policy in Russia 1900–1914

David MacLaren McDonald

Harvard University Press
Cambridge, Massachusetts
London, England
1992

This book is printed on acid-free paper, and its binding materials
have been chosen for strength and durability.

*Library of Congress Cataloging-in-Publication Data*
McDonald, David MacLaren, 1954–
United government and foreign policy in Russia, 1900–1914 / David
MacLaren McDonald.
p.  cm.
ISBN 0-674-92239-5
1. Soviet Union—Foreign relations—1894–1917.  2. Russo-Japanese
War, 1904–1905.  I. Title.
DK262.M44  1992
327.47—dc20
91-18993
CIP

For Lois and
to the memory of Gerhard Hildebrandt

# Acknowledgments

This study was sustained by financial, intellectual, and moral support. I was fortunate to have been funded by several organizations, to which I express my thanks: the Social Science Research Committee; the Maison des sciences de l'Homme, Paris; the Harriman Institute for the Advanced Study of the Soviet Union, at Columbia University; and the Association of Universities and Colleges of Canada, in Ottawa.

Intellectually, I am indebted above all to Leopold Haimson of Columbia University, an inspiring teacher, painstaking reader, and encouraging critic; like so many of his students, I have benefited greatly fron his attention and encouragement in the decade I have known him. I am also grateful for Marc Raeff's interest in and support for this project.

I should also like to thank István Deák at Columbia, B. V. Ananich and R. S. Ganelin in Leningrad, and V. I. Bovykin and Anatolii Georgiev in Moscow. Daniel Field and Walter Pintner offered helpful comments and suggestions for improvements. Of course, the mistakes that remain are in no way their responsibility. Much of my work is strongly informed by that of Frank Wcislo, who spent more hours than he would have liked in thrashing over various crises, autocratic and otherwise. I am also indebted to many friends and colleagues for all the discussions and arguments we had: Margaret Bearwood-Brummage, Dug Duggan, Burton Miller, Al Senn, Phil Swoboda, Dwight van Horn, Andy Verner, and Mark von Hagen.

Finally, thanks are due to those who, *nolens volens,* were compelled to live with the book and provided moral support at critical times—my parents, Al Pendleton, and, most of all, Lois, who saw how three years could last ten, and whose contribution to this work and my life would require another book to document properly. I dedicate this book to her and to the memory of a remarkable teacher, who first introduced me to the joys and challenges of studying Russia.

# Contents

United Government and
Foreign Policy in Russia
1900–1914

# Introduction

In 1904, Russia stumbled into war with Japan as the result of policies forced by Nicholas II and a group of personal advisers upon the minister of foreign affairs, the minister of war, and the minister of finances, S. Iu. Witte, who paid for his opposition with his ministerial portfolio in 1903. These and other officials saw this conflict as unnecessary and dangerous to internal order at a time of rising social unrest. Their worst fears were violently confirmed in the revolutions of 1905–1907, which almost overthrew the autocracy and transformed the nature of politics in imperial Russia.

The war with Japan and Russia's defeat hung over official and public life in Russia throughout the years that separated the revolution it spawned from the Great War. The terms "Tsushima" and "Mukden" entered discourse as evocations of the autocracy's bankruptcy. Moreover, the fashion in which the war and its origins were remembered by senior officials affected the foreign policy and "high politics" of late imperial Russia in ways that are often overlooked but that concerned the very bases of the autocratic order as it sought to reform itself in response to defeat abroad and revolution at home.

This book examines how memories of the war with Japan and its origins affected the course and making of Russian foreign policy from 1905 until 1914. After 1905 there was broad agreement among state officials and members of "society" alike—whatever their political orientation—that as in 1904, war abroad would bring the threat of renewed revolution at home. In official spheres, this perceived connection acted as arguably the most significant constraint on Russian policy at a time of growing instability in the Balkans, an area of special interest to official and nonofficial Russia. The link between the threat of complications abroad and domestic unrest was so compelling that after 1905 Russian statesmen sought to minimize by institutional means the risk of foreign entanglements. The most important such institution was the Council of Ministers, reformed in 1905 to act as a "United Government."

The council and its authoritative chairman were originally devised to unify a government riven by interministerial rivalries before 1905; it was felt that continued disarray would severely weaken state authority in the face of the threat presented by the elective State Duma that was ultimately granted in October 1905. However, the principle of United Government was invoked by successive chairmen—Witte, P. A. Stolypin, and V. N. Kokovtsev, in particular—to claim a role in the formation of the empire's foreign policy. This effort was of great importance to the future of the Russian state order, since it saw officials address the nature of their relationship with the sovereign emperor. As with foreign policy as a whole, the unification of government, the form it took, and its career until 1914 were all rooted in officials' responses to the prelude to the war with Japan.

Thus, the primary intent behind this book is to integrate the history of Russian foreign policy during these critical years into the growing discussion of the crisis confronting autocracy at the beginning of the twentieth century, as understood by senior imperial officials in particular. As a result, the picture of Russia's foreign relations offered here will be somewhat different from the prevailing interpretations in this often neglected area of Russian historiography.

Because of the nature of the concerns stated above, the treatment of foreign policy in the narrative is admittedly selective. The first part of the book deals with the origins of the war with Japan from the point of view of senior imperial statesmen and their attempts to come to terms with Nicholas's rejection of advice they felt it their professional duty to give, in favor of "upstarts" or "unofficial advisers" who encouraged Nicholas to believe that "bureaucrats" were usurping his autocratic power. The middle chapters discuss the lessons drawn from the prewar period as they were acted upon by the same statesmen Nicholas had ignored before 1904. The two most important of these lessons concerned the causal equation between foreign conflict and domestic strife, and the necessity of institutionally regulating relations between emperor and government, as embodied in the Council of Ministers reform. This reform emerges as a peculiarly "bureaucratic" response to problems confronting senior officials in 1902–1904, when Nicholas first rejected the counsel that many of them felt he was obliged to consult. The last part of the book examines the effort by successive council chairmen to integrate foreign policy formation into the purview of United Government, both for fear of domestic instability and out of a certain institutional logic that took hold as a semblance of routine reestablished itself during the years after 1907. This effort led to conflict, particularly between Stolypin and A. P. Izvolskii, but was ultimately decided in favor of United Government because of Nicholas's confidence in his assertive chairman. Ironically, Nicholas's growing mistrust of Stolypin's successor, Kokovtsev, and of the encroachments of cabinet rule on his power in general, undid both and helped create the conditions under which war suddenly became possible to contemplate in the summer of 1914.

I focus on those issues of importance in the general direction of Russian diplomacy before World War I whose resolution reflected the workings of autocracy. The view of the events treated here is that of actors within the imperial government, and particularly the Council of Ministers, rather than that of all statesmen concerned in any given issue. As a result, the treatment of the origins of the Russo-Japanese War or of the Bosnian crisis, for example, is more concerned with Russian officials' responses to events than with detailing the diplomatic negotiations arising from them.

Because of this focus, certain important determinants of foreign policy are omitted in the following discussion. The reader will find little on economic factors that influenced Russian foreign policy, or on military strategy, or, finally, on the increasing rigidity of the European state system and alliance structures in the years before the outbreak of the Great War. These have been amply discussed elsewhere.[1]

I have sought by this approach to incorporate the contributions of traditional diplomatic history into the literature on the history of the late empire, while proposing an alternative to treatments of Russian foreign policy that understand it as a variant of imperialism or of a social imperialism uniting domestic and foreign policies, based on comparisons with imperial Germany. The resulting work offers several new perspectives on the forces and concerns shaping Russian foreign policy in the years before the Great War.

While diplomatic histories have provided a clear account of the conduct of Russian diplomacy,[2] they have examined it in artificial separation from other developments within the empire, most notably the revolutions of 1905–1907, which are acknowledged only to the extent that they weakened Russia's political position in Europe. However, these works neglect to inquire how the revolutions and the reforms they evoked affected the procedures by which Russian foreign policy was decided. Instead, they state that foreign policy making was legally excluded from the institutional and legal reforms of 1905–1906—the emperor and his foreign minister continued as before to be the chief policy makers, to the exclusion of the Duma and more particularly of the Council of Ministers.

I shall argue that such a reading of these reforms dislodges them from the political contexts in which they were devised and fails to heed the way in which they were understood by those who drafted and implemented them. Moreover, there seems little evidence to suggest that these legal exclusions were felt by tsarist statesmen to be as binding as assumed by many historians of this period. Indeed, I propose that as a result of the reforms of 1905 and 1906, foreign policy ceased to be the exclusive province of the emperor and his foreign minister—if ever it was—and came to be governed to a larger extent by United Government and its chairman, who founded its claims to involvement in such matters on the necessity of coordinating *all* imperial policy in view of Russia's recently demonstrated domestic volatility, which could be reignited by external complications. As a result, in the place of a policy formed by consultation between the emperor and his foreign minister on the basis of more or less rational calculation, affected episodically by external and domestic events and actors, there emerges a policy governed to a larger extent by the exigencies of domestic reform through the increasing intervention of United Government. In addition, viewing Russia's post-revolutionary diplomacy as rooted in the lessons of the Asian war links on several levels two periods that are usually treated as discrete. New explanations emerge for the process and timing by which the Triple Entente took shape, much more gradually and for different reasons than is generally suggested. Finally, a new interpretation of Russia's Balkan policy is offered—one in which the origins of the Balkan alliances of 1912, and the decision to mobilize in 1914, are presented as the result of different considerations than is often argued.

While seeking to integrate Russian diplomacy into general conceptions of the empire's domestic life at a time of crisis, this analysis eschews the perspectives set forth by studies of Russia as an "imperialist" power. Recent studies are linked by the effort to place this policy in the context of one or another theory of imperialism—whether it is Lenin's notion of "Bonapartism" as the hallmark of Russian politics after 1907,[3] or one of the constructs set forth in German studies of the Kaiserreich under Wilhelm II.[4] While not denying the importance of structural or middle-term economic and social factors in guiding Russian foreign policy, I prefer to focus on the political mechanisms that mediated these broader forces and shaped in turn the outlooks of the actors who interpreted and responded to events in a much more specific context than these studies usually present.

Works based on theories of imperialism tend to proceed from an image of the central issues facing late imperial Russia that they have appropriated whole cloth from the late imperial intelligentsia. The most important of these is the historically irreconcilable relationship between "state" and "society."[5] From their various standpoints, these works present the state as trying to co-opt strategic elements of society through appeal to or acceptance of certain elements in a "national" agenda. The same processes of modernization that created these new social and political forces are seen as affecting materially Russia's definitions of its foreign goals. However, in making broader theoretical claims, these approaches often neglect the finer mechanics of causation and overlook the fact that imperial statesmen were highly reluctant to cede any voice at all to society in matters of foreign policy. While public opinion played an episodic role in discussion of foreign policy, as a state matter (*gosudarstvennoe delo*) such issues could be considered only by professional officials responsible to His Imperial Majesty.

The examination of United Government's role in foreign policy casts a revealing light on this last relationship (between the ruler and his highest official servitors), which serves as one of the central themes in this book, for it was precisely this relationship that came under question during the prelude to the war with Japan. The emergence of this issue bore upon the viability of the autocratic order in the early twentieth century and contributed to what has come to be called, appropriately, the "crisis of autocracy."[6]

The workings of this often overlooked relationship point to another element in the general crisis confronting autocracy in these years: the attempt by tsarist statesmen to define, through the creation of United Government, their political and institutional relations with the source of their authority—the sovereign emperor, Nicholas II. These attempts—undertaken in turn by Witte, Stolypin, and Kokovtsev—saw the extension to the highest administrative instances of a debate that had long been evolving within imperial officialdom. The central issue in this discussion was the nature of autocratic power—specifically, the degree to which it was personal and literally absolute in the hands of the tsar, and the extent to which it was bound by law. Before 1900, this debate had concerned relations between state and society. After the turn of the century, bureaucrats' attention was drawn to the figure of the sovereign himself.

The problem was defined by Minister of Finances Witte in 1900,[7] when he argued that the tsar's autocratic power was not totally unlimited; if it were, there would be no laws, "but rather a chaotic administration." Instead, "[t]he tsar is autocratic because it depends upon him to impart action to the machine, but since the tsar is a man, he needs the machine for the administration of a country of 130 million subjects, as his human strength cannot replace the machine."

Witte's was but the most succinct statement of a question that had concerned Russian administrators since the early 1880s,[8] and it assumed increasing significance in all areas, including foreign policy, before 1914. By 1900, many Russian officials had come to view the emperor as the fount of power and authority in the political order they served, while expecting him to honor the procedural dictates of—and their places within—the "machine" that was in place to mediate that power.

Several factors influenced the effort to define the relationship between state and ruler. There was the personality of Nicholas II and his views of his power and the government through which he exercised it.[9] In addition, Nicholas was served by a senior administration in which a variety of attitudes prevailed as to the nature of autocracy and the autocrat's ties to the machinery of state. These attitudes were in turn an amalgam of conflicting impulses: on the one hand, fealty to autocratic power as the source of the state's role in an empire defined by its national diversity and grouped into particularistic estates *(sosloviia);* on the other, a developing bureaucratic outlook or *mentalité,*[10] stressing professionalism, routine, and procedure as the hallmarks of good government, as opposed to the arbitrariness *(proizvol)* of personal rule.[11] The tensions between these outlooks, both of which defined autocracy in different instances, went unapprehended as long as they were seriously challenged by neither the Emperor nor civil society, which was becoming more self-assertive by the end of the nineteenth century. But they came increasingly to the consciousness of imperial officials when Nicholas began to flout long-held expectations in the period before the war with Japan, followed by the eruption of revolution in 1905.

Within this framework of crosscutting long-term and immediate causes, Russian officials faced two sets of tasks after 1905. They were forced to find a means by which to reconcile their own notion of autocratic power as the sole source of legitimate authority with the claims of society for a self-determining "nation" as the basis of Russian political existence. In the case of statesmen like Witte, perhaps, and Stolypin, certainly,[12] the two worldviews even assumed an uneasy if temporary coexistence. At the same time, they were hindered by the nature of their relationship with Nicholas II. Given Nicholas's power, this relationship necessarily consisted of both personal and institutional elements. As long as they were assured of Nicholas's "confidence" *(doverie)*—a notion with personal and institutional attributes—statesmen could act authoritatively with their colleagues in the bureaucracy and with the representatives of society. However, Nicholas's confidence was notoriously unstable, as successive statesmen found before and after 1905.

The role of this relationship was central to the history of the survival of the imperial order.[13] Efforts by statesmen to define their relationship with Nicholas II were a central aspect of the crisis of autocracy. Crucial to the failure of these efforts was the inability—itself a product of their ties to the "political culture" of autocracy, for lack of a better expression—to separate the person of Nicholas II from his role as the embodiment of sovereign power in the Russian state.

The years after 1905 can be seen as an attempt, initiated by Witte on the basis of his experience before 1903, to impose the obligation on Nicholas to rule exclusively through his "machine." The institutional vessel of this attempt was United Government—the creation of a cabinet headed by a powerful chairman, or premier. The career of this institution was itself a reflection of deeper-lying crises atop the imperial order. As many critics understood, and as Nicholas eventually came to agree, a unified cabinet headed by an authoritative chairman constituted at the very least a tacit limit on the emperor's power; this was recognized in the memorandum on which the council reform was based.[14] Because they concerned the state's *raison d'être* and officials' authority and professional identity, these implications were addressed only intermittently and often indirectly.

However, the "Russianness" of the means by which they sought to achieve this goal is indicated by the methods by which they promoted it. Each chairman's ability to impose his vision of the government's role rested ultimately on the emperor's confidence. When in favor, a chairman could be very successful, as long as he did not encroach on areas outside his purview. When not, his efforts to unify policy were doomed. The importance of Nicholas's confidence is indicated in the relative success of each council chairman in bringing the "excluded" ministries under council scrutiny. What is most interesting is that neither Witte, Stolypin, nor Kokovtsev—the most effective council chairmen—saw any paradox in the fact that their efforts to impose some sort of institutional rationality on the operations of the machine hinged ultimately on their personal relationship with Nicholas. Indeed, each emphasized the instrumentality of that relationship for their own institutional and political goals and accepted Nicholas as the source of all power mediated by the machine, since without Nicholas there could be no machine.

Nicholas's attitude toward the reforms and toward his government as a potential threat to his power was thus always key to the success of United

Government. The unpredictability of the emperor, and the fractiousness of the society and *narod* over which he ruled, created an atmosphere of instability. This instability only strengthened the urge of statesmen to bring foreign policy, the quintessential attribute of the emperor's sovereignty, under council control. For this reason, an examination of foreign policy decision making affords two perspectives: one on the pressures "from below" on "high politics" after 1905; and the second on how the system itself was viewed by officials and, tacitly, the emperor at a time of crisis within the empire and abroad. In the end, the shape that was to be taken by the autocracy depended on Nicholas himself; by 1914 he had shown his own limits for accepting reform—at the cost of a growing lack of confidence among the officials upon whom he still relied.

# · 1 ·

# The Witte Kingdom
# in the Far East

Rarely has a war been greeted with the lack of enthusiasm that met the Russian declaration of war on Japan in January 1904. In his memoirs Sergei Iulevich Witte, who long dominated Russian policy in the Far East, was struck by popular apathy toward the war. On the morrow of the war's outbreak, there was a "rather depressing" mass at the Winter Palace. Afterward, as the emperor was passing, a nearby general tried to elicit a cheer from the crowd: "this 'Hurrah' was supported by only a few voices."[1] Officials, including Witte, had opposed Emperor Nicholas's insistence on policies that they feared might provoke conflict with Japan. War Minister General A. N. Kuropatkin had often contended that too many resources were being expended in the Far East. Such efforts, he felt, were misplaced and even dangerous to Russia's vital interests, the "maintenance of domestic peace and order" and the defense of the western border.[2] By 1903, he worried that war in the Far East could "break the Russian Empire."[3] Such fears were widespread in official circles as domestic unrest grew throughout the empire.

The war itself would be fought in a distant hinterland, connected to the metropolis by an uncompleted railway through forbidding terrain. Action would occur in China, the hostility of whose populace had been vividly demonstrated during the Boxer Uprising of 1900. Russian agents in the area had since done little to assuage local ill-will. Indeed, when war came Russian troops occupied much of Manchuria in violation of a treaty proposed by the Russian government and signed in March 1902. Worse, the Russian government was unprepared for a war, despite Japan's frequent protests over Russian activity in Manchuria and Korea.[4] Japan's bombardment of Port Arthur on 25 January surprised officials in St. Petersburg and in Port Arthur itself. Moreover, the advent of war found Russia diplomatically isolated in the Far East. While Japan was allied with Great Britain, France had refused to recognize Asian conflicts as a *casus foederis* for the Dual Alliance.

Over the next eighteen months Russian land and naval forces sustained a series of defeats, culminating in the destruction in the Straits of Tsushima of the last disposable portion of the Russian navy. Hostilities concluded in the summer of 1905, with Russo-Japanese talks in the United States brokered by Theodore Roosevelt. The lenient terms of the Treaty of Portsmouth did not disguise the enormity of Russia's setback. In Russia, defeat brought in its train mounting unrest. Tsushima symbolized the bankruptcy of a state structure already assailed by workers' strikes, peasant unrest, growing liberal calls for reform and, finally, revolution.

Defeat in Asia had not been foreseen, but many Russian officials had feared the domestic consequences of an unpopular war. Although the origins of this war have been discussed in diplomatic and strategic perspectives,[5] few have examined these events in the context in which they were placed by Russian officials of the time, who saw them as part of a mounting social and political crisis in Russia.[6] In 1900, Witte explicitly addressed an important aspect of this crisis in a letter to a fellow minister:

> You say: the tsar is autocratic—he creates laws for his subjects, but not for himself. I—I am nothing—only a reporter, the tsar will decide, ergo no rules are needed; he who demands rules wishes to limit the tsar; he who doubts the correctness of decisions fears that the tsar will decide matters incorrectly . . .
>
> [This means that] each minister will contend *as convincingly as you* that he needs no laws at all, for he is only an executor, while the tsar decides. But then there would be no autocracy, but rather a chaotic administration. The tsar is autocratic because it depends upon him to impart action to the machine, but since the tsar is a man, he needs the machine for the administration of a country of 130 million subjects, as his human strength cannot replace the machine.[7]

The political hinge joining the emperor and his government was the ruler's *doverie,* often rendered as "confidence" or "trust." This term reflects the ambiguous nature of the authority emanating from the emperor, which combined personal and institutional elements.[8] One memoirist attributed Witte's success under Alexander III to his enjoyment of that ruler's "particular confidence."[9] In 1902, an official lamented "the Sovereign's mistrust [*nedoverie*] of the ministers . . . If he does not trust [*doveriaet*] one or another minister, then he must replace him."[10]

The years before the Russo-Japanese War witnessed the emergence of an often overlooked crisis in Russian government. Its symptoms were Nicholas II's increasing assertiveness in government accompanied by the increased influence of "unofficial advisers"[11]—figures such as Monsieur Philippe, Nicholas's brother-in-law Grand Duke Alexander Mikhailovich, and most important, "Bezobrazov and Co.," who played a key role in events leading to the Russo-Japanese War by interesting Nicholas in the political potential of timber concessions they held on the Yalu river in Korea. "Favorites" had been fixtures in Russian courts through the reign of Alexander I. By any legal standard, it was the autocrat's prerogative to rule through whom he pleased. However, Nicholas's sudden assertion of that prerogative threw many officials into a quandary, challenging expectations—ingrained through socialization and long practice—that they ought to be the exclusive mediators of the ruler's power. The favorites had their own view. In traditional conservative rhetoric, the most articulate of them decried the bureaucracy as an unnatural barrier between the emperor and his people. They urged Nicholas to wrest his power from the officials who had usurped it and to rule as a personal autocrat.

The resulting struggle in the highest councils of Russian government lasted until well into 1904. One of the central arenas for this contest was Russian policy in the Far East. Here, the "triumvirate" of Witte, Kuropatkin, and Foreign Minister V. N. Lamzdorf contended with "Bezobrazov and Co." Each sought Nicholas's support by attacking their adversaries as usurpers or interlopers, respectively. The Bezobrazov group's success and other developments by late 1903 led many officials to wonder whether Nicholas had any confidence in his government. The outcome of this struggle was critical for the autocratic order. In the short term, it led to an unwanted war. In the long term, the experience of the prewar years deeply impressed itself on the officials who felt they had lost to Bezobrazov and Co. and to Nicholas. They blamed the war for the eruption of revolution in the empire. Following the disasters of 1902–1905, the problems of domestic order, confidence, and foreign policy formation were intertwined in the minds of statesmen. Their views on the origins of the Russo-Japanese War stand as a necessary prologue to the political order and foreign policies of the postrevolutionary order.

## Sergei Witte and the Creation of the Kingdom, 1892–1900

At the turn of the century, Witte was unquestionably the dominant figure in Russian politics. Appointed minister of finances in 1892, he had aggressively extended his ministry's activities into such diverse areas as industrial development, rural economy, and local administration. The vigor and scope of these interests represented a marked departure from the narrowly economic concerns of Witte's predecessors. In the late 1890s, his authority had increased markedly with triumphs in bitter controversies over Russia's conversion to the gold standard and the role of the *zemstvo*.

Nowhere were Witte's influence and authority so entrenched as along the Trans-Siberian Railway and its branches in China. Construction on the trunk had begun under Witte's direction in the early 1890s. In 1896, the rail route was altered significantly when Witte engineered an agreement with the Chinese government for a shortcut through northern Manchuria and Mongolia.[12] From Harbin in Manchuria, a branch-line stretched to the harbors of Port Arthur and Dalnii (Talienwan) on the Liaotung peninsula. This area and the adjoining coastland formed the Kwantung Lease Territory, which had come under Russian control in 1898.

Virtually all activity on these lands—rail construction, commerce, administration—took place under the control of the Ministry of Finances (MF). The Chinese Eastern Railway Company (CER) oversaw the construction and operation of lines in Manchuria. CER merchant ships plied Manchurian rivers. The company had also amassed mining, telegraphs, and forestry concessions in the region.[13] The CER had close financial ties with the Russo-Chinese Bank, which enjoyed exclusive privileges in financing Russian enterprise in Manchuria. Both the railway and the bank were virtually wholly owned subsidiaries of the MF. A ministry "security guard" protected Russian interests in the area; this contingent was known as "Matilda's guard" in ironic honor of Witte's wife.

In the Far East, Witte even conducted his own foreign policy. It was Witte with whom the Chinese negotiated. Other governments sought his views on Russian interests in China.[14] He monitored Manchurian and Chinese affairs through a wide network of informants. CER administrators reported to him from Harbin. In Peking, he had a capable agent in his protege D. D. Pokotilov, the Russo-Chinese Bank agent and MF representative in the Russian embassy.[15] According to A. P. Izvolskii, Russia's envoy in Japan at the time, the MF attachés throughout the Far East constituted a separate foreign ministry whose agents corresponded secretly with Witte and "did not scruple to accept and maintain political ideas that were opposed to those of the official Russian diplomacy."[16]

Witte's sources even extended into Chinese government. He had a mutually profitable relationship with Li Hun-chan, a senior statesman in the Chinese foreign ministry. Li often expedited the resolution of diplomatic issues between the two states and had played a key role in gaining Chinese approval for the Manchurian diversion. He was rewarded for these services with liberal disbursements from the Russo-Chinese Bank.[17] A report in 1903 totalled the resources Witte had directed to the Siberian-Manchurian enterprise.[18] In 1897 income from the railway's concession area was 9.6 million rubles, while 92.7 million rubles were spent on the route and its logistical support. By 1900 these totals had increased to 21.9 million and 263.6 million rubles, respectively.

Contemporaries appreciated the extent of Witte's sway over the area. Izvolskii wrote, "taking Cecil Rhodes as a model, and copying his role as an 'Empire Builder', Count Witte made of this zone, which was subject to the exclusive control of his ministry, a domain over which he ruled with quasi-autocratic powers."[19] Another official alluded to Witte's "veritable kingdom in the Far East."[20] Both cited the railway administration and the security guard as symbols of Witte's sovereignty in Manchuria.[21] Witte's kingdom was regarded as part of the general aggrandizement of his institutional activity throughout Russia. Kuropatkin accused Witte of having "formed in his own ministry subsections of the other Ministries, such as Ways and Communications, War, Navy, Interior, Agriculture, and Foreign Affairs."[22] Izvolskii wrote in a similar vein of Witte's "State within a State," which duplicated other state agencies, while "deriving their powers directly and solely from this Minister." He felt constrained to add that these organs "were better organized, performed their functions more perfectly, and were imbued with a broader and more modern spirit than the corresponding Government services."[23] Witte's success also provoked harsher criticism, put most succinctly by V. M. Vonliarliarskii—one of the group known as "Bezobrazov and Co." Writing in 1910, he charged that "the direction of our Far Eastern policy was not confided to him, but was seized by himself willfully, or, say rather, usurped."[24] Regardless of their opinions, virtually all observers agreed on Witte's predominance in government by the end of the 1890s.[25]

Sergei Iulevich Witte had followed an unusual career for a senior Russian official.[26] Although the son of a career official he had come late to state service. Witte was already forty years of age when he joined the Ministry of Finances in 1889, following almost two decades of service as an executive in joint-venture railway companies in Malorossiia.[27] His abilities had brought him to the attention of officials in St. Petersburg.[28] Originally reluctant to incur the financial loss entailed by transfer to state service, Witte claimed to have been swayed by the stated wishes of Alexander III.[29] The emperor demonstrated his confidence in the newcomer when he named Witte minister of finances in 1892 after a brief stint as minister of ways and communications. He brought to MF a radically new vision of his ministry's role in Russia's economic and social development. Based on his reading of Friedrich List and on his view of the autocratic state, Witte's approach embodied a breadth and complexity that transcended what he dismissed as the narrow "departmentalism" of most officials.

The breadth of Witte's administrative outlook had been apparent in his original plan for the Siberian railway.[30] He envisioned the project as a truly great "matter of state," which would resolve many of the problems facing Russia. Overcrowding in rural Russia, painfully demonstrated in the recent famine, could be alleviated by state-organized settlement of the lands opened up by the railway. Construction of the line would stimulate heavy industry by creating demand for rails and rolling stock, and could be supported by trade in the markets to be created by the railway as it extended through the newly settled lands. A Siberian route could compete with the Suez Canal for the shipment of Chinese exports and imports, benefiting foreign trade. And Russian manufacturers would have advantageous access to the Chinese market. To direct this vast project, Witte had suggested the creation of a Siberian Railway Committee to circumvent potential obstructions by individual ministers; it would include representatives of interested ministries and a chairman to be named by the emperor.[31] Alexander III named his heir Nicholas to chair the committee, apparently at Witte's urging.[32] Nicholas had an interest in Siberia and the Far East dating to his travels there in the early 1890s.[33]

Witte's ministerial fiefdom in Asia had grown less by design than by his ability to adapt to changing circumstances. The arrangements binding the CER and the Russo-Chinese Bank to his ministry had been cobbled together following China's defeat in the Sino-Japanese War of 1895, when Witte had seen the opportunity for the Manchurian shortcut. To secure Chinese agreement to his plan, he arranged a loan for China's indemnity payments to Japan. The vehicle for the transfer of these funds was provided by the Russo-Chinese Bank. Finally, to overcome Chinese resistance to a foreign railway on Chinese territory, Witte had created the ostensibly private CER, whose shares had been bought up by the Russian Treasury. The Chinese official whose objections had been thus overcome was Li Hunchan.[34]

However, Witte's improvisational skill was also grounded in the departmentalism he claimed to deplore. His manipulations concentrated in his hands all levers for Russian policy in Manchuria. As events proceeded in an increasingly unstable Far Eastern political environment, Witte would sometimes find it difficult to persuade colleagues, and his ruler, that his ministry's and Russia's interests were congruent.

Witte's dominance of imperial political life also owed much to his success in the ministerial competition that was endemic to a system under the rule of a literally sovereign emperor. Given the emperor's absolute power, many factors—policy direction, institutional interests, and personality—overlapped in ministers' pursuit of the authority necessary to implement a given policy. This situation arose from the mutual isolation of ministries, which were individually responsible to the emperor. Since all authority flowed from the emperor, the critical task was to gain his confidence. This confidence armed the favored minister with the authority to ignore the jurisdictional boundaries separating individual ministries and spurred a particularly influential minister to seek to include as many areas as possible under his jurisdiction.[35] As a result, ministerial conflict was an inherent attribute of St. Petersburg political life. More important, this system guaranteed the emperor's autocratic power by making him the sole arbiter in all disputes. If any forces united this fissiparous ministerial structure, it was the unquestioned assumption that all authority flowed exclusively from the person of the sovereign.

The emperor's arbitrary power was often praised as the distinctive attribute of autocracy, ensuring that no one minister could usurp the power bequeathed to the tsar by God, dynasty, or history. The integrity and legitimacy of the autocratic order were held to depend on the exclusivity of the sovereign's power. This outlook had deep roots in Russian political thought. Its persistence until the end of the *ancien régime* reflected the logic used to reconcile the conflicting impulses underlying the mediation of autocratic power through a bureaucratic administration. Even Witte, who was often seen as a bureaucratic usurper, upheld the emperor's personal will as the motive force necessary to impart activity to the machine through which he governed. In fact, none of Witte's talents would have been realizable had it he not been able to cultivate a strong relationship with Nicholas II after the latter's accession in 1894. This relationship was the basis of all Witte's political success and, ironically, led to his political downfall in 1903.

Historians have long found Nicholas a conundrum.[36] The emperor who initiated the Hague Peace Conference also led Russia into two disastrous wars. The sworn upholder of autocracy, Nicholas promulgated the October Manifesto. Praised for his courtesy and grace, he was criticized for his inconstancy and his indecisiveness. Memoirs, diaries, and even political caricatures reflect the tensions within his character.

Nicholas came to the throne unexpectedly at the age of twenty-six, following the death of Alexander III in 1894. He was initially terrified at the prospect of ruling.[37] Nicholas's reaction was understandable; he had received little training in rulership. In addition, Alexander III harbored a low opinion of his son's capabilities[38]—a view shared by veteran officials who knew him[39]—and the two had clashed over Nicholas's inattention to his duties as tsarevich.[40] In his early reign, Nicholas struggled with the contrasts of character and appearance between himself and his father.[41] A physically powerful man, Alexander had ruled as *paterfamilias* over his household, the Romanov clan, and the empire with a firm, almost unconscious assurance in himself and his position as a personal autocrat. Although a reactionary, he confounded conservatives in such acts as his elevation of the *parvenu* Witte and the conclusion of the Dual Alliance with republican France.[42]

Nicholas was neither as physically imposing nor as self-assured as his father. If Alexander had ruled by temperament, Nicholas felt a personal distance from the new role that had befallen him.[43] He came to terms with these contrasts by adulating his father as the apotheosis of autocracy, a repository of all the attributes to which he himself aspired. One result of Nicholas's diffidence was a notorious indecisiveness. As one diarist noted, people said of the tsar, "that he has no character, that he agrees with each of his ministers in spite of the fact that they report the opposite of one another."[44] This behavior lent an increasingly bitter cast to policy debates as his reign wore on.

Related to Nicholas's indecisiveness was his aversion to controversy. His relations with his uncles, his cousin Wilhelm II, and many of his ministers were marked by a tendency to relent before strongly stated disagreement. His wife, Alexandra, upbraided him for this, advising him to "be firm . . . don't let others forget who you are."[45] Yet, however he felt about being tsar, Nicholas was jealous of the power he had inherited. He never decided precisely what his power as autocrat consisted in, but as much as anything, he saw it as a dynastic legacy which he was duty-bound to bequeath inviolate to his heir.[46] He was uncomfortable under the burden of sovereign power, but it was *his* burden to be borne alone. To protect this power, he often encouraged or tolerated divisions among his advisers, reserving to himself the role of ultimate arbiter.

He also achieved this position indirectly, avoiding the inevitable disputes that went with his position by allowing one minister to predominate among his colleagues. He thus found relief from the burdens of rulership, while diverting controversy from himself to the currently prevailing minister. Given the nature of bureaucratic politics, opposition would inevitably mount against the favored official, often taking the form of accusations that he had usurped the tsar's own power. To undercut an ascendant figure, others in Nicholas's court would urge him to reclaim his power from the overweening servant. By indulging such appeals or by telling individual interlocutors what they wanted to hear, he abetted a process through which there emerged several "Nicholases," each embodying a different ideal of autocratic power. As a result, the nature of the ruler's role as sovereign became an issue of debate among the various competing groups and individuals at the apex of Russian political life, while the notion of autocracy as a whole was under increasingly effective attack from outside the corridors of power.

Both patterns were evident in the trajectory of Nicholas's relationship with Witte, and later with P. A. Stolypin. Nicholas developed a reliance upon each minister, relinquishing almost total prerogative to him. Gradually, he came to resent the reliance he had fostered and would heed accusations that the minister was usurping his autocratic power, after which he undercut his erstwhile deputy.

Until 1902 Witte worked well with Nicholas. Witte's forcefulness, the breadth of his interests, and his close association with Alexander III inclined the young ruler to the finance minister. Witte also knew how to ingratiate himself with his master through adroit defenses of autocratic power.[47] Their relationship was especially close in Far Eastern policy, in which Witte had encouraged Nicholas's interest while the latter was still tsarevich.

This relationship was not entirely secure against the vagaries of bureaucratic politics, however. The growth of Witte's kingdom had brought him into conflict with the Ministry of Foreign Affairs (Ministerstvo Inostrannykh Del, MID), beginning with the decision to build the Manchurian diversion over MID's objections.[48] After having benefited from MID neglect or ignorance of Far Eastern issues,[49] Witte clashed with Minister of Foreign Affairs M. N. Muravev over Nicholas's decision in late 1897 to support Muravev's proposal for a Russian seizure of Port Arthur on the Chinese coast, despite Witte's vociferous objections.[50] This decision was Witte's first significant setback in Far Eastern policy. Witte's contempt for Muravev only sharpened the insult.[51] In early 1898, Witte asked Nicholas's permission to resign his post. Nicholas rejected this request, telling Witte, meaningfully, that he had confidence in him as minister of finance.[52]

Russian troops landed in Port Arthur in December 1897, leading to a protracted impasse as the Chinese government rejected Russian demands for the harbor and other privileges. But China's position was weakened by its need to meet the next Japanese indemnity payment. A resolution was suggested in February 1898 by the new war minister, General Kuropatkin, who proposed that a Russian loan to China be made conditional upon the granting of a lease on the southern Liaotung peninsula.[53] A branch from the Siberian railway could link the area to Russia. These terms were presented in Peking on 19 February,[54] but Russia lost its chief source of pressure when the Chinese government acquired a loan from a German-British group.[55]

At this juncture, Witte accepted the *fait accompli* of the seizure and proceeded to prove his worth to Nicholas by operating the political levers at his disposal.[56] He instructed Pokotilov to bribe Li Hun-chan and other officials to use their influence in favor of the lease proposal.[57] The agreement creating a Kwantung Lease Territory was duly signed on 15 March.[58] Witte thus earned Nicholas's "gratitude"[59] and demonstrated his indispensability in Far Eastern matters.[60] By July, Witte had consolidated his position with agreements extending the CER concession through southern Manchuria to the lease territory and giving the company control of Chinese customs in Talienwan, now renamed Dalnii.[61]

Witte's rivalry with Muravev was vexing, but his resolution of the Port Arthur imbroglio had demonstrated his superior ability in Far Eastern questions. He had reestablished his position with Nicholas, while saving his administrative kingdom from the ill effects he had anticipated from the decision to take Port Arthur. Witte's response to this challenge also showed the capacity for improvisation that had allowed him to build his kingdom in the first place. From the beginning of the Siberian project, Witte had reshaped the enterprise to take advantage of new circumstances, leading to the Manchurian diversion, the formation of the CER, and now the acquisition of Kwantung, which became the outlet for his ministry's enterprises in Manchuria. These improvisations also forestalled any possible suspicion of Witte's ascendancy from Nicholas, who had ratified piecemeal proposals instead of having to approve Witte's "empire" at one stroke.

However, the Port Arthur episode forced Russian officials to confront concern from other powers over the changes in the Chinese status quo. One result of this concern was a Russo-British agreement, signed in April 1899, which named the Great Wall as the boundary between their respective spheres of influence.[62] Witte had objected to this agreement as unnecessary, since Russia was "sated"[63] after gaining Port Arthur, but his real fear was that it would limit the Russo-Chinese Bank's sphere of operations.[64] These objections were overridden by Muravev and Kuropatkin, who contended that the new environment in China demanded agreement with Britain.[65] For Witte, there was consolation in British recognition of Russia's railway monopoly in Manchuria.

By the same token, the events from 1897 to 1899 obliged Witte to consider the international implications of his Far Eastern venture. The Manchurian shortcut had been an opportunistic decision to exploit temporary Chinese weakness, with little regard for other ramifications. After the taking of Port Arthur, Witte faced two threats to his kingdom: challenges to his control of Far Eastern policy from rivals in government; and foreign apprehension about Russian designs in China, based partly on the wide net of interests Witte had cast over Manchuria. Both threats materialized with the outbreak of the Boxer Uprising in the summer of 1900.

## Bureaucratic Politics and Far Eastern Policy, 1900–1902

After flurries of unrest in the spring of 1900,[66] violence in China became sufficiently serious by June that European governments began to form an international brigade to defend their legations in Peking.[67] Russia's role in this brigade became a problem, given the extent of its material interests in many of the areas affected by the rebellion. Significantly, Muravev now agreed with Witte on the need for friendly Russo-Chinese relations,[68] and advised Nicholas that in the interests of good relations with China, Russian actions in China should be limited and explained to other powers as a necessary protective measure.

In the midst of this deteriorating situation, Muravev suddenly died. His replacement was Count Lamzdorf, a longtime functionary in MID. Regarded as diligent, and exceptionally well-versed in the workings of his ministry, Lamzdorf was also seen as Witte's man.[69] Indeed, Witte took credit for this appointment;[70] a friend noted that he was "anxious" for Lamzdorf to succeed Muravev "because he himself would then, he believed, be able to exert a general directing influence over the entire business of the Tsardom."[71] Izvolskii wrote that Witte sought in Lamzdorf "an instrument entirely obedient to his will"; Lamzdorf "let himself be dominated in all matters by his great friend, and thereupon the two Ministries of Finance and Foreign Affairs were merged . . . in one and the same person."[72] While he now had an ally instead of a rival in MID, the spread of the rebellion into Manchuria confronted Witte with a new competitor, Minister of War Kuropatkin.

Witte and Lamzdorf wished to avoid for as long as possible a Russian military intervention in China for the sake of Russo-Chinese relations.[73] Witte also seemed interested in averting the threat to his ministerial interests in the Russian troops in Manchuria. Throughout June, Witte reinforced the security guards on the CER; he also requested the commandant of the Kwantung Lease Territory not to send troops into Manchuria unless requested to by him or the CER director.[74] Informing Kuropatkin of this request, Witte explained that he wished to avoid any incidents that could harm relations between CER officials and Manchurian authorities. By late June it was becoming clear that Witte's policy was failing. As rebellion spread, CER workers were ordered to Harbin.

On 26 June, Russian troops advanced into Manchuria,[75] a triumph for Kuropatkin, who had advocated forceful response to the rebellion. His impatience to "have done with Peking" had led Lamzdorf to protest to Nicholas that the general's attitude contradicted established policy.[76] In mid-July, Witte complained that Kuropatkin was exceeding his authority, conducting diplomatic negotiations, and forcing Russia too far into China. Witte had had to tell him "that he is the M[inister] of W[ar], not MID or MF, and that therefore he should appoint generals in our stead, or he should not step outside his role."[77] Later, Witte stated that "Lamzdorf and I fear Kuropatkin more than the Chinese." He lamented that Kuropatkin "stays very late with the Sovereign, taken up with war-games on the map."[78] Kuropatkin's access to the emperor was as galling to Witte as the presence of Russian regulars in Manchuria and exacerbated preexisting tensions between the two ministers.[79]

Witte had initially felt that the revolt would subside of its own accord before foreign forces could reach China.[80] As unrest continued unabated, however, Kuropatkin convinced Nicholas to send Russian troops from Kwantung to Peking, which was reached in early August.[81] Russian forces also moved from Kwantung into southern Manchuria and from Siberia into the CER zone in northern Manchuria,[82] where they suppressed popular disturbances through the autumn. By mid-August the entire CER returned to Russian control after interruptions due to rebel activity; service through southern Manchuria was restored by late September.[83]

Russian action had been decisive and extensive. By October, the Kwantung Lease Territory was under martial law, Russian troops were in Peking, and detachments were deployed in every major population center along the CER and the branch to Port Arthur, including Mukden, home of the Manchu dynasty. These actions caught Lamzdorf and Witte by surprise; Kuropatkin had said earlier that an invasion would not occur until at least September.[84] Again, Witte sought to make the best of a bad lot by suggesting to Nicholas that the occupied regions be pacified and evacuated as quickly as possible.[85] In addition to seeking the restoration of his control in Manchuria, Witte worried about the effects of Kuropatkin's actions on relations with Japan and Korea, and with Li Hun-chan, whom he had contacted in July.[86]

Thus, barely two months after Muravev's death, Witte faced a more redoubtable competitor in Far Eastern issues. Whereas Muravev had relied on diplomacy and on Witte's cooperation, Kuropatkin's command of the army gave him much more ability to act. Moreover, Kuropatkin was an imposing figure, hero of the conquest of Bukhara and a distinguished veteran of the Russo-Turkish War. Nicholas was inclined to him and the war ministry by the traditional Romanov interest in military affairs and his own happy memories of military service.[87] Witte was pragmatic enough to recognize the necessity of a *modus vivendi* with Kuropatkin. Still, this accommodation rankled, and Witte continued to seek ways to restore his dominance in Far Eastern policy. The political framework for the two ministers' rivalry was established in a circular note from Lamzdorf to interested governments on 12 August.[88] This note declared Russia's support for Chinese territorial integrity and a stable Chinese government. It also announced that Russia would seek a separate accord with China in matters of mutual concern, including the evacuation of Manchuria and the repair of the railway.

Shortly thereafter, Witte and Lamzdorf gained Kuropatkin's grudging agreement to an evacuation of Manchuria as soon as order was reestablished and the railway had been secured.[89] The Russian mission and troops in Peking were transferred to Tientsin in preparation for negotiations with a legal Chinese government. This decision was less Witte's victory than a consequence of Russian embarrassment at the rapacity with which the Russian component of the international contingent had subdued its sector of Peking.

The "separate agreement" was initially stalled by the lack of properly empowered Chinese government representatives.[90] To stabilize the CER concession areas in the meantime, the three ministers cooperated in arranging through their Manchurian representatives temporary accords with local authorities in October and November 1900.[91] These attached to each governor war ministry and MID agents, who vetted all new gubernatorial appointments.[92] The agreements were to stay in effect until a formal accord was reached with the Chinese government.

The months from August 1900 until March 1902 saw continuing disorder in Manchuria, dispute in St. Petersburg, and an international situation that increasingly restricted Russian room for maneuver in Manchuria. Witte and Kuropatkin continued to recommend diverging views on stabilizing and securing Russian holdings in the occupied provinces. Lamzdorf mediated this dispute and alerted his colleagues to important changes in the Far Eastern political environment, which were sufficiently compelling to foster a consensus between Witte and Kuropatkin, as reflected in the final Russo-Chinese agreement that was signed in March 1902.

The two ministers' disagreement was rooted in their differing institutional interests and experiences in Manchuria and China. As war minister, Kuropatkin defined his task as the defense of Russian interests in a foreign territory with a hostile populace.[93] To perform this task and to impose order on the restive Manchurian population, Kuropatkin insisted on Russian control over local Chinese authorities to be enforced by the maintenance of a military occupation for as long as possible.[94] Ideally, Kuropatkin sought the annexation of at least northern Manchuria as the only reliable guarantee for the security of Russian interests and subjects in China.[95]

Broad contacts and an institutional foothold in China and Manchuria inclined Witte to take a different view of the situation. The recent unrest forced him to accept at least a temporary Russian military presence to protect the CER in Manchuria, but it also challenged his previous control over Russian activity in the area.[96] His recommendations seemed directed as much toward ridding the area of Kuropatkin's troops as toward the restoration of good relations with China. He sought in both respects to reestablish the *status quo ante* for the CER and even to expand the company's holdings in Manchuria.[97] Witte argued that the success of the CER and associated enterprises showed the Chinese government's amity for Russia. Thus, as a gesture of Russian goodwill, he advocated a phased evacuation of Manchuria, to be completed when the CER was opened for regular traffic;[98] afterward, the CER security force could defend the railway lands.

The effort to conclude the "separate agreement" with China consumed thirteen months, from the initial presentation of a Russian draft accord to the Chinese government in February 1901 until the conclusion of a Russo-Chinese treaty in March 1902. In the interval, the original Russian demands were considerably diluted. The Russian government had sought control over troop numbers and Chinese administrative personnel in Manchuria, in addition to a considerable indemnity for material damages from the Boxer Uprising and its suppression, as a condition for evacuating the occupied territories.[99] But these terms were modified in the face two concerns that increasingly frustrated Russian ability to make such demands.

The first of these was the growing cost entailed by the ongoing occupation,[100] and it served gradually to drive Witte and Kuropatkin into a rough consensus on finding a stable settlement in Manchuria, including evacuation. In May, Witte noted that the "colossal expenditures" on the occupation threatened his industrial policies in central Russia.[101] He suggested that Russian goals be limited to protecting Russian interests in Manchuria, while abolishing the military administration. Privately, he complained that Kuropatkin's resistance to evacuation courted the risk of international and even military complications.[102]

The second was the international concern over Russia's ultimate aims for the occupied provinces. Chinese officials leaked confidential Russian communications to representatives of foreign governments, particularly those of Great Britain, Japan, and the United States.[103] Their protests allowed the Chinese to resist the initial Russian demands. As a result, Lamzdorf suspended the talks from the spring to the early autumn of 1901.[104] To increase pressure on China, he stated that Russia would retain full freedom of action in Manchuria until the security of Russia's railway and borders was assured.[105] At the same time, Lamzdorf was forced to take greater account of Japanese and British statements of concern at the continuing Russian occupation.[106] He raised this factor repeatedly in conferences and correspondence with Kuropatkin in particular.[107] By June 1901, Lamzdorf was insisting that Russia agree to evacuate the occupied provinces, given British and Japanese attitudes, as part of any agreement with China.[108]

Shortly thereafter, talks with China were resumed, but Russian demands were considerably less harsh than in the preceding February; now they were limited to Chinese recognition of the economic provisions of the Anglo-Russian treaty of 1899, in exchange for a phased evacuation of Russian troops from Manchuria to be completed by the summer of 1903, if no new complications arose—a condition attached at Kuropatkin's insistence. In addition, Chinese troop movements in Manchuria would be subject to Russian approval. To accompany this pact, plans were made for an agreement between China and the Russo-Chinese Bank, giving the latter the right of first refusal on resource concessions in Manchuria.

The final blow to a favorable "separate agreement" with China came in February 1902 with the conclusion of an alliance between Russia's two strongest adversaries in Far Eastern issues, Great Britain and Japan. In St. Petersburg, the British ambassador reported that in spite of official disinterest toward the news of the alliance, he had heard that the Russian government had "been greatly discomforted by it" and saw it "as a diplomatic check, if not a defeat," especially when a Russo-Japanese agreement had been within reach.[109]

Relations with Japan had been tense since after the Sino-Japanese War in 1895, when a joint French, German, and Russian *démarche* had forced

Japan to abandon an occupation of the Liaotung peninsula, which was taken by Russia three years later. These tensions were exacerbated by Japanese suspicion of Russian activity in Korea, in contravention of a Russo-Japanese treaty recognizing Japan's special interests there and barring Russian interference in Korea's chronic internal disorders.[110] Significantly, Japan had gone to war with China over the two states' respective rights in Korea. It was in recognition of this fact that Kuropatkin had suggested in June that Japan be offered a free hand in Korea in exchange for a Russian annexation of northern Manchuria. He had been obliged to relent because of Lamzdorf's and Witte's opposition.[111]

In late 1901, however, agreement with Japan had seemed possible with an ostensibly informal visit to St. Petersburg by former Japanese prime minister Marquis Ito. Ito brought proposals from his government demanding a free hand for Japan in Korea in exchange for similar Russian latitude in Manchuria.[112] Despite reports from Izvolskii that Ito's proposals represented Russia's last chance to reach agreement with Japan,[113] both Nicholas and Kuropatkin were disinclined to accept the Japanese offer.[114] As a result, Lamzdorf replied to Ito's proposals with a vague note that acknowledged Japan's special interests in Korea but stopped short of giving Japan *carte blanche,* while demanding Japan's recognition of Russia's freedom of action in Manchuria.[115]

This note, essentially a rejection of Ito's proposals, represented a defeat for Witte, who had counseled agreement with Japan in order to stabilize the Far East until the completion of the Siberian railway, after which Russia could dictate more favorable terms.[116] Without an agreement, Witte added, China could pit the two powers against each other, or military complications could result. He warned that war with Japan would be financially costly and would provoke negative reactions from an already restive society—this was a new and ominous note in the discussion of Far Eastern policy; it would assume a more prominent place in his and others' calculations as social unrest assumed growing proportions in Russia after 1902.

Russia's rejection of the Japanese overture led to the conclusion of the new alliance between Tokyo and London. Each power's fears of a possible Russian seizure of Manchuria had only been underscored by the conditions sent from Petersburg to Peking. The Chinese government quickly took advantage of the new situation. In mid-February, it sent to St. Petersburg a new draft accord that considerably modified previous Russian demands. Most notably, the Chinese draft abbreviated significantly the period for Russian evacuation, which was now to occur over twelve months.[117] The Anglo-Japanese agreement left the Russian government little choice but to accept the new Chinese terms. At the last moment, Witte bribed Chinese officials to extend the evacuation period to eighteen months,[118] literally buying time, but this was still insufficient for the full restoration of service along the CER.

The Russo-Chinese agreement was signed on 26 March 1902.[119] Russia agreed to restore all of Manchuria to Chinese authority. Russian soldiers would evacuate the occupied territories over three six-month periods, with southern Manchuria to be vacated first, by September 1902. For its part, the Chinese government recognized Russia's special position in Manchuria, according to the 1899 Anglo-Russian agreement. Any railway construction in Manchuria would require Russian agreement. At Kuropatkin's insistence, the Russian government promised to fulfill its obligations ''so long as no disorder arises and the conduct of other Powers does not prevent it.''

The agreement was a turning-point in the events leading to the war with Japan. Russia had undertaken specific obligations to evacuate Manchuria. While the condition regarding the maintenance of order allowed some flexibility, the treaty tacitly acknowledged Russia's loss of initiative in the Far East after the conclusion of the Anglo-Japanese alliance.[120] Neither Witte nor Kuropatkin was fully satisfied with the agreement; Witte was obliged to tolerate the continuing presence of Russian troops in areas under his control, while Kuropatkin accepted only reluctantly the idea of a Russian evacuation of northern Manchuria. Others questioned the political sense behind the treaty and called on Nicholas to renounce it. Raising what would become a persistent theme in future discussions of Far Eastern policy, Admiral E. I. Alekseev, commandant of Port Arthur and the Kwantung Lease Territory, told Kuropatkin in April 1902 that excessive ''tractability'' with China would only lead to new demands and could give rise to complications.[121]

Voices urging Nicholas to take a more assertive stand in the Far East also came from elsewhere. In Reval during the summer of 1902, Wilhelm II sent from the yacht *Hohenzollern* his famous message to Nicholas: ''The Admiral of the Atlantic greets the Admiral of the Pacific.''[122] In Russo-German discussions, the Russians stated that Japan's claims in the Far East aroused Nicholas's irritation for the interference they presented to his reign's mission of strengthening Russian influence in the Far East.[123] Still, in late 1902 Nicholas had yet to advocate any change in Russian policy toward Manchuria or Korea. But Far Eastern issues continued to sow controversy between Witte and Kuropatkin, especially as Kuropatkin continued to stall the evacuation promised in March 1902.

In the autumn of 1902, Witte went on an inspection tour of the Far East.

The report he submitted to Nicholas on his return was in equal measure a vindication of his policies since the inception of the Siberian rail route and a troubling picture of increasing checks on the government's freedom of action at home and abroad, all of which impinged on the far-flung organs of Witte's ministry. Still, the instincts for bureaucratic politics that had fueled his rise were also present; much of the report was a veiled attack on Kuropatkin and other opponents.[124] The report conveyed the paradoxical image of a spreading empire threatened by growing social unrest at home and the absence of coherent policy in an increasingly hostile Far Eastern environment. Thus, Witte defended the vision of his original memorandum on the colonization of Siberia through the use of the railway as having succeeded, but also called for an intensification of this policy in response to the growing "land hunger" whose effects had been demonstrated in recent agrarian disturbances in Poltava, Kharkov, and Saratov *gubernii*.[125]

Witte's observations on the situation in the Far East argued for adherence to the Russo-Chinese agreement regarding the evacuation of Manchuria. He defended the agreement as a necessary means to gain Chinese trust. He also continued his efforts to dislodge Kuropatkin's troops, arguing that the CER security guard could protect Russian property in northern Manchuria while growing economic ties fostered by the railway between Kwantung and southern Manchuria would guarantee peace there.[126] Alluding tacitly to his disputes with Kuropatkin, Witte wrote that confusion in St. Petersburg was mirrored in Manchuria, where Russian prestige was undermined by constant friction among the ministries' field representatives.[127] These effects were reinforced by the behavior of Russian military agents in Manchuria, whose arrogant conduct alienated the local population and courted the hostility of the Chinese government, to which authority in Manchuria had been transferred with the March 1902 agreement.

He added that the continuing occupation of southern Manchuria deepened the risk of complications with Japan, with whom relations were unresolved on a variety of issues.[128] Countering Kuropatkin and others who favored resistance to Japanese claims on Korea, Witte contended that present circumstances demanded at least a temporary renunciation of Russian interests in Korea.[129] Doing so would provide a basis for an agreement with Japan, which would then recognize Russian interests in Manchuria, thus eliminating a suspicion of Russia that dated to 1895. In the meantime, Russia could complete the eastern railways without fear of military complications. To underscore the importance of good relations with Japan, Witte cited his opponents' arguments that Russia should not make any concessions on Korea, and that since "war with Japan is inevitable in any event," Russia should attack before Japan became too strong.[130] He rejoined that such a war in the near future "would be a great disaster for us." Although Russia would undoubtedly emerge as the victor, "given the present situation, victory would be achieved at the cost of great sacrifices and would have a burdensome effect on . . . economic life."[131]

Witte's cryptic reference to "the present situation" was clarified in a letter to Lamzdorf in late November 1902.[132] Speculating on the possibility of war with Japan, Witte observed that victory would be very costly; "[b]esides this, and this is the main thing," a war for "distant Korea" would elicit little support from "Russian society," "while, on the ground of hidden dissatisfaction, those undesirable disruptive phenomena of our internal social life, which are making themselves felt during the present peaceful time, could be strongly exacerbated." These troubled thoughts joined for Witte the domestic rural disturbances of the autumn with affairs in Korea and Manchuria. This link between stability at home and foreign affairs itself resulted from the breadth of his ministry's involvement in all aspects of Russian administration. Other officials made the same connection between Russia's Far Eastern policy and domestic unrest. In December 1902, a pessimistic Minister of Justice N. V. Muravev, told Kuropatkin that Russia was entangling itself in Asia "only in order to get out of a difficult domestic situation."[133]

By the end of 1902, Far Eastern policy was again a prominent topic of debate. The approaching deadline for the second phase of the Russian evacuation, March 1903, provoked even Witte's disquiet about the safety of the railway, despite his persisting dispute with Kuropatkin. During the summer of 1902, Kuropatkin had proposed the retention of an occupation zone along the Amur to protect Russian shipping.[134] Others suggested hedging Russia's withdrawal behind a set of new Chinese promises to keep foreign interests out of Manchuria and to limit immigration into northern areas adjoining the CER.

Kuropatkin's proposals must have enjoyed Nicholas's support, as they served as the basis for two conferences during January 1903. The first, held at the MID on 11 January, treated Russia's future policy in the Far East. The second, a "special conference" convened on 25 January, included the participants in the MID meeting, as well as Kuropatkin, Witte, and representatives of the naval ministry. These meetings marked the final phase in the wrangling between Witte and Kuropatkin and served as the prelude to a final consensus in mid-February.

Both ministers had their own reasons for a compromise. On his trip to the Far East, Witte had concluded that Russia would require Chinese guarantees for its economic interests after evacuation.[135] Kuropatkin was pre-occupied by Russia's "troubling situation," which he blamed on excessive attention to Far Eastern affairs. He warned Nicholas that war was becoming likely in the west, where Russian forces had been weakened by demands in Asia. Like Witte, Kuropatkin also worried about "internal disorders" that could invite attack from abroad.[136] Kuropatkin had held such priorities since the Russian intervention in Manchuria. However, his misgivings about Russia's internal weakness were a new problem that preoccupied him and Witte increasingly in 1903.

At the 25 January conference, Kuropatkin and Witte initially appeared as far apart as ever.[137] The war minister repeated earlier calls for a con-tinued occupation of the parts of Manchuria traversed by the railway in order to create an area for Russian settlement and a permanent barrier against a Chinese influx.[138] Witte doubted the feasibility of these goals, given the international situation, the necessity for good relations with China, and the need to settle Siberia before looking abroad.[139] But he concluded, surprisingly, that when he took military considerations into account, he was forced to accept Kuropatkin's proposals.[140]

The conference supported Witte's claims to administrative predomi-nance in the occupied areas by resolving that "in order to avoid misun-derstandings both with the Chinese and in defining the competence of other Russian institutions remaining in the province," the military would be relieved of all administrative functions.[141] The conference also ratified the resolutions of the meeting of 11 January, including the demand for Chinese assurances that there would be no foreign intrusion into the evacuated areas. These were immediately to be submitted to the Chinese government. These resolutions constituted a considerable compromise by both minis-ters. Kuropatkin settled for a skeleton of the security measures he had previously envisaged. Witte, for his part, acknowledged the need for a continuing military presence to protect "his" district.

The conference also discussed relations with Japan. In the summer of 1902, Japan had submitted a draft agreement based on the discussions among Ito, Lamzdorf, and Witte in November 1901. According to Lamz-dorf, the Japanese had long sought a supplement to the existing under-standing on Korea, which dated to the mid-1890s. They were now willing to renounce any interest in Manchuria in exchange for a free hand in Korea.[142] The prospect of such an agreement elicited little debate. Al-though all participants agreed that Japan's demands were excessive, they also agreed fully that an understanding with Japan was necessary, if only to provide time for a buildup of Russian military strength. It was decided to treat the Japanese draft as a starting point for further discussions; the

Russian government would wait for Japan to reopen the talks before proceeding.[143]

Thus, after an often acrimonious dispute beginning in the summer of 1900, Witte and Kuropatkin had finally been brought together on a policy that both were compelled to accept. Witte, who had sought consistently to reestablish his administrative monopoly in Manchuria had recognized the necessity of military protection for his huge investment there. Kuropatkin had come to share Witte's views about the undesirability of any military complications in the Far East. If Witte understood the ramifications of a possible war as jeopardizing an increasingly unstable domestic social order, Kuropatkin was also concerned about the military complications in defending Russian territory on two distantly separate frontiers, of which the Asian was distinctly less important.[144] Both sets of concerns created a common ground on which each conceded somewhat to his erstwhile competitor, as demonstrated in the resolutions of 25 January. Most important, they agreed that even an unfavorable treaty with Japan was necessary to guarantee Russian interests in Manchuria.

The dominant member of the nascent consensus was Witte. His ascendancy was due to a variety of factors, chiefly the evolution of his kingdom, which began with the decision to undertake a Manchurian shortcut for the Trans-Siberian Railway. Two important consequences had resulted from this decision. First, Russian interests in the Far East were bound by a web of institutions under Witte's control. This network represented a huge capital and political investment, for Russia and for Witte himself. Additionally, in "gathering" his kingdom, Witte had developed a series of contacts in the Chinese government that had rendered him indispensable in Russo-Chinese relations. This had been trenchantly demonstrated in his actions during the Port Arthur episode and in the final phases of the negotiations that produced the Russo-Chinese agreement.

However, Witte's plans had been transformed since 1895. He had begun with a vision of relations with China based on an economic rapprochement to be fostered by the Manchurian railway. The railway's expansion drew him willy-nilly into the realm of foreign policy, obliging him to refine his views. But his goals in the Far East continued to be shaped by his outlook as minister of finances. After the Boxer Uprising, he was compelled to confront the international implications of his policy of peaceful penetration. He had to protect his economic interests and at the same time not provoke the other powers. Still, he entertained the possibility of maintaining Russian (and MF) economic sway over Manchuria with Chinese acquiescence.

The consensus among the three ministers was also founded on the acknowledgment that any policy had to balance their respective institutional interests and outlooks. Kuropatkin's decision to send troops into China and Manchuria was the last measure undertaken without consultation among the three ministers. After September 1900 Russian policy was the product of prolonged, often contentious, but collegial discussion among Witte, Lamzdorf, and Kuropatkin.

Yet, as Russia's Far Eastern policy was assuming a definite direction by 1902, a new threat was emerging to both aspects of the consensus that had been achieved among the three ministers—the substance of their policy and their methods for deciding it. Nicholas began increasingly to take an active role in the making of Russian policy. The results of his intervention were manifold and disastrous, leading ultimately to war with Japan and the revolution that followed it. The state reforms which came out of the revolution were shaped in large measure by the lessons officials drew from their memories of Nicholas's conduct in 1902–1904.

# · 2 ·

# The All-Out Bezobrazovshchina

The pressures for consensus between Witte and Kuropatkin had not come exclusively from abroad. As early as 1901, Witte noted in a letter, "We are having a bother here with Bezobrazov."[1] Shortly after, he elaborated on this comment:

> Bezobrazov, behind whom stands Vonliarliarskii—who has been mixed up in a whole mass of industrial affairs (he is probably losing money now)—and Albert have come to the conclusion not to make trouble with me, and so they have found it necessary to clear the way first . . . Since Bezobrazov is with the Sovereign no less than two times a week—*for hours at a time*—he, of course, talks all sorts of nonsense and shady plans. These conversations sometimes even spill over into action. Thus, not long ago, the Sovereign took fright over the fact that I was supposed suddenly to have *sold* all Siberia's minerals to the English.[2]

Nicholas had given enough credence to these charges to ask Lamzdorf and others about their veracity. Witte complained, "Not a word to me." Most significantly, Bezobrazov had suggested the transfer of the Chinese Eastern Railway to the Ministry of Ways and Communications. Witte closed on a worried note: "Bezobrazov is stirring up some sort of trouble, and it is hard to get at the truth given the Sovereign's character."

Kuropatkin recalled of the period beginning in late 1902 that " [t]he Korean adventures began after the Manchurian [ones] and were still more dangerous, for these directly affected Japan's interests in Korea. Here, Witte, Lamzdorf, and I worked together against Bezobrazov, Abaza, and Balashev, and would have vanquished them if not for the duplicitous role of Alekseev, who had supported these enterprises because the Sovereign favored them."[3]

Before 1903, Russia's actions in the Far East had been directed through consultation among the ministers most interested in the area, in this case Witte, Kuropatkin, and Lamzdorf. The emperor had as a rule ratified their joint recommendations with little hesitation. As in other areas of state activity, the formation of Russia's Far Eastern policy was exclusively the province of senior bureaucratic officials. In fact, since the reign of Alexander I, nonofficial advisers, or favorites, had played a negligible role in political life. Rulers had exercised strong control over their favorites, their immediate family, and their court. Even such a "personal" ruler as Alexander III had strongly disapproved of intervention in political discussions from unofficial quarters.

The closing of policy-making procedures within the ranks of the senior bureaucracy had developed in tandem with the professionalization of the administrative corps; the two processes reinforced each other in the development of a "bureaucratic" ethos incorporating certain ideals and expectations about procedures to be observed in policy making. Although there might be fierce debate over the nature of autocratic power, there was a widespread and tacit understanding among officials that they would be the exclusive agents in mediating that power. The rise of such nonofficial figures as Bezobrazov and Co. and the emergence of a new assertiveness in Nicholas's relations with officials posed in acute and increasingly conscious fashion the problem of autocratic power and authority as it related to its official mediators.

The bureaucracy's claim to be the exclusive channel between the ruler and the world outside his office, within Russia or abroad, came under increasingly critical scrutiny. To claim such a right, especially in foreign policy making, was to imply the existence of institutional restraints on the autocratic tsar. Witte's image of the mechanism interposed between the autocrat and his people demonstrated how far some statesmen had developed these notions. To state such views to Nicholas himself, however, would have been to invite career disaster.

## Bezobrazov and Co.

From late 1902 until the outbreak of the war with Japan in early 1904, Witte and like-minded colleagues in all branches of government found their views under increasing attack. In Far Eastern policy, these questions shaped the conflict between Bezobrazov and Co. and the opposing triumvirate—a conflict that affected in turn what foreign governments saw as Russian policy. The vagaries of this policy in fact reflected a bitter struggle in which the three ministers had to overcome their previous rivalry over traditional questions of administrative turf to confront a challenge to their very authority to make these decisions.

Ironically, Witte's predominance in the Far East buttressed opponents' claims that he had usurped what was properly the tsar's power. After late 1902, Witte, Kuropatkin, and Lamzdorf were unified by two tasks arising from the threat posed by Bezobrazov and his partners. They were obliged to defend the substance of their policy against their opponents' alternatives. They had also to justify the means by which they framed policy in the emperor's name, while their adversaries were telling Nicholas that he was in danger of losing his personal power to bureaucrats.

Success hinged on the attitude of Nicholas, to whom each side conceded the ultimate decision. However, mounting conflict between the two groups caused both to articulate with growing precision their definitions of their own and the ruler's role in what both groups persisted in seeing as an autocracy. Such debate overtook all areas of Russian political life during these years—one of Bezobrazov's chief patrons was Witte's chief rival in domestic policy, Minister of Internal Affairs V. K. Pleve. The outcome of this debate, war, provoked even graver effects within the empire, revolution. Memories of these events led all actors, including Nicholas, to draw from these years lessons that shaped post-1905 Russia.

The driving force behind Bezobrazov and Co. was supplied by A. M. Bezobrazov and V. M. Vonliarliarskii, whose backgrounds and careers lay well outside the bureaucracy. Bezobrazov was the son of a marshal of the Petersburg nobility.[4] His court contacts dated to his time in the Cavalier Guards, under Count I. I. Vorontsov-Dashkov, whom he served when the latter was Alexander III's minister of court. Bezobrazov's political views were those of his milieu, a convinced monarchism that exalted autocratic power and execrated bureaucracy. Even Witte, who called Bezobrazov "half-mad" admitted that he was an "honest" man.[5]

V. M. Vonliarliarskii was a *pomeshchik* from Novgorod *guberniia*.[6] He had been educated at the prestigious, and reputedly liberal, Alexander Lycée alongside many future senior officials. Vonliarliarskii had met Bezobrazov in the Cavalier Guards, from which he resigned after a scandalous marriage. In the 1890s he had published a modestly successful memoir of his service in the Russo-Turkish War. Like Bezobrazov and, interestingly, Witte, Vonliarliarskii had participated in the antiterrorist *Sviashchennaia Druzhina* ("Holy Retinue") after the assassination of Alexander II. In the early 1880s, still in his early thirties, he had retired to his estate.

Vonliarliarskii was a blend of postreform *pomeshchik* stereotypes. Like the self-reliant landowners who gave such vigor to the "landowners' movement,"[7] he farmed a modernized estate and was active in the local *zemstvo* with his friend and neighbor, future Duma president M. V. Rodzianko.[8] He had also invested in gold mines and Caucasian oil wells. Vonliarliarskii harbored a deep mistrust of the imperial bureaucracy and a particular animus for Witte, stemming from an industrial dispute in the mid-1890s at a factory he owned.[9] Despite these badges of modernity, Vonliarliarskii was an ardent believer in autocratic power conceived in the most personal terms. Recalling the years before the Russo-Japanese War, he wrote, "[f]or seven years A. M. Bezobrazov and I waited for the Sovereign to use the power in his possession: the Sovereign remained strictly a 'legalist' [*zakonnik*] and did not wish to rule the state 'autocratically', with the result that Minister of Finances Witte ruled without bearing any responsibility."[10]

The source of the conflict between Bezobrazov and his associates and the three ministers was a forestry concession on the Korean bank of the Yalu River, which Vonliarliarskii had acquired in 1897, hoping to found a Russian analogue of the East India Company.[11] After unavailing attempts to interest the ministries of finances and foreign affairs in his plans, he turned to Bezobrazov, who discerned the "vast strategical value of Northern Corea for the defence of our possessions in the Pacific."[12] Through Minister of Court Vorontsov-Dashkov, Bezobrazov brought the concession plans to Nicholas's attention in February 1898. Nicholas agreed to finance an expedition to reconnoiter the concession lands, under the direction of his brother-in-law, Grand Duke Alexander Mikhailovich. The concession was later bought by a court functionary with funds from Nicholas's personal cabinet.

For the next three years Vonliarliarskii and Bezobrazov sent Nicholas numerous memoranda on the concession. Transcending merely commercial interests, these notes stressed the strategic importance of northern Korea as a shield for Russian communications between Port Arthur and Vladivostok, and suggested that the concession be used to establish a Russian rear guard against Japanese expansion. These reports also criticized a "ministerial policy" that ignored Korea's importance to Russia as a barrier against Japan.[13] The antiofficial tone of these reports was consistent with the channels by which they reached the emperor; correspondence was delivered to Nicholas's valet by Vonliarliarskii's former batman. "[S]uch were the methods to which the Sovereign had to resort in order to receive information independent from the 'filter' [Witte]."[14]

The plans of the Yalu concessionaires were thwarted by a variety of factors. Russia's tense relations with Japan militated against the irritant represented by the Yalu concessionaires. Witte had little interest in fostering a project that could challenge the privileges of the Russo-Chinese Bank. In 1899 Witte scotched any idea of Treasury loans to the concessionaires, citing conditions in Korea and his doubts about the venture's viability.[15] He told one partner that he did not "regard the enterprise, which was conceived and conducted independently of him, and was even concealed from him, as serious, and that he therefore refuses to further it, either directly or indirectly."[16] In face of these obstacles, Vonliarliarskii and Bezobrazov let their plans lapse, feeling that the concession would be useless unless it formed part of a general Russian policy in the Far East.[17]

But when the outlook seemed bleakest Nicholas gave Vonliarliarskii cause for hope. At an audience on 2 May 1899, Nicholas allowed Vonliarliarskii to speak "from the heart."[18] For over two hours, Vonliarliarskii attacked Russian policy in the Far East and blamed Witte for "advancing misery" within Russia. Nicholas concluded the conversation by approving the work of the "staff," as he called the concession partners. The venture was resurrected in March 1900, as the East Asia Industrial Company.[19] According to Bezobrazov's draft charter, the company would be constituted to guarantee the achievement of "national interests" by placing most shares in the hands of chosen courtiers on behalf of Nicholas's cabinet. Such an organization would also help in "the struggle against bureaucratic and ministerial obstruction."[20]

As previously, however, events and Witte intervened to balk Bezobrazov's plans. At the request of a worried Minister of Court Baron V. B. Frederiks, Witte wrote to Nicholas on 2 June 1900 suggesting that only his ministry had the resources to achieve Bezobrazov's goals.[21] Shortly thereafter, the Boxer Uprising erupted, at which time Witte persuaded Nicholas to defer the question of the Yalu concession until China was pacified.

Bezobrazov awaited a decision until mid-July, when he lost patience. In a letter to Alexander Mikhailovich he attacked the policy of the "departments" that had entangled Russia in the Far East.[22] Bezobrazov's constant frustration with Witte began to crystallize into an overarching critique of the finance minister's authority and mode of action: "Sergei Iulevich has created a system which did not work even in peacetime, which weighed heavily upon the country's productive forces and gave birth to a mass of the dissatisfied and disenfranchised—in wartime, this system will automatically raise fears of state bankruptcy." The "infection" from this situation had even attacked the very center of authority—Nicholas was too indecisive. At such a crucial moment, Nicholas should prepare for action in the

Far East, but "[i]t seems that the master learns of everything only after the information has passed through the crude 'filter' of the appropriate departments."

This lament synthesized several themes in contemporary antistate rhetoric. Bezobrazov was venting a widely held view among rural nobles that agriculture had been bled white to subsidize industrial development. To such observers the "system" embodied all the ills plaguing Russia. Not only had it sacrificed Russian society to its own needs, it had imprisoned the tsar behind its filter. The depiction of Witte and his system was a trenchant rendering of a traditional motif in Russian political discourse in which the tsar was separated from his subjects by the wall of the bureaucracy.

Bezobrazov, Vonliarliarskii, and their sponsors at court had begun by advocating a strategic alternative to the official course. Repeated collisions with Witte had frustrated their efforts, leading to a refined critique of their adversaries. Given their backgrounds, they were predisposed to distrust Witte and to resent his policies. Now, they found that the system pressing on their rural estates also extended beyond Russia's borders. For them Witte became Russia's "evil genius."[23] All hope for undermining him lay with Nicholas, whom they sought to sway by contrasting their personal loyalty with the unreliability of the bureaucratic wall surrounding him.

Bezobrazov expanded this critique in late July in a memorandum on Russia's options after the Boxer Uprising.[24] He proposed that the East Asia Industrial Company's sphere of operations also include Manchuria, while excluding the possibility of cooperation with any other "active institution." Foreseeing resistance from "bureaucratic spheres," Bezobrazov recommended a company monopoly over economic activities in Asian areas outside Russia, to avoid the demoralizing spectacle of Russians disputes in front of "yellowskins." Thus, he suggested the formation of a conference *(soveschanie)* consisting of the company's executive under the emperor's chairmanship. This body would have the right of direct report to the emperor. A supreme order would be issued for the creation of a state secretary *(stats-sekretar')*, to serve as a liaison with interested ministries. This program was realized in its entirety by August 1903.

Despite Bezobrazov's efforts, the concession partners achieved little success in 1900. Events in Manchuria, the abortive Russo-Chinese agreement, and evidence of increasing Japanese sensitivity about Korea precluded serious consideration of Bezobrazov's proposals. Nonetheless, there was evolving a shadow government in the guise of the company, replete with its own executive body and policy papers, which constantly deplored Witte and the system that threatened Russia at home and abroad.

Bezobrazov and his colleagues believed that, as loyal personal servants of the sovereign tsar, they had as much right as bureaucratic officials to propose and make policy. They grounded this right in a view of autocratic power that stressed the instrumentality of the tsar's personal will. Vonliarliarskii, in decrying Nicholas's failure to rule "autocratically," put forth this view. Inchoate in their images of the system was an inversion of Witte's contention that the emperor could not rule without his machine.

At the same time, Nicholas tacitly encouraged their hope for success against the ministerial policy. Cabinet funds had been allocated for the Yalu concession. The emperor had also indulged antiministerial, or anti-Witte, complaints. Thus, if Nicholas continued to accept his ministers' recommendations for Russian policy, he was also listening to their opponents.

Bezobrazov's activities had little effect on Russian diplomacy in 1901. Talks continued with China, while separate discussions were initiated by Witte between Li Hun-chan and the Peking agent of the Russo-Chinese Bank. Interestingly, Witte's efforts seem to have been aimed as much against the Bezobrazov group as at protecting Russian and MF interests in Manchuria. A draft accord between the bank and the Russian government established Witte's direct control over the bank's activities in Manchuria, while noting the bank's "preferred right" to industrial concessions there.[25]

Witte's position seemed as strong as ever when in early 1902 he was made chairman of a special conference on agriculture. Bezobrazov was so discouraged at this news that he asked Nicholas's permission to "resume my liberty."[26] Significantly, Nicholas denied this request. But in late January, he ordered Bezobrazov to liquidate the East Asia Industrial Company. Bezobrazov asked for one last chance to reach agreement with Witte on unifying the Russo-Chinese Bank's forestry concessions on the Manchurian side of the Yalu with that owned by his partners in Korea.[27]

By 31 January, Bezobrazov had resigned himself to the impossibility of any accommodation with Witte. Repeating that "I deeply abhor and despise M. Witte and his system," Bezobrazov wrote a final apologia for the East Asia Industrial Company.[28] The company, he stated, had been meant not to operate for any one person's benefit but to put important areas into "reliable" hands. Witte had thwarted these plans, since he "did not sympathize in principle with . . . the possibility of receiving independent information, and of giving rise to competition for the Russo-Chinese Bank." With the Russo-Chinese agreement of March 1902, Witte seemed to have prevailed over Bezobrazov and his supporters. The Russo-Chinese Bank had preempted efforts by the East Asia Industrial Company to extend its holdings into Manchuria. The agreement with China was a "supremely" sanctioned expression of Russian intentions in the Far East. Bezobrazov disappeared from view until late 1902, by which time much had changed in the circumstances under which Russian policy was formulated.

Bezobrazov reemerged dramatically at the beginning of 1903, in circumstances that help explain the suddenness with which Witte and Kuropatkin agreed to bury their long-standing differences over Russian policy in the Far East. As the two ministers were reaching their understanding on 25 January, Bezobrazov was bound for the Far East with a two-million-ruble note of credit to be covered from the funds of His Imperial Majesty's Private Cabinet. Witte and Kuropatkin had reason to believe that Bezobrazov's star was rising. Indeed, Nicholas's behavior had undergone a marked change through 1902, just as officials were noting the increasing signs of unrest within the empire and the growing visibility of figures like Bezobrazov in the emperor's entourage.

### "Official" and "Unofficial Imperial Policies," 1902–1903

In late 1902, Kuropatkin brooded over the political situation: "We are living through a strange time. Turmoil grows. General dissatisfaction is also increasing. Unfortunately, information comes in from all quarters that this dissatisfaction extends to the person of the Sovereign. They treat the personality of the Sovereign with sympathy and love, but they are surprised and saddened by contradictions which occur in the actions of governmental authority. They hate very much the official and unofficial [shtatnye, neshtatnye] advisers of the Sovereign."[29] Since the spring of 1902 there had been severe outbreaks of peasant unrest in Kharkov, Poltava, and Saratov gubernii. The zemstvo movement had recrudesced. Student demonstrations had erupted in both capitals. And in April, Minister of Internal Affairs D. S. Sipiagin had been assassinated. So far-reaching was Witte's system that all of these strains impinged upon his hegemony in domestic policy, as well as in the Far East.

Sipiagin's death introduced a rival to Witte's predominance, the new minister, V. K. Pleve. While Pleve shared Witte's views about the state's role as a shaper of society,[30] the two differed over society's ideal structure and the means for achieving it. Witte stressed the role of industrial development as the motor for social development in an environment unfettered by such social distinctions as soslovie status. By contrast, Pleve sought an agrarian Russia in which peasant and noble estates were unified under the aegis of autocracy. These differences were reinforced by a mutual hostility, prompting observers in St. Petersburg to anticipate a bitter conflict in the near future—a not unattractive prospect for those bemused by what was seen as Witte's growing arrogance.[31] Such was the acrimony of this conflict that Pleve was soon in close contact with Vonliarliarskii, seeking an ally in his battle with Witte.[32] This alliance demonstrated the extent to which foreign policy and domestic politics overlapped as a result of Witte's dominant role in both.

As important as any of these developments was the change in Nicholas's conduct with his official servitors. For many, this was a central element in the crisis atmosphere of the period. By late 1902 there were abundant indications of the emperor's growing self-assertiveness as a ruler, seemingly in opposition to his own officials. As early as 1901, State Councillor A. A. Polovtsev had fretted that "the young tsar acquires an ever greater suspicion toward the organs of his own authority, and is beginning to believe in the beneficent strength of his autocracy, displaying it without preliminary discussion, without a thought to the general course of affairs." The only precedent Polovtsev could find for such behavior was the reign of Paul I.[33] While acknowledging Nicholas's right to seek alternatives to the "droning" of the ministers, Polovtsev complained that the tsar chose "nonentities" who wormed their way into his confidence. He concluded by noting that "the shortcomings of such a regime were felt by all monarchs who were outstanding . . . [they] sought to help by establishing proper consultative institutions" such as the Senate and the Committee of Ministers. "Today all of this is receding to one side and . . . is being replaced by whispering and evasion."

The mistrust imputed to Nicholas was demonstrated strikingly in December 1902 during the centenary of the Committee of Ministers, the State Council, and the court's Corps de Pages. Polovtsev, himself a member of the State Council, recorded and shared Witte's dismay at Nicholas's differing observation of the respective institutions' anniversaries. At the celebrations for the state institutions, the emperor "did not open his mouth." But at the celebration for the pages, "compliments were heard from the Sovereign, a number of extraordinary awards were strewn about," and there were a variety of ceremonies. Polovtsev asked, "Is it not clear that state advisers are annoying in the fulfillment of autocratic improvisations (for the most part randomly whispered), while the pages are blind executors of any sort of command?"[34] Another observer felt that Nicholas's behavior revealed that officials who been loyal throughout their careers "were under suspicion."[35]

Significantly, officials reacted to these events by criticizing Nicholas. On 28 November, Minister of Justice N. V. Muravev complained to Kuropatkin "about the Sovereign's mistrust of the ministers . . . the Sovereign wants to know the truth, but he seeks it in hallways, in dark corners . . . If he does not have confidence in one or another minister, then he must replace him—that is more correct."[36]

Nicholas's behavior troubled these observers because it brought into question the problem of the emperor's confidence, as Muravev had said. The issue struck to the very heart of these officials' sense of professional identity and legitimacy. It was the emperor's confidence that vested officials with authority in their governance of the Russian empire. Traditionally, bureaucratic conflict had consisted in a struggle for the emperor's confidence at the expense of one's competitors. Now a new note was entering officials' treatment of the idea. Confidence was emerging as the concept that defined the essence of the relationship between the emperor and the state structure designed to execute his will. In this connection, Polovtsev's comparison of Nicholas with Paul I was especially portentous, given Paul's reputation for arbitrariness and favoritism. Nicholas's conduct challenged senior officials' views of autocracy, which they had hitherto understood as a system operating under the rules and procedures that shaped their own professional environment. Although Witte and Pobedonostsev might have differed about the purpose or essence of autocratic power, neither doubted that his will would be executed by the state structure.

Officials' reactions to Nicholas's conduct showed how "bureaucratized" their worldviews had become by 1902. Such views had been entrenched by a half-century of practice. At the heart of this problem lay an issue that proved insoluble for these officials and their successors down to the Great War. In claiming that the emperor was obliged to rule through a bureaucracy sustained by his confidence, state officials were implying the existence of limits on a sovereign power that they held simultaneously to be vested in the ruler's person. As conservatives would point out time and again, such power precluded any attempts to bind it to institutions. When confronted with Nicholas's acceptance of this latter view, officials had no choice but to accept. This psychological and political *cul-de-sac* shaped in crucial fashion what Lenin and others referred to as the "crisis of the heights."

If Nicholas was coming to doubt his administration, inevitably the brunt of his suspicion was borne by the system's most powerful advocate, Witte. Nicholas's growing suspicion of Witte, encouraged by Bezobrazov and

Vonliarliarskii, was manifested in two instances that need only be mentioned in passing: the rising importance in agrarian questions and labor policy of Pleve's Ministry of Internal Affairs, in competition with Witte's Ministry of Finances; and the creation in late 1902 of a separate Merchant Marine, which had previously operated under MF auspices. It was now to be headed by Witte's foe, and a collaborator in the Yalu venture, Grand Duke Alexander Mikhailovich.[37]

Nicholas's apparent cooling toward his officials was accompanied by the emergence of what Kuropatkin called his "unofficial advisers." Witte complained that Monsieur Philippe was telling Nicholas "he has no need of advisers other than the representatives of the higher spiritual, heavenly forces with whom Philippe will put him into contact." Nicholas had become impatient of contradictions and insisted on his own decisions.[38] In recording these views, Polovtsev commented on Philippe's growing influence and alluded to "the other scoundrel," Meshcherskii. This aspect of Nicholas's behavior had important effects on Russia's policy in the Far East. Kuropatkin alluded to them when noting the "contradictions" in government actions, contradictions that became a primary cause for the war with Japan.

In early December 1902 Bezobrazov called on Kuropatkin, shortly after returning from a visit to Nicholas in Livadiia. Of the ensuing conversation, Kuropatkin remarked that "the words *I* and *the Sovereign* follow one another. The words *I* [Kuropatkin], *Witte,* and *Lamzdorf* are pronounced with a condemnation of these ministers' activity. Everyone is confused, no one understands anything, and only he, Bezobrazov, can save the Russian cause."[39] Bezobrazov announced that Nicholas was sending him to Port Arthur to oversee the concessions in Korea and Manchuria. He was also taking to Kwantung Commandant Alekseev Nicholas's authorization "to act by secret means against our promises in southern Manchuria." Foreign entrepreneurs were to be invited into the area; when they initiated operations, bandits obedient to Russia would attack and scatter the foreigners. Kuropatkin warned Bezobrazov of the complications entailed by such a plan. In his diary, Kuropatkin lamented that "parvenus like Bezobrazov are entangling our Sovereign in activity which is so unworthy of Russia, without his knowledge and permission, of course." Later that month, Kuropatkin reported on the conversation to Nicholas, who agreed that Bezobrazov's activity must not be allowed to create difficulties.

Witte already knew of Bezobrazov's voyage. Nicholas had ordered him to open a credit for two million rubles in Bezobrazov's name at the Russo-Chinese Bank.[40] On 18 January, Witte visited Kuropatkin to patch over a row that had erupted in the Siberian Railway Committee three days earlier.[41] Witte admitted his errors and suggested that both could accomplish more by mutual concessions, the results of which were made clear in their compromise at the 25 January conference,[42] a reconciliation probably facilitated by the two ministers' concern over Bezobrazov.

Witte monitored Bezobrazov's activities in the Far East using the very ministerial machinery that the latter had often criticized.[43] MF and CER employees were instructed to befriend Bezobrazov and report their conversations to Witte. These reports were wired in code to the MF chancellery, where Witte edited them for presentation to Nicholas. The reports were disquieting for Witte. Bezobrazov expatiated freely on Russia's poor position in the Far East. He attributed this to the "inimical relations of our ministries to one another" and claimed that he would soon resolve the situation.[44] Elsewhere, he posed as an expert on Russia's military position in East Asia. Most distressingly, he outlined his plans to establish a company headquarters in Fenhuanchen, an evacuated area close to the Yalu. This post would have its own stores, outposts in the bush, and an army brigade in civilian disguise to guard the concession.[45]

Witte supplemented surveillance with other tactics. He tried to co-opt Bezobrazov's partners in St. Petersburg, resulting in a letter from Vonliarliarskii to Nicholas, relating Witte's offer of aid in the acquisition of concessions in Manchuria currently controlled by a MF holding company, the Manchurian Mining Company.[46] According to Vonliarliarskii, the company was a MF counterweight to the East Asia Industrial Company, "which has the fortune to be in its sixth year of operation under the direct leadership of Your Imperial Majesty," thus tacitly accusing Witte of opposition to Nicholas. Witte also tried to discredit Bezobrazov by questioning his use of the moneys he had received. From Manchuria, there were reports of Bezobrazov's lavish expenditures—he was said to have spent approximately 300,000 rubles by mid-February on such items as a military hospital in Mukden, bribes to local officials, salaries for officers to head the concession company's military detachment, and even an Anglo-Chinese newspaper in Manchuria.[47] These reports were forwarded to Nicholas, leading to an investigation of Bezobrazov's accounts. However, Rear Admiral of His Majesty's Suite A. M. Abaza, one of Bezobrazov's allies at court, was able to blunt this attack, and Nicholas was "satisfied" with Bezobrazov's expenditures.[48]

By mid-February it was clear to Kuropatkin that Nicholas's support for the resolutions of the 25 January conference was beginning to waver. Nicholas also seemed to be turning on his ministers in favor of the "parvenus." On 15 February, Kuropatkin gave Nicholas a telegram from

Alekseev,[49] who wanted to leave a detachment of Cossacks on the Manchurian border with Korea and to transfer the troops evacuating Mukden to Kwantung. When Kuropatkin asked about this request, Nicholas, "becoming rather embarrassed," explained that Alekseev was answering a letter he had sent with Bezobrazov about the evacuation. Alekseev felt that Kwantung should be strengthened.

Kuropatkin observed that it had already been established that the danger of war with Japan would be lessened by conceding its freedom of action in Korea. He also mentioned the expense of transferring new troops to Kwantung. Nicholas insisted that Port Arthur was vulnerable because of the weakness of its garrison. Kuropatkin was forced to relent. Nicholas echoed Bezobrazov's view that Russian problems in the Far East owed less to Japan than to the discord among local agents of the Ministries of War and Finance; in these disputes he fully supported the Ministry of War.[50] These statements virtually overturned the agreement that Witte and Kuropatkin had reached on 25 January. Nicholas finally suggested that Kuropatkin undertake his own journey to the Far East.

The next day, Kuropatkin saw Witte,[51] who claimed that Nicholas was corresponding in cipher with Bezobrazov, a charge Nicholas had denied to Kuropatkin. He was angered that Nicholas seemed to trust Bezobrazov's reports more than his own report from the previous November, which Nicholas had yet to return. Reflecting on this conversation in his diary, Kuropatkin accepted Witte's contention that Nicholas had "grandiose" plans for Russia: to seize Manchuria, annex Korea, place Tibet under a Russian aegis, and similar designs on Persia and the Dardanelles. "[W]e ministers restrain the Sovereign in the realization of his dreams . . . he thinks that he is right anyway, that he understands questions of Russia's glory and well-being better than we. Therefore each Bezobrazov that sings along with him seems to the Sovereign to understand his schemes more correctly than do we, the ministers."[52] Kuropatkin reassured himself that even if Nicholas was disingenuous with the ministers, when he saw the real state of affairs, he would get rid of the Bezobrazovs and restore the ministers to their position.

Kuropatkin began to see the distinction between "official" and "unofficial" advisers, noted generally by himself and others in December, as specifically applying to Bezobrazov. Faced with the new challenge, Kuropatkin placed himself squarely on the side of "official" authority, regardless of his disagreements with Witte. Equally important was Witte's uncharacteristic self-effacement in seeking reconciliation with his erstwhile rival.

Thus, the consolidation of the triumvirate as a cohesive force in Russia's

Far Eastern policy can be dated from February 1903. Bezobrazov was no longer an ephemeral influence. Nicholas had expressed his "full confidence" in him, despite Witte's efforts to discredit him.[53] His views were now reflected in Nicholas's own and were even insinuating themselves into decisions by the emperor and Alekseev. What is more, both Kuropatkin's and Witte's reactions to these developments, and their attempts to explain them, reflected the standards and expectations they entertained about how the "Sovereign" ought to rule, as well as their own political dependence upon him. The best Kuropatkin could manage was to hope that this too would pass. As it turned out, it did not.

The following weeks brought further evidence of Bezobrazov's growing influence. He claimed to have the tsar's support for his plan to obtain more concessions in the area by reinforcing Russian troops in southern Manchuria as a lever in talks with China. To support this contention, he referred to a telegram from Nicholas authorizing the transfer of two regular brigades to the south.[54] Russian authorities in Manchuria and Kwantung were also becoming concerned by Bezobrazov. Alekseev sought confirmation of the legality of Bezobrazov's endeavors.[55] When Bezobrazov had first arrived in Port Arthur, the commandant had actively courted the emperor's favorite. In late February, he was increasingly worried by the expense and risks of Bezobrazov's plans, as well as the legal ambiguity of the East Asia Industrial Company's status.

By the middle of March, Kuropatkin was less sanguine about the situation than a month earlier. He noted in his diary, "the Bezobrazovshchina . . . has reached its apogee."[56] The very locution he used demonstrated how greatly the phenomenon disturbed him. On 3 March, Abaza had called on Kuropatkin with a message from Nicholas. The emperor wished to know Kuropatkin's views on increasing the strength of the "workers artel" on the Yalu by dressing three hundred soldiers in Chinese garb and concealing their weapons. Kuropatkin objected vehemently with a blunt attack on Bezobrazov: "he acts in the Sovereign's name and dispenses with the arrangements of all the ministers . . . Gogol's Khlestakov was a whelp and a boy compared to this Khlestakov of the early XX century . . . the enterprise on the Yalu, which could have become important to the state, was being made . . . into the Sovereign's personal enterprise which proceeded in contradiction to the Sovereign's measures and orders given by him to his ministers."[57]

Two days later, Kuropatkin saw Nicholas, who admitted that Bezobrazov was getting "carried away."[58] Nonetheless, Nicholas asked Kuropatkin to comment on a Bezobrazov memorandum from July 1901 giving a strategic appraisal of Russia's military position in the Far East.[59] Not surprisingly, Kuropatkin was highly critical of the document, which suggested, among many other things, that the Yalu concession be employed as a base for a guerrilla war against Japan.

In a characteristic diary entry from these weeks, Kuropatkin commented, "Witte, Lamzdorf, and I follow Bezobrazov's actions with anxiety and worry especially about the Sovereign's personal correspondence with this . . . adventurer."[60] Later, he observed, "two policies have arisen in the Far East—the 'Imperial' and the 'Bezobrazovian.'"[61] This was an accurate assessment, and it illustrates the systemic nature of the crisis that ministers confronted at the time. Despite disagreements over specific issues, Kuropatkin, Lamzdorf, and Witte shared the assumption that as ministers they should be consulted on the making of policy. Now, added to growing apprehension about rising social unrest, was the worry that the policy they had so laboriously arrived at was being undermined by Nicholas himself.

In fact, Abaza's role as Nicholas's messenger substantiated Kuropatkin's view on the emergence of "two policies." From March until the summer of 1903, Abaza played this part with increasing frequency. Given Nicholas's aversion to controversy, and Kuropatkin's objections to Bezobrazov's interference in policy matters, Abaza became an increasingly useful means by which the emperor could avoid imprecations for the actions of his favorites but present his ministers with decisions that were bound to elicit their displeasure.

In fact, Nicholas did not choose between the two groups that he had helped to foster. While agreeing with Kuropatkin about Bezobrazov's excesses, he offered continued support to the Yalu partners. Bezobrazov's journey to the Far East was probably meant to serve as a control on Witte's report, itself a symptom of Nicholas's mistrust of his ministers. Thus, Nicholas seems to have been raising an organized challenge to his ministers, or at least seeking an alternative to the monopoly they had thus far exercised in Far Eastern policy.

Less apparent was the fact that the ministers' efforts to thwart Bezobrazov and his partners were being presented to Nicholas as evidence of bureaucratic obstruction to the emperor's will. Kuropatkin and Witte were obliged to defend the government of His Imperial Majesty against the tsar himself, as Kuropatkin had done in the case of the proposed Yalu detachment. Nonetheless, Alekseev had with Nicholas's approval halted the evacuation of Manchurian provinces adjoining Kwantung.

In the meantime, Bezobrazov's presence in the Far East was becoming more troublesome for Witte. From Peking, Pokotilov relayed rumors from Mukden that Russian troops were being concentrated at Fenhuanchen and that the Japanese were on their way to the mouth of the Yalu.[62] Chinese officials feared that the Yalu enterprise could provoke a Russo-Japanese conflict on the Korean border. Other reports spoke of sporadic, often serious, clashes between the forestry's security force and Chinese troops, who saw these operatives as brigands, which was often the case.[63] There were indications at the end of March that the Chinese governor-general in Mukden was going to request military countermeasures in response to the consolidation of the Russian presence there.[64] These reports led Witte to demand a general discussion of Far Eastern policy to take place by the end of March.

Abaza too was pressing for such a discussion, to focus specifically on the Yalu forestry. In a note dated 13 March 1903,[65] he reminded the emperor that he had acknowledged as early as 1898 the concession's military importance, whereas the ministers opposed the project because they did not understand its strategic significance. Abaza referred to Bezobrazov's reports from the Far East as proof of ministerial resistance and predicted that when Bezobrazov returned, the ministers would resist him with "all the weapons their administrative cuirass" could supply. The more important Bezobrazov's information was, the more the ministers would seek to discredit him to avoid responsibility for their political errors. At the same time, Abaza contended, the Chinese and Japanese were watching "with profound joy the phases of the struggle engaged in by our official agents in the Far East."[66] They would certainly profit from this situation. Thus, Abaza concluded, a special conference was necessary to clarify the entire question. "It will be indispensable to bring the interested ministers to recognize the enormous importance of our present situation in the Far East, and to obtain from them what ought to be a conscientiously drawn-up program for work in common . . . when the enemy is at our doors, our patriotism should make us forget our various petty personal grievances."

The special conference requested by Witte and Abaza convened with Nicholas as chair on 26 March 1903, the first anniversary of the Russo-Chinese agreement.[67] It was ordered to discuss the "forestry matter on the Yalu" based on a report by Abaza, which was presented at the beginning of the discussion.[68] Also present were Grand Duke Aleksei Aleksandrovich, Witte, Lamzdorf, Kuropatkin, and Pleve. The presence of both Nicholas and Abaza was noteworthy. This was the first conference on the Far East that Nicholas had chaired in more than a year, lending Abaza's presence as *rapporteur* an added significance. It was also the first encounter in Nicholas's presence between the Yalu concession-holders and their ministerial antagonists.

Abaza's report attacked Russian policy in the Far East and the government's implementation of that policy in opposition to the expressed wishes of the emperor. The report cited Nicholas's old ties to the Yalu project, stating that he had appreciated its strategic import since the seizure of Port Arthur. With the present evacuation of Manchuria, the sovereign emperor had found the rear guard on the Yalu to be of special importance.[69] Thus, it was necessary immediately to organize the company proposed by the founders of the concession partnership for the establishment of this rear guard to protect the Yalu concession and the CER from Japanese or Sino-Japanese attack.[70]

Although he discussed the economic importance of the concession, Abaza's chief recommendations had political implications: the evacuation of Manchuria should be suspended; Russian troops should be stationed in the concession lands at equal strength with the Japanese troops in Korea; and foreign investors should be invited to participate in the project, thus obliging their governments to take an interest in the defense of their citizens.[71] Finally, Abaza argued that since the company would be promoting state interests, it should be headed by a special "state secretary."[72] This repeated recommendations by Bezobrazov in mid-1900. To these ends, the conference was enjoined to discuss the role of the MID in obtaining concessions, that of the MF in devising a charter for the company, that of the Ministry of War in the defense of the project, and general measures to overcome the prevailing "disarray" in state activity in the Far East.[73] In short, Abaza called for a *volte-face* in the policy that had been followed since March 1902, and in administrative methods that dated to the Boxer Uprising.

Nicholas's opening remarks supported Abaza's report. He favored the formation of a company that could exploit timber resources on both banks of the Yalu and check the spread of Japanese influence into Manchuria.[74] As expected, Witte, Lamzdorf, and Kuropatkin all voiced strong, if rhetorically hedged, objections to Abaza's proposals.[75] Witte stated that Russia's main task in the next five to ten years was to consolidate gains made in Manchuria and Siberia since 1895. This goal necessitated the maintenance of the best possible relations with China and Japan. By the same token, other interested powers must be given no grounds to suspect Russian aims. Any project with even hidden aggressive goals could be tragic for Russian interests. Therefore, any forestry company would have to be strictly private. Witte accepted Abaza's argument about foreign participation but warned that Treasury involvement would have to be strictly limited, given the great sacrifices that had already been made.

Lamzdorf doubted the legality of the Yalu concession. The foreign minister supported Witte's evaluation of the international situation, citing the vigorous protests his ministry had received from China and Korea about the concessionaires' conduct with local authorities. The same governments had expressed suspicion of the concession's ultimate aim. Japan believed that this activity was directly inspired by the Russian government. Lamzdorf also questioned Abaza's claim that halting Russia's evacuation would induce the Chinese to grant a concession on the Manchurian side of the Yalu. On the contrary, it would probably incite Chinese recalcitrance and countermeasures from Japan. Kuropatkin urged that the Yalu enterprise remain strictly private, with no military involvement. He criticized the plan to disguise soldiers as workers as both useless and dangerous, since it could provoke a rupture with Japan. A subsequent war could result in losses of almost a million rubles and thirty-five to fifty thousand Russian lives.

Passing over his colleagues' objections, Pleve merely echoed criticisms of the lack of administrative unity in the Far East. This remark aroused a spirited rejoinder by Witte listing the many successes of Russian policy over the last ten years. "All of this had been achieved by the unceasing collaboration of the Ministries of War, Foreign Affairs, and Finances, directed in their difficult work by the direct instructions of HIS IMPERIAL MAJESTY." The ministers might disagree at times, but this had never been manifest in the activity of the departments. Disagreement had always been resolved either by His Majesty's decision or in special conferences chaired by His Majesty.[76] This statement contradicted the facts of the previous two years, underscoring the role of Bezobrazov and Co. in unifying the previously divided ministers.

The conference's resolutions constituted a limited victory for the ministerial point of view. The MID was to investigate the legality of the existing concessions and work to confirm their claims. Together the foreign affairs and finance ministries were to seek a forestry concession on the Manchurian side of the Yalu. After the legality of the concessions was verified, a company would be formed under Russian law and in accordance with prevailing international agreements. Foreign investors would be invited to take a limited part. The new company would be strictly devoted to forestry and would be placed under the authority of the commandant of the Kwantung Lease Territory.

This victory was not unqualified. It was only by presenting a unified opposition to the political goals of the concessionaires that the triumvirate had been able to ensure that the forestry enterprise would remain a private commercial venture. Yet, they had been compelled to discuss the issue in a special conference. Abaza had spoken on issues in which the ministers had previously enjoyed a monopoly. They had also had to answer criticisms of the administrative effects issuing from their earlier squabbles. Indeed, to judge from the conference record, only the ministers' warnings of war with Japan helped bring Nicholas to their side.[77]

The ensuing weeks indicated that the conference resolutions were not unequivocal. At the end of March, Admiral Alekseev in Port Arthur emerged as a participant in Russian policy. During Bezobrazov's sojourn there, the admiral had expressed disquiet over his official position, his character, and his intrusion in administrative affairs. After Bezobrazov left Port Arthur early in March, Witte asked Alekseev to report these misgivings to Nicholas.[78] Alekseev asked the MF agent in Port Arthur to draft such a note, a copy of which was forwarded to Witte.[79] Alekseev accepted the idea of a commercial enterprise on the Yalu but warned that Bezobrazov's methods could lead to political complications. Despite Witte's repeated urgings, Alekseev never sent this report to Nicholas. Apparently, disappointed by Kuropatkin's repeated dismissal of requests for the improvement of Port Arthur's defenses, Alekseev went over to the Bezobrazov camp when promised the chance to report directly to the emperor on this question.[80]

In spite of Alekseev's position, the ministers were reassured of Nicholas's commitment to their policy in early April. Kuropatkin was then embarking on his own tour of the Far East and met Nicholas in Moscow.[81] The emperor asked whether "'that' Bezobrazov had called on him since his return." Nicholas "repeated firmly that the forestry affair on the Yalu should be a private matter . . . under the general supervision of Adm. Alekseev." Nicholas permitted Kuropatkin to erase the "traces" of Bezobrazov's activity in the Far East, including the withdrawal of the Cossacks from Fenhuanchen and the replacement of the more aggressive company agents, many of whom were army officers in active service.[82]

Kuropatkin's mission seemed to signal the initiation of a policy based on the 26 March resolutions. To judge from his meeting with Nicholas, Kuropatkin was being sent to Port Arthur to reassert ministerial control over activity in the Far East, and thus to minimize the risk of complications with China or Japan. However, even as Witte, Kuropatkin, and Lamzdorf set about implementing the 26 March policy, Bezobrazov had returned. Given Kuropatkin's impending departure, this event was significant. The war minister's absence divested the triumvirate of its most effective spokesman against the unofficial advisers. Witte was aware of Nicholas's waning favor for him.[83] Lamzdorf supported Witte but saw himself equally as the obedient executor of Nicholas's commands.[84] Kuropatkin was the only one of the three ministers who enjoyed Nicholas's full favor and did not hesitate to voice his concerns.

When he returned to St. Petersburg Bezobrazov learned of Kuropatkin's mission and its goal "of liquidating everything possible that was done by me."[85] To save the Yalu project, Bezobrazov sent Nicholas a barrage of memoranda including two reports that addressed Russia's strategic position in the Far East.[86] The reports repeated earlier proposals and went on to attack the ministerial policy as bureaucratic distortions of the emperor's intentions, in contrast to his own efforts to collect "trustworthy information," "*not fictions,*" on Russia's position in the Far East.[87] According to Bezobrazov, Russian actions had rested on the false premise that good relations with China could be gained by a policy of concessions such as the evacuation of southern Manchuria. To continue this policy would be dangerous, since Russia had lost face with a duplicitous Chinese government and had opened southern Manchuria to penetration by hostile foreign elements.

Bezobrazov blamed this situation on his bureaucratic opponents. "The desire one of our ministries has of wanting to do everything by itself" had led to a serious shortage of agents able to defend Russia's interests in southern Manchuria.[88] Bezobrazov concluded that the "Ministry of Finances must return to its natural role and not concern itself any longer with questions regarding security forces, as well as matters pertaining to the administration of [Manchuria]."[89] Elsewhere, he accused Kuropatkin of personal hostility to him because he had exposed flaws in military measures for the protection of the Russian border and interests in the Far East.[90] Despite outlays of two billion rubles and several military victories, "*we have lost our prestige and our self-confidence . . .* and are *on the eve of an economic, and perhaps, military defeat.*"[91]

Bezobrazov blamed both "natural" and "artificial" causes for Russia's plight. The natural problems were the obvious ones of the area's remoteness and underpopulation; both could be overcome in time. The artificial causes were much graver.[92] He accused the departments of pursuing an independent policy, based on unreliable information and an erroneous assessment of certain problems. Among the abuses he uncovered were the lack of economic management, conflicts among the overnumerous authorities, and "factual irresponsibility due to collegial procedures, in which there has been established a set of mutual compromises, not for the good of the cause, but for the interest of the departments." Finally, he wrote of "the solidarity of the departments in the struggle against any sort of accusation about their practical errors and their practical bankruptcy [*de-lovaia nesostoiatel'nost'*]."

Bezobrazov saw a simple solution to these problems. There had to be a departure from the "artificially created bureaucratic obstacles which are directed against the prestige and cause of the state, to the end of preserving the omnipotence of the ministers and their factually irresponsible activities."[93] He rejected the policies set in January and March. He called for an increase in Russian forces in the Far East; troops should be deployed along the rail-line in Manchuria and most densely in the south, since attacks were most likely to come from these quarters. The Chinese would become properly compliant when they realized that Russia refused to be duped and that Japan could not be enlisted against a newly strengthened Russian presence. In talks with Japan, Russia would be able to deal from a position of strength.

Next, he turned to the government's role in creating Russia's "difficult situation" on the Pacific coast. The concessionaires' businesses offered a "natural" [*zakonomernyi*] way out of Russia's difficulties.[94] Bezobrazov portrayed the concession as a defensive bulwark for Russian interests and "as the means for a successful transition to the offensive on the [Korean] peninsula when circumstances demand or allow it." The only impediment to the forestry's success would be "opposition proceeding from our governmental spheres."[95] Presently, the forestry was still too undeveloped to withstand such opposition. Nicholas was swayed by these and other arguments from Bezobrazov's circle. On 30 April he noted in his diary that he had seen Bezobrazov and Abaza "for a long time" during which the unification of Far Eastern administration had been discussed.[96]

The influence of the "Bezobrazovshchina" culminated in several telegrams sent to Port Arthur in Nicholas's name on 2 May. Alekseev was instructed to prepare for the introduction of new measures "under my immediate direction." These included barring the penetration of foreign influence into Manchuria, while encouraging Russian activity in areas of political and strategic import. Alekseev was also instructed to bring Russian military preparedness into accord with its economic and political tasks in Manchuria, thereby showing Russian intent to defend its exclusive position in the province. To these ends, the admiral was to concentrate in his person "supreme and responsible control over all departments in the Far East."[97]

At the same time, Bezobrazov was made state secretary, a rank of high degree usually awarded only after lengthy and distinguished state service.[98] This appointment was an ominous bellwether of Nicholas's changing views. The extent of this change was emphasized when Nicholas convened a special conference on 7 May to discuss the "executive aspect of several measures contemplated by the Supreme Will for matters in the Far East."[99] Writing several years later, Bezobrazov contended that Nicholas had been so struck by his reports that he decided to revise the 26 March conference resolutions.[100] Given the telegrams of 2 May, Bezobrazov's contention is disingenuous. The conference seems rather to have been intended to serve as a forum in which to confront Witte and Lamzdorf with a set of *faits accomplis*. This impression is reinforced by the fact that "State Secretary" Bezobrazov wrote the letter summoning Lamzdorf to the meeting.[101]

The conference was chaired by Nicholas. In attendance were Bezobrazov, Pleve, Witte, Lamzdorf, and Assistant Minister of War V. V. Sakharov, in lieu of the absent Kuropatkin. Also present as *rapporteurs* were Abaza and Major General Vogak, a former Russian military agent in Peking who had resigned his commission to join the forestry venture. The conference met to reexamine the decisions of the 26 March meeting, in light of progress in the forestry affairs during the Bezobrazov mission to the Far East. The true subject of discussion, however, was the whole course of ministerial policy, as was clear from the memoranda submitted to the conference by Vogak and Abaza. Vogak's report dealt with Russian policy in Manchuria; Abaza's with Japan and Korea.[102] Both excoriated the policies of concessions for conveying an impression of Russian weakness. This encouraged the Oriental powers to take advantage of a Russian position that was becoming increasingly vulnerable with the ongoing evacuation of southern Manchuria.

The first part of the conference was devoted to the status of the Yalu forestry concession. In March, the ministers had agreed to seek Chinese government permission for a private forestry concern on the Manchurian bank of the river. Discussion quickly became bitter debate between Bezobrazov and Witte over the operation's purpose and its political significance. Witte also used the exchanges to respond to the challenge posed by Bezobrazov and his partners.

After a sketch of the venture's history and activities, Bezobrazov turned to the conference journal of 26 March. He mentioned the desirability of obtaining a forestry concession on the Manchurian bank of the Yalu. Lamzdorf observed that the Chinese government could legally refuse to grant such a concession. Bezobrazov replied that Nicholas had already decided to claim it by "right of seniority" from his group's prior request.[103] At this point Witte entered the debate.

Witte prefaced his statements with the ambiguous declaration that he and Bezobrazov had already discussed the question and had no disagreements on its "substance."[104] Now, however, it was time to address the political and strategic goals of the venture, which was obviously not simply a private company. Witte noted that the company's ulterior aims had already been guessed in China and Japan. Thus, the matter had acquired an element of risk, and account had to be taken of the fact that "the external and especially the internal conditions of Russia are such that such a risk ought not to be ventured at present."[105] European Russia had already paid enough for the Far East; that and other factors had influenced the internal situation. A war could have "disastrous consequences."

Bezobrazov acknowledged this risk but felt that it ought not to be a decisive consideration, given the "right of seniority." Risk could not be limited by abandoning the area; it would only follow the retreating Russian presence.[106] Here, Bezobrazov raised Witte's Manchurian railway diversion as a comparable case: although its underlying goals had long been apparent, it had been completed successfully.[107] Now its security could not be guaranteed until the Yalu was occupied. Bezobrazov then seemed to shift his ground, stating that activity on the river would be limited to wood cutting.

Witte also pursued another rhetorical tack, to pressure Nicholas into recognizing the stakes of the discussion. Witte had stated that the question of the forestry's purpose was one "which nobody besides His Imperial Majesty can resolve."[108] Problems of political risk had been raised previously; each time the emperor had called a conference to discuss matters. In this case, there could be no doubt of the question's political aspect; "If His Majesty, regardless of the risk, is pleased to find that this matter is so important that the entire journal of 26 March be eliminated, then there will be no disagreement; if His Majesty is pleased to recognize the risk as serious, then the journal will maintain its force."

Writing later, Kuropatkin accused Witte of having displayed a "lack of civic courage" at this moment.[109] He contended that Witte's "agreement in substance" with Bezobrazov wholly contradicted his earlier views. According to Kuropatkin, once faced with the closeness between Nicholas and Bezobrazov, Witte tried to save himself by "playing politics" and toadying to the new favorite.

When seen against the meeting's immediate background, Kuropatkin's accusation misses the point of Witte's language. It is more likely that Witte was making a last-ditch effort to awaken Nicholas to the gravity of the steps he was countenancing. This would explain his reference to the domestic risks of foreign complications. He also seems to have been appealing to what Vonliarliarskii called the "legalist" in Nicholas, in his allusions to previous procedures that Nicholas had observed. Witte clearly did not regard the 7 May meeting as a properly constituted conference.[110] Given the extent of his intelligence network in the Far East, it is hard to believe that Witte did not know about the telegrams to Alekseev. Witte can be seen rather as having yielded to Bezobrazov's political aspirations in order to present Nicholas with a clear choice between two policies: one based on the disputed "right of seniority," with its attendant risks, the other based on the previously sanctioned conference journal of 26 March. Finally, Witte seems to have been forcing Nicholas, for whom strife and finality were equally distasteful, to make a final decision between the two groups and policies he had indulged and to understand where full responsibility for that decision lay.

Nicholas replied to these challenges with the statement that "concessions always lead to concessions,"[111] a phrase lifted verbatim from the reports of Bezobrazov, Abaza, and Vogak. He then asked Vogak to read his memorandum.[112] Vogak also criticized the policy of concessions. As a result of the March 1902 evacuation agreement, Russia's position in Manchuria and Kwantung was worse than before 1900. China and other powers had seen Russian conciliation as signs of weakness, since they had all understood the original entry into Manchuria as a *de facto* seizure of the territory. Further concessions would allow the penetration of foreign interests into Manchuria at Russian expense. In evacuating Manchuria, Russia must declare that it would cede its place to no one and state its willingness to support that stance "with weapons in hand." War could be avoided only by increasing military strength in the Far East. Vogak's and Abaza's memoranda gave no firm recommendations about southern Manchuria, but both implied that the railway to Port Arthur must not be left undefended. The rest of the conference was anticlimactic. Pleve remarked that these issues "did not become really clear until after the report of State Secretary M. A. M. de Besobrasow and the reading of General Vogak's note."[113]

The conference resolutions overturned virtually all of those taken in March. The legality of the Manchurian Yalu concession was secured through the claimed right of seniority. The formation of a company to operate the concession would await the clarification of this right, a tacit acknowledgment of the political thrust behind the project. Foreign capital would be invited after Russia consolidated its political and economic position in the region. Treasury participation in the project would match

Russia's interests and needs in the Far East. Finally, the company would seek all possible opportunities to expand its holdings in Manchuria. The only decision from 26 March left intact was the subordination of the entire operation to the oversight of Alekseev in Port Arthur.[114] Nicholas stated that these "supplements" superseded the 26 March journal.[115] Witte was reduced to refusing to sign the journal, claiming that such questions could only be definitively resolved upon the return of the minister of war.[116]

The *coup de grace* for Witte and Lamzdorf came at the end of the meeting; Bezobrazov was directed to read the telegrams sent to Alekseev on 2 May.[117] These concluded by ordering Kuropatkin and Alekseev "to determine together with State-Secretary Bezobrazov the essence of our politico-economic tasks in Manchuria and on the Pacific coast."

The 7 May conference heralded the advent of what came to be called the "new course" in Russia's Far Eastern policy. The meeting's outcome was a watershed in the course of this policy. Vonliarliarskii saw it as a triumph for his point of view and "the recognition of the necessity of removing from S. Iu. Witte unchecked and irresponsible sway over the F[ar] East."[118]

Kuropatkin's reflections on the conference indicated his own view of the means by which these decisions had been taken: "[T]he Sovereign had taken the 'new course' without consulting his ministers despite their opinion, trusting a gang of Bezobrazovs, Abazas, and Vogaks, supported by Pleve."[119] Its efforts to seal Manchuria from foreign penetration served to isolate Russia diplomatically; this decision had been taken without Lamzdorf's knowledge. At the same time the formulation of political and economic goals had been entrusted to Bezobrazov behind Witte's back.

Underlying Kuropatkin's and Vonliarliarskii's accounts of these decisions was the issue of the procedures according to which they expected Nicholas to act. Kuropatkin's statement echoed the protest against Nicholas's lack of "correctness" that Justice Minister Muravev had voiced in the autumn of 1902. It also pointed to the force that had brought the three ministers together: the challenge posed by the unofficial advisers to ministerial notions of the proper relationship that ought to obtain between the sovereign and his government.

This conception had a great deal in common with Witte's image of government as a mechanism on which the ruler depended. This outlook was opposed by that of Vonliarliarskii and Bezobrazov, who promoted an equally enduring conception of the tsar's personal power. The powerlessness of Witte, Lamzdorf, or Kuropatkin to do anything but voice their protests in ensuing months exemplified the problem inherent in their position: as imperial officials, they could act only with the sanction of the sovereign emperor. Thus, while contending that their office and expertise entitled them to be the ruler's exclusive agents in the formation and execution of policy, within that framework they too accepted the notion that it was Nicholas's power which imparted legitimacy to their activity. They were not able to apprehend the paradox underlying this definition of their position *vis-à-vis* the emperor and his power to resort to unofficial advisers at his pleasure.

The importance of Nicholas's confidence was made clear to Lamzdorf and Witte after the 7 May conference. On the following day, Bezobrazov wrote Lamzdorf in the emperor's name, requesting his signature on the conference journal. This document was highly critical of MID and MF obstruction in efforts to acquire a concession on the Chinese side of the Yalu.[120] On 11 May, Bezobrazov reported to Nicholas on two visits he and Abaza had paid Lamzdorf "in accordance with a received command," regarding the conference journal.[121] Lamzdorf stalled, pleading incompetence in economic and military questions, while warning that complications would result from the nonfulfillment of treaty obligations. He "tried several times to place the matter on personal grounds and to take offense at an intrusion into the business of his department." Lamzdorf even disputed the competence of special conferences to intervene in MID matters. He told his visitors that he intended to raise the question of "confidence." Bezobrazov replied, with some *Schadenfreude,* that he "did not understand this, since one could only trust God absolutely, and for convinced Catholics, the Pope as well."

At the end of May, Lamzdorf threatened to resign.[122] He was extremely distraught at the turn of events since 7 May.[123] At the last of many meetings with Bezobrazov during the intervening three weeks Lamzdorf gave his *"profession de foi."*[124] He defended his diligence and loyalty to the emperor and asked only "that Sovereign's will be stated to him directly and that he be permitted to state his own opinion in the same fashion." Again, he spoke of a loss of confidence, and asked to be allowed to rid Nicholas of a "disagreeable servant."

By this time, Bezobrazov and Abaza had become go-betweens for Nicholas and his ministers.[125] Lamzdorf's reactions showed his feelings about the irregularity of this situation. Nicholas's own sense of the incorrectness of these actions was indicated by his recourse to his new intermediaries to forestall unpleasant confrontations with the ministers whose policy he had undercut even as it was being elaborated. This behavior had been starkly evident on 7 May, when Nicholas had cloaked himself with his new state secretary, Abaza, and Vogak, shielding him from the recriminations of Witte and Lamzdorf.

Another result of the 7 May conference was also emerging. In examining materials sent him by Witte, Prince Vorontsov-Dashkov, Bezobrazov's erstwhile superior and patron, wrote, in the same vein as earlier remarks by Kuropatkin, of the "duality in the conduct of our policy in the East: official tsarist and unofficial tsarist."[126] Kuropatkin later spoke of an "indeterminacy of our policy."[127] This was in part the effect of resistance to the "new course" exerted by the two ministers in St. Petersburg. It also reflected the lack of organizational levers in the hands of the unofficial advisers for the execution of the new policies. Finally, it was an outgrowth of Nicholas's own persisting irresolution in this matter.

A step toward creating institutions to implement the new policy was taken on 31 May with the formation of the Russian Timber Partnership in the Far East.[128] The charter members included such familiar figures as Vonliarliarskii and Abaza, as well as members of court. In addition to organizational provisions, the charter traced the enterprise's descent from a company for the commercial exploitation of Russian America and northeast Siberia, which had functioned under the patronage of Paul and Alexander I: its employees had included officers in active service and had been accorded state rank. Significantly, the charter's history of this company remarked that under Nicholas I its agents enjoyed the right of direct report to the emperor. The parallels to the present situation were unmistakable.

With the creation of the Russian Timber Partnership after his elevation to state secretary, Bezobrazov had come far in fulfilling the objectives he had set forth to Nicholas in July 1900. Bezobrazov, Abaza, and their supporters had successfully outflanked their bureaucratic opponents, who were bereft both of the steadying influence of Kuropatkin, and, as Lamzdorf complained, of Nicholas's confidence.

By depicting the disunity of administration in the Far East, they had shown Nicholas the effects of the friction between Witte and Kuropatkin. They had encouraged the emperor's dissatisfaction with Russia's defensive posture in the Far East, offering an attractive alternative. They had reinforced their encouragement by urging Nicholas to reshape his relationship with his ministers and to rule on his own in the name of the "cause" his ministers had sacrificed to their own selfish institutional interests. Bezobrazov had turned the tables on Witte and Lamzdorf by positioning himself between them and the tsar; now, he was the filter through which they were obliged to pass before speaking with the sovereign.

# · 3 ·

# The Defeat of the Triumvirate
# and the Coming of the War

Despite Bezobrazov's impressive victories at the ministers' expense, few immediate changes in administration or policy followed the 7 May conference, resulting in a great deal of confusion. In Kwantung, Alekseev was unsure whether to proceed with the evacuation of Manchuria.[1] Although he favored annexation, he also feared Kuropatkin's reaction. Talking to Abaza in June, Witte and Lamzdorf called for a "clear and firm decision" on Russia's Far Eastern policy.[2]

In the Far East, Kuropatkin had seen signs of Nicholas's irresolution. In Harbin in early May, he had received copies of the telegrams to Alekseev announcing the "new course" in the Far East and was instructed not to proceed with the evacuation of Manchuria.[3] These instructions contradicted Nicholas's agreement in mid-April that Kuropatkin efface all traces of Bezobrazov's activity in the Far East. A second message told Kuropatkin to wait until Vogak joined him in Vladivostok before sailing to Japan.[4] He was now subject to the same regime as his colleagues in St. Petersburg, where Bezobrazov and Abaza were acting as monitors for Nicholas.[5] In Vladivostok, the war minister also received orders to go to Port Arthur after leaving Japan. There he would meet with Alekseev and Bezobrazov to discuss military and political issues in the Far East.

In Japan, Kuropatkin met with leading statesmen who expressed their concern over Russia's continuing presence in Manchuria and Russo-Japanese problems in Korea.[6] His responses were restricted by specific instructions Vogak had brought from Petersburg. He left for Port Arthur under the impression that while the Japanese would entertain some Russian claims regarding Manchuria, public opinion compelled the Japanese government to take a vigilant posture toward Russian actions in Korea.[7]

Kuropatkin arrived in Port Arthur in the third week of June. While in

Japan he had received a telegram from Court Commandant P. P. Gesse instructing him to prolong his stay there or to detour to Seoul before going to Port Arthur.[8] The delay was apparently intended to allow Bezobrazov to arrive in Port Arthur before him, giving Bezobrazov time for "a preliminary conversation with Alekseev."[9] In Port Arthur, Kuropatkin read the materials of the 7 May conference and received bracing evidence of Bezobrazov's status in a letter from his assistant minister, V. V. Sakharov.[10] This letter recounted a meeting at which Bezobrazov had declared that to reinforce troops in the Far East, Kuropatkin would have to abandon some of his plans for dispositions in western Russia. In his diary Kuropatkin noted that "this State Secretary is a surprising upstart." This information, combined with what he had learned in Japan, lent an increased vigor to his discussions with Alekseev and Bezobrazov over the next two weeks.

Bezobrazov too had cause for concern on his arrival in Port Arthur. His instructions for the upcoming talks were less supportive than he might have expected. Arriving in Port Arthur, he found a telegram from Abaza dated 11 June, a week after his departure,[11] informing him that Nicholas had decided to allow Japan "to take full possession" of Korea, up to the concession on the Yalu, to eliminate the possibility of conflict. Bezobrazov was to relay this directive to Alekseev. This decision seems to have been the result of Kuropatkin's initial report on the political climate in Japan.[12] According to Kuropatkin, neither Bezobrazov nor Alekseev mentioned these orders during the discussions at Port Arthur.[13]

From 10 to 28 June a series of conferences was held in Port Arthur. These meetings included Bezobrazov, Alekseev, and Kuropatkin, as well as the Far Eastern agents of the ministries of Foreign Affairs and Finances. The chief questions discussed were the evacuation agreement with China and such Korean affairs as the Yalu concession.[14] On each topic, Bezobrazov was refuted by the other participants. The resulting conclusions overturned the 7 May resolutions on each issue. An annexation of Manchuria, including the north, for which Kuropatkin had argued, was found undesirable.[15] However, the evacuation schedule in the Russo-Chinese agreement was held to be unfeasible without China's satisfaction of certain preliminary demands, including approval for Russian military posts at selected sites in northern Manchuria. Furthermore, a three year extension would be required to effect an appropriate increase of military strength in northern Manchuria and the Kwantung Lease Territory.[16] To diminish pressure from other powers demanding trading rights in Manchuria, the conference proposed designating certain "open" cities.

Throughout these discussions Kuropatkin sought to maintain Russia's military predominance in northern Manchuria. Equally persistently, the MF and MID representatives in Peking warned of Chinese intransigence on the observance of the evacuation agreement, and the growing concern of other powers about Russian reluctance to abide by it. Kuropatkin relented in face of these views. Bezobrazov played a marginal role, confined mainly to arguing for the retention of southern Manchuria as a Russian zone. Concerning the Yalu concession, Bezobrazov and two forestry company agents were isolated against the other participants. The question had become urgent because of Kuropatkin's findings in Japan and a recent Japanese request for Korean permission to open a port on the mouth of the Yalu.[17] Bezobrazov argued that the concession zones on both sides of the Yalu should be considered as bearing military and political significance; they should therefore be supported by the central government and its local agents. Also, he called for the maintenance of a military detachment in the vicinity of the Chinese concession area. He and his partners reassured the other participants that Korean apprehensions about the concession were dissipating, a claim disputed by the MID representative in Seoul.[18]

"After an animated exchange of opinions" it was agreed that the Yalu enterprise should be placed on an exclusively commercial footing. All active military officers and state officials were to leave the company, thereby removing any pretext for Japan to view the operation as military or political in nature. Alekseev endorsed this resolution in his capacity as official state overseer of the operation.[19]

Discussion of Korea was marked by a similar rift between Bezobrazov and the other participants.[20] Those present supported Kuropatkin's contention that, given Russia's military unpreparedness compared with Japan, all provocations must be avoided. According to Alekseev's information, Russo-Japanese relations were close to rupture. The participants determined that Russia should object to the opening of a Japanese port on the Yalu but should stop short of risking war. Bezobrazov saw this as yet another step in the policy of concessions. He felt that Russia should retain a free hand and acquire the ability to carry out reprisals. All conference resolutions were provisional, pending Kuropatkin's return to St. Petersburg.

The Port Arthur conferences represented renewed advocacy of the policy decided on 26 March 1903,[21] and a rejection of the 7 May meeting's resolutions. Not surprisingly, Bezobrazov claimed that these discussions achieved little of practical importance.[22] Learning of their results, Lamzdorf was overjoyed. In a letter to Witte, he wrote, "From the East—light—we shall see what the most honorable Aleksei Zlatoust brings us."[23]

Bezobrazov had failed at Port Arthur for all the reasons that he had succeeded with Nicholas. He had no departmental affiliation or expertise and felt isolated there.[24] Surprisingly, Alekseev was markedly cool to the 7 May policy, especially with regard to the Yalu venture. In addition, Kuropatkin made no secret of his hostility to Bezobrazov.

As was the case with the 7 May resolutions, no action followed the Port Arthur meetings. Instead, until late in July a stalemate set in between the triumvirate and Bezobrazov and Co. as Nicholas made no decisions. In a series of submissions to Nicholas, Witte and Bezobrazov in particular defended their respective policies in an effort to make Nicholas take a stand.[25] Still, when he returned to the capital in mid-July Kuropatkin felt that Bezobrazov had regained the emperor's favor.[26] This fact had caused concern in many circles. Even the archreactionary Prince Meshcherskii was said to have written to Nicholas, warning of a plot against the sovereign being conducted by the Bezobrazovs, Abazas, and "Nikolai Aleksandrovich."[27] This last was the emperor's name, and its inclusion may have been either a cryptic reference to the person of Nicholas as opposed to his role as emperor, or a significant slip of the pen by Kuropatkin as he recorded it in his diary.

The week of 24 July–1 August saw a rapid recapitulation of the turns taken over the preceding four months. Kuropatkin submitted to Nicholas his official report on the Far East, which was largely a critique of the Yalu operation.[28] He also insisted that the conference resolutions from 26 March were still valid, especially given the new tensions engendered by the Yalu concession. Discussing the Yalu's use as a rear guard, Kuropatkin questioned the value of a sparsely populated region miles from other Russian defenses. The only way to eliminate the provocative character of the concession would be to sell it to foreigners. The only other solution to this issue would be the creation of a strong Russian rear guard centered on Pyongyang in northern Korea, but this would entail excessive cost and political risks.

Bezobrazov had submitted his own reports on Far Eastern matters.[29] The most important of these proposed the creation in the Far East of a viceroy (*namestnik*) who would enjoy control over all military and political issues.[30] This post would reflect the administrative traditions of an empire whose growth had been predicated on the connection between the prosperity of the "periphery" and the presence there of *sanovniki* vested with "exclusive powers" by the "supreme authority." Bezobrazov's candidate for this post was Alekseev. According to Bezobrazov, rule through a *namestnik* would be "based on the personal confidence of the Sovereign and on his unmediated leadership of the cause."[31] The implications of this point were spelled out in the following paragraph: "this method gives the greatest intimacy between center and periphery . . . not by a bureaucratic route, but by a direct transfer to the locality of the combined authority of the departments."[32]

Once more, Bezobrazov invoked the themes of his critique of Russian policy in the Far East. In presenting a solution to the interministerial conflict he had documented in the spring, he was offering Nicholas full "personal" control over affairs in the east, in contrast to the "bureaucratic route," which impeded the sovereign's will. Nicholas accepted the offer. On 30 July, Nicholas issued an *ukaz* to the Senate, decreeing the creation of the Viceroyalty of the Far East, to be headed by Admiral Alekseev.[33] The viceroy would dispose of supreme military-administrative authority in all Russian provinces east of Lake Baikal. He would also be in charge of diplomatic relations with Korea, Japan, and China. This provision was probably inserted to forestall interference in the "new course" from Lamzdorf or Witte.[34]

Witte, Lamzdorf, and Kuropatkin learned of the *ukaz* only by reading of it in the official *Pravitelstvennyi Vestnik* the following day.[35] Speaking that day with Pleve, Kuropatkin expressed concern at the implications of Nicholas's method in taking this action.[36] Admitting previous knowledge of the *ukaz,* Pleve defended the way in which it had been enacted. Distrust of ministers and the publication of important acts without consulting them was consistent with "the principle of autocracy." Pleve continued with an unmistakable reference to the "Bezobrazovshchina." "On the surface, autocrats hear out their ministers, but people on the side almost always find a way into their hearts, or implant in the Sovereign a distrust of their ministers by depicting them as encroachers on autocratic rights." He recalled the examples of Speranskii and Pobedonostsev. Kuropatkin rejoined, "Speranskii and Pobedonostsev are not Bezobrazov." Pleve demonstrated an acute, if cynical, insight into the problem facing Kuropatkin; the sovereign's power allowed him to reject his officials whenever he pleased. Pleve himself had acted from this principle by cultivating the unofficial advisers in his larger struggle with Witte.

Despite Nicholas's coup, the three ministers met as previously scheduled on 1 August to discuss the Port Arthur meetings and Kuropatkin's reports on his recent journey. Bezobrazov was to attend this meeting, but Lamzdorf apparently arranged matters so as to avoid his presence.[37] As might be expected, the meeting endorsed the Port Arthur findings on continuing the evacuation—with certain Chinese guarantees—and the strictly commercial nature of the Yalu enterprise.[38]

These decisions could hardly have been better calculated to buttress Bezobrazov's arguments against the ministers. He had already given the emperor a blistering rebuttal of Kuropatkin's report and recommendations.[39] Now he could demonstrate active ministerial resistance to Nicholas. Another letter to Nicholas from Bezobrazov described a visit to Witte on 2 August to learn the results of the previous day's meeting "and generally to orient myself in the enemy's camp."[40] Bezobrazov denounced the ministers' resolutions and suggested appending his own opinion to the conference report, while hinting that he might not receive a copy of the journal from Lamzdorf, despite Nicholas's request that Bezobrazov be invited to the meeting.

On 4 August, Bezobrazov wrote Nicholas that Witte, as leader of the "triple ministerial alliance" was trying to bind Alekseev to the Port Arthur protocols.[41] Bezobrazov's influence was also evident in Nicholas's hesitation to ratify the conference journal, leading Kuropatkin to conclude that Nicholas was "standing fast for the Yalu and does not want to agree that that enterprise become totally private."[42] Finally on 15 August, Nicholas took the decision that Bezobrazov, Vonliarliarskii, Pleve, and others had sought for more than a year: he dismissed Witte as minister of finances and appointed him to the ceremonial position of chairman of the Committee of Ministers.[43] Bezobrazov knew of this decision before the fact. On 2 August, after visiting Witte, he had written to Nicholas, "I hope to use him for current necessities while *adhering* strictly to the instructions given me by Your Imperial Majesty, in particular: to consider him a very short-term actor. Please God!"[44]

Among the many reactions to the dismissal of the all-powerful minister of finances, the tartest and most accurate was an epigram making the rounds in St. Petersburg. "S. Iu. Witte, who had been ousted by the efforts of Pleve and . . . Bezobrazov, had departed 'spit upon and disfigured' [*oplevannyi i obezobrazhennyi*]."[45] Kuropatkin described Witte's fall with a naval metaphor.[46] The minister of finances had been sunk by three "mines," which, "had they been placed singly, would have had no effect, but placed simultaneously they produced an explosion." First, Grand Duke Alexander Mikhailovich had accused Witte of having gathered too much power, with "a set of ministries unto himself." He had thus disempowered or depersonalized not only other ministers but the autocracy itself. Next was Bezobrazov, who blamed Russian mistakes on the agreement that Witte had forged with Lamzdorf and Kuropatkin; errors could only be corrected when this agreement ceased to exist. The last "mine" had been set by Pleve, Muravev, and Pobedonostsev, who all denounced Witte to

Nicholas as a "red" for supporting such groups as the Finns, Armenians, Jews, and students.

Witte attributed his dismissal primarily to Bezobrazov's influence over Nicholas.[47] Bezobrazov had resented Witte's resistance to his plans in the Far East and felt that a more compliant successor could be found. Nicholas had come to see such recalcitrance as part of a larger pattern of disobedience.

Nicholas's motives can only be guessed at. Seen in retrospect, it can only have been a matter of time before Witte was dismissed: the economic and political ferment in the country seemed to prove the inefficacy of his policies. These had been consistently criticized by *pomeshchiki* and aristocrats in Nicholas's entourage, many of whom were materially affected by Witte's course. Other ministers resented Witte's arrogance and high-handedness. Nicholas himself must surely have wearied of constant friction with his most powerful minister. He was certainly displeased with the breadth of Witte's administrative reach. In informing Witte of his new duties,[48] Nicholas also enlisted Witte's help in dismantling the Ministry of Finances so as to simplify his successor's tasks. Nicholas referred specifically to the CER, the security guard, and the ministry's departments of education and railways as candidates for allocation to other ministries.

The creation of the Viceroyalty of the Far East, Witte's dismissal, and the reactions to both events comprise an important and often underemphasized dimension of what has been termed the "crisis of autocracy."[49] Other aspects of this crisis have been well documented in works dating to the immediate aftermath of the revolution of 1905–1907.[50] These works emphasize the pressures on the autocratic order from social and economic changes dating to the Great Reforms as they came to a head at the beginning of the twentieth century. When the tsarist administration is discussed, the "crisis" is held to have consisted in the crippling ideological and political divisions that beset a government faced with an increasingly restive *narod*. All of these developments did lend increased urgency to the fears of officials like Kuropatkin who felt a generalized atmosphere of crisis extending to the top of the order. But there is another aspect of the crisis: the perceived nature of the relationship and mutual obligations or expectations that obtained between Nicholas and his senior officials. Indeed, a "crisis of confidence" was overtaking the autocratic order; during the very period that autocracy's opponents accused the bureaucracy of standing between tsar and people, the emperor himself was behaving as if he shared these views.

Kuropatkin, for one, was alarmed by Alekseev's elevation to viceroy, which he perceived as a rejection of ministerial rule. In a lengthy audience on 2 August, Kuropatkin presented the ministerial case in response to Nicholas's revelation that the viceroy's jurisdiction included not only civilian organs, but all military forces east of Baikal, contrary to Kuropatkin's understanding.[51] This astonishing news led to a long and impassioned outburst in which the war minister vented frustration that had been building for months.

Kuropatkin began by acknowledging Nicholas's power and unique responsibility "before God and history." Because of this, imperial decisions were commands for the emperor's servitors. But, Kuropatkin continued, "having been placed by the Sovereign's confidence at the head of an important ministry, by law I had a responsibility for the correct flow of affairs in the ministry."[52] This was the "bureaucratic" view shared by Polovtsev, Witte, and others: the importance of law and "the correct flow of affairs" all set in motion by the emperor's "confidence." Kuropatkin applied this view to the viceroyalty: "[a]s Minister of War I had the right to hope that before the order of the subordination of an entire remote region was to be changed, my opinion would be heard. I did not hope for this opinion to be accepted, but it ought to have been requested, for precisely the fact that the opinion was not requested was evidence of distrust in his minister," who had studied this very issue in the Far East.[53]

Next, Kuropatkin turned to Bezobrazov's offenses. The state secretary had interfered in the confidential affairs of the war ministry, including military preparations on the western border. He had aired "the greatest secrets . . . in the streets." He had threatened Sakharov with a loss of favor if the latter refused to support the Yalu venture. He had saddled Kuropatkin with Vogak as a "nursemaid" and contrived to delay Kuropatkin's arrival in Port Arthur until he had spoken with Alekseev. The minister felt it his duty to "speak the truth to my Sovereign [about] . . . what turmoil Bezobrazovs bring into life, how they undermine authority." Bezobrazov "had formed a 'black cabinet' . . . even highly placed people were going to him in secret with their slanders." The result was disarray. "[N]obody knew whom to obey, where authority lay . . . all of this had a pernicious effect on the legitimacy of power . . . the Sovereign's distrust of the ministers was becoming a well-known fact and was discussed by the public."[54]

Kuropatkin asked to resign, since he obviously no longer enjoyed Nicholas's confidence. The emperor's only response was to note the absence of a suitable replacement. Kuropatkin persisted, promising to act as a commander in the event of war and to participate in the Committee on the Far East. He assured Nicholas that his "confidence in me would only grow when I ceased to be minister." Nicholas confirmed this insight; "It is strange, you know, but perhaps that is psychologically accurate." As Kuropatkin concluded in his diary, "by saying this the Sovereign confirmed in a way his distrust of ministers in principle."[55]

Kuropatkin's statements reflected the tension between his defense of procedure and what he called "turmoil," between the image of a ruler responsible only before God and history and that of one who also "ought" to have solicited Kuropatkin's counsel as minister. He was so bound by his outlook that he could do no more than ask to be replaced, given the loss of Nicholas's confidence. It does not seem to have occurred to him, as it did to Bezobrazov and others, that rule without exclusive reliance upon bureaucracy or ministers constituted a conceivable alternative to prevailing methods. Unlike Pleve, Kuropatkin lacked the ideological resources to reconcile the loyal subject with the professional minister.

Witte got caught up in a similar bind. As minister of finances, he had built an imposing and powerful "kingdom" or "system" extending from the Russian heartland to the Far East. Nicholas had recognized this fact in asking for Witte's help in dismantling the MF apparatus. The creation of this edifice had depended on Nicholas's support against Witte's competitors. Yet, Witte seems not to have understood that he might be held personally accountable when those policies faltered or that anyone but he would be the arbiter in judging their success. He had predicated his professional identity, and his relations with Nicholas on the notion that "since the tsar is a man, he needs the mechanism . . . for his human strength cannot replace the machine."[56]

Even in this formulation, it was the tsar who imparted motive force to the machine. Witte failed to anticipate the question implied by the inversion of his contention: what would happen if the man renounced the machine? To pose this question would have entailed questioning the very bases of his own authority in the autocracy. Indeed, he had owed much of his success to his ability to maintain Nicholas's confidence in a personal relationship. That he could accommodate simultaneously images of Nicholas as a personal sovereign and as the source of power mediated by the bureaucratic machine was indicated by Witte's success as a political infighter.

The closest Witte came to addressing this problem was in his memoirs, after Nicholas had twice rejected him. Here, he tied Russia's welfare as a state and an autocracy to the qualities of the ruler. In an obvious reference to Nicholas, Witte continued that it was difficult to maintain autocracy when the autocrat himself had shaken the state with unwise actions, especially at a time when the consciousness of the "popular masses" had grown with the encouragement of the liberation movement. Thus, he concluded, while his heart still loved autocracy, his mind and experience argued for limitations on the ruler—constitutions were a historical necessity.[57]

Officials' growing disapproval of Bezobrazov's activity, the prominence of Philippe or Meshcherskii, the disregard for "proper" methods, and finally, Polovtsev's comparison of Nicholas to Paul I testify that bureaucrats were ceasing to accommodate in their own minds the bifurcated image of tsar and emperor that dated to Peter I. Pleve saw this problem but praised it as an essential attribute of the "principle of autocracy." Speaking to Kuropatkin in early August, he had pointed to a symptom of the autocrat's arbitrary exercise of favor at the expense of his ministers, noting that this was the source of "the duality of actions" that had so troubled the triumvirate in trying to maintain a coherent Far Eastern policy at a time of growing international tensions.

"Duality of actions" was a tradition linked to the tension between the title of "tsar," with its connotations of divinely ordained personal and sovereign power, and the more legalistic "emperor," Peter's "first servant of the state." Peter's *fiskaly* and *ober-prokurator*, Catherine's *namestniki*, and even the *zemskii nachal' nik* of the 1890s were all channels for the direct transmission of the tsar's will. They could override or expedite the procedurally regulated actions of the state machinery—colleges, Senate, and ministries, all subordinate to the emperor.

The inability of many senior officials to accept what was, in fact, a legitimate exercise of autocratic power, which they in turn claimed to serve, demonstrates how far their own professional identity had evolved since the time of their grandfathers and how exclusive their understanding of autocracy had become. By the same token, their vulnerability to the attacks mounted by the unofficial advisers, and their own impotence when their views were rejected by Nicholas, suggest how much their views were informed by their experiences of preceding years. Their grandfathers had a worldview that admitted the possibility and legitimacy of an emperor acting "personally." Alexander III and Nicholas II, in their consistent reliance on state machinery, had created the conditions in which state officials expected to be the exclusive transmitters of the imperial will. When these expectations were thwarted, officials were forced to address the issue of Nicholas's confidence. This term more than any other captured the paradox that eluded them, because they founded their own activity on the instrumentality it connoted as the direct expression of the emperor's will. It was the crucial link by which the sovereign's power was transmitted to his administrative machine.

The central figure in this crisis was the ruler himself. His behavior after late 1902 perplexed both antibureaucratic actors who, like Vonliarliarskii, decried Nicholas as a legalist, and officials like Kuropatkin, who wrote of the emperor's "strange attitude to the law."[58] In fact, the creation of the viceroyalty combined with Witte's dismissal seemed intended to establish in institutional form what Pleve had called "duality of actions"—two separate and competing administrative structures between which Nicholas could act as *tertior gaudens* at his own pleasure.

By the middle of 1903 Nicholas was chafing at the limits he felt imposed on him by his own administrators. Bezobrazov and Vonliarliarskii had ably played on these feelings. They told him repeatedly that policies he personally favored had been consistently rejected by Witte, and later Kuropatkin. At the same time, Bezobrazov could convincingly warn Nicholas of the dangers of the "triple ministerial alliance" against Nicholas's own desires.

In late 1903, Pleve and Kuropatkin were discussing the rise of Bezobrazov. "Pleve said that the Sovereign had been extremely displeased with the ministers' opposition. One must not contradict him abruptly. That is why the Sovereign had turned to Bezobrazov."[59] Kuropatkin had reached a similar conclusion in August,[60] when he told Nicholas that Bezobrazov had served as a tool with which to break apart *(kolot')* the ministers. Now that this had been accomplished, the tool should be discarded. Indeed, Nicholas admitted to having had second thoughts about the creation of the viceroyalty: "it had even occurred to him that he had decided the issue of the viceroyalty *incorrectly* . . . But what was one to do? Now the question was decided . . . and account had to be taken of it."[61]

The repossession of his power seems, from his statements to Kuropatkin, to have been at least as important to Nicholas as the actual policy to be implemented: the correctness of the decision was not as important as the fact that he had made it himself. Thus, in the fall of 1903, Nicholas took personal and direct control over Russian policy in the Far East. Having overthrown the triumvirate, he had full leeway for action and a directly personal agent in Alekseev. Nicholas's view of his power, not as an instrument but as an end in itself, was reflected in his inattention to implementing the legislation on the viceroyalty. It also found expression in his curious neglect of the Special Committee on the Far East, which had been created at the same time. Nominally headed by Nicholas, with Bezobrazov, Abaza, Vogak, and Pleve as its members, this committee was supposed to advise Nicholas on the Far East; in fact it never met.[62] Having broken the ministerial trammels on him, Nicholas did not appear willing to create a new forum for potential resistance to his will.

Thus began the final phase in Russian policy before the war with Japan. Witte's kingdom had been cast down. The triple ministerial alliance had been liquidated, and Lamzdorf and Kuropatkin had now to deal with Nicholas as "conscientious secretaries," in Bezobrazov's phrase,[63] while Nicholas had his own conduit to the Far East through Alekseev and the Yalu partners. Beginning in August, 1903, Russia's international position became rapidly more precarious in face of a stiffening Japanese attitude. Within the government the sense of crisis and officials' dissatisfaction were exacerbated by Nicholas's methods for dealing with domestic and foreign problems. On all levels, state activity was marked by disarray.

In July, Russo-Japanese discussions had begun on the countries' interests in East Asia. The talks were conducted chiefly through Alekseev in Port Arthur and were dogged by constant delays as each new proposal was sent from St. Petersburg to Port Arthur, whence responses were returned to the capital for discussion and finally handed to the Japanese ambassador. Alternatively, decisions would be relayed to Port Arthur, and from there to the Russian envoy in Tokyo. By early October, Japanese spokesmen began to complain of the delays.[64] MID agents could only look on with trepidation. Lamzdorf was consulted desultorily by Nicholas, who did not even show him all salient documents when seeking his advice.[65]

By the middle of October, confusion in Russian policy was causing misgivings abroad. Lord Lansdowne, the British foreign minister, complained to the French ambassador that Russia's policy in Manchuria, where the occupation persisted, could only lead to suspicion of Russian motives. The ambassador apologized for France's ally by noting Lamzdorf's difficult position, which had been "considerably impaired" with the creation of the viceroyalty. "Not only did General Alexeieff's appointment encroach upon his functions as Minister of Foreign Affairs, but besides this the emperor had gone to the length of appointing M. Bezobrazof, who enjoyed His Imperial Majesty's special confidence to be a kind of special Foreign Minister to the new Viceroy, with direct access to His Majesty."[66]

In late October, Count A. K. Benkendorf, Russian ambassador in London, emphasized the confusion arising from the viceroyalty. "The result had been that the foreign policy of Russia at this point was no longer one and undivided. He evidently wished me to understand that many things happened for which Count Lamsdorff could not be held responsible."[67] When Lansdowne asked incredulously how understandings were possible when two countervailing influences were at work in Russian policy, Benkendorf could only answer that this was a passing phase.

Thus emerged a central irony in Russia's Far Eastern policy. Having rid himself of the troublesome ministerial restraints on his room for maneuver, Nicholas sought to rule through two parallel sets of institutions, one of which, the viceroyalty, was woefully incomplete. Characteristically, Nicholas's only clear decisions came during war scares with Japan, the frequency of which increased as autumn waned into winter amid an international atmosphere of increasing tension. Throughout all of these incidents, the most articulate of Nicholas's policy statements, which also indicated his view of the efficacy of his own will, was, "I do not wish war between Russia and Japan and will not permit this war. Take all measures so that there is no war."[68]

In the meantime, the two remaining ministers and the allies of Bezobrazov and the viceroy, continued to press sharply diverging policies upon Nicholas. Alekseev dismissed Japanese proposals as "impermissible pretension."[69] On the eve of the war itself, Abaza was still maintaining the line against a "policy of concessions." He recommended suspending all talks with Japan, because to the "oriental understanding," continuing them was an admission of weakness.[70] Nicholas seemed sympathetic to this view. On 15 December, at one of many special conferences on Far Eastern questions, he stated that present events recalled the situation after the Sino-Japanese War. At that time, Russia had firmly said "Back!" and Japan had obeyed. Now they had become yet more demanding. "All the same, it is a barbarous country. Which is better: to risk war, or to continue with concessions?"[71]

During these months, Kuropatkin resurrected his plan to annex northern Manchuria.[72] By late November, his concern for Russia's position had become so great that he proposed an agreement with China whereby Russia would receive northern Manchuria in exchange for relinquishing all of the south, including the Kwantung Lease Territory.[73] He was forced to acknowledge Nicholas's interest in Korea but sought to limit Russia's presence there for fear of provoking Japan. Kuropatkin's reports also indicated a renewed preoccupation with a problem that he and others had raised in late 1902—the possible effects of war upon Russia's domestic stability. Since 1902, Russia's domestic affairs had been overtaken by their own crisis, including a growing workers' movement, peasant revolts, student activity, and revived *zemstvo* activism. He asked Nicholas to make the concessions he proposed, to "avoid the possibility of internal disturbances in European Russia. A war with Japan would be extremely unpopular, and would increase the feeling of dissatisfaction with the ruling authorities."[74] Although a war against Japan would be winnable, it would entail great sacrifices, and given the remoteness of the region and obscurity of the war's aims to popular awareness, it would not enjoy the support of a surge of patriotism and popular enthusiasm, as had been the case in previous wars.

The instability of society and the army caused him grave misgivings. "We are now passing through a critical period. Internal enemies . . . are even invading the ranks of the army. Large groups of the population have become dissatisfied or mentally unsettled, and disorders of various sorts— mostly created by revolutionary propaganda—are increasing in frequency . . . If [the population is] asked to make great sacrifices in order to carry on a war whose objects are not clearly understood by them, the leaders of the anti-Government party will take advantage of the opportunity to spread sedition."[75]

Such concerns were widespread. At Nicholas's name-day dinner in December, Kuropatkin heard Grand Duchess Elizaveta Fedorovna describe the state of opinion in Moscow. "They don't want war, they do not understand the goals of the war, there will be no enthusiasm."[76] The governor-general of the Caucasus, the same Vorontsov-Dashkov who had been Bezobrazov's entrée to Nicholas, told Kuropatkin, "war must not be allowed . . . general dissatisfaction is growing . . . the question of a war could become 'dynastic.' "[77]

The converse of this view was the statement attributed to Pleve that to resolve present domestic difficulties, Russia required a "small victorious war."[78] Both views show a growing awareness among officials of a link between Russia's internal condition and foreign policy. All aspects of the growing crisis—internal unrest, foreign tensions, and Nicholas's overriding of his government—were joined in many minds. In November 1903, Justice Minister Muravev "expressed the opinion *that matters cannot proceed thus any further;* that the Sovereign should either admit that it is beneficial and necessary to return to the order that is established in law and continue to rule Russia with the help of the highest governmental authorities, or, if the Sovereign desires peace and the removal of responsibility from himself, then it will be necessary to move towards a constitution. The Sovereign himself will soon see the impossibility of ruling Russia with the help of . . . Meshcherskiis, and Bezobrazovs."[79]

During these months, pressure for Russian action was increasing from abroad. In September, the Chinese government had rejected demands for guarantees of Russian interests in the evacuated parts of Manchuria.[80] Talks with Japan continued, but were dogged by confusion, delays, and dissembling from the Russian side, while the United States and Great Britain joined Japan in protesting the continuing Russian military presence in Manchuria and the exclusion of foreign traders from this area. The situation became acute in October, when Alekseev upheld the unauthorized occupation of Mukden by the Russian military commissar there.[81]

Lamzdorf complained increasingly about Russian policy-making methods. "He ascribes special significance to the fact that the conduct of diplomatic negotiations in the Far East had been entrusted to the Viceroy. The representatives of all the Powers are unsure as to whom to address. They refuse to have accredited persons with the Viceroy."[82] He also bemoaned the impasse in the talks with China, which was now protesting the occupation of Mukden. Furthermore, he accused Alekseev of stalling the talks with Japan in order to gain time for military preparations. Alekseev's counterproposals for a recognition of Russian interests in Korea and special status in Manchuria appeared to Lamzdorf to treat Japan as an already defeated power.[83] Later, he even criticized the emperor's handling of matters. He was "upset by the Sovereign's opinion as to the possibility for him personally not to allow a war . . . The Sovereign told Lamzdorf that our powerful behavior in the Far East is advantageous, as it was the best pledge that there would be no war."[84]

Until a week before the Japanese attack on Port Arthur, Nicholas's statements echoed Alekseev's opinion that the Japanese proposals were "a sneer."[85] Nicholas dismissed them as "impudent."[86] At the New Year reception for the *corps diplomatique* in St. Petersburg, Nicholas "made use of such expressions as 'Russia is a big country' and 'there are limits to our patience'" in conversation with the Japanese envoy.[87] Despite such forceful talk, Nicholas continued to display indecision about which policy and whose advice to follow through late 1903 and the beginning of 1904. Conferences on Far Eastern matters were convened with increasing frequency through December and January. Kuropatkin and Lamzdorf participated alongside Abaza, while discussion usually addressed reports from Alekseev.[88] Both groups were given cause to lament the lack of a definite policy as Nicholas continued to vacillate.[89]

At the beginning of January, Alekseev received new proposals from Japan. These demanded that Russia renounce all interest in Korea and that a buffer zone be created in northern Korea to separate the two powers. Japan would recognize Manchuria as outside its sphere of influence if Russia pledged China's territorial inviolability and promised to respect the treaty rights of all foreigners in Manchuria. Added to these proposals was a postscript requesting a quick reply: "further delay in the resolution of the issue will be . . . extremely serious for certain governments."[90] On 15 January key officials met to discuss Russia's response. Disagreement between Abaza on one side and Lamzdorf and Kuropatkin on the other was so pronounced that two separate sets of conclusions were submitted to Nicholas, who was not in attendance.[91] By this time, however, Japanese resolve was such that even those compromises proposed by Lamzdorf and Kuropatkin would probably not have been accepted.

Nicholas himself seems only to have become deeply concerned about Russia's situation in the Far East on 23 January, when Alekseev received four coded telegrams from Lamzdorf containing the outline of the Russian reply. If local conditions dictated alterations, they were to be appended and the completed texts forwarded to Tokyo.[92] Finally, on 24 January, Nicholas "for the first time, expressed anxiety in regard to a possible war with Japan. Instead of the usual confidence that there will be no war, he said to me—slightly irritated—'the question of a war must be clarified more quickly . . . peace is well and good but this uncertainty is unbearable.'"[93] Within thirty-six hours, the Japanese "clarified" matters.

On the night of 25 January, a Japanese naval squadron attacked Russian vessels lying at anchor in the harbor at Port Arthur.[94] The Japanese government had given up waiting for a response to the proposals that had been submitted to Alekseev. The war came about for many reasons: Japanese sensitivity about Russian designs on Korea; concern among other interested powers about Russian intentions in Manchuria and China; inept negotiating; a refusal shared by Kuropatkin, Alekseev, Nicholas, and the Bezobrazov faction as well to recognize the degree to which Russian behavior was isolating the country diplomatically. However, the most striking aspect of the prelude to the war, as seen through the eyes of participants, was the total breakdown that overtook Russian policy making in Far Eastern matters.

After the outbreak of the war, Lamzdorf confided his bitterness to his friend and colleague Prince L. P. Urusov, the Russian ambassador in Paris. In a private letter, Lamzdorf wrote: "Everything that is happening was foreseen, foretold, documentarily proven beforehand; more than once I have supplicated our well-beloved Emperor to free me from my post—but nothing worked. The complete disorganization of our political activity in the Far East, the occult intervention of a pack of irresponsible adventurers and intriguers had to lead us to a catastrophe."[95]

This "disorganization of our political activity" was remarked by many officials. But these critics—Muravev, Kuropatkin, even Polovtsev—incorporated two other elements in their observations on the political situation as it deteriorated through 1902 and 1903. Whereas Lamzdorf questioned Nicholas's responsibility only implicitly, these critics found the tsar's rule through favorites to be unacceptable. In the context of Russia's activities in the Far East, it is important that, more than shared views about Russian policy, what had driven Kuropatkin and Witte together was the challenge to their prerogatives and rights as officials posed by Bezobrazov and Co.

Kuropatkin had been correct when he said that Nicholas had used Bezobrazov as a tool to "break apart" the ministers. Bezobrazov figured very little in events after September 1903. His plans for a great company to supplant the Ministry of Finances network was largely ignored by Nicholas. A company agent was left in charge of a forestry concession that operated only sporadically and with mounting debts.[96] By the end of November, State Secretary Bezobrazov had gone to Switzerland for health reasons.[97]

Nicholas had regained the power that so many said had been usurped by the bureaucrats. But in doing so, he had flouted the expectations and standards of his official advisers. To achieve his goal he had crippled the ministerial machinery in the Far East, without placing in its stead an equally effective mechanism or pursuing any other policy beyond a rejection of Japanese "impudence." It is striking that Nicholas's jealousy of his prerogatives overwhelmed all political considerations.

Another recurring theme in the remarks of Polovtsev, Muravev, and finally Kuropatkin, was the growing sense of being caught up in a broad crisis of the social and political order in which they lived and worked. Especially evident by the late autumn of 1903, when fears began to be voiced about the probable domestic consequences of a war with Japan,[98] these misgivings were linked with the growing prominence of the "Meshcherskiis, and Bezobrazovs" in the emperor's counsels. Such impressions were inextricably interwoven and reinforced in all sectors of Russian society as Russia suffered repeated defeats in distant Manchuria. After 1905, the words "Mukden" and "Tsushima" served as terse evocations in public opinion of the state's inability to fulfill even the most basic functions.

However, the sense of crisis was not limited to those popular and "social" forces that rose to such dramatic effect in the revolution that began in 1905. The events of 1904–1905, when the autocracy faced utter collapse, served to galvanize in the minds of many official actors a still inchoate critique of the relationship between the ruler and his government. Those in the state structure itself were indelibly stamped by the experiences of 1904–1905, when the causal nexus between war and revolution was glaringly demonstrated. The experiences of 1902–1904 were retrospectively reinterpreted by many officials to demonstrate the necessity of a new, expressly defined relationship between Nicholas and his government. The impact of this experience underlay many of the decisions and debates over foreign policy formation in the years after 1905.

The most important participant in the events leading to the war with Japan was unquestionably Witte. He had initiated the Russian drive into the Far East, and his success there had rendered him vulnerable to unofficial adversaries and Pleve, who focused their assaults on his bureaucratism, his "depersonalization of the autocracy," and his aspirations to undue prerogatives. Given the experience of building his kingdom and its collapse, it is no accident that in the autumn of 1905, Witte would be the most ardent proponent of United Government—in his version, the Russian equivalent of a cabinet, headed by himself as prime minister.

For the student of Russian foreign policy, the prologue to the Russo-Japanese War is instructive, despite its distance from the European theater to which Russian attention soon returned. In this regard, one of the enduring lessons of this war—which became a virtual axiom by 1908—was that the social fabric of the empire would not withstand the strains of war. The sense that social stability constituted a limiting factor on Russian freedom of action in international politics became the crucial aspect of the relation between foreign and domestic policy and politics between 1905 and 1914.

# · 4 ·

# The Lessons of War

By the summer of 1905 Russia's existence as an autocracy was threatened by defeat in Asia and revolution at home. The annihilation of the Baltic fleet in the Strait of Tsushima in May 1905 was a striking metaphor for autocracy's career since the war had begun. From November 1904 the *zemstvo* movement demanded with increasing insistence a national representative body to restrain or control an arbitrary and inefficient state structure. These demands were promoted by unrest among all groups in Russian society. At the left flank of the *zemstvo* movement was the intelligentsia-dominated Union of Liberation, which called for constitutional rule in Russia. Workers mounted a growing strike movement, first sparked by Bloody Sunday; intelligentsia agitation and success in the strikes themselves rapidly politicized the workers' movement, culminating in the creation of the St. Petersburg and Moscow soviets. The strikes isolated Nicholas in his suburban palaces; with rail service suspended, officials were forced to use riverboats to meet with the emperor. Meanwhile, the countryside was aflame with the most massive peasant *bunt* since the Pugachev revolt of the 1770s. Ironically, peasant violence was often aimed at the noble *zemtsy* who had initiated the rising unrest in 1904. A general on the Asian front noted in his diary the declining prestige of autocracy and the autocrat himself: "there is a caricature in Peter[sburg], in which the Sovereign is being flogged with his breeches down, while [Court Commandant] Gen.-Adjutant Gesse is diving at the breeches, trying to free him, as the Sovereign responds, 'Leave me alone, I am the autocrat!' "[1]

After temporizing since December 1904, Nicholas now conceded to advice that to save autocracy, he would have to grant a legislature in Russian government. To this end, a special conference was convened to create a Duma, whose existence and composition had been debated in-

tensely throughout 1905. The conference also discussed governmental reforms that would be necessitated by the Duma. Even more galling for
Nicholas must have been having to ask Witte to head the Russian delegation
at peace talks with Japan in Portsmouth, New Hampshire, in August.[2]

In the midst of these events, Nicholas signed a secret agreement with
Emperor Wilhelm during a private visit. In a manner recalling his earlier
conduct, Nicholas did not inform Lamzdorf of this act until six weeks
later.[3] The ''Björkö agreement'' was little more than a curious episode in
Russian diplomacy. However, when it became known, it revived memories
of events before the war with Japan. Equally important, the process by
which the agreement was undone, along with the events of the fall of 1905,
ushered in a period of retreat on Nicholas's part. Battered by military defeat
and revolution, Nicholas ratified a slate of measures which had the effect
of narrowing his prerogatives, no matter how much he protested his continuing status as an autocrat.

The governmental reforms in particular reflected officials' memories of
their relations with Nicholas before the war with Japan. The most important
such reform was the ''unification'' of government, which concentrated
executive authority in the Council of Ministers—widely referred to as a
''cabinet''—under a chairman who was called ''premier.'' These desig-
nations were not lost on contemporary observers; conservatives decried the
restriction of autocratic prerogative by the united council, and feared the
powers of the new chairman—whom they denounced as a ''Grand Vizier.''

The unification of government touched a problem central to autocracy.
The framers of the new regime flirted with the notion that limits might have
to be placed on the ruler—autocracy would have to be saved from the
autocrat. This impulse was certainly reflected in conservative fears of a
vizierate. However, by experience and outlook, virtually all officials upheld the idea of a sovereign autocrat. Such views were only strengthened
in the atmosphere of revolution. With state power under direct attack,
officials depended on autocracy to legitimate their own authority. The
reformers reached a murky resolution. While defending Nicholas's sovereign power, they sought to establish institutional control over its exercise.

According to the statute unifying government, the ministries of Defense,
Court, and Foreign Affairs were exempted from direct council scrutiny. But
these exclusions were vitiated by other parts of the statute and by the
general ambiguities pervading the whole post-1905 regime. Within days of
the council reform, the first chairman, Witte, was claiming a role in foreign
policy.[4]

The impulse to incorporate foreign policy under council purview persisted throughout the career of United Government. This impulse was based on conclusions drawn by officials from the Russo-Japanese War, which was seen to have resulted in part from disunity in government. After 1905 the widespread view was that war abroad would mean a recrudescence of revolution at home. As a result, Russian statesmen insisted on the necessity of a conservative foreign policy, as long as reconstruction continued within the empire. The arena in which these demands were stated, and in which the two areas of policy came to interact, was the Council of Ministers.

## Witte and the Unification of Government

In July 1905, as revolution in Russia intensified and hopes for victory in the east sank with the Baltic fleet at Tsushima, the imperial family embarked on a pleasure cruise in the Finnish skerries, where they were joined at Björkö by their German cousins. They were unaccompanied by any state official save the naval minister, Admiral Birilev.[5] On 11 July, while Nicholas was aboard the German yacht *Hohenzollern,* Wilhelm produced a draft Russo-German agreement for Nicholas's signature.

The Björkö agreement originated in private exchanges between Nicholas and Wilhelm dating to the autumn of 1904, a time of tension in German and Russian relations with Great Britain. The British government objected to the support offered by a supposedly neutral Germany to Russia's Asia-bound Baltic fleet, which had been dispatched to join the war against Britain's Japanese allies.[6] Russia and Britain were embroiled over the "Dogger Bank" incident, provoked when ships in the Baltic fleet had fired on English fishing boats on the North Sea, claiming to have sighted Japanese submarines in their midst.

Wilhelm had urged on Nicholas "a mighty combination of the three strongest continental Powers" against England.[7] While Nicholas was interested in finding a counterweight to British pressure, Lamzdorf warned that the German emperor was trying to interfere in the Franco-Russian alliance.[8] To placate Lamzdorf, Nicholas suggested to Wilhelm that France eventually be included in the coalition.[9] Wilhelm demurred, while continuing to press for a Russo-German treaty.

The treaty drafted by Wilhelm was brief.[10] Both parties agreed that if one were attacked by a third European power, the other would aid it with all the forces at its disposal; neither side would seek a separate peace. The treaty would take effect upon the conclusion of peace between Russia and

Japan and would be terminable upon one year's notice. As a concession to Nicholas, the draft stated that after the agreement took effect, Russia would inform France and invite its adherence.

Nicholas was apparently ill at ease about what he had signed.[11] When requesting Admiral Birilev to countersign the document, Nicholas asked whether the latter trusted him, then presented the document that both emperors had already signed. As Birilev complied, Nicholas covered the text with his hand. Nicholas kept the agreement secret until 30 August, when, at an audience in which he appeared "very much worried and even embarrassed,"[12] he revealed it to his foreign minister. Lamzdorf was taken aback, as he wrote to A. I. Nelidov, Russia's ambassador in Paris. He blamed Wilhelm's "insidious flattery" and statements to Nicholas that "he alone was his true friend and support" for the conclusion of a defensive alliance to which, in Wilhelm's opinion, France would "avidly adhere." Most distressingly, Wilhelm had received Nicholas's "*word* to conceal [the agreement] from *everybody* (of whom I am the first)."[13]

Nicholas was understandably susceptible to Wilhelm in July. Russia was losing a disastrous war with Japan—the result of policies he had pursued over his ministers' opposition. His power as autocrat was under discussion in official committees and under more direct threat in Russia's streets and countryside. Abroad, France had followed a refusal of meaningful support in the Far East by embarking on a startling *rapprochement* with Britain, Russia's age-old adversary. Wilhelm also made the most of Nicholas's insecurity. He appealed to his cousin's besieged monarchism, contrasting himself with the French leaders as political partners—since the latter "are not princes or emperors," they were not to be trusted fully.[14] When he presented the agreement to Nicholas, they were far from the countervailing influence of such officials as Lamzdorf. Wilhelm had avoided such influence throughout his discussions with Nicholas by conducting them through private correspondence. Nicholas had not kept Lamzdorf fully abreast of their progress, to Lamzdorf's evident chagrin.

At the audience on 30 August, Lamzdorf was immediately struck by the Björkö agreement's implications for Russia's foreign commitments. He warned Nicholas that the agreement's reference to a "third European power" could obligate Russia to enter a war against France.[15] In deference to Nicholas's support for the treaty, Lamzdorf suggested revising it so as to preserve the integrity of the French alliance. Before the treaty's ratification, Germany could consent to amendments eliminating any potential application to France. Alternatively, France could be prevailed upon to accept a revision of the alliance with Russia that would bring it into a "defensive triple alliance directed, obviously, against England."[16] Lamzdorf doubted the success of either alternative. Nicholas, however, insisted, "if the matter is handled *deftly* it will be possible to achieve."[17] Lamzdorf blamed this attitude on Wilhelm's "magnificent assurances."

The foreign minister regarded this *contretemps* as part of an older pattern: "This . . . is the new scrape into which we have fallen for no reason at all after so many strange adventures in the last two years. You can imagine how comforting it all is!"[18] Lamzdorf obeyed the letter of Nicholas's request to enlist French participation in the projected alliance,[19] but also recognized the futility of the agreement and looked for ways to rescind it with a minimum of fuss.[20] He was aided by the eruption in the fall of 1905 of a serious Franco-German dispute over Morocco, which was adjudicated at an international conference at Algeciras. In addition, Witte returned from Portsmouth, where he had successfully negotiated peace with Japan.

Witte had long supported the idea of a Russo-German agreement.[21] Returning to Russia from the peace talks in the United States, Witte visited Wilhelm at his hunting lodge, where he learned the general terms of the Björkö accord. Wilhelm assured Witte that the agreement would help realize Witte's goal of a "Continental Bloc."[22] Thus, on his arrival in Russia in mid-September, Witte was ready to support the agreement as Wilhelm had described it to him.

Witte's pleasure dissipated when Lamzdorf showed him the actual treaty. His reading of the agreement's implications for the French alliance coincided with Lamzdorf's, and he agreed with Lamzdorf that the agreement must be annulled.[23] To achieve this goal, they discussed impeaching the treaty's legality on the ground that it had not been countersigned by the foreign minister—in effect a statement that the Russian sovereign's signature was not sufficiently authoritative for this measure. In an extreme case, Witte and Lamzdorf envisaged leaving the Portsmouth treaty with Japan unratified, thus consigning the Björkö treaty to legal limbo by the terms under which it was to take effect.[24]

There ensued a campaign bent on pressuring Nicholas to renounce Björkö, while Wilhelm urged his cousin to uphold it. The German ruler contrasted German support for Russia with France's in the recent war and stressed that the agreement had been made "*before God.*"[25] Unwilling to trust Lamzdorf's strength of will with the emperor, Witte enlisted Grand Duke Nikolai Nikolaievich.[26] In the meantime, Nelidov's reports from France indicated that events in Morocco precluded any Franco-German agreement and furthermore that a Russian treaty with Germany would virtually destroy chances for a badly needed French loan currently under negotiation.[27]

Nicholas relented under these pressures. By late September, his letters to Wilhelm conditioned the agreement's ratification on a clarification of France's position in the projected bloc.[28] Matters came to a head with French demands for Russian support at Algeciras, an issue directly affecting the outcome of the loan negotiations. Although never formally renounced, the Björkö treaty became a dead letter when Russia voted with France at Algeciras.

The Björkö episode linked the periods before and after 1905. Lamzdorf placed the incident within the context of "the strange adventures" of the preceding two years. As before the war with Japan, Nicholas had acted without consulting his officials, to potentially disastrous effect. Equally important, Nicholas was persuaded to renounce Björkö at the very time that limits on his power were being discussed in an official conference—chaired by Senator D. M. Solskii—on legislative and institutional reforms to be undertaken in response to the year's revolutionary events. One of the conference's main tasks was to reform the structure of government in accordance with the new political conditions in Russia, acknowledged when Nicholas acquiesced in August 1905 to the creation of an elective Duma. This part of the conference's deliberations resulted in an *ukaz* promulgated on 19 October 1905 announcing the unification of Russian government under a reformed Council of Ministers, to be headed by an authoritative chairman.

Faced with the task of saving the autocracy, many of the council's creators acted to correct the vicissitudes they blamed for the war and the revolution that followed it. Judging from Lamzdorf's response to Björkö, the past was still psychologically recent for the reformers. Although Nicholas had forsaken his administrative machine in 1903, many officials—including Witte himself—now sought to oblige him to rule through it exclusively. But while imposing a bureaucratic reform on their weakened ruler, these officials were also sufficiently wedded to the principle of autocracy—by conviction, through socialization, and because of the threat to their authority "from below"—that they could not remove the autocrat from the center of the order. Thus, while wishing to harness the ruler to his machine on their own terms, officials were dependent on autocratic power for their political and professional legitimacy. This paradox would stalk the "heights" to the end of the old regime.

The council reform resurrected a problem faced by rulers and statesmen since the eighteenth century. There had been intermittent attempts to establish a legal framework for autocratic rule—a *Rechtstaat*—by legally defining the duties of officials in imperial service, while coordinating policy making and implementation in a council of senior officials who would meet with the emperor, from whose power their authority derived.[29] Such reform projects had acquired an increasingly bureaucratic cast during the nineteenth century, with the growth of an administration made up of officials whose outlook was conditioned by shared social and educational backgrounds in an increasingly institutionalized environment.[30]

All attempts had foundered on the effort to define legally the relationship between the emperor and his ministers, which implied limiting the ruler's sovereign power by placing it in a legal framework.[31] This paradox had emerged with bitter effect after 1900 when official expectations about the emperor's relationship with his administration had been flouted by the Bezobrazovshchina and similar developments in domestic affairs. The fact that rulers since Nicholas I had tended to govern through official advisers did not limit their ability to choose other channels for the expression of their will. By the same token, officials who had simultaneously evolved a bureaucratic conception of political authority through a half-century of practice had no conceptual defense from the tsar's assertion of his will against their expectations; they depended on the same power for their own authority.

Nicholas had also confounded those who had urged him to rule "autocratically" over his "unnatural" bureaucracy. Having established the viceroyalty and the Special Committee on the Far East, Nicholas demonstrated his own understanding of autocratic rule: while consulting Abaza and Alekseev, he also sought the counsel of Kuropatkin and Lamzdorf, thus retaining all initiative in his own hands. Such "parallelism," a longstanding complaint in the history of Russian (and Soviet) administration, was a formal outgrowth of the ruler's defense of his power against institutional restraints. Nicholas's behavior was rooted in a seemingly native understanding of the utility of administrative divisions for the maintenance of his own prerogative. By the same token, Nicholas's recourse to such institutional manipulations illustrated how bureaucratized or legalist was his own conception of his power, vindicating Vonliarliarskii's complaint that Nicholas did not rule sufficiently "autocratically." For their part, officials' objections to such behavior attested to an increasingly conscious distinction between two previously coexistent views of autocratic power: one exalting the personal and arbitrary nature of the tsar's sovereign power; another anchoring the state's legal-administrative structure in the legal sovereignty of the emperor.

The chronic insolubility of this problem was expressed in the coexistence by 1905 of two institutions stemming from previous reforms. The Committee of Ministers, formed by Alexander I, had become largely a ceremonial body, occupied with sundry legal and financial affairs, but with little real executive power, as Witte was aware when transferred there in 1903. There was also a Council of Ministers, which had enjoyed brief vitality after its creation by Alexander II. By law, this body could meet only under the emperor's chairmanship. It had been superseded by "special conferences" involving ministers with interests in a given matter.

The revolution of 1905 and the decision to create a state Duma introduced compelling new elements into ministerial reform. The topic had arisen in discussions leading to the disappointing *ukaz* of 12 December 1904.[32] In the course of debate on this measure, Witte drew up a draft *ukaz* entitled "Measures for the Improvement of the State Order," part of which called for "closer unification of the separate parts of government" under the Committee of Ministers, of which he was chairman. One observer saw this proposal as an effort by Witte "to assure himself of the direction of the entire state policy."[33]

In January 1905, Nicholas convened a special conference to discuss the unification of government activity.[34] The conference deliberated until April, in an atmosphere charged with growing unrest, which served in turn to spur discussion on the creation of a representative assembly.[35] Witte now called for the consolidation of all policy making in a reformed Council of Ministers and the abolition of the Committee of Ministers; as he would throughout the course of the reform, Witte argued for a strong council chairman.[36] Witte was opposed by Minister of Finances V. N. Kokovtsev, who adduced the historian A. D. Gradovskii to argue that the autocrat was better served by diverse opinions resulting from the existence of several high bodies of state.[37] Kokovtsev proposed retaining both the Committee and the Council of Ministers. He was quickly supported by the director of the state department of agriculture and landholding, the director of the imperial chancellery, and K. P. Pobedonostsev.[38] In view of the resulting impasse, Nicholas suspended the conference on 16 April 1905.[39]

Discussion was revived in August, by which time the domestic situation had gravely deteriorated. A memorandum on government organization by Assistant Minister of Internal Affairs S. E. Kryzhanovskii was submitted to Nicholas on 6 August, the day he had issued an *ukaz* approving a consultative Duma, thus raising the question of changes in state institutions to accommodate the new body.[40] Kryzhanovskii's memorandum[41] attacked the prevailing disarray in government: "one of the peculiarities of Russia's contemporary state structure is precisely the fragmentation of the separate ministries, which often passes over into a struggle among them."[42] Recent years were "full of examples" of "impermissible" opposition to the government from within and outside its ranks. Ministries often acted in total conflict with one another at all levels of state activity.

Drawing comparisons with the convocation of the Etats-Généraux in 1789, Kryzhanovskii warned that the new Duma would provide a potent forum for the expression of "united and fortified dissatisfaction," which would be aimed exclusively against the government. The French government's lack of a program had led to consequences that needed no elaboration. In Russia, events of the previous year demonstrated the fruitlessness of government action without a concerted policy.[43] Kryzhanovskii asked rhetorically whether the government would meet this struggle with its full armed capacity, or, an ironic allusion to the war with Japan, whether this would be yet another example of the state's "unpreparedness."[44]

Kryzhanovskii argued that governmental disunity under the new conditions could ultimately threaten autocratic power—which "must first and foremost be equally raised above all parties and *sosloviia,* over rulers and ruled"—since it could "inevitably be drawn into the struggle of the parties."[45] A "strong government" was needed to deliver the country from turmoil and to consolidate reform. The alternative was the "destruction of the legitimacy of power,"[46] which had already occurred in part, if that power did not maintain an appropriate "height." The "legitimacy of power" depended on the government that was its agent. The chief evidence of strong authority was unity, which was sadly lacking in government at present.[47]

Kryzhanovskii's solution was couched as inoffensively as possible: given the unanimity of goals to be expected in the Duma, he explained, it would be necessary to form a "uniform ministry or, as it is accepted to call it in the language of political doctrines, a Cabinet."[48] For Kryzhanovskii, the threat presented by the Duma overbore older objections to previous proposals for ministerial unification, which had warned of overcentralization of authority and the danger of the "establishment of a vizierate with a Grand Vizier at its head."[49] The new institution would function as an executive arm alongside the Duma. The "Supreme Representative" of both would be "the autocratic power." It would be freed from direct participation in "all the petty details of administration" and partisan conflict, ensuring its inviolability as the supreme head of the whole state, and not just of government, as in the West.[50] By implication, preserving "the legitimacy of autocratic power" demanded that the emperor be distanced from the governance of the empire.

Kryzhanovskii's recommendations placed unacknowledged limits on the emperor, while tacitly criticizing procedures followed during the preceding

four years. The Council and Committee of Ministers were to be amalgam-
ated into one council.[51] Individual ministerial reports (*vsepoddanneishie
doklady*) to the emperor "must be abolished"; these were the chief source
of "all the dissension and discordance of ministerial rule" in that ministers
felt no obligation to reckon with their colleagues, since on the day of his
report each minister was the bearer of Supreme Power. In the new order,
commands to ministers would be issued in the form of "supremely approved" conclusions from council discussions. The new council would
comprise all department chiefs and ministers.[52] To assure proper unity,
there should be a director of domestic policy who could "influence" the
selection of other ministers, although actual appointments would come
from the ruler.[53] However, even this prerogative was limited by a recommendation that, in the interests of unity, the chairman should have "the
right to present candidates for Ministerial posts" to the emperor.

In curious affirmation of his isolation from the events raging around him
and the memorandum's implications for his power, Nicholas wrote that he
found "much true and useful" in it.[54] He passed it on to the Solskii
conference on 27 August, responding to a request from Solskii, who echoed Kryzhanovskii's warning that the Duma must not become a forum for
resolving disputes between ministers.[55] The conference discussed the ministerial reform from late August until mid-October.

Discussion addressed two separate problems raised by Kryzhanovskii's
plan. Since the spring, official opinion had come to favor ministerial unification in principle.[56] One minister told the Austrian ambassador that the
"formation of a homogeneous ministry" had become "absolutely necessary," in order to prevent the Duma from expanding its competence at the
government's expense.[57] The minister also touched an issue that sparked
fierce debate in the Solskii conference when he added that the government
could rid itself of paralysis only by appointing a "leading minister."

Work on the reform languished until Witte's return in September.[58] He
entered the conference with a renewed authority, denoted by his new title
of count, a mark of the emperor's gratitude for his achievements at Portsmouth. Unlike many of his colleagues, he also had a clear idea of how
government ought to be unified. His language in the Solskii conference
recalled the Kryzhanovskii memorandum, with allusions to the Etats-
Généraux and the call for a cabinet.[59] But he brought his own emphasis to
the discussion by focusing on the role of the "chairman, also named the
Prime Minister." Throughout these discussions, Witte sought broad powers for the council chairman over the other ministers. In opposition to
Kokovtsev, he insisted repeatedly that the chairman be appointed from

among the sitting ministers and have the right to read all ministerial reports to the emperor.[60] When opposed on this point, he continued to demand that the council be informed of the content of all ministerial reports.[61]

On 4 October, Witte stated his full vision of the chairman's role. His model was legislation governing the Prussian cabinet from 1852, when the minister-president's powers were significantly broadened, until Bismarck's resignation in 1890. The example was well chosen, given officials' admiration for Bismarck and the tendency to see in Prussia an instructive parallel for Russia.[62] The Prussian legislation gave the minister-president the right to regulate all contact between individual ministers and the king.[63] Bismarck had apparently resigned when Wilhelm abrogated this decree.

In arguing for a strong "prime minister," Witte seemed to be seeking to control through law the relationship between the emperor and his government, as opposed to the rest of the council reform, which focused on the links between state and Duma. He stated this viewpoint during the revision of the Fundamental Laws in April 1906, when arguing: "[t]here is a basic article stating that the Russian state is governed on the firm base of laws. Once there is such an article, the interpretation of unlimited authority of rule no longer arises, for in reality the supreme power submits itself to law and is regulated by it. In Turkey, the state is not ruled on the basis of positive laws. There one may say that the authority of Government is unlimited, but here, since Emperor Alexander I, laws govern."[64] The autumn of 1905 was a propitious moment for the pursuit of his plans, given his new ascendancy as peacemaker and as the man held widely to be the only one capable of delivering Russia from turmoil. His arguments seemed designed to rectify the shortcomings in autocracy that had led to his downfall.

The mixture of institutional and personal ambition informing Witte's attempts to establish broad authority for the council was well appreciated by his opponents. Kokovtsev insisted frequently that ministers retain the right of individual report to the emperor. State Council member A. A. Saburov feared that the council could become "all-powerful, irresponsible, uncontrollable."[65] A. P. Ignatev and A. S. Stishinskii, defended the inviolability of autocratic prerogative and raised the specter of a "vizierate" in a minority opinion incorporated into the final report of the conference.[66]

Added to these reservations were personal animosity to and fear of Witte as "the coming man."[67] Most conference participants had had to deal with Witte during his heyday as minister of finances. His impending appointment as council chairman was common knowledge by this time. Therefore,

Kokovtsev and others were "working toward holding the powers of the Prime Minister within the narrowest possible limits."[68] But Witte and his opponents seemed to be driven together by Stishinskii's and Ignatev's wholesale rejection of any but the most minimally united government. At the same time, continuing revolutionary disturbances imparted a sense of urgency to the reform, given the simultaneous discussions of the legislation that resulted in the October Manifesto.

By early October, a grudging compromise was reached. Kokovtsev suggested ensuring cohesion within the council through the dismissal of dissenting ministers.[69] Witte relented on the right of individual report but insisted that all reports be communicated to the council,[70] while complaining "that the first minister was not being given those rights which ought to belong to him."[71] His efforts to gain an authoritative role for the prime minister continued to elicit protests from conservatives, who said that "this first minister" would be "a vizier, limiting autocracy."[72]

The conference's majority opinion countered this accusation, stating that the reform did not change "the existing Supreme guidance" of state administration. There was no "derogation of Supreme Power, neither in the establishment of procedures for the Chairman, nor in the prerogatives accorded him." The report added that whoever was appointed chairman would be by that fact "invested with the MONARCH's special confidence."[73] Therefore, there would be no need to waste time on documents and signatures for individual ministerial reports, as the minority had suggested. A demonstrated lack of confidence could harm the reform from its outset, in which case "it would be preferable not to undertake the reform."

The reform of the Council of Ministers was officially enacted on 19 October and reflected the rough compromise between Witte and his majority opponents based on the necessity for unified government.[74] The new body was put in charge of the "direction and unification of the chiefs of the departments, on subjects both of legislation and of higher state administration."[75] It included all ministers and department heads, under the presidency of a minister or some other person chosen by the emperor, who could also act as chair.[76] No measure of "general significance" could be taken by any senior official without reference to the council.

The council chairman could speak for all departments in the legislative organs.[77] He enjoyed the right of direct report to the emperor on all issues under council purview and in matters he thought to require the emperor's attention.[78] Council members were directed to provide him with "necessary" information and explanations, which he could introduce to council discussion.[79] Department chiefs were to give to the chairman in advance the contents of all reports to the emperor having a "general significance" or affecting other departments. These reports would be discussed in council or simply submitted to the emperor in the chairman's presence, if necessary.[80] Matters regarding the departments of Court, State Defense, and Foreign Affairs could be introduced into council when there was a supreme command "or" when the interested department recognized it as necessary, "or" when the matter affected other departments.[81] However, Article 19 reserved to the emperor the decision on all questions not receiving unanimous resolution in council.

Witte was named first chairman of the reformed council. On the eve of the council reform's announcement, Finance Minister Kokovtsev encountered an elder statesman, who lamented that "in the place of the tsar's autocracy, you are preaching the same autocracy, but only that of the First Minister or, in other words, the creation of the office of Grand Vizier."[82]

The new act and the reforms regarding the legislative Duma, the State Council, and civil liberties, had been the outcome of exceptional circumstances. The revolution had forced Nicholas to recall Witte to active service, and to consent to the inroads on his power contained in the reforms. The fact that the officials devising the reforms were reacting to exceptional circumstances also became the Achilles' heel of the new state structure. Witte had sought to mold the reform proposals in conformity with notions he held about the role of government vis-à-vis the emperor and the country at large. His opponents and colleagues in the Solskii conference, and later in the Council of Ministers, had views of their own about the nature of autocracy.

A. A. Polovtsev, for example, had shared the majority opinion in the Solskii conference on the necessity of a united government. But he retained an ambiguous understanding of the nexus between emperor and government that combined a bureaucratic worldview with a deep personal loyalty to the tsar and a fear (in the sense of "God-fearing") of the power he wielded. While supporting the council reform, Polovtsev could comment in his diary that the sovereign could consult with whomever he pleased; his will "after or without any conference" was still "holy."[83] Polovtsev's ability to entertain simultaneously—in Weberian retrospect—contradictory views was widely shared in high official circles, even after the experiences of 1902–1904. Many future ministers in the United Government would show by their actions that they shared this outlook in spite of the 1905 ukaz, especially as an air of seeming normality and routine returned to Russia after 1907.

Of course, the other critical factor in the reform was the attitude of Nicholas himself. Isolated at Peterhof by the disturbances, Nicholas was aware of the crisis besetting his empire. Yet he had only accepted Witte's draft of the October Manifesto and the ministerial reform after more than a week of concerted persuasion on the part of Witte and Grand Duke Nikolai Nikolaievich, who finally convinced him that the empire's survival hung in the balance.[84] Even in April 1906, during the revision of the Fundamental Laws of the Empire, Nicholas would insist on the retention of the adjective "unlimited" in the legal description of his autocratic power, despite the counterarguments of even conservative officials as to what had befallen that power the preceding October.[85]

Nicholas's assent to these reforms was less than whole-hearted. Witte learned that while he was urging the October Manifesto on Nicholas, the emperor had been holding private conversations with conservatives in search of a less distasteful solution.[86] On the day he had signed the legislation creating the Council of Ministers, Nicholas wrote to his mother: "It makes me sick to read the news! Nothing but new strikes in schools and factories, murdered policemen, Cossacks, and soldiers, disorder, mutinies. But the ministers, instead of acting with quick decision, only assemble in council like a lot of frightened hens and cackle about united ministerial action."[87]

From their inception, the reforms of October 1905 were vitiated by ambivalence on the part of their makers and by a lack of consensus on their meaning or permanence. Like the legislative Duma, the new council was based on an ambiguous and self-contradictory document. One observer wrote of the Duma, in terms which could apply equally to the council legislation, "[t]he result was . . . full of grand phrases and highsounding promises in which everybody could find what corresponded to his desire."[88] Witte's brief tenure as council chairman revealed the limits built into the new law and the critical nature of the relationship between chairman and emperor on which Witte had placed so much institutional weight. Nicholas frequently ignored his prime minister, going behind the chairman's back in his relations with Minister of Internal Affairs P. N. Durnovo, in particular.[89] Barely a month after the inauguration of United Government, a British diplomat observed that "although [Witte] is nominally at the head of a 'homogeneous government' the former departmental independence still appears to prevail in almost undiminished vigour."[90]

By early 1906, Nicholas had begun to regret the powers he had ceded in the fall.[91] At the end of January he wrote to Witte, "[i]n my opinion, the role of Chairman of the Council of Ministers should be limited to the unification of the ministers' activity, while all executive work should remain the obligation of the appropriate ministers."[92] Witte later analyzed Nicholas's implications for the chairman's relations with his adversaries at court and in the council: "and since the executive part may be carried out directly according to reports to the Sovereign or by the Sovereign's direct instructions, then by this means in all cases when one wished to get around an intractable premier, one left the head of government to one side and did what one desired without his knowledge."[93]

Witte blamed his rapid decline on D. F. Trepov, who as governor-general of St. Petersburg enjoyed daily contact with Nicholas and encouraged the latter's bent for behind-the-scenes actions. Witte also accused P. N. Durnovo in Internal Affairs of ignoring the October reforms as far as he was able.[94] Both had Nicholas's tacit support. When, in early 1906, Nicholas insisted on appointing A. V. Krivoshein and S. V. Rukhlov to the council over Witte's objections, the chairman sent a long letter to the emperor complaining of his differences with them, claiming that "[n]ow I am deprived of the possibility of unifying in proper fashion the actions of the Government." These recriminations were followed by a request to be relieved of his duties, which Nicholas rejected.[95]

When Witte repeated this request in mid-April, expanding upon his earlier complaints,[96] Nicholas "allowed" Witte to step down. Relations between the two had become extremely strained. Nicholas resented his premier's high-handed behavior in such cases as Kutler's draft land reform and the Duma electoral law and regretted having ceded so much prerogative to Witte in the first place.[97] As Witte noted in his resignation letter, he had been undercut by Nicholas virtually since his appointment as chairman. Witte had become further expendable after the conclusion of a large French loan, one of the chief reasons for his having remained council chairman as long as he had.[98]

Witte had learned the limits of his authority: his dismissal was still Nicholas's prerogative, exercised at Witte's expense in April, before the first Duma convened. Thus, despite all his efforts to concentrate the mediation of the sovereign's power in the office of council chairman, Witte was still dependent on Nicholas's confidence. The instrumentality of the ruler's confidence had been acknowledged as the basis of the council reform in the majority report of the Solskii conference. Even to Witte, the person of Nicholas as sovereign was still the source of the government's authority. Witte's efforts to reconcile the personal and institutional elements of autocracy meant that the emperor's confidence persisted as the *caput mortuum* of the post-1905 order.

Nowhere was the confusion more marked under the new regime than in the allocation of authority over foreign policy. Although foreign policy retreated to the background during these months of revolution and reform, views about the causes and consequences of the war with Japan, confirmed by the Björkö incident, had helped shape the council reform. Despite the almost exclusive focus on the reestablishment of domestic peace that dominated official concerns throughout 1905 and 1906, note had been taken of the problems presented by this area, particularly as they reflected the new status of the emperor's power. The ambiguities in the council reform were even more sharply reflected in the sphere of foreign policy making, touching, as it did, on the very essence of the emperor's sovereign power. As a result, the issue of foreign policy making in the reformed state structure received only desultory attention during the Solskii conference and its aftermath. Like so many of the period's reforms, references to foreign policy making during these discussion were ambiguous and contradictory. However, as United Government assumed a life of its own and turned to the reordering of the empire, these issues came under increasing scrutiny.

Interestingly, from the outset of his tenure as chairman Witte saw foreign policy issues as part of his portfolio. His memoir account of the Björkö affair distinguished between the period before October 17, when he was kept informally abreast of events by Lamzdorf,[99] and afterward: when "I had become Chairman of the Council of Ministers, I asked Lamzdorf—not out of friendly acquaintance but by right [*po pravu*]—about the status of the Björkö affair."[100] On 17 October, Witte sent a circular to the ministers, informing them of Nicholas's order that he "take measures for the unification of the ministers' activity before the confirmation of the legislation on the council of ministers."[101] An addendum to Lamzdorf requested him to keep Witte informed of "all major external events" with implications for Russia's internal condition.[102]

Although the Council of Ministers reform had segregated certain ministries from direct subordination to the council, the extent of this separation was unclear, even to the reformers. Thus, the Solskii conference report acknowledged "that affairs relating to the departments of the EMPEROR's Court and Appanages, state defense, and foreign policy should be under the direct conduct of the appropriate Ministers, and having agreed in general with such an assumption, the *chairman and the twenty-seven members* [of the majority] recognize it as necessary to foresee also those occasions when these matters must be brought into the Council of Ministers."[103]

These ambiguities were not clarified during the revision of the Fundamental Laws in April 1906. Only one article in the revised laws dealt with foreign policy: "12. THE SOVEREIGN EMPEROR is the supreme director of all external relations of the Russian State with foreign powers. The direction of the international policy of the Russian State is determined by Him also."[104] Historians often argue on the basis of this article that very little changed in the making of Russian foreign policy after 1905; as before, foreign policy was decided by the emperor in consultation with his foreign minister to the exclusion of other actors.[105] However, this interpretation overlooks the intentions of the framers of the new laws, which was to protect certain areas of state prerogative from encroachments by the new Duma. In regard to foreign policy, Witte stated this view explicitly at the Tsarskoe Selo conferences: "[i]t is necessary to exclude the possibility of the State Duma intervening in the affairs of the Ministry of Foreign Affairs . . . All external policy and international relations must belong to the immediate direction of the Sovereign Emperor."[106] Witte's primary concern was to distinguish the Duma's restricted legislative prerogatives under the October Manifesto from those that remained the exclusive province of the state as mediator of the emperor's will. This concern was evident in Witte's view of his own prerogatives in foreign policy and in those of his successors down to the Great War.[107]

Despite the best attempts of tsarist officials in the months after August 1905, the structure of the reformed government was still only formal. The elaboration of concrete relationships and practice took place within the framework laid down in October 1905 and April 1906, but the actual force of these laws was shaped by a wide array of factors, as officials sought to reestablish state authority at a time when autocracy had ventured into the *terra incognita* of quasi-parliamentary and cabinet rule. The unfamiliarity of new institutional circumstances was exacerbated by the continuation of revolutionary unrest and the relative absence of Nicholas as a decisive actor following Witte's resignation. Officials were forced to restore order in Russia at large while adapting to the new order in their own midst.

## Izvolskii, Stolypin, and the New Order, 1906–1907

On the day he resigned, Witte learned of one decision that would have a crucial bearing on the course and formation of Russian foreign policy in following years—the impending appointment of Alexander Petrovich Izvolskii to succeed Lamzdorf as minister of foreign affairs. Officially, Lamzdorf requested retirement for reasons of ill health.[108] The real reason was given in a letter by former Justice Minister N. V. Muravev, then

Russian ambassador at Rome: "having been the servitor of autocracy for forty years he felt incapable of turning a new leaf in his career faced with a new regime."[109] Lamzdorf had told the German ambassador that he had no wish to face "those people," in the Duma.[110]

Izvolskii represented a departure from the previous run of foreign ministers.[111] He had acquired little of his predecessors' experience for the minister's office. Although long regarded as a future minister,[112] by 1906 Izvolskii had not served for any extended time in the ministry's chancellery in St. Petersburg—in contrast to Girs, Lobanov-Rostovskii, and Lamzdorf—nor had he occupied any of the prestige embassies in Europe. Personally, Izvolskii was the opposite of the courtly, self-effacing Lamzdorf. The new minister was seen as highly intelligent, with a quick grasp of diplomatic niceties, but he was also known for an *amour-propre* and snobbery that fueled many anecdotes.[113]

The differences between the two ministers reflected their divergent career paths. Lamzdorf had owed his promotion to his mastery of the MID chancellery and the fact that Witte saw in him a pliant partner. By contrast, Izvolskii had spent most of his service abroad, after only three years of training in St. Petersburg from 1875 to 1878.[114] In fact, his long service abroad helped underline his status as an "outsider" in the MID. Still, Izvolskii harbored some links to ministry traditions. Like Witte's nemesis Muravev, Izvolskii had been Russian minister at Copenhagen—birthplace of Dowager Empress Maria Fedorovna—his post at the time of his appointment. As had all but two foreign ministers from the appointment of Gorchakov until 1916, he had been educated at the Alexander Lycée, an institution noted for the aristocratic antecedents of its students and for the liberalism and personal independence it inculcated in its charges.[115]

Izvolskii had a reputation for "liberal" or "*zemstvo*-liberal" sympathies. He sprang from a modest *pomeshchik* background of the sort that had provided so many *obshchestvennye deiateli*. He came to his ministerial chair with the feeling that the recent reforms had "endowed Russia with a complete constitutional system," which was "frankly accepted by all those, including myself, who represented the Moderate Liberal Party . . . [which] had taken the name of 'Octobrist.'"[116] Part of his reputation derived from the letter he delivered to Nicholas from the dowager empress, in October 1905, in which Maria Fedorovna was said to have advised Nicholas to grant a constitution.[117] Izvolskii later claimed to have sought "to convince [Maria Fedorovna] and through her to convince the Czar of the necessity of making concessions to the reasonable demands of the moderate liberal party."[118]

If Lamzdorf had resigned his post at the prospect of dealing with "those people" in the Duma, Izvolskii defined his role foursquare within the framework of the new regime. Foreign Ministry Councillor M. A. Taube credited Izvolskii's appointment as minister to his views on reform, which Nicholas had first encountered during Izvolskii's mission on behalf of Maria Fedorovna in late 1905.[119] Izvolskii's "reputation as a 'reformer'" caused his appointment to be widely greeted in the press and Duma circles.[120] The need for a foreign minister able to deal with the new Russian politics was cited by Izvolskii himself. In April 1906—before his appointment[121]—Izvolskii speculated during "private" talks at the Quai d'Orsay on the probability of Lamzdorf's following Witte into retirement.[122] He felt that Lamzdorf's successor would have to be able to deal with the new assembly. Izvolskii also attributed his appointment to his interest in domestic affairs as a result of the revolution of 1905.[123] As Taube observed, Izvolskii "had striven to stand before the first Russian 'Parliament' in the capacity of the first 'constitutional' Russian Minister of Foreign Affairs."[124] During the first part of his tenure—as head of an ostensibly "excluded" ministry—he threw himself into "cabinet"[125] discussions of domestic policy.

These claims were not disingenuous. Soon after his appointment, he created MID posts to act as liaisons with the Duma[126] and the nonofficial press.[127] He championed the cause of the Duma within the Council of Ministers and participated in discussions for the creation of a "mixed" cabinet—to include leading "public men" (obshchestvennye deiateli) as well as officials—after the dissolution of the first Duma in the summer of 1906. Izvolskii's views of the new order were evident in his choice for assistant minister, N. V. Charykov—a pomeshchik from Saratov guberniia whose family had long been involved in zemstvo activities.[128] Charykov too had spent most of his career abroad and sympathized with the course of reform in Russia. Offering Charykov the post, Izvolskii wrote that he saw in him someone "belonging to the traditional circle of Russian landed nobility which dominates, and I hope will continue in the future to dominate, our representative institutions."[129] Izvolskii also had wide contacts among liberal circles.[130] In November 1905 and in the summer of 1906, he tried to convince his liberal friends of the need to accommodate the government so as better to resist the destructive forces of the revolution.

His outlook on autocracy, like many officials', had been significantly shaped by the period before the war with Japan. He had witnessed the Bezobrazovshchina as Russia's envoy in Tokyo, from whence he had sent frequent warnings about Japanese sensitivity to Russia's intentions in Korea. His experiences led him to believe that what he called "despotism" was accompanied by "incoherence, if not contradiction in the conduct of affairs," leading to "irreconcilable" decisions from the "supreme leader." In his mind, "the Russo-Japanese War came from this."[131] These problems could be overcome under the new regime.

Izvolskii's view of his role was also reflected in an approach to his relationship with Nicholas that was diametrically opposed to the submissiveness that had often characterized Lamzdorf. Thus, in 1907, on the eve of Nicholas's departure to Swinemünde for his first meeting with Wilhelm since Björkö, Izvolskii wrote to the Russian ambassador in Vienna that his and Bülow's presence at the meeting would undoubtedly provoke "some fantasizing commentaries and deductions." Nevertheless, he was happy to accompany Nicholas: "it will suffice that you recall what took place at Björkö, and that must be avoided at any cost."[132]

In his first months as foreign minister, Izvolskii was preoccupied with Russia's domestic situation. Rather than acting as chief of diplomacy, Izvolskii concentrated on his duties in the Council of Ministers, under Witte's successor and one-time adversary I. L. Goremykin, a former minister of internal affairs of decidedly conservative views. During the late spring and summer of 1906, the council faced a Duma dominated by Kadet and peasant deputies intent on passing a land reform and other measures unacceptable to the government, both in their content and in the prerogatives they claimed for the legislature. Tensions between the government and the Duma culminated at the beginning of July, with the prorogation of the first Duma, an abortive attempt to include "public men" in the government, and the replacement of the Goremykin ministry with one under the chairmanship of Minister of Internal Affairs P. A. Stolypin.

Izvolskii's involvement in these events was important in shaping his attitude to the relationship between government and Duma, and in the development of his relations with the "cabinet." His very participation in these events was significant, given his ministry's status and Nicholas's misgivings about the role taken by his foreign minister.[133] The crisis over the dissolution of the first Duma also showed for the first time that Russia's internal political condition was an important element in its international position.

The council under Goremykin failed to meet the expectations Izvolskii had voiced in Paris. Instead of a remedy for administrative incoherence, Izvolskii found the council to be a "heterogeneous" body whose chairman "took no pains to conceal the little respect he had not only for the Duma but even for the Council of Ministers, considering that institution a useless innovation and [making] his colleagues to understand that he called them together merely for the sake of form."[134] Izvolskii's letters to Russian ambassadors abroad were preoccupied with the impasse between the Duma and the government, which he criticized for a "pitiable unconsciousness or ineptitude"[135] in its dealings with the legislature.

Izvolskii's contempt for his council colleagues was heartily reciprocated. Kokovtsev derided Izvolskii's proposals for accommodation with the Duma, which he attributed to an excessive concern with Russia's image and standing abroad, even at the risk of domestic upheaval.[136] In council meetings, Izvolskii often found himself isolated against his more conservative colleagues.[137]

Izvolskii demonstrated his commitment to the new institutions during the July crisis. In late June he had begun to advocate the formation of a cabinet "capable of seeking an understanding with the moderate elements in the assembly."[138] In early July he gained Nicholas's permission to negotiate with leading moderate Duma deputies for the formation of a mixed cabinet, based on a note drafted by several deputies at a meeting arranged by Izvolskii.[139] These talks, in which Stolypin joined, lasted into the third week of July.

Izvolskii's efforts were not simply an outgrowth of his liberal sympathies. As foreign minister, he drew close connections between the Duma crisis and Russia's position as a great power in Europe. Of immediate concern were the effects of the crisis on Russia's standing in Europe: Benkendorf had raised this problem in June.[140] Izvolskii used this argument when persuading a reluctant Nicholas to permit him to take part in council discussion of domestic problems. After vouching for the conservatism and loyalty of landowner-deputies, Izvolskii "drew the Emperor's attention . . . to the impression produced by our internal crisis upon foreign cabinets and European public opinion."[141] Western distaste for the Goremykin cabinet and lack of confidence in Russia's ability to gain a state of normality "obstructed in advance any steps we might take in our foreign relations" and impeded Russian access to European money markets. The last part of this statement was a reference to Kadet efforts to forestall the French loan to Russia before the opening of the Duma; this plan had been only narrowly averted by Witte before his resignation.[142]

Izvolskii's concern over the July crisis was also based on considerations of longer duration. In early May, he had written to Prince L. P. Urusov, the ambassador in Vienna, of his worries about the domestic situation and the inevitability of a clash with the Duma: "What will be the result of it? Today, no one can predict it, but it is certain that we are entering a very troubled period which will impose on us more than ever the absolute necessity of being on good terms with everybody." For these reasons, he advocated consolidating the existing understanding with Austria-Hungary on upholding the *status quo* in the Balkans.[143]

Thus, by the summer of 1906, Izvolskii had integrated his views on Russia's options abroad with his ideas on the course to be followed in domestic policy. To Izvolskii, Russia's foreign policy had to take into account the empire's domestic stability and strength. Russian prestige in Europe had been grievously diminished by the Japanese defeat and was being eroded by Russia's internal crisis, as demonstrated in the difficulties in securing the French loan. These difficulties had occurred despite Russian support for France at Algeciras and the fourteen-year-old Dual Alliance. In addition, the government's inability to assure order in domestic politics was itself a symptom of weakness, further exacerbated by a cabinet that was unwilling or unable to meet the challenge posed by revolution. These considerations dictated a policy of "remaining on good terms with everyone."

Significantly, Izvolskii saw only one solution: cooperation with the moderate liberal elements in the Duma. His belief that Russia could not recover its international position until a working arrangement was established between the government and the Duma lent a radically new cast to official Russian thinking on foreign policy. Izvolskii's commitment to the preservation of the Duma also cemented his relations with the other "outsider" in the Goremykin cabinet, Minister of Internal Affairs Peter Arkadevich Stolypin.

Stolypin's appointment as council chairman was crucial to the consolidation of what had been left unresolved in the governmental reforms of 1905–1906. In many ways, he played the role after 1905 that Witte had before the revolution. Both came relatively late to the higher reaches of state service. Both achieved positions of political preeminence at times of vulnerability for Nicholas. And both came to political grief from conflicts with the emperor over their authority as statesmen and the principles on which it was to be defined. But Stolypin established to the fullest extent the prerogatives of the post for which Witte had sought such wide authority. Armed with the confidence of a singularly insecure Nicholas, Stolypin made the position of council chairman into the *de facto* premiership of a truly united cabinet.

Most important, Stolypin's elevation to premier represented the resurrection of the ideas that had dominated the reform discussions throughout 1905 but that had lapsed under Goremykin: the conviction that society as represented in the new legislative institutions was a factor in state life and that the challenge to state authority posed by the new conditions demanded a united government under an assertive chairman. Unlike Witte, Stolypin did not develop these ideas pell-mell. By the time he assumed his duties as council chairman, he had very definite views on the role of this position. At least part of his outlook can be attributed to his own career experience, as can his acceptance of the new representative institutions and the relatively unfettered press that faced his government.

Stolypin was born in 1862 into a landowning noble family.[144] Educated in the early 1880s at St. Petersburg University, he entered the Ministry of Internal Affairs before completing his studies. From the perspective of his subsequent career, two posts he held before becoming minister in April 1906 were of especial importance. In the late 1880s he served as marshal of the nobility in ethnically mixed Kovno *uezd*, an area numbering Lithuanians, Poles, Jews, Germans, and some Russians among its inhabitants. His service in this area is often cited to explain his manifest Great Russian nationalism which bemused or distressed some of his colleagues and other observers.[145]

After a promotion to *guberniia* marshal, he was made governor of a neighboring *guberniia* in 1902. The next year he was sent to Saratov, a hotbed of *zemstvo* activism and social ferment.[146] Stolypin served there just before and during the first part of the revolution. In April 1906 he replaced P. N. Durnovo as minister of internal affairs. The sudden promotion to ministerial dignity of a provincial official who had not served in the capital in over twenty years was dramatic. As one of his assistants later observed, "Stolypin was Fate's darling."[147]

Stolypin brought to St. Petersburg two sorts of experience of which he availed himself throughout his tenure as chairman. As marshal of the nobility and as governor he had formed relatively broad links within local "society" during the most dramatic period of growth in *zemstvo*-based activism. These contacts seem to have affected his views of this part of society as a potential political actor.[148] Thus, Stolypin never seemed to feel—as did Goremykin or Kokovtsev in 1906—that the Duma was expendable as a representative of society. Despite the failure of his attempt with Izvolskii to form a mixed ministry, and the dissolution of the second Duma, his reform of the franchise and electoral procedures in the dramatic measures of 3 June 1907 showed his concern for finding a viable social and political partner for the state as much as it illustrated his desire to crush the revolution once and for all. This impulse was also evident in the stated intent of his famous land reform to create a small-holding rural constituency with a stake in the political order.

To assert all of this is not to equate him with a British prime minister or a premier in the Third Republic. His frequent recourse to the emergency powers provided by Article 87 of the Fundamental Laws bespoke a high-handedness, and an assertion of the superiority of "state" vision, which were incompatible with precepts of parliamentary rule. In assessing his role as premier, we must compare him with his German and Austro-Hungarian counterparts who, like him, rejected notions of ministerial responsibility to their respective chambers while recognizing the necessity of working with them, and also had an active awareness of public opinion as an important barometer of social ferment in a postrevolutionary time.[149] In these traits, as well as in his professional background and career, he differed markedly from the majority of his ministers and his own aides in Internal Affairs.

The other enduring element in Stolypin's provincial experience emerged in his relations with the council itself. As a governor, one of his tasks had been the "unification of the administrative apparatus."[150] Indeed, the role of governor, as the local delegate of central authority, was easily transferable to the functions of council chairman. This was especially the case at a time of continuing political tensions, when the empire as a whole must have looked like a macrocosm of Saratov during Stolypin's tenure there.

Certainly, Stolypin deplored the disunity and passivity of Goremykin's council.[151] Like Izvolskii, Stolypin criticized Goremykin's refusal to recognize "any sort of unified government," and the attitude that "the whole government is the tsar alone, and that he will say what we will execute, but so long as there is no clear instruction from him we must wait and be patient." This statement also contained an assertive view of the prerogatives of the council and its head in relation to the emperor. Elsewhere, Stolypin contended that United Government was necessary to lighten the sovereign's burdens.[152] In fact, the conditions under which he accepted his appointment as premier bespoke his views on United Government. Before agreeing to take the new position, Stolypin insisted upon the dismissal of two well-known reactionaries in the former cabinet—A. S. Stishinskii and A. A. Shirinskii-Shikhmatov—while reserving the right to pursue discussions on the mixed cabinet.[153]

As became increasingly evident during the two years following his appointment, Stolypin was committed in equal measure to the reestablishment of order by cultivating strategic social support,[154] and to cabinet rule under an authoritative premier. On 3 June 1907, faced with a recalcitrant and relatively leftist Duma, Stolypin used the activities of some Social Democrat deputies as a pretext to invoke the emergency powers accorded the government under Article 87 of the Fundamental Laws. In his *coup d'état*, Stolypin enacted a restricted electoral franchise that accorded predominance to noble landowners in the countryside and propertied elements in urban Russia. The third Duma seemed initially to vindicate Stolypin's calculations. Dominated by deputies from the moderate-liberal Octobrist party and self-styled "moderate rights" from the rural gentry, the new Duma presented the chairman with a viable partner in rebuilding Russia on the basis of cooperation between "state" and "nation," as he and his Duma constituents understood the terms.

The question of whether he actually succeeded in creating a homogeneous government is not so important as has been suggested.[155] What is striking is Stolypin's effort as chairman to make the Council of Ministers the exclusive instance of decision making, with the aim of developing a program of political reform and reconstruction based on a consensus worked out through discussion among all the ministers.[156] By law, all matters affecting the activity or competence of more than one ministry were to be treated in the council.[157] It is a measure of Stolypin's energy and success in establishing the council's role as a policy-making forum that by 1909 a "Small Council" was created to deliberate the most important issues. Routine decisions were left to the larger council, to which many ministers had long been sending their assistants.[158]

Undoubtedly, the atmosphere of urgency informing the council's activity during the period from Stolypin's appointment until 3 June 1907 nurtured the habit of collegial consultation among the ministers and contributed to an aspiration to consensus in policy matters. Kokovtsev recalled of this period, "all of us had to follow intently the struggle with revolutionary outbursts in various localities in Russia, since Stolypin gave all of us the full possibility to be always and fully abreast of events, and none of us had the right . . . to say that he did not take part in the resolution of ongoing matters or did not bear responsibility for the decisions that were taken."[159]

Izvolskii wrote of these events in much the same vein, characteristically taking credit for drafting many of the council's legislative projects, since he was the only minister with intimate knowledge of the workings of "a constitutional and parliamentary regime." He also commented on his interest in the elaboration of Stolypin's land reform legislation of November 1906—not a topic one would expect to find in a diplomat's memoirs.[160]

These and other accounts also attest to continuing efforts by Stolypin and some of the ministers to make the Council of Ministers a "solid" body. Izvolskii was asked by Stolypin to stay on as foreign minister in the summer of 1906 because Stolypin knew "that he could count on my hearty cooperation in carrying out his program of reforms and in preparing the ground for future harmony between the Duma and the Government."[161]

Kokovtsev cited the ongoing discussions of electoral laws in late 1906 to describe the growth and the novelty of cabinet solidarity. In these talks, Izvolskii was the only opponent to a substantial reform of the laws that had produced the unworkable first Duma; he doubted the legality of such revisions without the assent of the Duma. Although often critical of Izvolskii's liberalism, in this instance Kokovtsev commented approvingly that Izvolskii kept his misgivings to himself—not even broaching the question with the emperor—and even helped draft new legislation.[162]

By 3 June 1907 Stolypin was able to assert the principle of cabinet unity as a prerequisite for tenure in a ministerial post. Shortly thereafter, State Comptroller P. Kh. Shvanebakh was forced to resign owing "to the insuperable differences of opinion between him and the head of the government." Shvanebakh had objected strenuously to Stolypin's attempts to reach an understanding with the second Duma. He had carried this battle into the State Council, earning the reproaches of his fellow ministers for having breached professional discretion. Although Nicholas was said to sympathize with Shvanebakh's distaste for the legislature, his "unshaken faith" in Stolypin proved to be a decisive obstacle to the comptroller's intrigues.[163] His ability to gain this dismissal stood in marked contrast to Witte's frustrations with both Nicholas and dissident ministers in his council.

By all appearances, Nicholas did indeed support the council and the principle of United Government as implemented under Stolypin. This was particularly evident in a supreme rescript addressed to Stolypin on New Year's Day, 1907.[164] The message praised Stolypin as chairman of the Council of Ministers, "which is under your leadership," for the council's work in the restoration of order in Russia.

Stolypin's ability to win Nicholas's confidence was bolstered by the growing respect of most of his colleagues. Several aspects of his personality seem to account for his success with Nicholas and the other ministers. War Minister A. F. Rediger recalled that "[a]t that time . . . Stolypin produced the best impression on me: young, energetic, with faith in Russia's future, [he] set about reforms decisively."[165] Kokovtsev traced Stolypin's personal and political ascendancy to August 1906. On 12 August, his summer home was the target of a bombing that, although sparing Stolypin himself, injured many others, including two of his children. In recalling this event, Kokovtsev noted Stolypin's "surprising self-possession." The chairman's *sangfroid* under this attack and its effects on "his personal situation" led to a change in attitudes toward him "not only at Court and in broad circles of society, but also among all the members of the Council of Ministers . . . In a word, Stolypin in some way grew at once and became the generally recognized master of the situation."[166]

It was this combination of "moral authority," as Kokovtsev called it, and the energy described by Rediger that led to the rapid consolidation he accomplished within the council—especially when seen against the background of its history under Goremykin and the longer-term habits of ministerial fracture. His newfound authority also allowed him simultaneously to seek a solution to the impasse with the Duma, which permitted its preservation—albeit in truncated form—and the maintenance of the principles on which it had been founded, from an official's point of view.

By the beginning of 1908, Stolypin appeared in large measure to have reestablished order in Russia and to have laid the groundwork for lasting cooperation between his government and the centrist third Duma. The 3 June measures had evoked a harsh outcry from Kadet ranks and those further to the left. Misgivings had also been voiced over his recourse to Article 87. But both had largely subsided or been politically nullified by the end of 1907. His ability to unify the cabinet, create a relatively pacific Duma, and maintain Nicholas's support seemed to justify Kryzhanovskii's statement that Stolypin was "Fate's darling." In ensuing years, he would expand the scope of his authority by intervening directly in foreign policy making, for reasons that were rooted in his experiences in dealing with the revolution in 1905–1907 as governor in Saratov, minister of internal affairs (a portfolio he retained after August 1906), and chairman of the Council of Ministers.

Thus, in October 1908 Stolypin was able to demand that Izvolskii account to the council for Austria-Hungary's annexation of Slav-populated Bosnia-Herzegovina, with the purported approval of the Russian government. Izvolskii was to find to his chagrin that the reforms set in motion in 1905, which he had supported, ultimately created a new environment within which even the minister of foreign affairs—despite Article 12 in the Fundamental Laws—was no longer able to operate with the same latitude as his nonconstitutional predecessors. When he had embraced the Russian parliament and membership in Stolypin's cabinet, Izvolskii had really ensured that his own actions and policy would be subject to the same sort of critical scrutiny that he had applied to Goremykin and Stolypin.

# · 5 ·

# The Building of a
# Foreign Policy Consensus

The confusion that characterized the post-1905 order within Russia also affected Izvolskii's earliest efforts to define the empire's external policy. After an initial preoccupation with domestic events, Izvolskii soon turned to the problem of devising a diplomatic position for a Russia that had been terribly weakened by war and revolution. As with the Duma and the Council of Ministers reform, the course and the making of foreign policy were beset by the ambiguity that pervaded all of Russian politics until order was firmly established in mid-1907.

Like the *coup d'état* of 3 June 1907, which established the bases for constitutional and social stability in Russia, the Anglo-Russian agreement of August 1907 marked a key juncture in the development of a new foreign policy for postrevolutionary Russia. The agreement itself was modest: it regulated outstanding issues regarding Britain's and Russia's interests in Asia, including a partition of Persia into spheres of influence, separated by a neutral zone. But many observers at the time and afterward regarded this agreement as a reflection of Izvolskii's liberal proclivities and a major reorientation of Russian diplomacy.

An examination of the motives behind the agreement, and the way support for this departure was mobilized, indicate that it emerged from the same lack of definition that dogged domestic policy until 1907. In fact, Izvolskii and other statesmen found themselves developing simultaneously a new course for Russian policy and new procedures for making it. The following discussion concentrates more on the process by which the Anglo-Russian entente found acceptance within Russian government, than on its implications for prewar diplomacy. In both regards, the background to the agreement laid the bases for the Bosnian crisis as it affected the making of foreign policy under United Government.

## The Making of the Agreement with Britain, 1906–1907

The revolution's effect on Russian foreign policy went beyond the appointment of a liberal foreign minister. The war and the subsequent revolution forced all Russians with an interest in foreign policy to reformulate their conceptions of the bases and directions of that policy, given the changes that had occurred within the country. The effects of these changes on the understanding of diplomatic issues were evident in the so-called orientation debate within government and society over the requirements and goals of Russia's foreign policy. This debate revolved around the ideological and political bases upon which Russian foreign alignments were to be founded at a unique conjuncture in Russia's foreign and domestic political circumstances.

The transformations of 1905–1906 within Russia coincided with an unaccustomed latitude in its international relations. The recent war had demonstrated the geographic limits of the French alliance and the extent of British determination to resist the expansion of Russia's presence in Asia. The Dual Alliance had been further undermined by France's entry into the Entente Cordiale with Great Britain in 1904. Indeed, the central European empires had offered greater support than France during the war. Germany had maintained a benevolent neutrality, to the extent of courting complications with Britain, while Austria-Hungary had honored the 1903 Mürzsteg agreement on the *status quo* in the Balkans, despite Russia's difficulties in Asia. Even Russia's long-standing enmity with Great Britain had shown signs of abating before the war with Japan when talks began between the two governments concerning their interests in the Far East and Central Asia.[2]

Thus, when he took over the Ministry of Foreign Affairs in 1906, Izvolskii enjoyed a theoretical freedom for maneuver unmatched since the late 1880s. This latitude aroused discussion in many quarters of the best policy for Russia to pursue. Although the debate echoed similar discussions during the 1850s and early 1890s, the terms of discourse were dramatically recast as participants now founded their views on interpretations of the revolution's meaning for Russia's foreign relations. This element had been inchoate in the forebodings of Kuropatkin and others about the domestic ramifications of war with Japan. After 1905, all observers viewed foreign policy against the backdrop of domestic events.

Many conservatives favored returning to a policy of defending the "monarchical principle," in the tradition of the Holy Alliance or Bismarck's Three Emperors' League. However, if these earlier alliances had been aimed at containing the spread of democratism in Europe, the revolution had led many conservatives to believe that ferment had now reached into Russia.[3] Unsurprisingly, State Comptroller Shvanebakh was a strong exponent of such views. In a visit with British Ambassador Sir Arthur Nicolson, Shvanebakh indulged in "a strong denunciation of the alliance with France, which he characterized as having been disastrous to Russia."[4] Nicolson reported further that Shvanebakh was not alone in his views.[5]

Shvanebakh attacked the French alliance for the risk it had brought of alienating Germany. Russia had benefited little from the relationship, beyond gaining easy credit for the construction of the Siberian railway and "artificially" to "create industry." Shvanebakh examined the utility of the alliance against the background of recent events in Russia: "the union with France was doubtless welcome to the revolutionary elements in Russia, but it was condemned by all who wished to preserve the established order of things . . . all that was solid and durable in Russia had been introduced on German models and from German sources, and at this moment especially, it was clearly to the interest of the Russian government to draw more closely to Germany." Shvanebakh hoped for a revived "alliance of the three Emperors, who together would assist each other in the maintenance of the monarchical principle and in the preservation of peace in Europe."

Shvanebakh's jeremiad restated enduring themes in the rhetoric of Russian conservatism. Compared to older statements on foreign policy, Shvanebakh's critique was novel for the links it posited between Russia's foreign orientation and domestic political order. But this causal connection was shared throughout the entire political spectrum after 1905.[6] Furthermore, Shvanebakh's was not the sole statement on behalf of a monarchically oriented policy based on "les soucis d'ordre intérieur."[7] In January 1906 Lamzdorf wrote to Nicholas that "in view of the threatening development of the revolutionary movement in Russia it was necessary to consider a friendly unification of all conservative forces in Europe, relying above all on the German Empire."[8] Although Nicholas expressed interest in this proposal, little came of it. The note came barely two months after the resolution of the Björkö episode. Lamzdorf's earlier protestations about the sanctity of Russian obligations to France had been overcome by the tide of revolution. Conservative hopes thus met a setback with the conclusion of the August 1907 Anglo-Russian agreement. It was seen by many as a definite realignment of Russia's ties in a more liberal direction and as a defeat for conservatives in Russia.[9]

At first glance, the conservatives' failure is surprising. Given their high standing and Nicholas's own undoubted sympathy for the monarchical principle, proponents of a *Dreikaiserbund* in defense of autocracy should have been well placed to press their recommendations. However, the Nicholas of 1906 was neither the same figure nor in the same situation as he had been before 1905. Indeed, until 1911, Nicholas seemed curiously absent from political activity, to the consternation of Russian monarchists and foreign observers alike. In June 1907, when Nicholas sent a much-publicized telegram to Dr. A. I. Dubrovin, expressing his gratitude for the loyalty of the right-wing Union of Russian People, publisher A. S. Suvorin remarked dryly: "This is seen as the Sovereign's independence. To send such a telegram in secret from Stolypin—is that really independence?"[10] As late as 1910, a French ambassador complained of the inaccessibility of the Russian ruler, who had greatly curtailed even his ceremonial activities since the war with Japan.[11]

Although still the source of authority within the imperial government, as both Witte and Shvanebakh knew only too well, the Nicholas who reigned during these years lived in the shadow of Tsushima, the revolution, and perhaps even Björkö. Ruling without, or despite, his government had proven disastrous at every turn. Given his diffidence toward his power, it is not difficult to imagine his relief at finding an effective statesman like Stolypin to lead Russia out of turmoil. With infrequent exceptions, from October 1905 until early 1911 Nicholas can be seen as having retreated into the role of "legal" sovereign, despite increasing conservative complaints about the overweening conduct of his officials, particularly Stolypin.[12] During the constitutional and political crises confronted by the imperial government—from the *coup d'état* of 3 June 1907 until the "Western *zemstvo*" affair of 1911—Nicholas steadfastly ignored such advice and supported Stolypin against attacks from spokesmen who claimed to be protecting autocratic power from encroachments by officialdom.

Nonetheless, Nicholas had not become a constitutional monarch on the model of Edward VII; his confidence was still the critical element in bureaucratic politics—again, as Witte and Shvanebakh could attest. And he had placed his confidence in Stolypin, giving him the authority to impose on his colleagues, and on Russia, his views as to how government ought to work. As some noted, these views stood in contradiction to those espousing an untrammeled and personal autocrat as the source of Russian unity and strength, but even these complaints were without avail as long as Nicholas supported his council chairman. Moreover, the longer Nicholas remained "absent" from government, the more views such as Stolypin's on the workings of government assumed a legitimacy sanctioned by practice. Ironically, conservatives demonstrated their faith in the undiminished power of personal autocracy by advancing their views through the same channels that had proven so effective for Bezobrazov and Co.[13] Their very failure attests as eloquently as the Anglo-Russian agreement to the new role assumed by Nicholas.

Conservative calls for a monarchical alignment were opposed by those members of society whose representatives formed the dominant coalition and its Kadet loyal opposition in the third Duma. These spokesmen also viewed Russia's foreign interests through the prism of the domestic political order. They favored closer ties with Britain and France in the belief that such ties would strengthen the tentative parliamentarism established with the State Duma.[14]

Discussion of Russia's future orientation was important not for the alternatives it set forth—as has been suggested—but rather for what it indicated about the new environment in which that policy would have to be made. Thus, conservatives' failure reflected a dissonance between their hopes for the autocratic order and the role assumed by the cynosure of these hopes, Nicholas II. By the same token, the terms in which debate was couched showed how widely observers of all stripes shared a view in which domestic politics and foreign policy were directly linked.

Although Izvolskii had predicated acceptance of his appointment on Nicholas's assent to his general program,[15] he faced a new political environment in which to promote it. Nicholas's retreat created a relative vacuum atop Russian government. Within this vacuum all officials, including Izvolskii, were compelled to adapt to the new arrangements devised in 1905–1906. In the short term, Nicholas's absence rendered Izvolskii and others vulnerable to conservative complaints, since it was possible that Nicholas might weigh in on their side at any moment.

As a result, when Izvolskii was finally able to direct his attention to Russia's foreign policy, he was obliged to seek support for his program within the government. This fact, and the means by which he solicited such support, reflected in turn his view of himself as a constitutional minister in a cabinet. This view had been reinforced by his intimate involvement in council discussions of domestic issues throughout 1906–1907 and by his growing partnership with Stolypin, to whom he saw himself bound by inexperience in bureaucratic circles and political outlook.

Izvolskii's commitment to the new "constitution" and to "cabinet," and the prevailing ambiguity of the role of both in foreign policy, was demonstrated at a Council of Ministers meeting on 17 August 1906.[16] Izvolskii asked the council to discuss "which international treaties and agreements . . . are subject to the scrutiny of the legislative institutions before their ratification by the SUPREME AUTHORITY." He was raising this question since existing laws were "insufficiently definitive."[17] He observed that many treaties contained articles affecting areas normally under the purview of the legislature.

The council quickly concluded that even in these cases the Fundamental Laws clearly stipulated that all treaties regardless of their nature "are subject to the exclusive jurisdiction of the Supreme Authority."[18] The protocol, however, added in a different vein that according to Article 14 of the Council of Ministers statute "such international acts which concern not just the Ministry of Foreign Affairs, but also affect the interests of other departments, are submitted to the preliminary scrutiny of the . . . Council before their presentation for the confirmation of YOUR MAJESTY."[19]

This resolution was an early indication of Stolypin's and the council's understanding of the legal basis for their role in foreign policy making and was consonant with the attitude Witte had expressed at the inception of United Government in 1905. It came at the height of Izvolskii's own involvement with council work, between the negotiations for the mixed cabinet and the promulgation of the land reform in November 1906. In addition to the council resolution, more informal causes led to a situation in which figures like Stolypin and Kokovtsev came to expect council involvement in foreign policy decisions virtually as a matter of course. These expectations took shape during the intragovernmental discussions that led to the agreement with Britain in August 1907.

When he became minister in May 1906, Izvolskii's immediate goals appeared to be relatively simple. Uppermost was the necessity of disentangling Russian policy from its problems in Asia by securing its eastern frontiers against potential conflicts. When this had been accomplished, Izvolskii felt, Russia could return to its "historic" interests in Europe.[20] His first step was to open discussions with the British government for the regulation of the two states' conflicting interests in Asia. Parallel talks were also begun with Japan. The proposed agreement was by no means as revolutionary as some of Izvolskii's conservative critics maintained. Limited agreement had been reached by the two powers concerning China in 1899, and talks on Central Asia had begun before the war with Japan. In February 1906 Lamzdorf accepted a British proposal to resume these talks.[21]

The resumption of the talks with Britain, and the issue of partitioning Persia into zones of influence, occasioned the first determined resistance to Izvolskii from General F. F. Palitsyn of the General Staff. Through the autumn of 1906, Palitsyn raised repeated objections to Izvolskii's plans to pull back from an active policy along the Asian borders. Palitsyn was apprehensive about possible German reaction to an Anglo-Russian agreement, particularly possible complications on a western border that was much more dangerous than the east, precisely because Germany was Russia's chief potential adversary.[22] The general also distrusted England's ultimate intentions, given its traditional hostility to Russia.[23] In both cases, Russia's present vulnerability militated against a policy so fraught with potential complications.[24] Finally, Palitsyn objected to Izvolskii's proposal for a delimitation of spheres of influence, particularly in Persia; Britain could exploit temporary Russian weakness to bar any future opportunities for expansion southward.[25]

These arguments created problems for Izvolskii. Nicholas shared Palitsyn's misgivings about Britain's traditional enmity toward Russia,[26] as did some of Izvolskii's cabinet colleagues.[27] This resistance led to a hiatus in the Anglo-Russian talks until early 1906, giving Izvolskii time to canvass other members of the government for their support.[28]

When a new conference met on 1 February 1907, agreement had been reached on the necessity of entente with Britain.[29] Here, Izvolskii acknowledged resistance to the idea of partitioning Persia. He also noted the view that there were opportunities for Russian penetration all the way to the Persian Gulf. However, he continued, "the events of the last years have . . . shown the unattainability of this plan" and demonstrated the necessity of eliminating causes for conflict with England.[30] Palitsyn and the rest of the conference now accepted the principle of partition.

The meaning of "the events of the last years" was clarified in following months. In April 1907, at a meeting on Russian interests in Afghanistan, Izvolskii stated that "the general state of affairs which was created as a result of the war, and the internal turmoil that followed, compelled us to renounce any plans that are in insufficient accord with the real powers of the country."[31]

By 11 August, on the eve of the final signature of the Anglo-Russian agreement, Izvolskii was depicting the accord as part of a program by which "Russia must be assured of peace from Kamchatka to Gibraltar for about ten years . . . there will occur complications, and we must be ready to speak, or else we will be in the position of a half-forgotten Asian power."[32]

Izvolskii had expended great effort to sway his colleagues.[33] The basis for their agreement had been the lessons of the recent war and revolution, along with the acknowledged need to subordinate Russia's foreign goals to the demands of domestic reconstruction. So compelling were these arguments that Palitsyn had agreed to the necessity of partitioning Persia for the sake of an agreement with Britain. In April, Kokovtsev had given his own reasons for seeking an understanding with England; "[t]he lessons of the past convince [me] of the necessity of conducting an exclusively realistic [*real'naia*] policy."[34]

Presiding at the 11 August conference, Stolypin stated the view of most of the government in evaluating the Anglo-Russian accord; his observations remained the basis of his outlook on foreign policy for the rest of his tenure as premier:[35]

> [T]he successful conclusion of the agreement with England represents a truly great matter of state. Our internal situation does not allow us to conduct an aggressive foreign policy. The absence of fear from the point of view of international relations is extremely important for us since it will give us the opportunity to dedicate with full tranquillity our strength to the repair [*us-troenie*] of matters within the country.

Thus, by August 1907 Izvolskii had established a consensus on Russia's foreign policy among the leaders of the government. This consensus had little to do with Russia's orientation as understood by public opinion; it sought the best foreign conditions for the paramount task of restoring order within Russia, at a time of extreme military weakness. Palitsyn's final acceptance of the partitioning of Persia attested to the urgency of these demands. Equally important was the fact that Izvolskii had had to forge such a consensus in support of his policy. This search for support reflected his convictions about cabinet rule, while creating expectations among his colleagues about their role in foreign policy matters, which assumed greater weight, given their views on the interaction of foreign policy and domestic events.

As it turned out, various participants understood this consensus in very different terms. Thus, although the reasons behind the agreement with Britain appeared clear to those at the 11 August conference, when instability erupted in the Balkans in early 1908, the underlying disparities between the views of Izvolskii and the other participants—particularly Stolypin and Kokovtsev—came glaringly into view. These discrepancies took center stage during the Bosnian crisis.

The agreement with Great Britain was neither directed against Germany, nor reflective of Izvolskii's "liberalism."[36] It was seen simply as a means to eliminate potential complications in Asia. In addition, Izvolskii's Anglophilia was effectively limited by Nicholas's lingering suspicions of Russia's long-time foe, his sympathies for Germany as an exemplar of the "monarchical principle,"[37] and, finally, Stolypin's admiration for Germany.[38] Moreover, the policy Stolypin endorsed was one of equilibrium or disengagement from all foreign entanglements, in deference to Russia's domestic needs. Since the beginning of his ministry, Izvolskii had also stressed the need for good Russo-German relations "as an essential factor of our foreign *and domestic* policy."[39] During the negotiations with Britain, he had also conducted talks with the German government, for an agreement on Baltic issues and also to allay German suspicions of the Russo-British entente.[40]

Even in August 1907, however, there were signs that the agreement about the "realistic" direction of Russian policy was not unequivocal. One can distinguish between a "consensual" outlook, as set forth by Stolypin, and the policy that Izvolskii soon began to pursue on his own authority, without consulting his colleagues. This distinction only came to light when Russia confronted its first foreign policy difficulties after the war with Japan, in the winter of 1908.

## The Limits of Consensus: Izvolskii and the Council, 1907–1908

During the earliest phases of the Anglo-Russian discussions, and in dealing with fellow officials, Izvolskii was motivated by several impulses that set him apart from his colleagues. Undoubtedly, his liberalism made the prospect of an entente with Britain more palatable than it would have been to his predecessors. The securing of Russia's Asian borders served as the issue around which the consensus within the government crystallized, with most other participants seeing this stabilization as the beginning of a larger program of disengagement abroad, for domestic needs. At the same time, Izvolskii used the Anglo-Russian talks to pursue a goal that he did not raise directly in the intragovernmental discussion of the agreement with Britain: the regulation of the Straits Question so as to permit the egress from the Black Sea of Russian naval vessels. This aspect of the "Eastern Question" had long been a point of discord between Russia and Great Britain.

The status of the Straits under international agreements had been studied in the foreign ministry during the Russo-Japanese War, particularly after Tsushima.[41] In all reports on possible revisions of the Straits regime, under which Russian warships were forbidden to exit from the Black Sea, the attitude of the British government was identified as the critical factor for a favorable resolution. The issue lapsed with the end of the war with Japan and the redirection of official attention to the revolution in the fall of 1905.[42]

From the outset of the talks leading to the August 1907 agreement, Izvolskii had sought to link the problems of the Straits and settlement in Asia. On 25 August 1906 he received a memorandum which set the considerations that seem to have informed his subsequent efforts to turn the Anglo-Russian entente to ends he had not raised with his colleagues. This note, "on the question of an agreement between Russia and England,"[43] supported an accord, "given the present political situation," and pointed to other benefits that might be expected from it.[44] Among these was the possibility of a "favorable resolution" of the Straits Question. According to the memorandum, the issue would become increasingly important, given the possibility of complications that could arise in the Balkans with the ferment engendered by the "national movement" there.[45] Disputes among the "Christian peoples" could require Great Power intervention, most probably a naval demonstration. Russia was the only power unable to exert its influence in such a case. The talks with England presented an opportunity to end this debility.

These issues were discussed at a conference held in September 1906 to define Russia's goals in the impending negotiations with Great Britain.[46] In addition to his general objections to an Anglo-Russian accord, Palitsyn warned against pursuing such a complicated goal when Russia was so weakened. Kokovtsev stated that the decline in Russia's international position must be accepted along with its consequences for Near Eastern policy; this argument was to become an increasingly troublesome point of dispute in the future development of the consensual policy. Notwithstanding these demurrers, Izvolskii continued to portray the agreement with Britain as a way to free Russian forces from commitments along the empire's southern and eastern frontiers. Writing to Palitsyn, Izvolskii added that this would "allow us, when the time comes to apply [these forces] to the resolution of those great historic tasks which we have in the Near East."[47]

Even as consensus was building for a realistic Anglo-Russian agreement, Izvolskii continued unilaterally to seek a solution to the Straits Question and ensure Russia's ability to act in the Near East "when the time came." Russian diplomats broached the issue in London in the fall of 1906.[48] In March 1907 Benkendorf sought, ostensibly unofficially, British Foreign Secretary Sir Edward Grey's position on the question.[49] When asked by Benkendorf a second time, Grey acknowledged the harm to Russia of England's opposition to the opening of the Straits. He told Benkendorf "that if permanent good relations were to be established between the two countries . . . England must no longer make it a settled object of its policy to maintain the existing arrangement."[50]

Izvolskii was "highly satisfied" with the outcome of these inquiries and encouraged in his view of the agreement as an opportunity to strengthen Russia's role in the Near East.[51] The disparity between this view of Russian interests and that of his colleagues was evident, if unacknowledged, at the conference on 11 August 1907. Thus, while Izvolskii recognized the importance of domestic needs in speaking of "peace from Kamchatka to Gibraltar for about ten years," he also foresaw "complications in Europe" in which Russia must be prepared to act or to sink to "the position of a half-forgotten Asian power."[52]

Stolypin meanwhile had concentrated on the agreement's importance for domestic "repair."[53] The differences in these two views appear to have gone unremarked at the time. The Balkans were relatively quiet. Russian diplomacy—Nicholas's meeting with Wilhelm at Swinemünde and the Anglo-Russian agreement, both in 1907—indicated that Izvolskii was pursuing the policy of disengagement on which a consensus had formed. Indeed, several Russian diplomats abroad criticized Izvolskii for a policy that seemed based on a fear of Germany and a desire to get along with everybody.[54]

Izvolskii continued to explore the questions he had raised with Grey. Armed with the English agreement, he met the Austro-Hungarian foreign minister, Count Alois Aehrenthal in Vienna in September 1907. Izvolskii spoke "highly confidentially . . . about the future of Russian policy in regard to Turkey. My Russian colleague is up to nothing other than eventually resolving the Straits question in the Russian sense!"[55] Reporting on these conversations to Nicholas, Izvolskii placed them in the context of the Austro-Russian entente on the Near East.[56] Given Turkey's instability, it was good for both partners to consult about their respective goals should complications arise. Aehrenthal had avoided any direct response, by referring to the thorny nature of the question Izvolskii had raised.[57] According to Izvolskii, Aehrenthal promised to inform his Russian counterpart should the Dual Monarchy contemplate any concrete measures, specifically the possible annexation of Bosnia and Herzegovina.[58]

Izvolskii's council partners did not know of his initiatives in London and Vienna. This secretiveness stands in contrast to his general course in the discussions preceding the agreement with England, during which he seemed to approach policy making as a procedure based on collegial consultation. Nevertheless, on finding his colleagues agreeable only to part of his aims for the English agreement, Izvolskii appears to have simply decided to obviate this impediment by recourse directly to Nicholas for support of his own particular policy.

The underlying tensions between Izvolskii's views on Russia's foreign goals and those which had predominated in the conferences of 1907 were brought to light by the first real challenge to Russian foreign interests since the revolution. In January 1908 Aehrenthal announced plans for the construction of a railway through the sanjak of Novibazar—with Austro-Hungarian backing—which would link up with trunk lines leading east to Turkey and south to the Aegean.[59] Izvolskii saw this announcement as "a serious blow" to Russia's position in the Balkans, portending Austria's "political ascendancy" there.[60] This in turn posed a threat to the Balkan *status quo* that the two powers had agreed to uphold.

The Aehrenthal announcement came at a time of alarming instability on Russia's southern frontier. Tensions were rising on the border between Turkey and Persia. In the Balkans, the problem of the Christian population in Macedonia—and Turkish abuses—had raised the possibility of armed intervention by Bulgaria.[61] These developments were discussed at a conference on 21 January 1908, which saw the first indication of the divergence of Izvolskii's views from the "consensual" views of Russian interests, and of disagreement over the procedures by which such matters should be decided. In both respects, this conference foreshadowed directly the events of the following autumn.

Stolypin presided at the meeting in his capacity as chairman of the Council of Ministers. Also in attendance were Izvolskii, Palitsyn, Kokovtsev, Naval Minister Dikov, Assistant War Minister Polivanov, and Assistant Minister of Foreign Affairs Gubastov. The conference began with a briefing by Izvolskii, who outlined the aims of his activity since taking over the foreign ministry.[62] These turned out to be quite different from those he had set forth in the months before the conclusion of the Anglo-Russian agreement. Thus, he noted that two years previously the great issue facing Russia had been the Far East. This had been resolved by agreements with Japan and Britain. In pursuing these agreements "significant meaning had always been attributed by [Izvolskii] to the consideration that Russia could find itself in the near future face to face with serious complications in the Near East" at any time. "Russia's historical tasks in the Turkish East and the traditions of our past will put [Russia] in the event of such complications, into an especially difficult position. By not taking part in them, she risks at one blow the fruits of centuries' long efforts, forsaking the role of a Great Power, and taking the position of a secondary State, whose voice is not heeded."

Turning to the "troubling symptoms" of the present moment, Izvolskii discussed the southern border briefly before dealing at length with the Balkan situation. There, the chief problem was the lack of progress in improving the lot of the Macedonian Christians,[63] a situation which had provoked Bulgarian threats. Izvolskii criticized his predecessor's "protective" policy in the Balkans; Lamzdorf had sought to uphold the *status quo* by simultaneously restraining Bulgaria and supporting entente with Austria. This negative policy could not resolve Balkan issues in accord with "Russian historical interests," even if it did manage to "freeze" matters. These interests had recently been dealt a serious blow by Austria-Hungary. Having resolved its own internal crises, this power now felt able to pursue its long-hidden "egoistic" urges for "economic and cultural . . . but in reality, of course, also political ascendancy in the Balkan Peninsula."

It now appeared probable that the Dual Monarchy would even contravene the letter of the "Mürzsteg program" by supporting Turkish resistance to judicial reforms in Macedonia. Under these circumstances, it was likely that Turkey would be compelled to implement reforms in Macedonia only by a military demonstration. In this event, the only Great Power whose cooperation Russia could rely on would be England. The failure of the reform would seriously harm Russia's prestige as "the traditional defender of the oppressed Slavic nationalities of Turkey."

At this point, Izvolskii stated that the English ambassador had hinted at the possibility of a closer *rapprochement* between the two states, given their shared interests in the Near East. He speculated on the "alluring prospect" of joint military actions with England in Turkey, which could lead to "brilliant results" and help achieve "Russia's historical goals." But here, he drew back somewhat, acknowledging that this course could also reopen the "Turkish question" in its entirety.

Turning to concerns over the Caucasian border, Izvolskii warned that the Asian and Balkan aspects of the Turkish problem were closely connected. Aggressive action in the south might serve as a signal for action in the Balkans, especially by Bulgaria, which was already preparing for a conflict. Victory by either Turkey or Bulgaria could demand Russian intervention. Izvolskii closed by saying that Russia had to decide beforehand on its position in case of "the approaching complications."

> Ought she to regard them passively, to do everything to avoid difficulties and not to be drawn into the struggle? One could not expect success and the proper protection of Russian interests by this course. By taking such a position we will emerge diminished from the future political crisis, we will no longer be a Great Power. Or, perhaps, we are presently in such a state that we ought to renounce an active policy no matter what happens.

Only in closing did Izvolskii allude to previously acknowledged limits on Russian policy. His report was instead a renewed advocacy of the policy he had advocated throughout 1906 and 1907, only to be reminded by his colleagues that such a policy was beyond Russia's present capabilities. Now, as before, he praised the agreement with Britain for the opportunities it offered rather than for the peace it had secured in Asia—the factor that had persuaded his colleagues. Central to his arguments were notions of Russian prestige, and the defense of Russia's "historical interests" in a Balkan sphere now destabilized by Austria-Hungary.

The novelty of direction and emphasis in Izvolskii's remarks was immediately evident in Kokovtsev's and Stolypin's responses. To judge from his equivocal closing sentence, Izvolskii anticipated resistance from this quarter. Before the two ministers replied, it emerged that logistical considerations would severely curtail the ambitious measures proposed by the foreign minister. The military representatives all spoke strongly against any active policy either in Asia or the Balkans. Neither the army nor the navy was sufficiently restored from revolution and defeat to carry out the tasks projected in Izvolskii's proposals.[64] After these revelations, Stolypin and Kokovtsev addressed the substance of Izvolskii's report.

Kokovtsev spoke first,[65] expressing surprise at the tenor of Izvolskii's arguments and at how such important questions had come to be raised. Kokovtsev confessed that "the subject of today's conference is absolutely new for him," despite the importance and complexity of affairs in the Near East and the possibility of war with Turkey. Describing how Izvolskii ought to have proceeded, Kokovtsev said: "The Council of Ministers, which was unified by the *ukaz* of 19 October, 1905 remains in full ignorance. Meanwhile, the Government as a whole will bear a well-deserved responsibility before the Monarch and public opinion if events take an unfavorable turn . . . in the given case [Kokovtsev] is disturbed by the circumstance that a question of such exclusively serious state significance was not put to the assessment of the united government."

Kokovtsev then assessed Russia's alternatives. As in 1907, he referred to Russia's internal weakness, which precluded any "aggressive" measures on the southern border. Moreover, any Russian involvement in the dispute between Persia and Turkey would "be incomprehensible to popular consciousness," as it would entail the spilling of Russian blood for the sake of an Islamic state. Kokovtsev shared Izvolskii's concerns for Russian interests in the Balkans, which he saw as much more "substantial," but simply suggested that the foreign minister create a diplomatic environment in which Russia would not be forced to act alone in the Balkans.

Izvolskii responded to Kokovtsev's procedural objections: "during the last two years, not only had he not concealed, but he had constantly indicated the possibility of serious complications in the Near East."[66] He contended that the agreements on Asian questions had been concluded for these reasons. Izvolskii's argument revived differences that had been glossed over in the 1907 conferences, or, to Kokovtsev's view, had been resolved in favor of a policy of external pacification.

Izvolskii then asked whether he could depart from the "protective policy to which Russia had hitherto adhered, or can he speak with the firmness befitting the Minister of Foreign Affairs of a Great Power who is assured of the possibility for it to uphold its interests decisively."[67] To proceed without this assurance would be "an unreasonable risk." Izvolskii, while conceding the final decision to his interlocutors, seemed tacitly to recognize the difference between his present opinion and the limits on Russian policy as expressed in 1907.

Stolypin reserved to himself the last words in the conference protocol.[68] He seconded Kokovtsev, expressing his "embarrassment at the lack of information for the Government" about the issues that Izvolskii had raised. Indeed, he felt, "panicked terror at the thought that the Government might not be informed of matters which had come face to face with the most serious events. All matters of state importance should be maturely considered in the midst of the Council of Ministers . . . the defeat in the Far East had been provoked in part by the fact that there had been no unity among state actors." Stolypin told Izvolskii summarily that he could not expect any support for his proposals.

> A new mobilization in Russia would lend strength to the revolution out of which we are just beginning to emerge . . . At such a moment one could not decide on an adventure or even to display initiative in international affairs. In several years, when we have achieved full pacification, Russia will again begin to speak its former language. Any policy other than a purely defensive one would be at present the delirium of an abnormal Government, and would bring with it danger for the Dynasty.

He ended with a statement of the limits within which Izvolskii would have to proceed, while mollifying him with an appeal to his abilities. If there were serious complications in the Balkans, Russia would have to trust in Izvolskii's abilities. "There is now in his hands a lever without a fulcrum, but Russia must have a respite after which it will become stronger and again occupy its appropriate rank as a Great Power."

In reacting to Izvolskii's report, Stolypin and Kokovtsev stated bluntly their understanding of a principle that had been established formally and informally since the advent of United Government: that the Council of Ministers was to be consulted on foreign policy in instances where it might affect the interests of one or the other ministries. This principle had first been set forth in the Solskii conference's report on the unification of government, and provision for it had been made in the *ukaz* on the council; it had been asserted by Witte in October 1905 and by the Council of Ministers in August 1906. Kokovtsev's invocation of the Fundamental Laws grounded this principle in law. It also had a strong basis in practice. Since the autumn of 1906, the chairman had been included in discussions of these matters. In August 1907 and January 1908, this involvement had received formal sanction through his chairmanship of special conferences on foreign affairs. This understanding had been abetted informally by Izvolskii, who had honored it in his claims to membership in a cabinet in questions of domestic policy and in forging the ministerial consensus in support of the Anglo-Russian accord.

Stolypin stated explicitly the connections he saw between foreign policy and the methods by which it was to be determined. Forgoing Kokovtsev's legalistic approach, he stressed instead the significance of unified decision making by blaming its absence for Russia's defeat in the recent war, a view Izvolskii had also expressed in 1906.[69] At the same time, Stolypin articulated an expanded understanding of the necessity of cabinet rule, beyond the bounds originally envisioned by most of the council reformers with the exception of Witte. This broader vision of the prerogatives of United Government had developed almost spontaneously in the intensive activity marking his tenure as chairman since the summer of 1906. While a great deal of effort was spent during these months fencing off areas of legislation from the Duma, relatively little attention was paid to the relations at the heights of the administration, especially as concerned the "excluded" ministries.

Such inattention to the legal distinctions governing relations with these ministries can be traced to several factors. At the outset of Stolypin's ministry the pressure of revolutionary events had precluded any systematic examination of the limits of the council's purview over the rights of individual ministries. The stipulations set forth in the legislation on the council in this regard were elided in the urgent atmosphere of the last phases of the revolution.

The tendency to ignore institutional boundaries—and the resulting expansion of council prerogatives—was only reinforced by the strength of Stolypin's personality and convictions and the respect they inspired among his fellow ministers. This was not simply the moral strength of the victor over the revolution. He had enjoyed at several critical moments demonstrations of Nicholas's confidence, thus implying supreme sanction for his view of government. When his view had been challenged, Nicholas had supported Stolypin, strengthening his authority and validating his understanding of his role as chairman. This understanding rested on a broad vision of the interrelationships linking all areas of political activity at a time of extreme precariousness for the Russian state. Central to this vision was his own feeling of responsibility for ensuring a political environment in which the political arrangement of 3 June 1907 could be given time to develop.

Now Stolypin and Kokovtsev were asserting this expanded view of council prerogative in foreign policy, despite the fact that the cabinet *per se* had not often served as a forum for the discussion of such issues.[70] Their claim sprang from the intimate connection Stolypin posited between the possibility of war abroad and a renewed eruption of unrest at home, arousing a "panicked terror" at the prospects set forth in Izvolskii's report. These connections had been an important element in support for the Anglo-Russian agreement in 1907. Given the links between foreign and domestic events in this view, any activity abroad necessarily affected the interests of the other ministries, and thus demanded council involvement in the making of foreign policy.

Significantly, Izvolskii accepted, or did not resist, Kokovtsev's and Stolypin's statements on behalf of their expanded vision of United Government. Some ministers reacted less passively to such claims. In 1907, the head of the excluded war ministry, General A. F. Rediger, actively opposed what he saw as an attempt by the Council of Ministers to intrude in his ministry's affairs.[71] These efforts were only partially successful; by early 1908, Stolypin and the council chancellery participated in and even initiated the discussion of military matters.[72] By early 1908, Izvolskii too began to bridle, at least privately, at the council's claims on him.[73]

The 21 January conference revealed the differences within the consensus that had coalesced around the Anglo-Russian accord—differences which continued to develop in Izvolskii's pursuit of a policy that had been rejected before the making of the agreement. The differences expressed reflected divergent perceptions of Russia's ability to pursue an active policy abroad. Izvolskii insisted that Russia reclaim its status as a Great Power, lest it be relegated by inaction to a secondary position in the chief arena of its foreign interest. For his part, Stolypin was primarily concerned by the fact that the empire had just "begun to emerge" from revolution; the present decline in

Russia's stature was a necessary, if temporary, cost of domestic renewal.

These divergent views of Russia's interests and abilities to pursue them were rooted in Izvolskii's and Stolypin's differing perspectives on Russia's condition. Since the middle of 1907, the foreign minister had become less involved in domestic affairs, while devoting more attention to the husbanding of Russia's position in Europe. A perfectly understandable development, Izvolskii's increasing attention to his own responsibilities drew him away from the council and made greater room for the development of his own individual ideas about Russian policy. Certainly, he identified personally with Russia's international stature[74]—he saw Aehrenthal's announcement on the sanjak railway as a personal attack.[75] His advocacy of an active policy may also have been spurred by persistent rumors about his own shaky position as foreign minister. These had first surfaced in early January, reaching a crescendo with press attacks on the foreign minister after Aehrenthal's announcement.[76]

As might be expected, Stolypin's views of Russia's foreign interests were shaped by his position as minister of internal affairs. He was still preoccupied with the effects of the revolution "out of which we are just beginning to emerge." The potential effects of a "new mobilization" precluded even the risk of complications abroad. Stolypin also had more immediate difficulties in early 1908. Part of his program of domestic renewal had been the convocation of a Duma elected by a propertied majority with a stake in the reestablishment of internal order. The government had introduced to the third Duma a broad program devised to effect a reconstruction of Russian society: an agrarian reform, the restructuring of local administration, educational reform, and the granting of some religious tolerance under the law. Despite a cooperative centrist majority in the lower chamber, the difficulty of Stolypin's task was indicated by the fact that all of these bills were debated throughout the four and a half year existence of the third Duma. Indeed, this Duma had itself opened on a note of bitter controversy over the wording of its formal address to Nicholas.[77]

By late January 1908 conservative disaffection with Stolypin and his Duma allies had spilled over into attacks from the conservative and reactionary press. In his archreactionary *Grazhdanin*, Prince V. P. Meshcherskii called for the abolition of the Council of Ministers and the post of chairman because the "institution . . . is a limitation of the Sovereign's autocracy."[78]

Added to this friction was the public reaction to the announcement of the Austro-Hungarian railway project.[79] Despite the legal segregation of foreign policy from Duma deliberations, and despite the generally limited influence of public opinion in foreign policy—even after the abolition of most censorship in 1905[80]—the press and the Duma fractions sought at times to intervene in the discussion of foreign policy. One famous instance of such efforts was the Duma delegation visit to England in 1906; there were similar visits to France. However, at certain junctures, the government seemed genuinely to heed and even actively to have sought the support of public opinion and the Duma majority in foreign policy questions.

Izvolskii spoke of public opinion's influence to Sir Arthur Nicolson at the height of the press campaigns against the Austrian railway project. Confessing dismay at the ferocity and unanimity of the public reaction to Aehrenthal's announcement, Izvolskii told Nicolson that the effect of public opinion depended on how he presented a case to Nicholas. Usually, these instances were overlooked, but "if as in the present instance H.M. were told that the press was echoing a deep national feeling then the Emperor w[ou]ld certainly give heed to it."[81]

With regard to the Duma's role in the discussion of foreign policy, several factors combined to mitigate the separation of imperial matters from those legally under the legislature's scrutiny. First among these was a general solicitude in government about the relative tranquillity of society after 1905–1907, especially in the circumstances of the working relationship that Stolypin was forging with the Duma center. More important was Izvolskii's own attitude to public opinion and the Duma. He was known to be "exceedingly sensitive to newspaper attacks."[82] Izvolskii also set store by the views of society; he had seen his appointment as ushering in a new relationship between his ministry and Russian society. Thus, while continuing, as Lamzdorf had, to use the semiofficial *Rossiia* as an outlet for foreign ministry statements, he also cultivated contacts with the press, even giving off-the-record briefings on current policy.[83]

When he had become minister Izvolskii had created a new press department in the ministry. This body compiled press reports from foreign and Russian newspapers and forwarded them to the emperor. "Izvolskii hoped that by this means he could manage to inculcate in Nicholas a constitutional way of thinking."[84] At the same time, informal contacts were maintained between foreign ministry officials, including Izvolskii on occasion, and members of the centrist fractions in the Duma.[85]

As a rule, public opinion—the major daily newspapers and journals of Moscow and St. Petersburg—and most Duma members devoted little attention to matters of foreign policy. In his famous essay "Great Russia," P. B. Struve criticized the relative neglect by Russian radicals and conservatives alike of Russia's foreign tasks.[86] Although the Duma fractions had incorporated foreign policy positions in their respective programs, their treatment of such questions was desultory and generally supportive of the course set in 1906–1907.[87]

This quiescence came to an abrupt end with Aehrenthal's announcement of the sanjak railway. The government was sufficiently concerned by this reaction to undertake a series of increasingly serious and public palliative measures that demonstrated both a responsiveness to the views of opinion, and the prevalence of the Stolypin/Kokovtsev line elaborated on 21 January.

In February, Izvolskii sent a representative of the foreign ministry to Moscow to inform confidentially members "of representatives of Moscow political and social circles and also the major press organs about the state of affairs in the Near East."[88] At about the same time, Izvolskii "in the presence of P. A. Stolypin and V. N. Kokovtsev" appeared before a closed session of the Duma's Commission of State Defense "on the issue of the direction of our foreign policy."[89] The fact that the new Austro-Hungarian initiative was aimed at the Balkans struck a very sensitive nerve in observers and political actors on both sides of the divide separating government and society. Pan-Slavism and its offspring "neo-Slavism" or "neo-panslavism"[90] had deep roots in Russian political thought and were shared by official and unofficial actors alike.

Russian nationalism and its pan-Slav or neo-Slav components served as a link between state and society. The generation in government or on the Duma benches had come of age during the Russo-Turkish War in the late 1870s. This war had been provoked in part by the efforts of Russian volunteers—like Tolstoi's Count Vronskii—to help Serbia gain its final independence from Turkey. The conflict led to a war that ultimately saw the liberation of Bulgaria from direct Turkish rule. For such figures as Izvolskii, P. N. Miliukov, or Prince E. N. Trubetskoi this war had come during adolescence and had elicited their first feelings of national patriotism for Russia as liberator of the Slavs.[91]

Trubetskoi described the atmosphere of "crusade" that permeated Russia during the war: "[t]he reading of the Supreme Manifesto on the declaration of war is one of the most meaningful experiences in all my life—I was thirteen years old then, but I only sensed Russia with such strength with all my being as I sensed it then one time in life, at the beginning of the great European war in 1914."[92] Not only did the war show Russia as the liberator of its Slavic kinsmen; in many memories, it endured as a rare moment in which state and nation acted together for a truly national cause.

Stirrings of interest in Balkan questions had begun before Aehrenthal's declaration. In early January, Struve had published "Great Russia" in the first issue of *Russkaia Mysl'* and called for the active penetration of Russian economic and cultural influence into the Balkans to satisfy deep-seated "national" and "tribal" drives.[93] The agreement with England had created the possibility of a return "homeward" for Russian foreign policy. This point of view was strikingly similar to Izvolskii's assessment of the possibilities presented by the 1907 agreement.

Struve's article was but one sign of a growing attention within civil society to Russia's Balkan policy. Several organizations were formed at this time to promote the expansion of economic and political ties among Slavs.[94] Among the participants in these organizations were Octobrists like Alexander Guchkov and F. E. Lvov, in addition to Kadets like Miliukov, Maklakov, and Struve. Stolypin himself seems to have shared such interests. In May 1908 he attended a reception in honor of visiting delegates to the Slavic Congress taking place at the time.[95]

Government sensitivity to public response to the sanjak railway announcement was signaled by a speech given by Izvolskii to the Duma in April 1908.[96] Beginning his address, Izvolskii acknowledged the "perfectly natural" interest of the Duma and "broad circles of society" in recent events in the Near East: "affairs on the Balkan peninsula strike particularly sensitive strings in every Russian heart."[97] Much of Izvolskii's speech was couched in phrases echoing literature on the Balkans that had been circulating since the late 1870s, with references to "Russia's vital historical traditions" and its "historical role" in defense of its fellow believers and "fellow tribesmen."[98]

While alluding to such outlooks, the speech itself reflected the viewpoint taken by Stolypin and Kokovtsev on 21 January. Referring to the recent outcry over the sanjak railway, Izvolskii declared that his duty as foreign minister was to remember that his goal was not to win "diplomatic victories" but to attain "the state's real interests with the removal of everything that could lead to dangerous complications."[99] Russia's task in the Balkans was to promote the welfare of the young states and to protect the Christian population in Macedonia. Therefore, instead of protesting the railway project, Russia had responded with its own plan to benefit the Balkan states. (Izvolskii had proposed a railway to run along the Danube basin to the Adriatic.) At the same time he had presented new proposals for reforms in Macedonia. These *démarches* had been attacked as "half-measures" in the press, but Izvolskii, in an appeal for the Duma's support, made clear the limits on Russian capacity for stronger actions: "I think that each of you, each a reasonable Russian, is imbued with the conviction that no matter how necessary the introduction of the Macedonian reforms, Russia cannot be subjected to the possibility of war-like complications for the sake of this goal."[100]

Izvolskii devoted the rest of his speech to a defense of his policy in the Near East, which he portrayed as an outgrowth of Russia's historical goals, while stressing Russian "disinterestedness" in any gains for itself. In outlining what might be referred to as the "Stolypin policy," he accented its "national" character in deference to his audience. "[W]e ought not, we cannot undertake anything that would lead to an armed conflict with anybody, for Russia needs peace above all, needs a restoration of its strength after the external and internal shocks of the last years."[101]

Izvolskii's Duma appearance was an event of manifold significance. The very fact of his appearance indicated something of the Russian political climate during this period, in which pragmatism was emphasized at the expense of a strict adherence to the formal legal provisions for excluding foreign policy from Duma discussion. Certainly, there was no legal basis for Izvolskii's appearance. In 1906, the council had decided to bar the Duma from any discussion of foreign affairs. But the rigor of the Duma's exclusion from the treatment of such matters was vitiated by several factors. Due to ambiguities in the 1905 reforms, the Duma and the State Council held limited budgetary authority over the otherwise excluded ministries. Izvolskii's first appearance before the Duma, in March 1908, had been occasioned by a bill to raise the Russian mission in Tokyo to embassy rank, which would entail unanticipated expenses. By the same token, the pretext for Izvolskii's 4 April appearance was the submission to the Duma of a special commission report on the MID budget for 1908.[102]

The foreign minister himself was sensitive to public opinion and supported the idea of a strong Duma. His sympathies for the Duma as a forum for the discussion of foreign policy were stated in a Council of Ministers meeting in May 1907, when he informed his colleagues that Nicholas had given him "a general order regarding the possibility in cases of need for addresses by the Minister of Foreign Affairs in the legislative institutions, with explanations about one or another issue of foreign policy."[103]

There is also reason to believe that the April appearance was supported by Stolypin and the council. On 21 January, Stolypin and Kokovtsev had insisted that they be consulted on foreign policy matters. The extent to which this insistence was observed after the conference was indicated by the presence of the two ministers when Izvolskii addressed the Defense Commission on 12 February. The council discussed a similar appearance during the Bosnian crisis the following autumn.[104] Indeed, Russia's ambassador in Rome, N. V. Muravev feared a possible "limitation of imperial prerogative" from the minister's "new habit" of discussing foreign policy "on the parliamentary tribune," which he linked to Stolypin's "dependency relation" with the Duma.[105]

Muravev's statements were a conservative's criticism of the relations Stolypin had cultivated with the third Duma. This body, with its solid centrist majority, was intended by the council chairman to serve as the national partner in the passage and implementation of the broad and intricate program through which he intended to regenerate Russia after the revolutions of 1905–1907. What Muravev called Stolypin's "dependency" had been highlighted by conservative press campaigns against the premier concerning a variety of issues in early 1908. Leaders of the majority Octobrist and moderate right coalition in the Duma were seeking a larger role in the decision of such national questions as defense policy.

From this point of view, Izvolskii's appearance can be seen as an expression of government goodwill and confidence in the sobriety and responsibility of the dominant coalition, as well as a sop to their self-images as aspiring statesmen. Izvolskii's appeals to the "reasonable Russian men" in his audience, and his stress on the necessity of avoiding complications in order to proceed with Russia's restoration "after the external and internal shocks of the last years," were designed to appeal to the Duma majority. The core of this group had first formed during the fall of 1905 in opposition to the revolution's excessive violence; it now stood as a proponent of reform at a measured pace, based on cooperation between state and society.

Thus, by April 1908, Stolypin had succeeded in bringing the principal bases of Russia's foreign policy back to the position he had envisaged in August 1907: an end to the possibility of complications abroad and Izvolskii's agreement to consult with the council in future decisions. He did not disagree with the thrust of Izvolskii's ultimate goals. He himself noted that the time would come when Russia could "speak its former language." But for the near future, internal reform was his exclusive concern. For this reason, the Council of Ministers and its chairman had to be informed of new developments beyond Russia's frontiers.

Stolypin's success was apparent at the end of May 1908, when he accompanied Izvolskii and Nicholas to a meeting with a British party headed by Edward VII at Reval. There he participated in intergovernmental discussions. A report by a member of the British delegation—filtered by a preternaturally English outlook—attested to the nature of Stolypin's position: "I was informed on the very best authority that when invited by the

Emperor to accompany His Majesty to Reval, he told the Emperor that it must be distinctly understood that he went to meet a Constitutional Sovereign as the first Minister in a Government based on constitutional principles, to which His Majesty at once assented."[106]

Thus, the sanjak railway crisis provoked the articulation of new questions about the mechanism by which Russia's foreign policy was to be set. Most of these questions had been latent in the agreements and disparities that characterized Izvolskii's and Stolypin's respective views about the pact with Great Britain. They were cast into sharp relief by Izvolskii's response to Aehrenthal's announcement at a time of political tensions in Russia. Izvolskii's speech to the Duma and Stolypin's presence at Reval seemed to indicate that Stolypin's view on these questions had triumphed. By the following autumn, all these questions reemerged more acutely with the advent of new trouble in the Balkans. These events came close to precipitating the sort of "external complications" that Stolypin had been so anxious to avoid.

# · 6 ·

# The Bosnian Crisis and the
# Triumph of United Government

On 24 September 1908, Emperor Franz Josef of Austria-Hungary officially notified his Russian cousin of his decision to annex the provinces of Bosnia and Herzegovina.[1] Although the Dual Monarchy had occupied and administered these provinces and the sanjak of Novibazar under the Treaty of Berlin since 1878, they were formally part of the Ottoman Empire. As an area of predominantly Slavic population, they were also of interest to neighboring Balkan states, particularly to politicians and press commentators *(publitsisty)* who harbored dreams of incorporating these provinces into "Greater Serbia." In Russia, officials and the public reacted with outrage to the absorption of their "Slavic brethren" into "Germanic" Austria-Hungary. Finally, the change in at least the formal *status quo* established by the Treaty of Berlin also raised cries for compensations on the part of other Balkan states and an effort by the Russian Ministry of Foreign Affairs to bring the annexation before the court of a European conference before officially recognizing the Austro-Hungarian action.

The Bosnian crisis was nasty, even by Balkan standards. The Balkan and European tensions it engendered raised the threat of war. The crisis was exacerbated by the combination of traditional rivalry between Russia and the Dual Monarchy and a strong personal antagonism between Izvolskii and Count Alois Aehrenthal, which imparted a special acrimony to efforts to restore civil relations between the two states. The two foreign ministers held sharply variant political outlooks, not least in their views on "whither Russia" after 1905. Aehrenthal had spent much of his career in St. Petersburg, where he had cultivated close contacts in conservative circles. Even after returning to Vienna, Aehrenthal maintained ties with Stolypin's and Izvolskii's *bête noire*, P. Kh. Shvanebakh, sharing the latter's scorn for Izvolskii's "liberalism."[2] Despite these tensions, calm was eventually achieved in March 1909, after strong German pressure on the Russian government to recognize the annexation as it stood or face unspecified consequences.

Equally important, the conduct of Izvolskii and, indirectly, Nicholas in the events preceding the Bosnian crisis led to harsh controversy within the Russian government. Stolypin and the Council of Ministers were confronted by Izvolskii with a *fait accompli,* which portended complications in an area of acute interest to Russian policy and public opinion, and in direct contravention of the substance and procedures for foreign policy that had been laid down emphatically in the 21 January conference. Both on the European stage, and within the United Government, the Bosnian crisis had effects that shaped the course of Russian policy until the outbreak of the Great War.

## Izvolskii and the Origins of the Crisis, July-September 1908

The Bosnian crisis resulted from the aftermath of the sanjak railway declaration of January 1908 and the recrudescence of political instability in Turkey-in-Europe. During the spring and summer of 1908, there were Austro-Russian discussions aimed at reestablishing the two states' entente on upholding the *status quo* in the Balkans. A Russian *aide-mémoire* submitted to Vienna in late June focused on these two issues as topics for future negotiations and raised the questions on which the Bosnian crisis ultimately turned.[3] Referring to the Dual Monarchy's possible annexation of Bosnia-Herzegovina, the note claimed that this issue bore a "European character" and thus could not be "regulated by a separate entente between Russia and Austria-Hungary." But the note acknowledged that the same conditions applied to issues of interest to Russia, particularly the Straits regime.[4] Russia was prepared to discuss such issues in a spirit of friendly reciprocity.[5] As soon became evident, Izvolskii was chiefly interested in these latter issues.

Having publicly upheld the view imposed upon him by Stolypin in January 1908, Izvolskii still entertained the political desires he had expressed at that time. In mid-July, he spoke of the talks with Austria and of Russia's Balkan interests to the German ambassador, who promptly relayed his notes to his Austrian colleague.[6] The "leading idea" in Izvolskii's policy was the maintenance of the Balkan *status quo.* "Russia seeks nothing for itself"; the days of dreaming about Hagia Sophia had passed. However, Izvolskii alluded to one aim that he wished to attain "eventually"—"the attainment of the right of free passage through the Dardanelles" if this could be achieved "without complications." This passage was highlighted in the Austrian copy of the report.

New urgency was lent to the Austro-Russian negotiations with the outbreak of the Young Turk revolution in July, which provoked disturbances throughout the Balkans. On 21 July 1908 a special conference met to discuss Russian measures should the Turkish situation deteriorate.[7] As in January, military action was held to be beyond Russia's present capacities. Izvolskii's remarks at this meeting reflected his own growing divergence, in response to the opportunities offered by the new developments, from the policy laid down by Stolypin in January. Thus, while acknowledging that "we must not embark on an adventure," he added that the European political conjuncture had become more favorable for Russia. Reviving his position on 21 January, he stated that the agreement with Britain had removed an obstacle in the Near East, a circumstance of "special significance,"[8] given the possibility of complications there.

In mid-August, the Ministry of Foreign Affairs received Aehrenthal's response, dated 14 August, to the Russian *aide-mémoire*. This note outlined the bases for a possible entente on Balkan affairs. It advocated the maintenance of the Balkan *status quo* "so long as circumstances permit" and supported the Russian proposal for an entente to guard against possible complications in the Balkans.[9] As concerned the occupied provinces, the Dual Monarchy was willing to contemplate a withdrawal of its troops from the sanjak of Novibazar but regarded Bosnia and Herzegovina "as territories which we have possessed for thirty years, into which we entered by virtue of an international mandate, and which we have conquered by force of arms." If "imperious circumstances" demanded it, these provinces would be annexed. This statement constituted a rejection of the Russian claim that the disposition of these territories was a European issue. The Austrian note proposed that Russia "observe a benevolent and friendly attitude" to such an act; at the same time, it declared Austrian willingness to participate in "a confidential and friendly exchange of views" regarding the Straits. Thus, the Austrian response ignored the Russian claim that the disposition of Bosnia-Herzegovina was a European question, while demurring on the Straits.

As the summer wore on, Izvolskii began once again to press the desiderata he had been obliged to renounce on 21 January. Through the Austrian ambassador, Count L. Berchtold, he sought a private meeting with Aehrenthal, to coincide with a sojourn in Carlsbad during late August and early September.[10] The encounter was apparently clinched by Aehrenthal's note, a spate of newspaper reports, and a dispatch from the Russian military attaché in Vienna indicating the impending annexation of Bosnia and Herzegovina.[11] From Carlsbad on 20 August, Izvolskii outlined his reactions to Aehrenthal's note in letters to Charykov and L. P. Urusov, the Russian ambassador in Vienna. He commented that the Austrian note seemed to confirm rumors that the Dual Monarchy was seriously contemplating an annexation of Bosnia and Herzegovina.[12] This impression was strengthened by the monarchy's pledge to evacuate the sanjak and by conversations with Berchtold, who gave vague responses to Izvolskii's questions about causes that might prompt an annexation.

Given these circumstances, Izvolskii favored meeting with Aehrenthal to discuss the conditions for an annexation and to determine "through personal conversation" Vienna's plans and compensations that might be demanded.[13] In these letters, Izvolskii insisted that any discussion of annexation must also include the issue of the Straits—"these two questions are already connected as of today."[14] Ironically, he privately recognized the chief difficulty of linking the two issues: "the annexation of Bosnia and Herzegovina will be a material fact," while a resolution of the Straits Question would bear "an abstract and secret character."[15] This disparity came back to haunt Izvolskii throughout the autumn.

The two ministers met in Berchtold's palace at Buchlau on 3 September. Izvolskii was guided in these talks by a letter from Charykov, dated 28 August, which predicted that an Austrian annexation of Bosnia-Herzegovina would bring many benefits to Russia.[16] Russian interests would not be affected. Indeed, Austria-Hungary's stated intention of evacuating the sanjak allayed fears of further expansion and removed a long-standing pressure point against Serbia and Montenegro. Moreover, the annexation would bring into the Hapsburg lands "Orthodox Serbs who have long sympathized with us." These changes would lead to the "appearance of neo-Slavism" within the monarchy and would complicate its relations with the Balkan states and Turkey. Assuming that the annexation would entail revision of the Treaty of Berlin, Charykov listed compensations to be demanded for the Balkan states.

Since the beginning of the summer, and especially since receiving the Austrian *aide-mémoire,* Izvolskii's aims had changed rapidly. The anticipated annexation of Bosnia and Herzegovina coupled with his views of Britain's changed attitude seemed to offer him purchase in his negotiations on extending the Austro-Russian Balkan entente. The "resolution" of the Straits issue suddenly seemed achievable, and Izvolskii now reverted to the policy that had been rejected on 21 January. The only initiates of his plans were Charykov, Urusov, and Nicholas.[17] Stolypin learned of Izvolskii's new plans only when it was too late to affect them.

Izvolskii was able to contemplate his dramatic change of course because of the support he enjoyed from Nicholas. The emperor, who had been largely absent from the discussion of foreign policy since the middle of 1906, now emerged as Izvolskii's co-conspirator in seeking a resolution of the Straits issue and personal revenge against Aehrenthal for the sanjak railway project. Izvolskii had taken this act as a personal slight.[18] Nicholas agreed with Izvolskii's view of Aehrenthal's duplicity: "He knew Baron d'Aehrenthal very well, and had always considered him to be a straightforward gentleman anxious to act in accord with Russia in all Balkan matters. The tortuous course which he had pursued of late showed his Excellency in a different light."[19] Elsewhere, Nicholas stated his intention to "disengage" himself from the entente with Austria, "not at one blow, but also without fail."[20] Nicholas's support for Izvolskii's plans was a critical element in the events that resulted in the Bosnian crisis.

An atmosphere of mutual animosity characterized the conversations at Buchlau. The interview began with Izvolskii blaming Aehrenthal "for the break of the Entente" and the consequent necessity of a Russian *rapprochement* with England.[21] After a series of exchanges of similar tone, talk turned to the Aehrenthal's note of 14 August, and particularly the question of Bosnia and Herzegovina. Determining what exactly transpired at the Buchlau talks is rendered problematic by the bitterness of the crisis that resulted from it, and by differences of fact and emphasis in the two ministers' respective accounts of this meeting.[22] In the end, each came away convinced that he had forced his counterpart to accept his position.

Aehrenthal maintained the position set forth in his 14 August note. He told Izvolskii that "the Austro-Hungarian government had irrevocably decided on annexation"[23] and demanded that the Russian government "finally take a position on this so often ventilated question." After some resistance, Izvolskii answered that Russia would take "a friendly and well-disposed posture" toward an annexation.[24]

Izvolskii proceeded from the assumption, stated in his correspondence with Charykov, that the annexation of Bosnia-Herzegovina would constitute a substantive revision of the Treaty of Berlin and was thus a European question. Accordingly, Izvolskii stated his conditions for Russian support of Austria-Hungary in revising the Berlin Treaty. He told Aehrenthal that in agreeing to the annexation, he could not "lose sight of special Russian interests," or of the effects on the Balkan states and Turkey resulting from the impending "modifications of the Berlin Treaty."[25] He therefore proposed territorial and political compensations for the Balkan states and Turkey to forestall complications from the annexation,[26] but he reserved the greatest demands for Russia.

Denying any territorial ambitions in Turkey, Izvolskii proposed that Austria-Hungary promise to observe a benevolent and friendly attitude should Russia request the free passage through the Straits of individual Russian warships and those of other Black Sea riverain states. Aehrenthal conditioned his government's cooperation in this question on Russia's support when the annexation occurred.[27] Izvolskii was "very glad" at this statement.[28] When Aehrenthal inquired whether he had raised this question with the British government, Izvolskii answered that he was hopeful of good results in London.[29]

The Russian minister now addressed the question that subsequently became a point of dispute with Aehrenthal. In his reports on the conversations, Izvolskii contended that his proposals about the Straits and compensations for the Balkan states were "conditions" for Russia's benevolence toward the annexation of Bosnia-Herzegovina.[30] In Aehrenthal's version, Izvolskii anticipated no significant Turkish resistance to these "eventual modifications of the Berlin Treaty."[31] When Izvolskii asked about the possibilities for the realization of his proposal on the Straits, Aehrenthal remarked that negotiations among Turkey and "the Cabinets" would be necessary and added that "there could be no more talk about Bosnia and Herzegovina." It was only after coming to a preliminary agreement on these topics that Izvolskii asked when the annexation might take place.[32] Aehrenthal answered vaguely that it would probably occur in early October, new style.

Having resolved the main points of concern, the interview drifted into a denouement. Izvolskii was in high spirits and spoke about the present European situation in terms that sound ironic in the context of the afternoon's talk and of his earlier differences with Stolypin and Kokovtsev. Izvolskii declared that "for at least twenty years Russia is . . . dependent on a policy of peace." Its only role could be that of a conciliator. He had been forced to improve relations with England but only in Asian questions; this relationship had no meaning in Europe. He also protested his good will toward Germany.[33]

Izvolskii's euphoria pervaded the immediate aftermath of the Buchlau meeting. He wrote to Charykov, "we can be fully satisfied with the results I have achieved," which accorded entirely with the conditions Charykov had outlined on 28 August.[34] Charykov was to argue before Nicholas that the monarchy's decision had been taken for many reasons, including the wish to end Franz Josef's reign with a territorial acquisition "even at the cost of a renunciation of broader plans in the future." Austria-Hungary would never have relinquished the two provinces. A negative Russian response could only take two forms: "a fruitless protest" or threats "which could lead to hostile actions."

Thus, Izvolskii continued, "the path of compensations and guarantees I suggested seems to me incomparably more useful." "With luck and a skillful conduct of the matter" the Straits regime could be changed to Russia's benefit, without having to await the "liquidation of the Turkish empire." Austria had agreed to this change, and it was possible that Germany might as well. Compensations for the Balkan states would raise Russian prestige there, even when it became clear that there would be no war over the two provinces. Finally, Austria's breach of the Treaty of Berlin would complicate its relations with Turkey, the Balkan states, and the other Great Powers.

Izvolskii closed with instructions that were revealing both for their concerns and for what they omitted. Charykov and the director of the ministry's press department were to prepare, "and in the decisive moment direct," the press, "which could easily go onto a false path."[35] Special attention was to be paid to *Novoe Vremia*. In these dealings, Charykov was to conceal the agreement. He was to say that the Dual Monarchy had decided upon an annexation and Russia had found out about it in good time. Due to Russian insistence, Austria-Hungary had agreed to evacuate the sanjak. To protest these measures was useless, since there would be no war for them. Thus, compensations had been demanded. These instructions carried no mention of the Council of Ministers or Stolypin.

Before reporting to Nicholas, Charykov set out to determine the formal means by which Izvolskii's "conditions" would be implemented. In a telegram to his superior (who was vacationing in Bavaria) on 6 September, he was still under the positive impression of Izvolskii's "magnificent" report.[36] Charykov also felt that "after some further preparation," there could be "success" in the Straits Question. He suggested the convocation of a European conference to discuss the proposed revisions of the Treaty of Berlin; this demand could be included in the official reply to the Austrian note of 14 August.[37] Aehrenthal might even prefer a conference to the risks of a unilateral annexation. He closed by requesting Izvolskii's views on these issues.

On 8 September, Charykov submitted Izvolskii's letter on the Buchlau meeting to Nicholas.[38] The emperor was "extremely satisfied" and "values in particular" Izvolskii's proposed resolution of the Straits Question, which would represent "the solution to an age-old problem." Nicholas told

Charykov, "I will remember 8 September 1908."[39] Naval Minister Dikov was also elated with the proposed solution of the Straits issue. Charykov noted that approximately one quarter of the Berlin Treaty would have to be revised and asked again whether this would best be achieved through a conference or by a simple bilateral agreement.[40] Nicholas already supported the conference strategy.

The emperor had also raised, as had Izvolskii, the problem of "preparing our press for an appropriate attitude to this question."[41] Charykov reported Izvolskii's instructions and assured Nicholas that two reporters "are in our hands." To enhance this control, at Charykov's suggestion, Nicholas had appointed one as a delegate to an international conference on literary property. His compliance had thus been secured for a "mere courier's allowance."

Events seemed to be unfolding smoothly for Izvolskii. On 10 September he wrote Aehrenthal from Bavaria, promising a speedy Russian response to the Austrian *aide-mémoire*.[42] The next day, in a letter to Charykov, he discussed the conference proposal and betrayed some of his intentions in going to Buchlau.[43] While he agreed that a conference should meet to discuss revisions of the Treaty of Berlin, a proposal from St. Petersburg at this time would put Russia in an unfavorable position, particularly at home, where the idea of such a conference was unpopular. It would look much better if it were a response to Austria's action. "It is much more favorable for us to lay responsibility . . . for the violation of the Berlin Treaty on Austria." This would "naturally" raise the question of a conference, and Russia could act as defender of the Balkan states. Aehrenthal had resisted a conference.[44] Izvolskii would canvass European views on this issue.

Again, Izvolskii urged the "preparation" of public opinion. His recommendations were now more thoroughgoing: Charykov should influence other papers as well as *Novoe Vremia*, and should also speak with Guchkov and Miliukov, who had a good grasp of Balkan issues. Finally, a week after Buchlau, he told his deputy to inform Stolypin and "the chief ministers" of what had occurred. They would "of course" agree that it would be "madness" to aggravate relations with Austria, and thus with Germany, and to risk war over the annexation.[45]

On the face of it, Izvolskii had every reason to be well pleased with his recent activity. By his lights, he had forced Aehrenthal to accept sweeping conditions in return for Russia's goodwill toward the annexation, already decided on, of Bosnia and Herzegovina, while having gained Aehrenthal's agreement for a similar benevolence toward a rectification of the Straits issue. Indeed, it appears that Izvolskii had been laying a trap with which to obtain European sanction for his proposals, most notably on the Straits Question, while forcing Austria to a conference "in the role of the accused."[46] Not least, he had ingratiated himself with Nicholas.

Most puzzling were Izvolskii's belated and off-hand instructions to inform Stolypin, especially after his elaborate provisions for the preparation of public opinion. Possibly, Izvolskii was presenting Stolypin and the council with a *fait accompli* to vindicate the policy he had propounded on 21 January. Given these circumstances, and Nicholas's pleasure, his instructions on public opinion seemed designed to forestall procedural objections from Stolypin and Kokovtsev.

Whatever Izvolskii's intentions, 11 September marked the brief high-water mark in his career. Virtually overnight, events turned against him everywhere. The first intimation of the impending debacle arrived in a letter from Urusov in Vienna. The ambassador reported a confidential conversation with "an old friend," a German diplomat who had seen Aehrenthal the previous week.[47] Aehrenthal boasted that he was "abreast of everything that happens in Russia" and that he enjoyed influence in "the official world of Petersburg." Aehrenthal believed that Izvolskii "did not have a long career before him." In support of Aehrenthal's claims, Urusov noted Shvanebakh's ties with the Austro-Hungarian minister.

In mid-September, Izvolskii went from Bavaria to Paris, to start rallying support for a European conference to discuss the annexation. On his way, he met with his German counterpart, Baron V. Schoen, in Berchtesgaden on 12 September, to discuss the Buchlau interview. Izvolskii repeated earlier statements about the change in Britain's attitude, and the two discussed possible compensations for Germany's agreement to Izvolskii's Straits proposals. Schoen stated that his government had no reason to oppose this measure if it received proper compensations.[48] In Paris, however, Izvolskii received more bad news in a letter from Aehrenthal, dated 30 September, new style, informing him "very confidentially" that the annexation would take place on 7 October, new style.[49] Other governments would be notified on that date. Aehrenthal closed by noting that given Izvolskii's statements at Buchlau, he was sure of Russia's sympathetic and benevolent attitude.

In St. Petersburg, Izvolskii's instructions had been followed to good effect. Rumors of the annexation had put the press "in full cry against this fresh act of Austrian diplomacy" at Slavdom's expense.[50] But even this success evaporated on 17 September, when Charykov informed Stolypin and the other ministers about the meeting at Buchlau.[51]

## Stolypin and the Assertion of United Government, 1908–1909

A "Special Private Conference" attended by Stolypin, Kokovtsev, Rediger, Dikov, and a General Staff representative, met on 19 September. Its official purpose was to consider Izvolskii's draft reply to an Austrian note of 14 August.[52] This note depicted the annexation of Bosnia-Herzegovina as a violation of the Balkan *status quo*, hitherto upheld through Austro-Russian agreement, and asserted that as a European issue, it was subject to the scrutiny of the signatories of the Treaty of Berlin. While noting the grievances of the Balkan states, the draft approved the Austro-Hungarian pledge to evacuate the sanjak. There followed a list of conditions for Russian acceptance of the annexation. These included compensations for the Balkan states and the right for Russian and other Black Sea riverains freely to send their warships through the Straits. Austria-Hungary would also be obliged to exert its influence in Berlin for a favorable solution of the Straits issue.

The conference discussed this note only after criticizing Izvolskii's conduct at Buchlau. Stolypin and Kokovtsev expressed their "extreme chagrin" that the United Government had learned so late "a matter of such immense national historical significance." The annexation bore implications for "internal political conditions" and threatened future complications.[53] Charykov reported the conference's mood to Izvolskii: "negotiations could lead to great complications in the Near East and should have been made known beforehand to the Council of Ministers, which is now evidently deprived of any opportunity to introduce substantial alterations in the current dealings with Baron Aehrenthal and of lending a different direction to this question."[54] These statements repeated the charges leveled at Izvolskii on 21 January 1908.

Stolypin and Kokovtsev agreed with Izvolskii that Russia would be unable effectively to oppose the annexation and that Russia should act as protector of the Balkan states at a conference. But they parted company with the foreign minister over the conditions for Russia's approval of the annexation. In a new statement of the limits governing Russian policy, Stolypin and Kokovtsev stressed "the inappropriateness for Russia of any risk of external complications which had been so favorably eliminated by you in the Far and Near East."[55]

In defense of his superior, Charykov maintained disingenuously that the delay in informing the council was due not to a departure from "close contact with the members of the Council of Ministers," but rather to the exceptional circumstances under which the talks had occurred. He added that the draft reply to Vienna was subject to a final definition, after discussion by "the united government."[56] The inefficacy of Charykov's efforts was indicated when he notified Izvolskii in his report that on the next day he and Stolypin would report to Nicholas, aboard the imperial yacht *Shtandardt* in the Finnish skerries. Charykov seemed to concede the legitimacy of the ministers' view when he argued that it would not be a significant alteration of Russia's attitude should the reply to the Austrian *aide-mémoire* place more distance between the Russian and Austro-Hungarian governments, while stressing its role as protector of the Balkan states. The ministers had also agreed that Charykov should draft a circular about a European conference as a "worthy and peaceful way out," while preparing the Balkan states and Turkey for such a conference. Finally, Nicholas was to be asked to recall Izvolskii from his European tour.[57]

Thus, by 19 September, Izvolskii had lost his initiative in two critical spheres. Aehrenthal's letter had deprived him of the little time he had to coordinate a European response in support of Russia's view that the annexation was a European matter, and thus subject to the approval of the Berlin signatories. More significant, however, was the shift in his relations with Stolypin and the United Government.[58] Stolypin and Kokovtsev had asserted the council's role in policy making and had also disputed Izvolskii's measures, devising an alternative course of action. Charykov's report forwarded a text of the draft telegram, drawn up by himself and Kokovtsev; the telegram's concluding passages would be sent after Stolypin's approval.[59]

The reasons for the strength of the ministers' response to the news of Buchlau and its consequences are clear. Despite the resolutions of 21 January, Izvolskii had acted unilaterally in an area of notorious political instability that was seen by government and society alike as an area of historic Russian interest. Stolypin was so exercised by Izvolskii's act that he threatened to "tender his resignation to the Emperor," if Izvolskii continued his negotiations.[60] Stolypin's threat pointed at least obliquely to Nicholas's part in these events. Having been aware of Izvolskii's initiative and expressed his great satisfaction at the results from Buchlau, the emperor had also given Charykov permission to inform the other ministers of these developments.[61] The passivity or duplicity Nicholas exhibited in the weeks that followed is striking. As tensions grew between Izvolskii and Stolypin before the former's return to St. Petersburg in mid-October, Nicholas seemed to support both.

From Paris, Izvolskii responded quickly to Charykov's report of the 19 September conference. In a telegram on 21 September, he defended both his policy and his ministerial independence.[62] He disputed the opinion that his talks with Aehrenthal had been "dangerous." Aehrenthal had presented the annexation as a *fait accompli*. He had known that Russia would not contemplate war on such a basis. The protest suggested by the conference could lead to such a clash. He then defended "the course set forth by me, endorsed by the Sovereign Emperor." It did not ally Russia with the monarchy. His draft response had merely warned Austria of the annexation's international ramifications and had proposed the route "for a peaceful and favorable way out for us and the Balkan states." Still, he was prepared to accept Kokovtsev's draft. He suggested that Russia refrain from a response until the annexation, after which a circular could be sent to all the powers.

Turning to his relations with the United Government, Izvolskii insisted that his talks in the West were too important for his immediate return to St. Petersburg. He added "that the decisive condemnation of my actions by the conference, and the intrusion into the purely technical area of my negotiations will prompt me immediately upon my return to discuss whether I ought to petition [for] dismissal" from his post. At the same time, Izvolskii was seeking Nicholas's support in his dispute with the council. He asked permission to continue his visits abroad "where I am awaited with impatience" to prepare for the convocation of a European conference. An immediate recall could be misinterpreted, which would be "especially dangerous in the present critical circumstances."[63]

However, the tour on which Izvolskii had placed such hopes failed to provide any meaningful results. Already, press reports were surfacing in Europe about the coming annexation. Within a week of receiving Aehrenthal's notification, Izvolskii was confronted with events that redoubled the pressure upon him. On 23 September, Bulgaria unilaterally declared its independence from Turkish suzerainty, a substantive alteration to the Treaty of Berlin.[64] This action preempted one of the compensations Izvolskii had extracted from Aehrenthal and deprived him and Russia of the opportunity to sponsor Bulgarian independence. The timing of the declaration led to the inevitable suspicion that Aehrenthal had stolen yet another march on Izvolskii.[65]

Soon afterward, Aehrenthal sent to St. Petersburg a draft of the annexation announcement, which noted Russia's friendly agreement.[66] This statement was also leaked to the other European powers.[67] Finally, on 24 September the Russian government learned officially of the annexation in a letter to Nicholas from Franz Josef.[68] The letter summarized Aehrenthal's reasons for the measure but also referred to Russian agreement to an annexation dating to the 1880s. Neither Izvolskii nor Nicholas had known of these precedents.[69]

These events inaugurated a period of deepening confusion and retreat in Izvolskii's efforts to salvage his position. While Charykov and Stolypin were telling foreign representatives that Izvolskii had been asked to return to help prepare a response to the annexation,[70] Izvolskii pressed on with his effort to establish an agenda for a European conference.[71] His task was complicated by his efforts to shore up his position with Nicholas and Stolypin.

On 29 September, Izvolskii sent Nicholas a telegram outlining the delicacy of his position.[72] Disparaging Aehrenthal's announcement of Russian support for the annexation as "Jesuitry," he complained that attacks in the Russian press had placed him in "an extremely burdensome position." Press attitudes had impeded the achievement of his dual task: "the peaceful outcome, which is so necessary for us, of the present crisis, and the guarantee of Russian and Balkan interests." Therefore, Izvolskii requested permission to appear in the Duma, as the only worthy means to "restore the truth." If Nicholas agreed, "it would be desirable to acquaint the public with this intention." Nicholas agreed to the request, but no date was set for the appearance.

Abroad, Izvolskii sought almost desperately to convince his counterparts in London and Berlin of the necessity of a conference. Sir Edward Grey's reaction was lukewarm to his proposals about the Straits and the conference.[73] In his pleas, Izvolskii cautioned that the future of the Anglo-Russian entente was in the balance.[74] He warned that Nicholas was "by training and education not on the Liberal side." His support for reforms in Russia depended on his being convinced that they were working. "In the same way, it would be fatal to a good understanding with England" if it turned out that it had blocked a resolution of the Straits Question.[75] Izvolskii gave Grey to understand that his own position was at stake because of his association with the agreement with Britain. Grey still did not promise to support the Russian proposals; he considered Izvolskii implicated in the Austrian annexation decision.

Proceeding from London to Berlin, Izvolskii met a stonier response to his conference agenda. Despite warning of a possible world war to be feared from Balkan responses to the annexation, Izvolskii was unable to extract from his hosts support for a conference or German mediation in Russia's grievances against Austria-Hungary.[76] Throughout Europe, Izvolskii complained constantly of the "bomb" Aehrenthal had detonated at his expense.[77] His diatribes underscored the damage to his own position, especially given the new conditions in Russia.[78] He reproached Aehrenthal for not taking seriously the strength of public opinion and the fact that he was "a constitutional minister."[79] Since Buchlau, Izvolskii had been preoccupied by public opinion. After an initially well-managed and favorable reception of the conference proposal, the press had quickly become more critical of the foreign minister.

By the time of the annexation declaration most newspapers even rejected the idea of opening the Straits. Many argued that, given the weakness of the Black Sea fleet, opening the Straits would ultimately be harmful to Russia's interests. Kadet and Octobrist organs, as well as the powerful *Novoe Vremia,* all focused on compensations for the Balkan states and passed over any possible Russian demands.[80] The press's unrest reflected that of society. In mid-October, Stolypin's Ministry of Internal Affairs had barred a public address on Balkan matters by the pro-Slavic Professor Pogodin.

Izvolskii was aware of the public mood in Russia. A worker in the Russian embassy in Berlin described Izvolskii's situation: "His discouragement was greatly increased by the news from the President of the Council of Ministers . . . who informed him that public opinion was greatly incensed" at the annexation. He was also depressed at the prospect of explaining these events when he returned.[81] Calling himself a "fallen man," Izvolskii spoke openly in Berlin of his probable resignation.[82]

These declarations indicate the strength of Izvolskii's view of his status as a "constitutional minister." His concern about public opinion overwhelmed what should probably have been a greater concern for the attitude of Stolypin, who had had to weather the storm in Russia. This concern appears to have occurred to him only on the eve of his return from Berlin and may have compelled his last attempt at a vindication of his position before public opinion and the council.

On 12 October, Izvolskii gave an interview to *Novoe Vremia* in which he acknowledged the outcry in Russia. He seemed to accept the validity of this response when condemning the Austrian measure as affecting "the vital interests of Slavdom."[83] But, he continued, "I have a tribune upon which I can explain all of my policy . . . the State Duma. I hope that the Sovereign Emperor permits me to appear . . . Then the country will judge me." If, as is likely, the foreign minister sought to defend himself against Stolypin and the council by direct appeal to "the country,"[84] he reckoned without the degree to which circumstances had changed in St. Petersburg. His interview only added to his difficulties.[85] Charykov said that any statement by Izvolskii to the Duma "would have to be the work of the whole Cabinet, and there was no immediate prospect of its being delivered."[86]

At the same time, Stolypin and Kokovtsev discussed the last month's events with Berchtold, distancing themselves from Izvolskii.[87] Both ministers gave a surprisingly frank account of events, including the late date of Charykov's revelations and the proceedings of 19 September. According to Stolypin, the annexation had not been so much a surprise as the fact that it had been unilateral. Bosnia-Herzegovina had been seen as a European question until the arrival of Izvolskii's draft reply to the Austro-Hungarian aide-mémoire. Stolypin insisted that "according to notions here . . . it was totally excluded" that Izvolskii could agree to this. Such an act would constitute Russia's "unilateral acquiescence" and would "always be seen and branded as a betrayal of Slavdom." Aehrenthal recognized the rift between Stolypin and Izvolskii and instructed Berchtold to inform the chairman and Kokovtsev directly about Austria-Hungary's activity, given Izvolskii's continued distortion of the events at Buchlau.[88]

Thus, Izvolskii's return to St. Petersburg on 16 October came under less than auspicious circumstances.[89] According to Kokovtsev,[90] there was a meeting of the Council of Ministers at this time, where Stolypin confronted Izvolskii with rumors that he had consented to the annexation of "two Slavic provinces." Izvolskii apparently deflected Stolypin with the statement "that he had absolutely definite instructions from His Majesty not to discuss in the Council questions of foreign policy."

Clearly, Stolypin was able to overcome Izvolskii's resistance, for on 25 October the council met to discuss "on Supreme orders," as Stolypin stated, "the questions of Bosnia and Herzegov[ina] and . . . the appearance of the M[inister] of F[oreign] A[ffairs] in the St[ate] Duma."[91] This meeting began with a lengthy apologia by Izvolskii.[92] He recapitulated the policy he had outlined in January, alluding to his previous warning that unexpected developments in the Near East could leave an unprepared Russia in the ranks of secondary powers. He now stated that he had concluded the agreements with England and Japan "[i]n order to untie my hands." As in January, he referred to the unpopular agreement with Austria he had "inherited." He added that if hitherto Austria had been restrained by fear of Russian strength, Aehrenthal had now become sure of Russia's weakness. The result had been the sanjak project, which Izvolskii had been able to counteract. Izvolskii claimed—not entirely accurately—to have first heard of the annexation while he was in Carlsbad. He told the council that his alternatives had been hedged by a series of preexisting Austro-Russian understandings dating to the late 1870s on the monarchy's right to annex the two provinces.

Izvolskii depicted the Buchlau meeting in a different light from that conveyed in his reports.[93] He claimed to have told Aehrenthal that the annexation was a European issue and would thus entail a general review of the Treaty of Berlin; "in particular I indicated the Straits." Izvolskii now told the council that he had added, "Of course, this entire conversation was occurring unofficially"—contradicting his previous accounts of the meeting. Thus, he continued, Aehrenthal had announced the annexation, while "by unattractive means" creating the impression that Izvolskii had agreed to it.

Since he knew that Russia would not fight for the return of the provinces, Izvolskii continued, he had tried to gather the other powers for a discussion of the annexation. This effort had been undercut by an Austro-Turkish agreement. He apologized for not anticipating the ensuing, albeit exaggerated, "indignation" in Russia. The monarchy had only consolidated what it possessed already. At the same time it had relinquished the sanjak and had "compromised its mor[al] role" in the Balkans. "But, of course, the excitement of Russian society is a fact and it must be reckoned with and therefore the matter cannot be further conducted in a calm, practical direction."

Assessing possible responses to the annexation, Izvolskii rejected any protest, since "it would be war."[94] Rather, Russia should continue to push for a conference. Although Austria-Hungary had agreed only to a conference that already recognized the annexation, Russia could continue to request a more substantive meeting, while avoiding a formal recognition of the annexation. Izvolskii finished by saying that he would be prepared to promote these arguments in the Duma.[95]

At this point, Stolypin took the floor.[96] He began by stating that it was "unclear . . . why the Council is finding out about this so late." He had learned of these events from Charykov on 17 September; the participants in the 19 September meeting had been told only that Russia would recognize the annexation if Turkey agreed and if it led to no European incidents. Stolypin's response at that time had been "heatedly" to declare that such important decisions must not take place "behind the government's back." He had rejected any compensations at Turkey's expense, since these could lead to war, and asked Charykov "to declare that Russia could not agree with this and did not desire to enter into any negotiations with Austria."

Interestingly, the only significant variation in the two records of this meeting—the protocol and the official journal submitted to Nicholas— concerned Stolypin's statements about the prerogatives of United Government.[97] The journal account, was much more emphatic than the protocol in this regard; in the former, Stolypin complained about Izvolskii having bypassed the Council of Ministers, "which had been summoned by the law (Fundamental Laws, 1906 ed., art. 120), however, for the direction and unification of the M[iniste]rs' actions." This version of Stolypin's statements expanded on the public reaction to Izvolskii's lack of response to an act "which had been directed against the vital interests of Russia, in the capacity of the Slavic Great Power." Possibly, Stolypin amplified his original remarks in the course of editing the journals after the conference. Very probably, the difference between the two variants represented a direct claim upon Nicholas by Stolypin for a role in such decisions. The emphasis on this claim would be understandable in a document meant expressly for Nicholas's perusal. By late October, Stolypin had probably realized the degree to which Nicholas was complicit in what had occurred "behind the government's back." He may also have been seeking, in his appeal to law, to forestall any efforts by Izvolskii to claim his ministry's exclusion from council scrutiny.

Stolypin was also not so ready as Izvolskii to downplay the reaction of public opinion, which he invoked to support his view of the course Russia should pursue. Russia did not want war, but at the same time there was "no need to go to a conference and enter any negotiations."[98] The hostility of Russian opinion was primarily due, Stolypin felt, to its ignorance of the key documents. He interrupted his discussion of public opinion to remark that the foreign minister's resignation "would be fatal as a sign that Russia is going on to the path of war." Having rejected any possibility of war, the council decided that Russia would simply refuse to recognize the annexation, as public opinion demanded. State Comptroller Kharitonov suggested that it would better to "drag out the matter and stall it."[99]

Discussing Izvolskii's declaration to the Duma, Stolypin stated that such appearances should be infrequent, and only when their success was assured beforehand, "especially in questions of foreign policy." "This is dangerous. Political thought is not developed. A discussion could incite a war," while a condemnation could compromise Izvolskii at home and abroad, and "could push onto the practical path of parliamentarism." Therefore, if Izvolskii were to address the Duma, provisions would have to be made to ensure a good reception. In particular, the "parties" would have to be prepared. "Since 3 June, 1907, I have quit talking with the Kadets. Now it is possible to rely on the rights and Octobrists." There was no need to seek the support of the "lefts"—"for one cannot conduct two policies— one for internal policy, and a second for foreign."[100]

Izvolskii apologized for his indiscretion in Berlin about the Duma declaration, "I did not have control of my nerves." He suggested that he resign and that this act be attributed to his "excessive liberalism, my wish to appear before the Duma." Stolypin dismissed this: "That is extremely undesirable, to inflame passions, and especially on the grounds of internal disagreements."[101] Stolypin was having his own problems with the conservative nobility over local reform. They too had seized upon the government's incompetence in the Bosnian annexation.[102] Therefore, the chairman needed a display of unity and strength in his government. Since, in his view, policy should be consistent, Buchlau would have to be recognized; Aehrenthal could not be publicly labelled a liar.

Kokovtsev criticized Izvolskii's statement in Berlin while agreeing to that he should appear before the Duma, "but, of course, with preliminary staging"; also, the council would have to know what Izvolskii would say.[103] The council had discussed this subject before Izvolskii's return and had decided "unanimously" that a speech was impossible at present.[104] Other speakers suggested waiting until circumstances improved. Although some raised the question of the appropriateness of the declaration in the context of the Fundamental Laws, this point did not constitute a primary issue. Instead, the ministers were concerned by the future course of negotiations, the unpredictability of the foreign minister's reception, and the possibility of providing grist for the Duma opposition. In deciding to delay the declaration, it was also established that the council would be able to set the timing and approve the contents of this speech.

The 25 October conference restated the concerns and outlooks expressed on 21 January and 19 September. At the same time, this meeting marked the final step in the integration of foreign policy making under the rubric of United Government. At previous meetings, objections about the obviation of the council had appeared as criticisms of Izvolskii's negligent conduct. Now, Stolypin advanced a forceful argument that Izvolskii was responsible to the council, and that this was prescribed by the Fundamental Laws.

Probably the most immediately evident effect of this meeting was the abrupt and explicit subjugation of major foreign policy decisions to the findings of the "cabinet," as represented by Stolypin and often Kokovtsev. Discussing these events in retrospect, Kokovtsev told Sir Arthur Nicolson that "during all the latter phase of the South Eastern question, M. Iswolsky had taken no steps without consultation with the Russian Cabinet, and the latter was responsible for everything which had occurred."[105]

The "latter phases" to which Kokovtsev had referred had been created by Russia's continuing refusal to recognize the annexation, as decided on 25 October. Over the ensuing months, the danger of a Balkan war grew with tensions between Austria-Hungary and Serbia, whose government continued to demand territorial compensations for the annexation of Serbian irredenta. By March, the situation had become critical. As a result, Germany, in a strongly worded note, exhorted the Russian government to recognize officially the annexation and to encourage Serbia to modify its posture. This note hinted at the possibility of war, prompting Izvolskii, the council, and even Nicholas to see it as a veiled ultimatum.[106]

Throughout these months, Stolypin strengthened the council's role as the key institution in policy making. Stolypin and Kokovtsev began to speak much more authoritatively on foreign policy issues. In December, the minister of finance told a German visitor that he and Stolypin had always opposed Izvolskii's plans for the Straits as compensation for the annexation, an error that Izvolskii now recognized. Kokovtsev also revealed that Izvolskii had twice offered to resign—he retained his position only "under the condition that he do what Stolypin and Kokovtsev want."[107] Conversations between Berchtold and Stolypin in February also indicated the latter's awareness of ongoing developments and his ability to speak for the Russian government in international questions.[108]

Izvolskii's statements also reflected the new situation in Russian government. Discussing the possibility of international complications, Izvolskii echoed Stolypin's outlook in noting the danger of revolution in Russia from a war abroad.[109] However, until the final phase of the crisis, it was also apparent that Izvolskii was resisting his new status to a certain extent. Thus, when on Aehrenthal's instructions, Berchtold spoke of Balkan matters with Stolypin, Izvolskii protested the "snub" vehemently.[110] These rifts within the Russian government were no less evident in the field. The Russian envoy to Serbia was reportedly "disgusted with his department not knowing which foot to dance on," a problem he blamed on the contradictory instructions he was receiving from Izvolskii and Charykov.[111]

These divisions dissipated in the face of the German "ultimatum." The Council of Ministers met several times to discuss the response, in council sessions and at a conference attended by Stolypin and several other ministers.[112] The forums chosen and the decisions reached indicated Stolypin's ascendancy. Later, he noted that when the German note arrived, he had been ill, "but as he wished to share the responsibility of the reply that would be given," he had met informally with some colleagues to impress upon them the necessity for peace, and thus capitulation.[113] The outcome of the meeting, and the way in which it was reported all bore Stolypin's stamp. Thus, Izvolskii informed Nicolson of Russia's decision, in language evocative of Stolypin's:

Russia did not want a war. She was just beginning to bring order into her finances, was reorganizing her army, and internal unrest was quieting down. A war would throw back all the progress effected, and would probably revive all the troubles from which Russia was just emerging. The whole matter was thoroughly threshed out during the Cabinet meeting which lasted three hours . . . Three or four years hence, Russia would have so far recovered herself as to be able to speak in a different tone.[114]

The red thread running through all discussions of foreign policy since 1905 had been the causal connections in official thinking between foreign war and domestic unrest. This belief informed all discussion of Russia's foreign policy until 1914. Such a view was also shared in society. With the news of the German note in March 1909, one diarist noted, "God grant that there be no war, there would be another revolution."[115]

However, there was also another element in Stolypin's understanding of the internal ramifications of foreign affairs. This involved the government's relationship with society in the press and the Duma. This relationship was much different, and more intricate, than the strict mechanism underlying the image of the elemental potential of the *narod*. There can be little doubt that the public outcry in the fall of 1908 carried weight in the council.

The history of the early third Duma was partially determined by efforts to build a bridge across the gulf between the state and that part of society represented in the lower chamber's majority. In the meetings of 19 September and 25 October public opinion was cited as a significant consideration. Its role must be seen in the context of Stolypin's ongoing attempts to work with the majority bloc he had formed for the enactment of his program of internal "repair." By the spring, this cooperation had become even more necessary to Stolypin, in light of the decision to seek State Council approval for the controversial legislation on the navy's General Staff in the form issued by the Duma.

The foreign ministry had expended a great deal of effort to cultivate a favorable response to the events of September and October. The council's decision to allow Izvolskii to appear in the Duma to explain the Bosnia affair, despite the threat of "parliamentarism," indicates the lengths to which the government felt compelled to placate educated society. This was not an easy task. It was originally decided on 11 November that Izvolskii would speak to the Duma in the second week of November. He did not actually appear until 12 December.[116] MID representatives had already met with members of the center-right Duma majority on 31 October and 9 November. But these efforts yielded little success.[117] On 17 November, Taube represented the MID at a meeting with Duma leaders, at which he revealed the nineteenth-century Austro-Russian agreements and Izvolskii's attempt to gain concessions for Russia and the Balkan states. Once again, in spite of these revelations, his audience could not promise support in the Duma for Izvolskii.

Finally, on 10 December, Izvolskii himself met with Guchkov for the Octobrists, Balashov from the "moderate rights," and other leaders from the center. He told them the contents of his declaration, which the Duma members finally promised to support.[118] After these negotiations Izvolskii spoke before the Duma, which supported his declaration.[119] These meetings and the decision to allow Izvolskii to address the Duma were more than the simple "preparation" of opinion. These transactions were based on an area of genuine accord between the government, the Duma center, and even the Kadets. The annexation had been a blow to all of them in the same way as the sanjak railway announcement in January. It represented the incursion of Austrian *cum* German interests and power into an area of unique interest to Russia as the Slavic Great Power.

The solicitude for Russia's position *vis-à-vis* both the Dual Monarchy and the Slavic states was shared by virtually all Russians of Stolypin's, Guchkov's, Miliukov's, and Izvolskii's generation. Thus, while reproaching Izvolskii for ignoring the council, Stolypin had also been outraged by the annexation of two Slavonic provinces. Much of this philo-Slavic sentiment was tied up with memories of Russia's role as liberator of the Slavs in the nineteenth century, and particularly in the war against Turkey in the 1870s. Interwoven with these memories of the glorious war and what many called Russia's "historic mission" was the way the Russo-Turkish War had been concluded. "It is painfully memorable to each of you gentlemen under what conditions this treaty [of Berlin] was concluded . . . which destroyed a good half of those results which [Russia] had achieved not so much for its own benefit as for the benefit of the Slavic nationalities of the Balkan peninsula."[120] Izvolskii was not merely indulging rhetorical flourishes. During the sanjak episode, the German ambassador, Pourtales, noted that many Russians blamed Germany for covertly supporting Aehrenthal's *démarche*. He now heard frequent "reproaches about Germany's conduct during the Russo-Turkish war and the Berlin Congress."[121]

In his disagreements with Izvolskii, Stolypin had never questioned his ultimate goals. He had questioned their timing, insisting that their achievement was ancillary to the complex process of rebuilding Russia, even should Russia become a second-rate power. In January 1908, he had stated that Russia would then be able to regain its proper role or, as he put it to Nicolson, "in two or three years she would be able to speak in European affairs with a very different voice from what was now the case."[122] Even in February 1909 he had occasionally hinted that if Serbia were invaded, he would have the Duma's support for any measures needed to save that country.[123]

This ordering of priorities was apparently a basis for cooperation between the government and the leaders from the Duma majority. In late 1909, Guchkov expounded his views on foreign policy to Nicolson. Like Izvolskii's in March, his language reflected Stolypin's influence. "For two years," the leader of the Octobrists said, "peace is essential to Russia, and it is for that reason that I have approved the policy of Monsieur Iswolsky . . . But in two years Russia will be able to speak in a very different tone than she has of late been able to employ."[124]

This harmony of views would be important in two regards. First, it served as the area of intersection between the views of the government and those of the part of society with which it cultivated cooperation; both accepted for much the same reasons the necessity of subordinating foreign goals to domestic reform. In addition, this agreement served as evidence of the emerging cooperation between both sides in the state-Duma agreement. The government was able to bolster its support in the Duma at a much needed time, especially in conjunction with the ministerial crisis following the Bosnian affair in the spring of 1909. At the same time, members of the Duma majority coalition could feel that they were participating in the framing of a "national" policy for the new Russia.

The resolution of the Bosnian crisis in March 1909 represented a watershed in European and Russian affairs. In the Balkans there began a period of increasing tensions set afoot by the annexation of two provinces dear to the irredentist dreams of Great Serbian nationalists. In Europe, the crisis and its outcome saw the division of the powers into two "camps,"[125] the Triple Alliance and the still developing Triple Entente. Although Britain and France had not gone so far as Izvolskii had hoped in support of Russia's claims, the German *démarche* at St. Petersburg had demonstrated the nature and strength of Berlin's support for Vienna.

Within Russia, the crisis brought a quick and definite end to a debate that had been engaged in with varying degrees of intensity since August 1907. The debate had revolved around what its participants saw as the connected issues of Russia's capabilities and interests abroad and the success of domestic pacification and reform. The events of January 1908 to March 1909 demonstrated the force with which domestic conditions affected foreign policy. Although the ironclad binding of war and domestic disorder was a crude equation, it was widely held and dominated Russian foreign policy making until January 1914.

More complex and significant was the institutional aspect of this debate—the claim asserted with growing insistence and success by Stolypin and Kokovtsev for the inclusion of the council in the determination of Russia's foreign policy. This claim was rooted in the formative experiences shaping the evolution of United Government and of the office of council chairman as a seat of authority in government. By October 1908, Stolypin and Kokovtsev had won their point—the domestic risks in Russia's foreign policy were such as to warrant the discussion of these questions in the body which had been "summoned by the Fundamental Laws" to unify policy.

Stolypin's success in pressing this claim was reflected in rumors during the crisis and its aftermath. In December 1908 the newspaper *Rus'* reported that a special commission had been created for the discussion of foreign policy.[126] Composed of the foreign minister, representatives of the Council of Ministers, and diplomats, its decisions were said to be forwarded to Stolypin for approval. In late January 1909, *Svet* reported rumors from "bureaucratic circles" that discussions were afoot for the "unification in the hands of one single person of the higher internal and external direction of the country."[127] The article referred to a plan for "the re-establishment of the old position of Chancellor . . . or the transmission of the functions of the Minister of Foreign Affairs to the President of the Council of Ministers." These rumors resurfaced in the spring and connected Stolypin's name with the post of chancellor.[128]

Certainly, Stolypin was an indispensable factor bringing foreign policy under the purview of United Government. His insistence on the necessity of peace and the avoidance of any foreign initiatives by Russia are the most enduring themes in this debate. Equally important was the role he envisioned for the council as the coordinator of policies in a Russia undergoing restoration from revolution. So compelling was his vision that he was able to override seemingly legitimate protestations of independence by the heads of the excluded ministries. In so doing, he imprinted Russian government with his interpretation of the Fundamental Laws. This reading stressed the paramount necessity of the unification of government, to the exclusion of interpretations like Rediger's, which sought to preserve the separation between the emperor's ministries and the state's.

From this point of view, Izvolskii played at least as important a role in the debate over the making of Russian policy. Since joining the council in 1906 he had consciously distanced himself from his predecessors' approach to the office of foreign minister. He had often been a passionate partisan of the new constitutional order and had been an active member of the council during the months of feverish work leading to the final accommodation reached on 3 June 1907. Even at the height of his disgrace, he continued to insist that he was a constitutional minister. In the same vein, he sincerely sought the support of the Duma and public opinion in ways that Lamzdorf would have abjured.

More important was Izvolskii's method of dealing with his council colleagues in foreign affairs questions. From the first suggestion of the agreement with Britain, he had actively courted his colleagues, creating the impression that such consultation was connected with their membership in the united council. Kokovtsev's and Stolypin's remarks on 21 January were trenchant testimony to the strength of the impression he created. He had contributed further by rarely appealing to an exclusivist interpretation of the Fundamental Laws. It is difficult to envision Lamzdorf or Muravev accepting the rebukes heaped on Izvolskii in January or October 1908. Izvolskii's compliance, if not always willing, reflected the novelty of political arrangements in the post-1905 era and the force of the lessons adduced from the period before the war with Japan—an era to which both Stolypin and Izvolskii had referred in similar terms, deploring the lack of governmental unity.

Of course, the central figure in these events, if only by default, was Nicholas. Nicholas's role during the years 1906–1908 was fraught with the irony and ambivalence that characterized both his reign and the career of the state order after 1905. His withdrawal from active intervention in government after 1905, also attested by the curious futility besetting conservative efforts to sway him to a German "orientation" in defense of the "monarchical principle," helped consolidate the situation in which United Government was able to claim and take control over foreign policy making. His absence from politics, coupled with Izvolskii's own constitutional and cabinet proclivities, were directly contributory to the forging of the consensus on foreign policy goals first seen in the Anglo-Russian agreement of 1907, and finally in the assertion of cabinet rule during the Bosnian crisis.

However, Nicholas's ambivalence toward the new order was evident in his connivance with Izvolskii during the prelude to and immediate aftermath of the Buchlau interview. It is possible that Izvolskii, frustrated by Stolypin's resistance to his plans for the Near East, appealed independently to Nicholas, who had known of Izvolskii's independent goals for the Straits since the fall of 1907. With Nicholas's approval, Izvolskii went to Buchlau in full confidence that, with Britain's support, he could win his goals for the Straits. It was only when confronted with the possibility of Stolypin's resignation that the emperor relented and supported the claims of United Government.

Although it is impossible to find a definite reason for his surrender to Stolypin, several factors were probably responsible for this turn. First among these must be the obvious defeat of Izvolskii, and by extension Nicholas, perpetrated by Aehrenthal in 1908. This defeat was yet again, as in the Far East and the revolution, directly tied to actions taken "behind the back" of his government and, like previous episodes, helped to drive him back into political retreat or passivity. Indeed, the popular association of the Bosnian annexation with Tsushima is revealing in this regard.

Also important were Stolypin's forcefulness, certainty of vision, and apparent success in managing the pacification and "repair" of Russia during these months. In domestic affairs, the emperor seems to have left the problems of reform to Stolypin. In fact, Nicholas did not attempt to assert his power until the height of the Naval Staffs crisis during the late spring of 1909. Significantly, after some hesitation, he overruled Stolypin but insisted that he continue as chairman, in spite of conservative fears that the chairman's views and methods infringed on the autocrat's power. Indeed, an article in the British press by Witte's friend C. J. Dillon reported the "Conservative" apprehension that Stolypin was undermining the tsar's prerogatives, noting that he had brought into the council "the three Ministers of War, Marine and Foreign Affairs, whom the Constitution expressly emancipates from Cabinet control."[129] In the making of foreign policy, Nicholas's distance from events may well have dovetailed with Izvolskii's own views of his role as a minister in the cabinet and induced Izvolskii to seek a consensus among his colleagues in support of his policy.

Until early 1914 Russian policy continued to bear the imprint of Stolypin's outlook on foreign affairs. This is testimony to the effectiveness with which he asserted his views. If Russia had joined the Triple Entente, this was only in the eyes of advocates of closer relations with Britain. In fact, until late 1913, Russian policy continued to reflect the concerns of Stolypin and Kokovtsev, that because of internal disarray Russia needed peace at all costs. The agreement with the United Kingdom went hand-in-hand with good relations with Germany. Both served to stabilize potential areas of complications on Russia's frontiers.

While Russia might once again "speak in its old voice," this possibility was still several years distant. In order to assure observance of these strictures, it was necessary that foreign policy, with its potential effects on domestic order, be subject to the scrutiny of the body that had been created to coordinate and unify policy—the Council of Ministers, under the authority of its powerful chairman.

# 7

# The Apogee of
# Stolypin's Chairmanship

The aftermath of the Bosnian crisis avoided foreign complications, but lent new strength to developing domestic problems. Days after the final establishment of his role in the discussion of foreign policy, Stolypin confronted the first significant challenge to his government and its institutional underpinnings. Although not concerned with foreign policy, the ministerial crisis brought about by the Naval Staff controversy[1] had most probably gained strength from the diplomatic "Tsushima"[2] with which the Bosnian affair had concluded. Exhausted and ill, Stolypin was absent from the capital until the middle of April. His conservative adversaries capitalized on this circumstance to mount an organized assault in the State Council on the overweening activity of the council chairman at the expense of the autocrat's power.

Forced to return to St. Petersburg in defense of his policy and position, Stolypin took the significant step of gaining the agreement of the Council of Ministers to resign collectively should Nicholas support the conservatives in the State Council.[3] The crisis soon subsided, but not without enduring effects. The constitutional and diplomatic crises spurred conservatives to urge that Nicholas dismiss Stolypin. This effort, combined with widespread blame of Izvolskii for the Bosnian debacle led to speculation about the imminent resignation of the cabinet or Izvolskii and its probable effects on Russian diplomacy. Rumors of Izvolskii's retirement and the identity of his successor themselves reflected the intersection between the constitutional crisis and the general orientation of Russian foreign policy.

After a brief period in late March when Charykov appeared to be Izvolskii's likely replacement,[4] the name of I. L. Goremykin, formerly minister of internal affairs and chairman of the Council of Ministers, emerged as the probable future minister of foreign affairs.[5] Goremykin, in Berlin at the time, was said to have confirmed reports that Izvolskii had offered his resignation and that he was to be his successor.[6] This possibility was held in part to be connected with the Naval Staff crisis and the fate of the entire Stolypin cabinet.[7] It was linked in turn with expectations of a rightward shift in Russian politics, leading to St. Petersburg's realignment in favor of Berlin and Vienna.

The attempts to unseat Stolypin came to naught. It could well be argued that despite the threat to his position which had appeared during the constitutional crisis and Nicholas's veto of the Naval Staff bill, the chairman was as strong as ever. Certainly, this was the opinion among supporters of the conservative fraction in the State Council.

For the first time since Witte's tenure as council chairman, the epithet of "vizier" was attached to the office.[8] One conservative observer wrote in his diary in 1910, "[t]his lord [vlastelin] seats everywhere people who are mediocre and obedient to him. Such are—Sazonov in Foreign Affairs, Kasso in Education and Guchkov in the Duma. All of this is lined with petty personal interests, careerist aspirations and—alas—servility.[9]"

The most interesting critique of the ministerial crisis and its implications came in an anonymous memorandum presented to the emperor in 1909.[10] This document focused on the alloy of personal and institutional interests that had combined to make the post of council chairman strong enough to threaten the power of the emperor himself. Having examined the 1905 council reform in practice, the writer observed that "the authors of the new statute on the Council of Ministers and its relations to the Tsar" had acted "with the design of seizing the most possible power into the hands of the Chairman of the Council of Ministers." As a result, ministers had been demoted to "the role of bureaucrats subordinated to him," while the tsar's own "executive power" was more restricted than that of the German emperor. The latter was at least able to name his own ministers and to receive reports from them directly.[11] While not initially apparent, limitations of the emperor's power had grown increasingly visible with each year. Now, there was a widespread feeling "that the power of the Sovereign has fallen under the control of the Council of Ministers and its Chairman, without which He can neither name a Minister, nor give him orders."

The new statute had created a bureaucratic dictatorship, "which has appropriated to itself a part of the Tsar's Autocratic power." Indeed, Stolypin was said to have stated that "the Sovereign reigns [tsarstvuet], but I rule [upravliaiu]."[12] But the problem was not Stolypin: "[he] has done what anybody else in his place would probably have done, he has at one and the same time become carried away by the interest of the task before him and personal *amour-propre.*"[13] The author blamed Witte, who had drafted the original statute. The only solution would be to abolish the post of chairman, which had become raised above the council, and to have the emperor himself preside at council meetings.[14]

This critique described concisely the problems inherent in the post of chairman of the Council of Ministers. The Bosnian crisis had illustrated the author's argument. Stolypin had insisted on Izvolskii's obligation to consult with him and the council in important matters of foreign policy. Part of Stolypin's success had been due to the fact that the foreign minister had long entertained ideas similar—if not as rock-ribbed—to his about the relationship between the council and its individual ministers, including the excluded minister of foreign affairs. Rediger had complained about Stolypin's urge to integrate all ministries into the council, calling it a "delusion of grandeur"—a phrase repeated elsewhere in the fall of 1909.[15]

Crucial to Stolypin's success, however, had been his relationship with Nicholas. The writer of the anonymous memorandum had been entirely correct both to point out the central role played by the political relationship between emperor and council chairman and to attribute its origins to Witte. Yet, in 1909, this relationship still worked in Stolypin's favor, giving him the authority to impose his political and institutional views on fellow ministers, even over their protests.

In September 1908 he had threatened to resign over Izvolskii's conduct of the Buchlau negotiations without his knowledge; in April 1909 he had threatened the resignation of the entire council to extract from Nicholas a positive resolution of the Naval Staff bill, although this threat had ultimately failed. In both cases, Nicholas had more than ample legal grounds, even under the new Fundamental Laws, to support a more narrow reading of council and Duma prerogatives. Stolypin's opponents in the State Council had asked the tsar to do precisely that in the spring of 1909. However, Nicholas continued to support his chairman.

Any explanation of Nicholas's continuing confidence in Stolypin must include several factors. Nicholas had "retreated" since 1906 from the active rule he had espoused before the revolution. As during those years, and in the Björkö episode, his intervention in policy in 1908 had led to failure. After a brief display of his authority in the Naval Staff issue, he relapsed into the position of semipassive observer. Moreover, the same moral authority and strength of personality that had so impressed his council colleagues during the revolution and afterward could well have buttressed Stolypin's position with the emperor, who had a history of relying on strong advisers.

The chairman could also point to the success of his reform program. Russia had been pacified; a working arrangement had been established with the representatives of society; the agrarian reform seemed to present a solution to rural unrest; and an air of normality was gradually entering imperial political life. Most of all, Stolypin's program and his forthrightness in its pursuit had protected Nicholas from the burden of involvement in the acrimonious and threatening events that had menaced the empire, both within and abroad, during the last four-odd years.

Nothing indicated so markedly the personal *cum* institutional nature of the relationship between Stolypin and Nicholas as the emperor's statement in a letter to the chairman at the height of the ministerial crisis in April 1909: having rejected Stolypin's recommendation that he ratify the Duma bill which had provoked the controversy, Nicholas wrote, "there can be no question of confidence or no confidence."[16] Although the ruler's confidence was indispensable in the success of any imperial statesman, in Stolypin's case confidence was being accorded in a vastly different institutional setting than that of 1903 or 1906. Whereas Witte had never persuaded Nicholas to support his claims for dominance as premier within the council, Stolypin had asserted a vision of United Government that Nicholas had supported at critical moments since 1906.

The chairman's continued enjoyment of Nicholas's confidence had profound institutional repercussions, for it—combined with Nicholas's passivity—rendered authoritative Stolypin's view of the council chairman's role in relation to individual ministers. Here, too, the writer of the memorandum had ably spelled out the implications of this situation. In service of internal reconstruction and out of a persisting solicitude for social peace, Stolypin had indeed unified government and subordinated the other ministries to his views, imparting in the meantime a general and coherent cast to Russia's internal and external policies. The Bosnian crisis, however, had also demonstrated the potential for independent action by one minister with Nicholas's support. Thus, after the resolution of the ministerial and Bosnian crises, Stolypin turned his attention to the related problems of defining Russian foreign policy and choosing a successor to Izvolskii.

The Bosnian crisis seemed to open once more the question of Russia's foreign orientation, as was evident in the rumors and speculation surrounding Izvolskii in the spring of 1909. Izvolskii had promoted active cooperation with Great Britain in the defense and extension of Russia's position in the Near East. This understanding of the 1907 Anglo-Russian entente was central to the policy he had pursued in spite of Stolypin and the council, culminating in the Bosnian crisis. By the same token, many conservatives felt that Germany's support for Austria-Hungary in the recent crisis demonstrated the fruitlessness of Izvolskii's policy. These observers began once more to advocate alignment with Germany, both with the hope of detaching Germany from Austria and in the earlier interests of monarchical solidarity.

Stolypin favored a middle path between these alternatives, which demonstrated the degree to which he subordinated external relations to the exigencies of domestic reconstruction. In August 1907 and throughout 1908, he sought peace above all for Russia through understandings intended to forestall the possibility of complications wherever they could arise. Thus, he had interpreted the agreement with England in purely defensive terms and had advocated a policy of nonintervention in the Balkans. In the wake of the Bosnian crisis, he seems to have sought to set right relations with Germany, which had been severely strained since Izvolskii's arrival at Pevchevskii Most. At the same time, Stolypin remained a convinced advocate of the agreement with Britain.

His support for this policy took two forms. First, he emerged in the spring of 1909 as an authoritative spokesman on foreign policy issues.[17] He had assumed this role in May, while Izvolskii was absent from the capital. The significance of Stolypin's new position was underscored by the fact that Charykov, who as assistant minister would normally have been the authoritative Russian official in foreign affairs, deferred publicly to Stolypin as the decisive actor in such questions.[18] In May, Charykov was appointed ambassador to Turkey; the Porte was notified of this appointment by Stolypin.[19]

Stolypin's new role in foreign policy became more apparent after Izvolskii resumed his duties as foreign minister. In early June, Stolypin accompanied his colleague to a meeting of Nicholas and Wilhelm aboard the German imperial yacht *Hohenzollern*.[20] Of course, one of the topics discussed was the German ultimatum in March. German reports of this meeting noted Stolypin's "sympathy" for good relations with Germany, and distinguished the moderation of his views from those of Izvolskii. Still, Stolypin was by no means a Germanophile in the style of a Goremykin. In late August he spoke on European affairs with Sir Arthur Nicolson.[21] Stolypin noted that "the Extreme Right parties were discontented, but the latter were strongly opposed to any understanding with England and were sturdy advocates for an alliance with Germany." Such circles felt that England was trying to weaken Germany by pitting it against Russia. For his part, Stolypin wished to see the United Kingdom and Germany reach agreement on naval questions. He also expressed concern over future developments in southeastern Europe, given Turkey's internal weakness and Austria's intentions. Russia's policy in the Balkans from 1909 until 1912 reflected these concerns.

In tandem with his newly elevated profile in the diplomatic counsels of St. Petersburg, Stolypin turned to the other question raised by the Bosnian crisis—the independence that had been exercised by Izvolskii at such grave risk. He resolved this problem in his own way with the selection of a successor to Izvolskii and the transfer of Charykov to Constantinople. Rumors of Izvolskii's resignation in the spring of 1909 had not been unfounded. This action had been under discussion since the autumn of 1908, when Stolypin had rejected such a measure, for fear that it would signal Russia's shift to "the path of war." In March 1909 Izvolskii had requested Nicholas's permission to resign, but was turned down,[22] chiefly for lack of a qualified replacement.[23] The implications were obvious—Izvolskii was now to serve as a caretaker of his ministry until a successor was found.

The first indications that changes were afoot in the Ministry of Foreign Affairs came in late May 1909, when Charykov was replaced as assistant foreign minister by Sergei Dmitrevich Sazonov. This move was immediately appreciated as constituting the appointment of Izvolskii's eventual successor.[24] According to Sazonov, he was told by Izvolskii upon his arrival from Rome—where he had been serving as Russian minister to the Vatican—that Izvolskii's resignation had been decided in principle, and that Sazonov had been designated to succeed him.[25]

There ensued a period of fifteen months that served as a sort of interregnum at Pevchevskii Most. Sazonov attributed the delay to two causes.[26] Since Izvolskii had no wish to retire, an appropriate embassy had to be found for him. In addition, once the inexperienced Sazonov had been chosen as a successor, he would need a lengthy transition period during which to learn the procedures and problems of heading the ministry. Thus, during a personal leave taken by Izvolskii in the spring of 1910, Count Berchtold wrote to Vienna that senior officials in the Russian foreign ministry were treating this as Sazonov's "test period" preceding receipt of his "diploma" as Izvolskii's successor. Now, Izvolskii would only have to await the availability of an "appropriate" embassy.[27]

Sazonov's internship ended in September 1910, when an opening appeared at the Russian embassy in Paris. Izvolskii went to France and Sazonov stepped into his place at the MID. Like Izvolskii's own elevation to the minister's post in 1906, Sazonov's was regarded as a political appointment, but reactions also indicated the changed nature of the politics that had determined it. Sazonov was not eminently qualified for his new position; he came to the ministry from a relatively junior position with little of the chancellery experience that had traditionally been considered a prerequisite for the foreign minister.

Here the similarities ended. Izvolskii had owed his appointment to the patronage of the dowager empress and his own well-known sympathy for the reforms of 1905–1906. Sazonov enjoyed no such imperial patronage, and his views on the Duma or the constitutional changes undergone by Russia were little known.[28] However, virtually all observers pointed to the importance of his family relationship with his brother-in-law Stolypin as the key factor in his elevation. Indeed, it appears that on the eve of his official confirmation in September, there was a period of resistance on the part of "Court circles and Far Right circles" who feared that "Stolypin family" would gain too much power through this appointment.[29] Perhaps the most trenchant evaluation of the new appointment came from the wife of Justice Minister Shcheglovitov, who remarked of the joint naming of Sazonov and Education Minister Kasso to the council, "the tsar does not know them, they were appointed by telegraph. Stolypin plays the role of the Grand Vizier."[30]

The nature of the new relationship between foreign minister and council chairman was most starkly illustrated in the spring of 1911. Sazonov fell ill with a serious throat infection that necessitated his absence from his post until November. As his illness grew graver, speculation grew that he would have to be replaced.[31] "Cabinet members" told Berchtold that such speculation was "entirely baseless"; Sazonov's assistant, A. A. Neratov, was fully capable of fulfilling his duties, and "he is moreover covered by the personality of Herr Stolypin, who will be asked in all important questions of foreign policy," as he had been since "Herr Iswolsky had demonstrated his inability during the Annexation crisis."[32]

Stolypin's control of the new foreign minister was also reflected in Russian policy. Sazonov debuted as foreign minister during a visit by Nicholas to Potsdam in late October 1911.[33] The main topics discussed at these talks were a possible link between Russian railways in northern Persia and the "Berlin to Baghdad" line, as well as the extent to which Germany was prepared to separate itself from Austria-Hungary in Balkan affairs. The meetings were even more important from the point of view of what is now called "atmospherics." Speaking with the German ambassador in St. Petersburg, Stolypin expressed his pleasure at the final elimination of the mistrust that had so recently reigned between the two powers.[34] At the same time, he sought to reassure Russia's partners in the Triple Entente, as it was coming to be called, that no major reorientation was forthcoming in Russian policy.[35]

In foreign policy, Stolypin consistently defined Russia's needs very simply and directly. In 1909, he stated in a famous interview that Russia needed "twenty years of peace."[36] He had held this view throughout his conflict with Izvolskii over the direction and control of foreign policy. Explaining the reasons for the Potsdam discussions, Stolypin assured the French ambassador that their countries "need peace" and that Russia was doing "everything possible to assure it." Germany knew that the Dual Alliance was "untouchable." "Nothing has changed, and nothing will . . . but one still had to try to arrive at a *modus vivendi* in matters that could imperil relations between Russia and Germany."[37]

Writing to Izvolskii in the summer of 1911, Stolypin stated his thinking yet more clearly. Izvolskii had sent Stolypin an analysis of the threats to peace in Europe, outlining the responses that Russia should be prepared to undertake. Stolypin's answer expressed his perplexity at this advice: "You know my views: we need peace, war during the next years, especially for reasons the people would not understand, would be fatal for Russia and for the dynasty."[38] Thus, Sazonov's appointment was significant from several points of view. Stolypin had obtained a trustworthy colleague who would tailor Russian foreign relations to Stolypin's own understanding of the empire's needs and capabilities.[39] The fact that he had secured the elevation of "his" candidate demonstrated the solidity of his relationship with Nicholas, and the authority flowing therefrom.

Furthermore, it appears that Stolypin was instrumental in the other significant appointment made in May 1909—that of N. V. Charykov as ambassador to Constantinople. This embassy was one of the most important in the imperial foreign service, situated in the cockpit of Balkan politics. Charykov's political ties with Stolypin dated to September 1908, when he had cooperated with the chairman in the development of an alternative position to that set forth by Izvolskii after Buchlau. Charykov's subsequent relationship with the foreign minister seems to have been strained, a fact which did not escape the notice of diplomatic observers.[40] Charykov's appointment to Constantinople heralded the advent of a new Russian policy in the Balkans. Upon arriving in Constantinople, Charykov was frank in describing the course to be taken by Russia in the Balkans during the near future. His program was to effect a rapprochement between Turkey and the individual Balkan states, first in economic relations, with the ultimate intention of restoring normal political relations.[41]

Later, there were reports that Charykov had advised the Serbian representative that good relations were essential among the Balkan states, as the only way in which to erect a "natural barrier" against intrusion by outside forces. He said that this was "one of the chief tasks of his mission in Constantinople."[42] These statements and others by Charykov are seen to have been the first steps in the creation of the Balkan alliance that fought the war of 1912.[43] Historical accounts of the alliance's formation rightly stress Russia's role in these developments. However, these accounts are also led by the subsequent outbreak of the Balkan wars to interpret the underlying intent of Russian policy as revanchism in response to the Bosnian crisis. Thus, having been bested in the annexation crisis and its European aftermath, Russian diplomacy sought to forge from the individual Slavic Balkan states—two of which had their own grievances from the crisis—a potent weapon with which to strike Austria-Hungary when the need arose.

The outcome of the Bosnian crisis and Stolypin's ascendancy point to a different argument, however. Even after the peaceful resolution of the Bosnian crisis, the political situation facing Russia was not reassuring. Turkey was still volatile, owing to the ebb and flow of the Young Turks' attempts to master power. Of more concern was the fact that weakened authority in Constantinople vitiated Turkish efforts to maintain order in the restive European provinces. This fact only added to the threat of general instability in the wake of what was still widely seen in Russia, Serbia, and Montenegro as a unilateral breach of the *status quo* by the Dual Monarchy. Furthermore, the prospect of instability hung over a geographical area in which Russian public opinion—including Stolypin's partners in the Duma —had expressed vocal support for Russia's historical role as the Slavic Great Power. Complications in this area could well lead in the foreseeable future to a war which Stolypin felt would spell domestic disaster for the empire.

Thus, Stolypin faced the necessity of reestablishing stability in the Balkans, more from the demands of internal tranquillity than of righting the altered balance of power there after the annexation. One solution would have been to reestablish the Balkan entente with Austria-Hungary. As first established in 1897, this agreement had been intended by both parties to put the Balkans "under glass" until the anticipated collapse of Turkey.[44] However, Stolypin had not been entirely impervious to the sentiments provoked in Izvolskii and Nicholas by Aehrenthal's methods in the autumn of 1908. While Charykov was first explaining Russia's new policy in Constantinople, Stolypin was telling Sir Arthur Nicolson that "he had no confidence whatever in Austria" and that he did not trust Aehrenthal.[45]

Seen in this light, a Balkan league, to include Turkey, would have answered Stolypin's political needs. It could put the Balkans "under glass" without Austrian cooperation, and thus assure the peace Russia needed. This did not exclude an anti-Austrian thrust—certainly it was meant to serve as a "barrier" to Austrian expansion into the area. By the same token, all the prospective partners, with the exception of Bulgaria, had reason to be hostile to the Dual Monarchy. But this sentiment could be used as a point of persuasion in favor of the league, to enable effective resistance to future Austro-Hungarian "adventures" in the area. Above all, it would give Russia, as the alliance's sponsor, effective control over questions of war and peace in a notoriously unstable area at a time when it needed peace at all costs.

In pursuit of such a policy, Stolypin had in the Ministry of Foreign Affairs two important figures—Sazonov and Charykov—upon whom he felt able to rely. But the authority that allowed Stolypin to take these steps ultimately proved to be his political undoing and that of the policy he promoted. In like fashion, the reasons for which he had obtained Sazonov's promotion ended by compromising the policy he envisioned, with unfortunate effects on the future of United Government and Sazonov's position respectively.

Although he was assassinated in September 1911, Stolypin's authority was severely weakened at the very time that Berchtold was reporting his importance in Russian foreign policy. In March, Stolypin confronted a renewed attack on his position as chairman—resulting in a serious setback in his relations with Nicholas—when the emperor gave his adversaries permission to oppose him in a State Council vote. The immediate cause of Stolypin's difficulties was the "Western *zemstvo*" crisis,[46] which ended by bringing into sharp focus the relationship between Nicholas and his premier. Stolypin's attempt to introduce institutions of local government in the western provinces, structured to make them politically trustworthy, provided a lightning rod for building conservative disaffection with the high-handed methods of the chairman. The crisis itself was provoked when Nicholas, in response to appeals from the right in the State Council, allowed members of that chamber to vote with their "conscience" on this issue.[47] As a result, the bill went down to an embarrassing and threatening defeat for Stolypin, which "rocked the bureaucratic world."[48]

This setback led Stolypin to demand an audience with Nicholas, where it became evident that Nicholas was beginning to heed charges that Stolypin was encroaching on his prerogatives.[49] Lurking behind the entire conversation, as recorded by Stolypin, was the image of the vizierate, increasingly invoked by conservatives to decry Stolypin's usurpation of power properly belonging to the tsar. Thus, when Stolypin complained of intrigues by "reactionaries,"[50] Nicholas asked, "[a]gainst whom? You or me?" Stolypin tried to efface this distinction by stating that one could not divide "the steward and the master." This metaphor, with its image of rule through an intermediary bore interesting parallels to the image of the grand vizier circulating in conservative attacks on Stolypin. When Stolypin declared that he would resign, given Nicholas's lack of support, Nicholas told him that there could be no question of Stolypin's resignation, since "there is no substitute for [Stolypin]." Although the audience came to no conclusive outcome, Stolypin ended his notes in a troubled mood, again with unconscious allusions to the image of the vizierate: "I felt that the Sovereign believes that I shield him, that somehow I am standing between him and the country."

The "western *zemstvo*" affair shook all the institutional relationships on which "3 June Russia" was founded. To force passage of the legislation, Stolypin invoked the emergency powers provided him by Article 87 of the Fundamental Laws, by which he suspended the legislature and enacted the *zemstvo* bill by decree. This act aroused criticism from those Octobrists who still cooperated with the government and a rift with their leader, Alexander Guchkov, who had been an ardent partisan of the Stolypin program. Most importantly, the crisis confronted Nicholas with the extent of his dependence upon his premier. The deterioration of this relationship had been exacerbated by Stolypin's demand that Nicholas expel from St. Petersburg Stolypin's two most bitter conservative foes—P. N. Durnovo and V. F. Trepov—who enjoyed close ties with Nicholas, forcing the emperor to make an unpleasant choice. Although the immediate results of these measures seemed to leave Stolypin untouched in his authority, both he and others knew that "he would not long remain in his post."[51]

The confrontation with Nicholas apparently led Stolypin to reexamine the legal and political bases of his position as chairman of the Council of Ministers and the bases of state administration in Russia as a whole. In 1957, Professor A. V. Zenkovskii published a document that he claimed to have taken in dictation during May 1911, in the aftermath of the Western *zemstvo* crisis.[52] The document took the form of a report to Nicholas, proposing interesting correctives to administrative structures, based on Stolypin's five years at the head of the government. The report analyzed the workings of every ministry and made extensive proposals for their overhaul.

Stolypin's most interesting comments, with regard to foreign policy, were those concerning the Council of Ministers, its chairman, and the Ministry of Foreign Affairs. Stolypin proposed that the chairman be appointed by the sovereign, to whom he would be directly responsible. All other ministers would be appointed by the chairman, who "should be responsible for all Ministers whom he has proposed to the Sovereign." He added that their reports to the emperor should only be made "upon a preliminary agreement with the Chairman."[53] All of these proposals recalled Witte's recommendations for the chairman's powers in the fall of 1905. Equally significant, Stolypin recommended that the minister of foreign affairs be "obliged to inform the Chairman" about the international situation and foreign attitudes toward Russia, in order to ensure the coordination of domestic and foreign policies.[54]

These proposals represented the codification of Stolypin's *de facto* achievements as chairman of the Council of Ministers. At the same time, they embodied Stolypin's recognition of the need to establish legal forms for these achievements, given the behavior of ministers such as Izvolskii. The binding of all ministries to the council, and the broad authority that Stolypin claimed for the chairman's office, had been sources of complaint from the excluded ministries since 1907. Stolypin had often and successfully invoked the principle of unity in council activity as a *sine qua non* of governmental organization. The emergence of separate "small" and plenary council sessions also attested to the body's broadening purview as it had developed under Stolypin. With the exception of Kokovtsev and the minister of war after March 1909, V. A. Sukhomlinov,[55] the council over which Stolypin presided was composed of either his appointees or sympathizers with his policies for the reconstruction of Russia.

Significantly, this reform project, particularly its provisions for the chairman's right to nominate ministers and to vet their reports to the emperor recalled Witte's earlier efforts to confront the problem of regulating the relationships among the council, its chairman, and the emperor. Despite differing approaches to ministerial organization, attributable to Stolypin's longer experience as council chairman, both men's visions of the council and the premier's role in relation to it and the emperor were congruent. The outstanding parallel in Stolypin's and Witte's views of cabinet rule was the crucial weight they assigned to the nexus between emperor and council chairman. Both sought to make the office of chairman the sole channel regulating the relationship and contacts between the emperor and the world outside; the chairman *qua* prime minister would harness the emperor's sovereign power, and in so doing would direct it to the tasks designated by policy.

In fact, those critics who labelled Witte and Stolypin "viziers" struck to the heart of the problem facing these statesmen and the tsarist order after 1905. On the one hand, the creation of an elective legislature raised more trenchantly than previously the question of the source and legitimacy of the state's authority. In defense of the state's continued primacy, imperial officials were forced to derive this authority from the sovereign emperor, as the Fundamental Laws vividly attest. Yet, on the other hand, the experience of Witte and others before 1905—and that of Stolypin, particularly in 1911—had shown them the distinction between Nicholas as the sovereign source of state authority and as the actual person of the ruler.

It might be suggested that both Stolypin and Witte were casting about for a way to separate these two aspects of imperial power or, as conservatives suggested, to limit Nicholas's power within the bounds of a sovereignty regulated under law. However, because of their own beliefs about the workings and integrity of the autocracy, they were unable to pose the problem in precisely this fashion. Instead, they tried to oblige Nicholas to rule exclusively through his machinery of state. In their view, the council chairman would act as the exclusive point of engagement between the emperor's sovereign power and the administrative machine, thus allowing them to retain their necessary source of authority but under circumstances and in institutions they controlled.

Ironically, this view of the chairman's role only heightened the instrumentality of the emperor's confidence as the variable on which the rest of the political system's activity depended. Yet, it was crises of confidence that brought down Witte and Stolypin in turn. Witte's experience of the withdrawal of Nicholas's confidence had ultimately led him to conclude years later that, given the possibility of such emperors as Nicholas, a constitution was probably inevitable for Russia. Stolypin never reached this conclusion, if his reform plan can be accepted as his political testament. While seeking the institutionalization of a strong chairman on the lines first suggested by Witte in 1905, Stolypin also believed in autocracy to the extent that he seems to have accepted the necessity of imperial confidence as the *sine qua non* for a government's existence.

Indeed, the formal and substantive congruity of Witte's and Stolypin's attempts to integrate the sovereign emperor into the top reaches of the state structure through an obligatory relationship with the council chairman attests both to the persistence of a problem first identified in high official circles before 1905 and to the enduring inability of tsarist officials either to separate the personal, arbitrary tsar from the legal, sovereign emperor or to find an alternative basis for legitimate power. Thus, the link between emperor and administration embodied in the idea of "confidence" became both the linchpin and the tragic flaw of autocratic government after 1905, largely through the efforts of those who were trying to save it. This paradox was invisible to tsarist statesmen because of the very nature of late imperial bureaucratic culture, for lack of a better term, and stands out as one of the underlying, and often undetected, elements contributing to what Lenin termed the "crisis of the heights" in imperial government on the eve of its demise.

The closest Stolypin ever got to actively proposing substantial limitation of the emperor's personal power had come in March, when he compared his relationship with Nicholas to that between a "master" and his "steward." Although the image is cryptic, it does imply a certain passivity on the part of the former, who entrusts the latter with the active administration and disposition of his estate. Confronted with the limits of this relationship, Stolypin, a good son of the autocracy, could only react by proposing the further tightening of the channels leading to the emperor, thereby preventing the possibility of intrigues from quarters beyond his control. Nevertheless, he was resigned to the fact that his tenure as chairman was to be limited after the Western *zemstvo* crisis.

In spite of his ultimate failure, Stolypin had refashioned the shape and habits of Russian government. The procedures and ethos of United Government had developed piecemeal within the vague frameworks bequeathed by Witte and Goremykin, and under the pressure of revolutionary events and their consequences in the form of the settlement reached after 3 June 1907. Although many of the practices that had developed under Stolypin had never received explicit legal sanction—*ergo* his reform project—they had been ingrained by practice and abetted by Nicholas's abstention from government and Stolypin's enjoyment of his confidence. The presence of Sazonov in the council, Stolypin's role in the conduct of Russian foreign policy after the fall of 1908, and the very binding of Russia's foreign aims to the exigencies of consolidating the post-1907 order were all evidence of the extent to which Stolypin's views had gained acceptance in official Russia, and even at Tsarskoe Selo.

However, if these institutional arrangements had been grounded through constant usage, they still required the personality of a Stolypin, enjoying Nicholas's confidence, and the respect of his colleagues to ensure that United Government continued to function with the vitality and coherence that had marked its career since 1908. This crucial aspect was to be absent during the chairmanship of Stolypin's successor, V. N. Kokovtsev.

Stolypin's fall from favor had inevitable effects on Sazonov's position, tied as he was so intimately to Stolypin's authority. This in turn affected the course of Russian policy during a period of advancing instability in the Balkans and increasing political fracture within Russia. These effects were enhanced by the institutional flux that overtook his ministry during the years after 1909. From 1909 until 1914, virtually every Russian mission in Europe saw a turnover in its chief personnel, including the transfer of Charykov and Izvolskii to Constantinople and Paris, respectively, and Sazonov's own appointment as minister. Generally, this was the product of attrition. Most incumbents—Nelidov in Paris, Osten-Sacken in Berlin, and Urusov, who had extended his stay in Vienna because of the Bosnian crisis—were well into the years when retirement could be expected. Other transfers had lasting effects, especially the appointment of N. V. Gartvig— despite or perhaps because of his name a fervent sympathizer for the "Slavic cause"—to head the Russian mission in Belgrade.

The resulting situation became increasingly difficult for Sazonov, especially as Stolypin's own authority waned between February 1911 and his assassination in September. Although he enjoyed close ties with the council chairman, the factors that had led to his appointment as minister undermined his stature within his ministry. Taube remarked of Sazonov that he was a sympathetic, highly moral, and honest character, unmarked by any of his predecessor's "snobbism." But, all the same, he was a weak minister, "producing the impression of an unprepared student who had climbed into a professorial chair."[56] A diplomat whose views usually differed greatly from Taube's came to much the same conclusions: "It was very easy to get on with him . . . but he did not give the impression of a great statesman and I always thought it was a mistake" to appoint him minister "at such a critical time."[57]

These attitudes toward Sazonov were reflected in an alarming independence on the part of many Russian agents abroad, including Izvolskii. Interestingly, when the latter had acceded to the ministry, he had encountered few of the same problems among his subordinates abroad. This was probably due in equal measure to his long acquaintance with most of them, his undoubted intelligence, and the early accomplishments of his ministry. Sazonov received little such cooperation. After Stolypin's death in the fall of 1911, Charykov undertook a serious unilateral *démarche,* which Sazonov was forced to repudiate publicly. Gartvig rarely followed orders from St. Petersburg,[58] preferring to pursue his own political ideals. And Izvolskii conducted intrigues in Paris while hectoring Sazonov through the diplomatic pouch, complaining of a lack of proper information.[59]

What authority Sazonov did enjoy was tied in many ways to the stature of Stolypin and later of Kokovtsev, who succeeded Stolypin as council chairman. Thus, ironically, in tying the foreign minister firmly to the Council of Ministers, Stolypin also abetted the degradation of the latter's authority in the implementation of a policy now largely dictated by Stolypin. The result was to undercut the effectiveness of the foreign ministry as an instrument for maintaining peace abroad on Russia's terms.

When Stolypin died, Sazonov demonstrated his recognition of the "cabinet" considerations behind his appointment by allying with Kokovtsev in many matters. But he gradually began also to state views that he had concealed during the first period of his ministry. To contemporaries, the most obvious of these were his strong Russian nationalism and a fervent embrace of Orthodoxy unusual in his predecessors, as well as an "extreme Anglophilism and a sentimental love for the 'little brothers' " in the Balkans.[60] The outlooks implied in Taube's ironic locution played a major role in Sazonov's ministry.

# 8

# The Unraveling of
# United Government

The years from 1911 to 1914 were a period of both continuity and gathering crisis in Russian foreign policy. On one hand, these years saw the policy-making procedures developed by Stolypin assume abiding institutional form, as did the entire framework of political relationships that had emerged under the 3 June system. On the other hand, important changes occurred in the nature of the relationships among the component parts of this framework. The period began with Stolypin's assassination in the autumn of 1911. Although his authority had declined since the preceding spring, his death represented nevertheless a visible and irrevocable break in the history of post-1905 Russia. As if to emphasize the importance of Stolypin's death, the man chosen to succeed him, Vladimir Nikolaevich Kokovtsev was in all respects the antithesis of the late chairman.

Under Kokovtsev, the institutional structures Stolypin had forged remained formally intact. As chairman, Kokovtsev insisted, like Stolypin, on the necessity of unity in government and on the crucial role of the chairman *vis-à-vis* the council and the emperor. He continued Stolypin's attempt to govern with the Duma and State Council as channels to the support of society. Yet, the relative weight of the various components in "3 June Russia"—emperor, council, chairman, society, and, for lack of a better word, the people *(narod)*—changed markedly after 1911, largely because of Nicholas's reemergence as a political actor after Stolypin's death. This change brought in its train a series of consequences, including a veiled attack on United Government, with the formal preservation of the council, and a rapid deterioration in relations between the government and the Duma, as well as increasing unrest among the *narod*.

Abroad, barely eighteen months after the resolution of the Bosnian crisis, the Balkans relapsed into instability with the outbreak of war between Italy and the Ottoman Empire during the summer of 1911. Originally fought over Turkish possessions in northern Africa, the war soon spread tensions to the Balkans, which became the cynosure of European attention with little remission for the next three years. The period was marked by two inconclusive wars and bitterly conflicting territorial claims advanced by the Balkan nation-states. The wars and their ramifications drew Russia and Austria-Hungary into disputes that were further envenomed by memories of the Bosnian crisis. These memories, as held by Nicholas, Sazonov, and society, spurred the Russian decision in July 1914 to mobilize in support of Serbia against the Austrian ultimatum after the assassination of Franz Ferdinand.

If any attribute characterizes this period in historical retrospect, it is irony, much of which originated with Nicholas himself. In order to prevent the reemergence of a high-handed chairman, he appointed a successor whom he undercut by condoning dissent within the council before dismissing Kokovtsev in January 1914 and replacing him with the figurehead of I. L. Goremykin. Two weeks after dismissing Kokovtsev, the emperor "administered a little lecture to his Ministers, impressing upon them the necessity of acting together as a united Government," in cooperation with the Duma and State Council.[1]

In the same vein, concern for domestic instability led Russian statesmen to broker a Balkan alliance intended to "freeze" the area after the collapse of the Austro-Russian entente in 1909; the allies flouted Russian intent and embarked on wars that Russia was too weak to prevent. Later, Russia was unable to support the unexpected success of its protégés, out of continued adherence to the perception among Russian officialdom that the risk of war abroad could provoke a renewed revolutionary outburst. These events, and Russian inability to act decisively in them, brought a turnaround in official thought on foreign policy and its domestic consequences. Thus, in July 1914, Sazonov advised Nicholas to aid Serbia against Austria-Hungary; otherwise "Russia would never forgive the Sovereign."[2] When these words were spoken, the streets of St. Petersburg were crowded by the largest wave of strikes since 1905. Perhaps the crowning irony of this period was the image of an autocrat embarking on a "national" war.

## V. N. Kokovtsev as Chairman: Institutionalizing Stolypin's Legacy

Reflecting on his confrontation with Nicholas in March 1911, Stolypin saw only two ways out of the situation that had been created by the Western *zemstvo* crisis: a reactionary cabinet or a bureaucratic one "under the banner of previous policy."[3] Stolypin continued, "[e]vidently the second course will be chosen and Kokovtsev will be appointed." His prediction was realized in September 1911, when Nicholas appointed Kokovtsev to succeed the assassinated Stolypin as chairman of the Council of Ministers.

Vladimir Nikolaevich Kokovtsev was indeed a bureaucrat. Unlike Witte or Stolypin, Kokovtsev was a creature of official St. Petersburg. After graduating from the Alexander Lycée in 1872, at the age of nineteen, he had risen steadily through the ranks of the bureaucratic establishment.[4] Joining the Ministry of Justice from the lycée, he became a senior assistant in the prison administration in 1878. In 1890 he moved to the State Chancellery, and in 1896 he became Witte's assistant in the Ministry of Finances. In 1904, he was named minister of finances after the death of Witte's successor, Pleske, serving in that capacity under Stolypin's chairmanship after a brief stint in the State Council.

Kokovtsev brought to his new post none of the attributes that had distinguished Witte and Stolypin. He lacked their broad vision of Russia's needs and of the state's role as an agent of transformation. Neither did he dispose of any of the force of personality that Witte and Stolypin had used to such effect both with their fellow ministers and Nicholas. Indeed, Nicholas seemed to have selected him precisely because he was the quintessence of St. Petersburg chancellery life[5]—a fact underscored by the formal language of his reports and the stiff legalism of his administrative outlook. When Kokovtsev visited the imperial family at Livadiia after being named chairman, the empress stressed this contrast, berating him for "always making comparisons between yourself and Stolypin. It seems to me that you greatly esteem his memory and attribute too much significance to his activity and his personality."[6]

The empress was unwittingly correct. Kokovtsev's career as chairman was a bureaucrat's attempt to continue what he saw as Stolypin's legacy. However, the circumstances surrounding his appointment and Nicholas's experience with his powerful predecessor conspired to erode that legacy until United Government came to be honored, ironically, only in foreign policy.

When Kokovtsev took over as chairman, his views of cabinet rule had changed markedly since 1905. In early 1905, Kokovtsev had opposed Witte's attempts to unify government. Once United Government had been accepted in principle, he fought a rearguard action in the Solskii conference against Witte's efforts to institute a strong chairman. By January 1908, however, he had become a convinced advocate of United Government, largely because he admired Stolypin as much as he distrusted Witte.

Despite his support for cabinet rule, Kokovtsev enjoyed little success in maintaining unity in the council. As one critic observed, "the idea of 'United Government' remained only in his imagination, as well as in his endless—intolerable in their length—explications to the Council of Ministers."[7] His efforts demonstrated both the degree to which the council had become established as an institution for some and the limits of United Government in a political environment that had been negatively shaped by Stolypin's manner, as much as it was held together by his authority.

Stolypin's conflict over the Western *zemstvo* issue with Nicholas, the State Council, and the Duma in 1911 had only emphasized the fragility of the results of his five years' "stewardship." While he had sought a working partnership with the "responsible" elements in the legislative instances, his forced passage of the Western *zemstvo* bill had dealt the *coup de grâce* to this relationship by leading his erstwhile partners to ask whether he wished to cooperate with his Duma allies, or to dictate to them in the name of "state interest."[8] Kokovtsev would be forced to deal with a Duma in which there was no dependable majority. Stolypin had also left him a Council of Ministers that had been united only by being Stolypin's men: the members were either appointed upon Stolypin's recommendation or had generally been forced to observe his insistence on cabinet unity.

Kokovtsev's position as incoming chairman was thus complicated from several viewpoints. His colleagues owed him no allegiance. There were indications that Nicholas had come to believe allegations that Stolypin had encroached on his prerogatives. Most important, Kokovtsev had alienated many of his fellow ministers in his capacity as minister of finances. His chairmanship was to be dogged by older disputes with figures such as War Minister V. A. Sukhomlinov and the director of agricultural administration, A. V. Krivoshein.[9] And whereas Stolypin had enjoyed the authority to enforce governmental unity, Nicholas's waning support of his new chairman further undermined the United Government.

None of this was apparent during Kokovtsev's first months as chairman. On the contrary, he moved quickly, with Nicholas's approval, to consolidate in characteristically formal fashion the principle of United Government as it had been articulated by his predecessor. Significantly, the immediate occasion for these actions was provided by a foreign policy issue that arose at the time of Stolypin's death, coupled with Sazonov's absence from Russia due to a prolonged illness.

Stolypin had died shortly after the outbreak of war between Turkey and Italy. In addition to its ramifications for the territorial *status quo* in the Balkans, this conflict threatened Black Sea shipping, which was critical to

Russia's grain trade. In Sazonov's absence, the Ministry of Foreign Affairs was directed by A. A. Neratov, a long-time "inventory item" in the ministry's chancellery.[10] One diplomat noted that, while conscientious and diligent, Neratov had "neither the breadth nor the authority" to direct Russian diplomacy.[11]

Neratov's lack of authority probably encouraged the Russian ambassador in Constantinople to pursue a new plan to resolve the renascent Straits Question. The so-called Charykov *démarche* proposed a bilateral Russo-Turkish resolution of the Straits issue, which would allow Russian Black Sea warships to assist, if necessary, in the maintenance of the *status quo* in the Balkans and the territories adjoining the Straits. Charykov had argued to Neratov in mid-September that Turkey's current difficulties created a favorable situation for a resolution of the Straits Question.[12] Charykov's plan also had support from Izvolskii, who nevertheless warned that Charykov "with his characteristic impatience" might press matters too quickly.[13] As late as 29 September, Neratov seems to have permitted Charykov to explore Turkish attitudes toward his plan.[14]

But by 1 October Neratov changed his position. In the face of rumors from Constantinople, and understandable international interest in the rumored Russo-Turkish agreement, Neratov denied having ever authorized Charykov to propose such far-reaching measures in the name of the Russian government.[15] Nonetheless, Charykov continued to pursue his plan, now a broader Russo-Turkish agreement also to include a general Balkan rapprochement and other questions between the two states.[16]

There are several possible explanations for Neratov's change of heart. Obviously, international attitudes on the Straits had changed little since 1909, especially given the volatility of the Near Eastern situation with the Italo-Turkish War. Like Charykov, he may initially have been attracted by the opportunity offered by Turkey's circumstances; while denying support for the Charykov *démarche,* he had complained that Russia had never benefited from any of the numerous changes in the Near East in the previous thirty-five years. This had led "Russians" to wonder whether or not they could not at least gain a moral satisfaction of age-old desires or dreams. The wish to grant "public opinion" such "moral satisfaction" had guided Russian initiatives in this instance.[17]

Neratov's shift was also probably due to Kokovtsev's having caught wind of Charykov's activities in Constantinople.[18] On 20 October, Kokovtsev sent, with the emperor's permission, a long letter to Neratov,[19] "in confirmation of personal discussions with Your Excellency," in which he set forth "considerations and suggestions inclined toward a more precise regularization" of future relations between the Ministry of Foreign Affairs and the Council of Ministers.[20]

In the first part of the letter, Kokovtsev set forth his reading of the council statute of 19 October 1905 in the context of the previous six years of practice, which had broadened considerably the council's role, even with regard to the excluded ministries. Thus the foreign ministry was a member of the council, which was obliged to discuss all measures of "general significance." In addition, the chairman was to be informed "without delay" of all important events and measures in each ministry, and to be given beforehand all ministerial reports to the emperor "having a special significance, or affecting other departments." If the chairman deemed it appropriate, he could refer these matters to the council. Interestingly, this is the article that Kokovtsev had resisted so strenuously in 1905.

Here, Kokovtsev stated explicitly the statute's application to Neratov's ministry: "the relations of the Ministry of Foreign Affairs to the Council are defined by the aforementioned resolutions . . . on common bases with the other departments."[21] He acknowledged certain distinctions governing the excluded ministries—largely to do with the procedures by which their concerns were to be introduced to council discussion—but concluded with his own interpretation of these distinctions: "it is definitively stipulated that matters of foreign policy which affect the other departments should be brought to the discussion of the Council of Ministers."

Kokovtsev gave his version of the history of relations between the Ministry of Foreign Affairs and the council to illustrate his contention that practice had "diverged" from the "prescriptions of the Legislator" insofar as the Ministry of Foreign Affairs had occupied "a somewhat special" position that was "not altogether corresponding to the law."[22] The Bosnian crisis was the climactic point in this account. Lamzdorf had held aloof from the council, a situation that had continued at the beginning of Izvolskii's tenure.[23] But under Izvolskii council discussion of issues concerning the Ministry of Foreign Affairs was replaced by "private conversations" between Izvolskii and Stolypin or special conferences including these and other "interested" ministers. Kokovtsev regarded such discussions as extensions of council activity. This depiction gave a revealing insight into the degree of personal influence exercised by Stolypin as chairman; by implicit contrast, Kokovtsev was now appealing to this precedent as a basis for his attempt officially and formally to establish the obligation of the Ministry of Foreign Affairs to continue this relationship.

Kokovtsev's treatment of the Bosnian crisis placed it within his understanding of the original mandate of United Government.[24] He noted that while until 1908 the council had borne responsibility for the "general course of state administration," it had been barred from discussing "the most important questions of our foreign policy," despite the fact that these affected other departments and Russian interests "in the most vital fashion." This situation lasted until the autumn of 1908 and the "memorable meeting" at Buchlau, which resulted in the Austrian annexation of Bosnia and Herzegovina. "This failure of Russian policy" had provoked dissatisfaction among the patriotically inclined part of Russian society.[25] As a result, the Ministry of Foreign Affairs changed "its habitual practice" and renounced its "unilateral responsibility for taking one or another decision in the area of our foreign relations."

Hereafter, Izvolskii informed Stolypin of all matters in his ministry, and there were more frequent conferences of interested ministers for the discussion of foreign policy issues. After Sazonov's appointment, this practice continued, "and, perhaps, received more development."[26] But, according to Kokovtsev, even such conferences were an unsatisfactory replacement for discussion in the council of questions that affected the other ministries. Council discussion of such issues would be useful "for there is without doubt, an organic link between a state's foreign and domestic policy. This condition is so generally known, that it does not require detailed evidence, moreover the necessity of coordinated actions by the whole government in the area of our foreign relations is confirmed almost daily by the events of international life."[27] Kokovtsev cited examples ranging from the Italo-Turkish War to the current revolution in China, all of which had effects on Russia's economic and social well-being.

In light of all these considerations, Kokovtsev had "thought it my obligation in the post of Chairman of the Council of Ministers to report to HIS IMPERIAL MAJESTY, that I consider it necessary always to be informed in detail about the course of our foreign policy." He had told the emperor that he ought to have the right to introduce foreign policy discussion to the council, since such issues "affect the interests not only of the Ministry of Foreign Affairs." Kokovtsev argued to Nicholas that ministers who did not participate in special conferences on international affairs objected to a situation that deprived them "of the opportunity to bear the responsibility laid upon them as Members of the united government."[28] If true, this statement reflected the degree to which United Government had gained acceptance within Stolypin's council.

Finally, Kokovtsev appealed to pragmatism. With Stolypin's death, the conferences that had met previously would be composed of only four members, since he was now both council chairman and minister of finance.

If one considered further that the two military ministers were consulted specifically for the "clarification" of technical matters, discussion in such conferences "would consist merely in the exchange of opinions between myself and the Minister of Foreign Affairs."[29]

Kokovtsev was soon writing Neratov to inform him that Nicholas had granted his petition on procedures for foreign policy discussion. Neratov was to inform Kokovtsev of foreign policy issues bearing "general significance." Such questions would now be treated in the Council of Ministers. Finally, and significantly, Nicholas granted Kokovtsev, as council chairman, the authority to introduce such questions into council discussions. Nicholas had agreed to these proposals, telling Kokovtsev that such procedures would facilitate his task in deciding these questions. He would now be able to evaluate them on the basis of the detailed conclusions of the Council of Ministers.[30] The day after the dispatch of this letter, Kokovtsev informed the council of Nicholas's decision.[31] Neratov then apprised the council of foreign developments since the previous spring.

Within a month, Kokovtsev reported to Nicholas that the change had produced "direct benefit, imparting to our measures that consistency and orderliness which are so necessary." According to Kokovtsev, Neratov also acknowledged the benefits of the new order, and the chairman expressed the hope that Sazonov would take the same view on his return.[32] These events, and their treatment in Kokovtsev's arguments, were the institutional completion of Stolypin's efforts to bring foreign affairs under the purview of United Government. Characteristically, Kokovtsev sought to formalize a process that had evolved under his predecessor as *ad hoc* responses to a series of emergencies. Kokovtsev's letter lent structure to the piecemeal process by which Izvolskii had been obliged to consult with Stolypin and the council.

Especially noteworthy was Kokovtsev's description of the Bosnian crisis. Here was, for him, the classic illustration of the connection between foreign policy and domestic politics. He remembered it both as a diplomatic failure for Russia and as a blow to Russian "national consciousness" and the relations between state and society upon which the entire reconstruction process rested. Permeating this perspective was Kokovtsev's own rendering of Stolypin's view of the Council of Ministers as the area in which all strands of policy came together and were coordinated, to avoid any chance for destabilization within or outside Russia during the reemergence from revolution.

In the context of Charykov's efforts to exploit Turkey's distress to Russian advantage—at the risk of upsetting the Near Eastern *status quo*—

Kokovtsev's concern for establishing firm control over such matters is understandable. This factor can only have been emphasized to his view by the temporary presence of the unauthoritative Neratov at the Ministry of Foreign Affairs. At the same time, his request to Nicholas reflected his own method of operation: if Stolypin had gained the rights now requested by strength of personality, coupled with Nicholas's confidence and the sheer "force of events," Kokovtsev sought the emperor's formal sanction of a procedure that had emerged in practice.

Kokovtsev's acquisition of the "authority" granted him by Nicholas can be seen as the high-point of institutionalized rule in Russia after 1905. Nicholas had granted him as council chairman the formal authority to intervene in foreign policy on a footing equal with the minister of foreign affairs. Furthermore, according to Kokovtsev's account, the other members of the council wished to play a role in policy formation as part of their responsibilities in the council.

However, it was the contrast between Stolypin's informal methods and the more legalistic approach of Kokovtsev that ultimately vitiated the governmental unity achieved on paper by Kokovtsev. He never was able to establish with Nicholas the same degree of confidence that his predecessor had; indeed, his bureaucratic outlook demanded a "regularization of procedures" with a faith in their self-sustaining nature to make them operate. In relying on a strictly legal delineation of rights and responsibilities, he neglected, or could not address in the post-Stolypin political conditions, the critical problem of Nicholas's confidence. It was precisely on this element that Stolypin's authority had hinged.

In November 1911 Kokovtsev still seemed to enjoy the emperor's confidence; indeed, Nicholas seemed to have relapsed into the semipassivity that had characterized much of the Stolypin period. He had approved Kokovtsev's proposals for council authority over an area that was the quintessence of his sovereignty. The new chairman's continued success would be determined by this confidence and how it was perceived by his council colleagues, many of whom had reasons to hope for its erosion.

The immediate consequences of Kokovtsev's petition to Nicholas seemed to herald a smooth transition for the new chairman. The Charykov *démarche* came to an abrupt end with the return of Sazonov in late autumn. Stopping in Paris en route to St. Petersburg, Sazonov denied categorically that Charykov had ever had instructions from Pevchevskii Most to seek an opening of the Straits; his initiatives had been purely personal.[33] To emphasize this disavowal, the Russian government recalled Charykov from Constantinople in late February 1912.[34] For the time being, Kokovtsev's often expressed desire for peace was fulfilled.[35]

Kokovtsev's honeymoon was short-lived. As one observer noted, he headed a government "some members of which were politically unsympathetic toward him and disinclined to follow his directions."[36] The inchoate tensions in the council he inherited became increasingly divisive over the first nine months of 1912. The Duma had already become more oppositional, with the defection from the pro-government benches of much of the Octobrist fraction, after Stolypin's forced passage of the Western *zemstvo* bill. Relations between government and Duma would become even more strained with the elections for the fourth Duma in the fall of 1912. Finally, the beginnings of renewed unrest among the urban working population were instigated with the news in the spring of 1912 of the Lena Goldfield massacre. The labor movement grew in fits and starts, reaching a massive peak in the summer of 1914, exacerbating rising tensions between state and society.

## The Decline of United Government, 1911–1914

The bitterest and most abiding conflict within the council was that between Kokovtsev and Minister of War Sukhomlinov.[37] This friction dated from 1909 and Sukhomlinov's efforts to extract funding from the Ministry of Finance. Kokovtsev entertained a thoroughgoing contempt for what he considered the laziness, irresponsibility, and lack of professionalism manifested by the minister of war.[38] In April 1912 the two clashed openly, before the council and the emperor, when Sukhomlinov lost his temper at a meeting of the Duma's Commission of Defense; pressed to answer questions for which he either had no answer or considered beyond the body's purview, the minister took umbrage and stalked out.[39] Although Kokovtsev was not a fervent supporter of the new legislative arrangements in Russia—he had caused a furor in 1907 by declaring from the Duma tribune, "Thank God, we have no parliament!"—he had become convinced of the necessity of good relations with the body. These had been seriously jeopardized by Sukhomlinov's action.[40]

This *contretemps* provoked a scandal that soon extended to the emperor, when both ministers were at Livadiia. After being scolded indirectly by the emperor for trying to discuss Sukhomlinov's actions during a reception, Kokovtsev received an audience. This meeting turned into a lengthy diatribe by Kokovtsev against Sukhomlinov.[41] Ultimately, the chairman stated that if Nicholas was dissatisfied by relations between Kokovtsev and Sukhomlinov, "then allow me to quit my double post."[42] Nicholas neither accepted his resignation nor dismissed Sukhomlinov. Stolypin had used this threat several times to the desired effect; Kokovtsev's acceptance of Nicholas's nonresponse was really the first blow to United Government. In the capital the existence of sharp divisions among the ministers—not just Kokovtsev and Sukhomlinov—became common knowledge.[43]

By the late summer of 1912, divisions within the council had become grave, and Kokovtsev's own position as chairman was anything but secure. Matters were brought to a head by a confrontation between Kokovtsev and the one minister he had helped appoint, Stolypin's replacement in Internal Affairs, A. A. Makarov.[44] The issue was Ministry of Internal Affairs intervention in the elections to the fourth Duma. Kokovtsev felt that the ministry's governors were too preoccupied with preventing the election of liberal candidates. Makarov defended his ministry's effort to influence the elections and added that the matter was exclusively the concern of the Ministry of Internal Affairs, not the council.[45] Kokovtsev brought the matter before the council, which supported Makarov's contention—"[b]y this time a totally unfavorable attitude toward me had begun to be established in the Council."[46]

In addition to his waning authority within the council, there were also signs that his relationship with Nicholas was going to be much different from his predecessor's. Already, the emperor had shown signs of restiveness with the existing political order. Early in the year, Nicholas had pressed Kokovtsev and Makarov to take more strenuous measures against the press, which was finding abundant grist in the emergence of Rasputin as a figure close to court.[47] When the ministers spoke of the difficulty of bridling the press, Nicholas declared, "I simply do not understand—is there really no possibility of executing my will?"

Nicholas's displeasure with the Duma was also increasing: he did not reprimand Sukhomlinov for his truculence toward the body, and he transferred the able Polivanov out of the war ministry. Kokovtsev had had to expend great effort to persuade Nicholas to receive a Duma delegation at the end of the third session; his address to the delegation was highly critical.[48]

The emperor finally did dismiss Makarov, but it was out of displeasure with his "attitude to my wishes" in press matters.[49] Nicholas accompanied this news to Kokovtsev with an offer of the embassy in Berlin. Interestingly, Nicholas presumed that the dismissal of his appointee would be unpleasant for Kokovtsev—probably a backhanded allusion to Kokovtsev's advocacy of ministerial unity. To succeed Makarov, Nicholas chose N. A. Maklakov, an intimate of Prince V. P. Meshcherskii,[50] who had reentered Nicholas's favor, itself an indication of Nicholas's growing displeasure with the post-1905 regime. Most probably, this was Nicholas's attempt to rid himself of his chairman with a minimum of acrimony.

The divisions in the council seem to have arisen at least in part from a collective sense that this was an opportune time to defy the will of the chairman, a sense abetted directly and indirectly by Nicholas. At about this time, Kokovtsev lectured a meeting of the council on the necessity of the preservation of ministerial unity despite the rancor that sometimes accompanied council resolutions: "once the matter is solved . . . it is a decision of the United Government and of course not one of its members has the right to protest against it."[51] He stressed this point because a dissenting minister had written to an influential person in Livadiia with the intent that the matter come to the emperor's attention. This was but one of many incidents that were repeated with increasing frequency during Kokovtsev's tenure. In each instance, Nicholas commiserated with Kokovtsev over the violation of ministerial unity, while taking no measures against the offending party.

These events created growing fracture in the highest official spheres. The situation was burdensome not only for Kokovtsev but also for Sazonov, who still accepted the principle of United Government and the procedures established by Kokovtsev in his absence. In light of the new role the council had acquired in foreign policy, Sazonov's alliance with Kokovtsev only served to isolate him further in the council. As a result, he became more sensitive than before to the pressures of guiding Russian policy in a European situation that was becoming increasingly critical and to the demands of public opinion, which grew both in response to European tensions and generally as part of the newly oppositionist posture of society in the fourth Duma period. Both lines of fracture—within government and between state and society—came starkly into view during the autumn of 1912, when the long-expected war in the Balkans finally erupted.

Russian sponsorship of an alliance among the Balkan states, which was finalized during the first half of 1912, had arisen from several contradictory motives. Often seen as an attempt to fashion a weapon for revenge against Austria-Hungary after the Bosnian crisis, Russian support for the alliance seems, in the light of Stolypin's reactions to the same events, rather to have been intended as a replacement for the broken Austro-Russian entente, to ensure the maintenance of calm in the Balkans without Austria's partnership. In this way, complications could be avoided in this sensitive area and, by extension, political peace could be assured in Russia. This line of argument dominated statements by Kokovtsev, Sazonov, and Neratov during this period and was a motif in the foreign ministry's correspondence with its agents in the Balkans.[52]

After Stolypin's death and Sazonov's return, however, this policy was modified because of several factors. Foremost among these was the view common to Sazonov and others of the Balkan states as Russia's "little Slavic brothers," and Russia as the "firstborn" Slavic power, which fostered the notion that Russia could control the actions of these states once they had been brought together in a league.[53] This attitude was embodied in a provision in the Serbo-Bulgarian alliance that named the Russian emperor as arbiter in any territorial disputes between the two after joint actions.[54]

Another factor hindering the achievement of St. Petersburg's aims was their distortion by Russian agents abroad. The most flagrant offender in this regard was N. V. Gartvig, the Russian agent in Belgrade. He was an unabashed exponent of a strange composite of virulently Austrophobe, Anglophobe, and pan-Slav views, who actively sought to convert the league into a military and aggressive alliance. From the outset of talks for the formation of the Balkan alliance, he characterized its natural goals as the "final reckoning" of "the Slavs" with Turkey.[55]

Finally, the pact itself was brought into being by the prospect of Turkish difficulties resulting from the latter's losses in the war with Italy. The resulting multilateral alliance, centered on a Serbo-Bulgarian pact and including Montenegro and Greece, was hardly defensive. It contained provisions for the division of Turkish territory and for joint mobilization against the Ottoman Empire.[56] Virtually on the morrow of the conclusion of the Serbo-Bulgarian treaty, warnings of its aggressive intent were relayed to St. Petersburg by Russian agents in the Balkans.[57]

When French president Poincaré, who learned of these agreements in early August, confronted Sazonov about their aggressive purport, Sazonov could only give "assurances that their objective was the maintenance of the *status quo*," and that the allies would not mobilize or declare war without Russian approval.[58] This faith in Russia's ability to restrain the allies persisted until the outbreak of the war and was yet another reflection of the paternalism in official and unofficial views of the Slavic states.

As the autumn of 1912 approached, signs of impending war aroused alarm in St. Petersburg.[59] In early September, Sazonov sent telegrams to Sofia and Belgrade,[60] in an attempt to restrain the Balkan allies. He stated that when the agreement had first been suggested, it had been greeted as putting an end to "internecine struggle between two Slavic peoples." The desire to aid this goal "compelled us to pass over in silence several other articles," despite the "serious doubts" they had inspired. As a check, Russia had accepted the role of ultimate arbiter in any disputes that might arise between the two parties. However, he warned, if the two states used the agreement to attack Turkey, Russia would be guided solely by its own interests. These warnings were repeated by Kokovtsev, who told the Serbian ambassador that "Russia under no circumstances would go to war. Rather would he resign as minister-president than sanction such a policy."[61] This advice was contested in Belgrade by Gartvig, who said publicly "that he was disgusted with M. Sazonoff's policy"; it was "incomprehensible" to him that Russia was now trying to halt a movement that it had been preparing for years.[62]

Despite Russian warnings, the Balkan states went to war against Turkey at the end of September 1912. Sazonov was in Berlin, en route to Russia from visits to Britain and France, when he heard of Montenegro's declaration of war on Turkey. A German official noted, "the report . . . made a visibly depressing impression on the Minister."[63] The chief concern of Russian and other sympathetic observers of the Balkan conflict was that the small states would prove no match for Turkish forces. Talks opened between Russia and Austria-Hungary in September and October in search of a means by which to localize the conflict and to assure the preservation of at least a semblance of the *status quo ante.*

Contrary to expectations, the war saw a series of stunning successes by the Balkan allies; by the end of October, Bulgarian forces were pushing toward Adrianople, while the Serbs were nearing the Adriatic coast. These developments cast the Balkan situation in a different light, and European talks began on the nature of the territorial settlement when peace was made. Once again, as so often before, the chief discussants were Russia and Austria-Hungary, which was concerned that if Serbia gained an outlet on the Adriatic, an important economic lever for controlling its restive neighbor would be lost.

Russian reactions to the war demonstrated the disarray that had overtaken government in preceding months. During October and November, Kokovtsev and Sazonov disagreed over Serbia's claim to an Adriatic port; more seriously, the two ministers faced a crisis when Sukhomlinov decided unilaterally to mobilize the southern units of the Russian army. The first of these disputes demonstrated the growing effect of public pressure on Sazonov, who had to be restrained by Kokovtsev. The second showed the degree to which ministerial unity had decayed over a foreign crisis. Both were exacerbated by the absence of Nicholas from the capital until the middle of November.

Since 1909, the political setting in Russia had changed in two significant regards. Public opinion was much more antigovernmental than in 1909.

This was reflected in the composition of the newly elected fourth Duma, in which the working majority formed by Stolypin in 1907 had broken down into a less manageable series of small blocs.[64] In addition, official and public responses were stamped by memories of Russia's humiliation in the Bosnian crisis. Public opinion had become sufficiently vociferous that foreign governments began to take account of it. Beginning in late 1908, the French embassy compiled a twice-weekly "Review of the Press," gleaning articles of interest from publications of all political stripes.[65] Such considerations had even influenced the Balkan allies' timing of their declaration of war; on Guchkov's advice King Ferdinand of Bulgaria insisted to the Serbian government that war not begin until the elections to the fourth Duma.[66]

The war itself was eagerly anticipated in Russian society. The Austrian *chargé* reported on the renewed activity of Slavic societies; donations were solicited for the Red Cross and "aid societies"; the departure of a group of Bulgarian officer-trainees had been the pretext for "fraternal demonstrations"; public speakers implored the government not to leave the Slavs "in the lurch."[67] At first, Sazonov resisted this pressure. In a circular to Russian representatives in Europe, he proposed exploiting public restiveness for Russian interests.[68] Noting the frequent reproaches for his policy of cooperating with Austria-Hungary to localize the war, he stated that he was equanimous to such attacks "to the extent that there has been created the deceptive idea of a radical discord between official and unofficial Russia." This apparent rift had eased Russia's position by allowing it to persuade other cabinets of difficulties in contending with public opinion.

However, by early November, the press outcry had become particularly insistent, especially in support of Serbian demands for an Adriatic port. Commentary on the Balkan war had also been strongly anti-Austrian, an implicit criticism of the Russian government's talks with the enemy.[69] Such criticism seems to have affected Sazonov. In the first week of November, he gave interviews to Russian newspapers, in one of which he complained that the Russian press was not properly supportive of the government.[70]

Sazonov's sensitivity to the press was apparent in his official handling of the Serbian port question. In mid-October, when the success of the Balkan allies was first becoming apparent, he raised the possibility of granting Serbia limited access to the Adriatic as part of the postwar settlement. Returning to St. Petersburg after seeing Nicholas at Spala, Sazonov stated that he had been told to assist the Slavs "without involving Russia in any serious entanglements"; at the same time he was on record as supporting full cooperation with Austria-Hungary in support of the *status quo*. The monarchy was unlikely to support the idea of hostile Serbia's having access to the Adriatic.[71]

By the third week of October, Sazonov began more actively to promote the idea of a Serbian port, arguing that it would never threaten Austrian interests. He suggested that the Serbian port serve as the entente powers' *quid pro quo* for the creation of an independent Albania supported by the Triple Alliance.[72] He promised Austrian representatives that concession in this matter—even in exchange for the monarchy's economic monopolization of the Balkans—could lead to a more secure Balkan entente between the two powers.[73] Kokovtsev was speaking at this time of a purely economic port for Serbia.[74]

By the very end of October Sazonov was suffering under various pressures. Gartvig was holding a militant line in Belgrade;[75] the Serbian envoy in Berlin had said that Russia would support strongly the claim to an Adriatic port; and public opinion was becoming increasingly outspoken in support of Serbia. He wired Gartvig that Russia would never risk a war over the question, a position that he soon stated publicly.[76] With foreign representatives, Sazonov took a harder line, reminding them that much had changed since 1908–1909: "Russia would not let herself be humiliated a second time. That would be war."[77] He began to inquire about the position that the British and French governments might take should Austria-Hungary attack Serbia, since Germany had indicated that it would support the monarchy.[78]

Sazonov's and Kokovtsev's positions were beginning to diverge sharply. While Sazonov was taking a firmer stance on a port for Serbia, Kokovtsev's statements were more conciliatory. In a long conversation with an Austrian diplomat, "in his capacity as *chef* of the Russian Government, who also bears in large part the responsibility for foreign policy,"[79] Kokovtsev suggested that the issue could be solved by a compromise that would put the port under international administration, thus placating Austrian concerns, while giving Serbia an economic maritime outlet. He added that he had Sazonov's full agreement.

Similar differences of emphasis between the two Russian ministers had been noted on the eve of the war,[80] and continued to be remarked upon during the discussion of the Serbian port issue.[81] Observers were particularly impressed with the variability in Sazonov's language and demands for the Serbs. Undoubtedly, he was responding in part to the pressure of public opinion; his references to the changes in Russia's resolve since 1909 echoed viewpoints expressed in the press.[82]

The influence exerted by public opinion can only have been enhanced by two other circumstances. Since the preceding summer, the head of the foreign ministry's Near Eastern department had been Prince G. N. Trubetskoi, who had returned to the ministry after a leave of six years.[83] During his retirement, he had been a prominent publicist for the "Slavic cause," as a collaborator with his brother in the publication of *Moskovskii Ezhenedel'nik*. He enjoyed broad contacts in liberal circles. As a publicist, he had complained that public opinion was insufficiently reflected in the formulation of Russia's foreign policy.[84] Moreover, the intensity of public interest in the Balkan settlement had grown markedly in the wake of the allied victories over Turkey.[85]

Finally, the differences between Kokovtsev and Sazonov can be attributed to their differing goals. As finance minister and chairman of the council, Kokovtsev seemed more concerned with the threat of complications than his colleague; the tensions generated by the war had affected the value of Russian papers abroad and stock markets at home.[86] Thus, he searched more openly for a rapid and peaceful solution. Sazonov seems to have had conflicting aims. On one hand, he wished to convince Serbia—whose demands had been encouraged by Gartvig—that Russia would not risk war over the port issue. On the other, he seems to have been influenced by the widely seen parallels between present events and the Bosnian crisis, in connection with the position taken by Germany and the entente powers.

Although the differences between the two ministers had been over tactics more than actual policy, they came together in mid-November, when both suggested that Serbia must have some form of economic access to the Adriatic, the details of which would be discussed at the international conference on the settlement of the war.[87] However, as Sazonov repeated, "the question of a port under Servian [*sic*] sovereignty was not one in which Russian interests were so engaged as to justify, if taken by itself, her going to war." Their agreement was in part a response to the increasingly militant anti-Austrian sentiments they faced in the Council of Ministers, especially on the part of Sukhomlinov. According to some reports, there had been conflict in the council over how far to support the Balkan states' territorial claims.[88]

There emerged in the council a "war party," which sought a more assertive posture by Russia in defense of its Balkan allies and interests.[89] Especially vocal in advocating this view was Minister of Agriculture Krivoshein, who inverted long-standing arguments that Russia could not risk the domestic repercussions of war. Krivoshein maintained that it was necessary to "believe more in the Russian people and their age-old love for the homeland, which was greater than any accidental preparedness or unpreparedness for war."[90] Krivoshein's argument reflected a fundamental disagreement with Kokovtsev about the internal state of Russia and its future course. In 1913 these differences would inspire a campaign led by Krivoshein to unseat Kokovtsev.

Recalling this confrontation, Kokovtsev wrote that these meetings "demonstrated clearly my isolation and even my full helplessness." In addition, the council was deeply divided. Some ministers were "profoundly indifferent" to all events, "while the others . . . conducted a policy that was clearly inimical to me . . . [These] had the Sovereign on their side." This was not due to any inherent bellicosity in the emperor— Kokovtsev felt that Nicholas was "deeply pacific." However, "he liked the elevated mood of the Ministers of a nationalist bent. Their exaltative sing-song about the boundless loyalty of the people and its indestructible might . . . pleased him more."[91] In foreign policy issues this opposition was led by Sukhomlinov, who brought matters to a head at the end of the first week of November, when he ordered a partial mobilization of Russian troops on the Austrian border.

Kokovtsev saw Sukhomlinov's move as an illustration of the latter's irresponsibility and as evidence of the degree to which unity had ceased to exist in the Council of Ministers.[92] According to Kokovtsev, Sukhomlinov telephoned on the evening of 9 November, with the message that Nicholas wished to see him and Sazonov the following morning; the war minister claimed not to know the subject of the projected audience. Thus, on the morning of 10 November, Kokovtsev and Sazonov met with the minister of communications, Sukhomlinov, the chief of the General Staff, and Nicholas. When it emerged that the three civilian ministers were unaware of the reason for the conference, Nicholas announced that a military conference had decided to mobilize the Kiev and Warsaw Military Districts and later to mobilize the Odessa district. He added that this measure was directed exclusively against Austria-Hungary, and not against Germany. Sukhomlinov informed the conference that mobilization orders were now ready and would be sent after the meeting. In what seems to have been an apologetic aside to Kokovtsev, Nicholas stated that Sukhomlinov had wished to move the previous day, but that Nicholas had requested a delay in order to discuss the measure with the ministers who ought to be alerted.

An angry Kokovtsev accused Sukhomlinov of concealing from the emperor that a mobilization could lead to war with both Austria-Hungary and Germany. Contradicting Nicholas, Kokovtsev contended that the two Germanic empires could not be treated separately. Furthermore, since the mobilization would take place without proper warning for France, Russia might have to face the consequences on its own. Kokovtsev then questioned the entire basis for Sukhomlinov's proposed measures and insisted to Nicholas that "the War Minister had not had the right even to discuss such an issue without consulting with the Minister of Foreign Affairs and with me."[93] Sazonov supported the chairman. Nicholas agreed to cancel the mobilization orders.

Although Kokovtsev's is the only detailed description of these events, other accounts testify that such a measure was under consideration, and that the issue added to the tensions in St. Petersburg at this time.[94] Diplomats in western Russia, and in the capital, reported rumors of a mobilization for the first two weeks of November.[95] It was widely felt that "military circles" were pressing for a strong stand against an anticipated Austrian aggression on Serbia.[96] Finally, the war ministry was obliged to deny publicly that there would be any mobilization.[97]

After their clash with Sukhomlinov, and in response to foreign concern over the mobilization rumors, Sazonov and Kokovtsev took a much more measured stance on the Serbian port issue. It is likely that Sazonov softened his insistence on a Serbian port when confronted with the threat of war in Sukhomlinov's abortive mobilization effort. Although there was no official explanation for Sazonov's retreat, some observers felt that Kokovtsev and the minister of internal affairs feared that war would still threaten the internal stability of the empire.[98]

A Council of Ministers meeting in December discussed Austria-Hungary's continuing pressure on Serbia.[99] Sukhomlinov proposed "military precautions." Sazonov and Kokovtsev objected that any incautious measures could lead to a general war, in which there would be no guarantee of support from the entente powers. In addition, the armed forces were ill-prepared, and "the internal state of the country is far from the inspired patriotic mood which would allow one to count on a mighty upsurge of national spirit and a vital, direct sympathy." These arguments were still convincing in the council. The limits of Russian flexibility having been reached and demonstrated, the Serbian claims were referred to the conference for the settlement of the peace, which convened in London in December.

Still, if Kokovtsev and Sazonov had resolved their differences, the Serbian port issue and the attempted mobilization attested to disunity in Russian government. Even if he had relented, Nicholas had flouted Kokovtsev's expectations of decision-making procedures and his views on the council chairman's authority. It had only been at the price of a confrontation, in fact, that Kokovtsev had been able to demand and win recognition of his rights as chairman. In addition, Sazonov's solidarity with Kokovtsev had been shown to be vulnerable to his concern for Russian prestige and to the influence of public opinion.

In the short term, Kokovtsev's ascendancy seemed to be reestablished in the outcome of the Serbian port dispute. Shortly after the resolution of this controversy, he gave the "throne speech" at the opening of the fourth Duma.[100] Approximately half of this speech was devoted to Russia's foreign policy and the international situation. Dominating these statements was Kokovtsev's view of the enduring internal necessity for Russia to continue a policy of peace at all costs. Equally significantly, this speech represented the first discussion of foreign affairs in the Duma by a council chairman.

However, in the longer course, the forces sapping Kokovtsev's authority in the council continued to operate unchecked during the spring of 1913. The most important among these factors was Nicholas's relationship with Kokovtsev. Again, as in April 1912, Sukhomlinov had incurred no enduring disfavor by his actions in November. There were also signs of a new self-assertiveness on the part of the emperor, particularly the rising prominence of Rasputin and the renewed influence of Prince Meshcherskii, who had long been out of contact with Nicholas. Nicholas was beginning to chafe at what he saw as unseemly limitations on his ability to act, much as he had on the eve of Witte's dismissal in 1906. Thus, he complained to his minister of the court, Baron F. F. Frederiks, "I no longer have the right to do what I find useful, and I am becoming fed up with that."[101]

## Nicholas and the Reassertion of Autocratic Power, 1913–1914

The event that probably persuaded Nicholas to take a more active role in government was the celebration of the tercentenary of the Romanov dynasty. There were many observances all over the country connected with the occasion, most of which emphasized the mystical and historic links among the dynasty, the tsar, and the devoted Russian *narod,* first demonstrated in the election of the Romanovs to the throne in 1613. Much as he had done in different circumstances in 1902, Nicholas ignored those members of his government who accompanied him on this tour.[102]

Kokovtsev noted a growing attitude at court that the ruler should reclaim his role as autocrat, dispensing with the post-1905 political system; this feeling was only reinforced by the experiences of March 1913, which were seen as demonstrations of the depth of popular devotion to the autocrat.[103]

The Sovereign's journey was evidently given the meaning of a "family" celebration of the House of Romanov, and the "state" character was in no way accorded a fitting place . . . in the Sovereign's intimate circle the notion of government or its meaning faded into the background, while the personal character of the Sovereign's rule emerged more sharply and in greater relief, and . . . the view became apparent that the government made up some sort of "partition" between [emperor and people], in some way impeding their mutual rapprochement.

Now, there emerged a cult of Autocratism *(Samoderzhavnost')*.

Reflecting on these developments, Kokovtsev confronted the problem that had undone Stolypin and Witte. He felt that his growing loss of authority with Nicholas and the government might be due to his own lack of prestige.[104] More probably, the new order had been undercut by its own success. "[T]he experiences of revolutionary times . . . were succeeded by the following seven years of internal tranquillity, and made a place for the idea of the greatness of the Sovereign's personality and a faith in the unlimited devotion of the popular masses to him as God's Anointed." The new state structures and the legislature were unpleasant reminders of changes that need not have occurred. Signs of this new attitude in court circles were also apparent in the emperor. Nicholas began to complain to Kokovtsev about the latter's interference in foreign affairs.[105]

The evident wavering of Nicholas's confidence in his chairman did not go unnoticed by other ministers. By mid-1913 the council had split into two main factions with Kokovtsev caught in the middle and supported only by Sazonov.[106] There were many pretexts for opposition to the chairman, but in none of them did Kokovtsev receive any support from Nicholas against his colleagues. Sukhomlinov's defiance had been read aright by the other ministers.

Thus, while United Government continued to be honored formally, council meetings only demonstrated the extent to which matters had reverted to their pre-1905 configuration. The council's only seeming purpose was to serve as a standing "special conference" within which interministerial alliances could be contracted and activity against Kokovtsev could be pursued. The disintegration of government unity was paralleled by a downturn in relations between government and the fourth Duma. Throughout the spring of 1913, there were frequent expressions of noncooperation and antigovernment sentiment from all sides of the legislature.[107] Matters reached a crucial turn with the "ministerial strike" of the late summer, in which the ministers, in uncharacteristic unison, refused to appear in the Duma until a formal apology was made to Kokovtsev for insulting remarks from the right side of the house during a speech.[108] While ostensibly a show of governmental solidarity in the face of pretensions by the Duma, the measure also served to convey the feeling among conservative ministers that the Duma was an unnecessary attribute of state life.

The rift between state and society had long been apparent in foreign policy matters. Sazonov was blamed for having displayed unnecessary weakness in the face of Austrian obduracy regarding the territorial claims of the Balkan states.[109] When Russia's conciliatory stance in the Serbian port issue was made known in December 1912, press reports described the decision as "worse than Tsushima" or a "diplomatic Mukden."[110] As the peace conference on the Balkan wars dragged on in London at the end of 1912 and in early 1913, Sazonov was subjected to increasingly harsh attacks in the press and in the Duma. These criticisms reached a climax in the campaign of "Slavic banquets" and public demonstrations in connection with Montenegro's unilateral seizure of Scutari in the spring of 1913.[111] The demonstrations were so serious that they were banned in mid-April.

The memory of these outbursts particularly impressed Sazonov.[112] He was sufficiently sensitive to the reproaches that he held a private meeting with interested Duma deputies, reading them the relevant diplomatic documents concerning Russian actions.[113] Criticism of Sazonov had become so strident during the late spring, with the outbreak of the second Balkan war, that an imperial rescript was issued in his name, declaring the emperor's gratitude and approval for his minister's policy.[114] Sazonov's sensitivity to public opinion seems to have been genuine. He shared with many publicists a sympathy for the "Slavic cause." Instructing Benkendorf on Russia's position at the London conference, he had written, "[i]t is important for us . . . to achieve the reinforcement of the independence . . . of the peoples whom we have called to life, who are our natural allies in Europe."[115] Added to this was his memory, shared by much of the public, of the Bosnian crisis as a blow to Russian prestige.

During the months from the outbreak of the first Balkan war through the spring of 1913 and the eruption of a new war in the Balkans, Sazonov seemed to strain at the limits on his freedom of action. In the council, he had allied himself with Kokovtsev, whose chief concern was the maintenance of peace at virtually any cost for the sake of domestic stability. At the same time, during the discussion of the Serbian port issue in the preceding fall, he had been confronted with French and British diffidence toward Russian interests in the Balkans. He had also seen the impressive solidarity of the two central powers. Finally, he was forced to explain to the nation the reasons for Russian restraint in the area of their "historical" interest. Public opinion may have been willing to accept Stolypin's statements about the need for patience in 1909, when most moderates had accepted that revenge would be deferred until strength had been restored at home through the cooperation of the state and the nation. Now, with the chasm between these two elements growing daily, impatience for a national policy was increasing in equal measure. Paradoxically, the proponents of United Government found themselves under pressure from above and below, because of the apparent stabilization of political life that had occurred under Stolypin's chairmanship.

Thus, the Russian government found itself through 1912 and the first part of 1913 forced by a sense of internal weakness to continue Stolypin's policy of restraint. This meant having to react to events as they occurred, a position that was maintained by Kokovtsev, and more grudgingly by Sazonov, out of a continuing feeling that the advent of war would spark the recrudescence of revolution. However, this policy, and the defense of United Government mounted by Kokovtsev in November 1912, had acquired an artificial quality. This was partially a reflection of the weakness and bureaucratic shortsightedness of Kokovtsev, who was more enamored of the letter than the deed—as seen in the increasing contrast between the rights he had won for the council in October 1911 and the decay of ministerial unity. It was also a symptom of Sazonov's own growing restiveness with a policy that he was coming to regard as inadequate and injurious to Russia's international stature.

## The Fall of Kokovtsev and the Liman Affair, 1913–1914

The resolution of many of the problems that had arisen during Kokovtsev's chairmanship—both in the Council of Ministers and in foreign policy—came in late 1913, with the simultaneous unfolding of the "Liman von Sanders crisis" and the final undermining of Kokovtsev's position as chairman of the Council of Ministers. The Liman affair decided both Nicholas and Sazonov on the impossibility of any understanding with Germany. Kokovtsev, as council chairman, played an active part in the resolution of the dispute. Ironically, the circumstances enabling him to play such a role—the fact that he was in the West when the incident arose—allowed his adversaries in Russia to mount the campaign that sealed his political downfall.

The crisis was provoked by what struck many as a minor event. In the autumn of 1913, the German and Turkish governments announced that General Liman von Sanders was to be appointed commander of an instructional army corps stationed in Constantinople.[116] Sazonov reacted strongly to the news, contending that the presence of a German commander in the Turkish capital would put the area, and the Straits, under German control.[117] This view was amplified in what appears to have been an inspired press campaign that included, for a change, *Novoe Vremia*.[118] It soon became clear that Sazonov was going to make the Liman appointment a major issue. He told the British *chargé* that this question "would put the value of the Triple Entente to the test."[119] In such statements he noted the lack of support the entente had provided Russia "in the course of the recent Balkan complications."[120]

During the first phases of this crisis, Sazonov pursued two tacks. Through November and December, he sought British and French support for joint *démarches* to the Turkish government, indicating entente concern at the appointment. He also sought to persuade Berlin of the gravity with which he regarded the Liman appointment. To this end, he made use of Kokovtsev, who was returning to Russia after talks in France for a loan to construct strategic railways in the west of Russia. Stopping in Berlin in the first week of November, Kokovtsev met with German officials and was granted an audience with Wilhelm.[121]

Kokovtsev's report on these meetings indicated as much about his insecurity as chairman in late 1913 as about the substance of his discussions in Germany.[122] The most striking feature of his report was a prefatory apologia for the chairman's involvement in diplomacy. This passage stands in sharp contrast to the tone in his letters to Neratov in October 1911. Describing the purposes of his trip abroad, the chairman explained, in characteristically circumlocutory fashion, his role in dealings with foreign counterparts: "Above all, I cannot conceal before Your Majesty, that in my discussions with various state actors abroad, I had involuntarily [*ponevole*] to exceed the limits of the actual task laid upon me."[123] Foreign leaders were unversed in the "peculiarities" in Russian government regarding "the limits on the power and prerogatives of the Chairman of the Council of Ministers." Thus, they raised all sorts of questions touching on all areas of Russian political life: "foreign state actors make no substantial distinction between the Chairman of the Council of Ministers and the person who directs foreign policy according to the Supreme inscriptions [*nachertaniia*] of Your Majesty, since they proceed from the supposition that the Chairman of the Council of Ministers should be sufficiently informed of all questions which affect the vital interests of the country and cannot decline discussions about their substance."

Underlying this excursus was a defense of his position and duties as chairman, even with regard to foreign relations—a vestige of the outlook he outlined in October 1911. He wrote further that, given his interlocutors' assumptions about his position, he could either renounce discussion beyond the immediate sphere raised by his mission, or he could participate in such discussions, explaining as best he could Russia's position. Not surprisingly, he had chosen the latter course, which he hoped would not displease Nicholas. Again he felt obliged to explain: "I was inclined to such a conclusion by my close participation in all questions of our foreign policy, both according to the direct instructions of Your Imperial Majesty, as well as to my close relations with the Minister of Foreign Affairs, who always draws me into the discussion of major questions affecting the state's external relations." He also feared that Western officials might interpret his refusal to discuss political questions as evasion.[124]

Part of Kokovtsev's submissiveness in this report can be explained by the German response to his protests about the implications of the Liman mission. His hosts met these statements with consternation. Bethmann-Hollweg simply insisted that given the political situation in Turkey, the chance of the mission's being able harm Russian interests was remote.[125] Bethmann and Wilhelm also introduced a justification, which Kokovtsev relayed to Nicholas. His discussions had "left me with the impression that this matter had already arisen in the spring of the current year."[126]

Apparently, Wilhelm had raised the question of the Liman mission with his cousins Nicholas and George V in personal conversation during the festivities for the marriage of Wilhelm's daughter the preceding May. Wilhelm said he had broached the plans for the mission and neither of his cousins had raised any objections. Obviously, Kokovtsev could not question the word of a ruler. In the German account and in his own report of this conversation there is no record of his having done so. In his memoirs, however, he claimed to have reminded the German emperor that Nicholas had not been accompanied in May by Sazonov, who had never been informed of this conversation and Nicholas's purported agreement to the Liman mission.[127] He also claimed to have stated that a change in the military training regime in Turkey "could in no way be stipulated by the verbal agreement of two monarchs, but must be secured by a special exchange of written notes."

After Kokovtsev returned to Russia, Sazonov continued talks with the German and Turkish governments through representatives in Constantinople and Berlin. At the same time, he impressed repeatedly upon the representatives of the entente powers the significance he attached to a satisfactory resolution of this question.[128] The strength of Sazonov's reaction bemused his colleagues in Paris and particularly in London, in view of the fact that a British admiral had been named to head a naval training squadron, in much the same capacity as Liman was to serve in the Turkish army. Sazonov's anger was not dissembled. As negotiations for a solution of the Liman question proceeded sporadically through December, the Russian government began to discuss possible measures to back its point of view. On 23 December, Sazonov addressed the issue in a report to Nicholas,[129] which was striking for its anti-German tone and for the decisive responses it proposed to the Liman mission.

According to the foreign minister, the talks in Berlin had been characterized by contradictory explanations and a refusal to make any binding pledges.[130] He agreed with Ambassador Sverbeev in Berlin that the Germans were simply delaying the issue in order to prevent unified action by "the Powers of the Triple Entente," hoping thereby to confront them with a *fait accompli*. Given Berlin's intentions, Sazonov recommended a set of possible actions should the Russo-German talks fail. First, the Russian government should report to the other two entente powers that the Russo-German talks seemed unlikely to produce a satisfactory outcome. Possible joint military measures would have to be decided in agreement with France and Britain and with the Russian military ministries. For his part, Sazonov recommended that the entente powers seize and occupy "certain points in Asia Minor" and declare that they would remain there until their demands were met.

Sazonov admitted that such an action could lead to complications; if Germany acted, the focus would move from Turkey to Russia's western border "with all the consequences flowing therefrom."[131] He emphasized the gravity and the consequences of the choices facing Nicholas and his government. He noted that should Russia insist on the implementation of its demands, account must be taken of the risk of "European complications, although the probability exists that a firm resolve not to retreat from the position taken by us will be sufficient for us to receive the satisfaction due." But if Russia simply decided to reconcile itself to the fact of a German command in Constantinople, "our concession will be tantamount to a major political defeat and could have most fatal consequences."

These consequences were spelled out by Sazonov purely in terms of the European political situation. Concession to Germany in this instance would not prevent growing claims by that power and its allies; even now, their tone was becoming less conciliatory in all questions concerning their interests. Conceding on the Liman issue could also create the "dangerous conviction" in London and Paris that Russia was prepared to concede in all questions for the sake of peace. Such an outcome would destroy what little unity the Triple Entente possessed. Indeed, as it was, the French were more interested in financial agreements than in protecting Russia's political interests. All three powers would have to pledge themselves through agreements with the "opposite camp," which was Germany's goal.[132] For Russia the result would be diplomatic isolation. Therefore, Sazonov concluded, the military ministries should be consulted on the possible risks in this question, and talks should be opened with the other entente powers. If they counseled concessions, the risks of unilateral action would probably be prohibitive. If they supported Russia's views, complications must be avoided, but Russian interests should be firmly defended.

Sazonov listed recommendations to be discussed at a "special conference under the chairmanship of State Secretary Kokovtsev," along with representatives of the military bodies and general staffs.[133] He proposed that the conference determine Russia's present ability to use compulsion in defense of its position. Furthermore, discussions should be opened to establish the extent of French and English support for the joint occupation plan; the necessity in these talks of avoiding a conflict that would create an "all-European war," while persuading the other two powers of the equal necessity for a firm defense of Russian interests; an escalating series of entente measures against Turkey before undertaking any military acts; and military preparations, since it was politically crucial to support the demands with force quickly.[134]

This report marked a major departure in Sazonov's thinking on foreign policy. He was now willing to countenance the possibility of war as the price for defending Russia's credibility as a Great Power. Although conceding the undesirability of this war, he depicted it as a possible consequence of the necessity of Russia's demonstration to the central powers that its interests must be respected. He also placed Russia firmly within the orbit of the Triple Entente, seeing Germany as the adversary along with Austria-Hungary.

On 31 December, the special conference requested by Sazonov met under Kokovtsev's chairmanship. This was to be Kokovtsev's last involvement in such matters. Also in attendance were Sazonov, Sukhomlinov, Naval Minister Grigorovich, and General Zhilinskii from the General Staff.[135] The meeting began with Sazonov reading the conclusions of his memorandum to Nicholas. Discussion turned immediately to further possible measures that might persuade Turkey and Germany to renounce their agreement, including a financial boycott of the Porte by the entente powers—a prospect which all admitted would not appeal to the French government. In treating a possible joint entente seizure of selected points within the Ottoman Empire, Sazonov played down the threat of war with Germany. The necessary ingredient would be English participation; Germany would not fear the prospect of a simple Franco-Russian action but would hesitate if England were to support the dual allies. Interestingly, as a foreshadowing of July 1914, Sazonov predicted that in the case of a conflict between Germany and the Dual Alliance, the United Kingdom would doubtless intervene should the allies suffer reverses.[136]

As he had done since 1907, Kokovtsev emphasized the simple risk of war entailed by Sazonov's proposals. He asked whether war with Germany was desirable, and whether Russia could fight. He supported the boycott proposal but doubted the likelihood of French support. He concluded by recommending that Russia avoid any "direct" measures that might lead to a war. All three military spokesmen challenged Kokovtsev, casting doubt on the probability of German intervention. Even if this should occur, although war was undesirable, it was "fully permissible."[137] For the first time since before the war with Japan, the antirisk argument with its implications for domestic stability had failed to circumscribe the policy alternatives that Russian statesmen were willing to entertain.

The conference resolutions reflected this viewpoint. They advocated the continuation of talks with Turkey and Germany until their failure was undeniable. Thereafter, the Russian government would take a series of increasingly compulsive measures in conjunction with France and Britain, as proposed in Sazonov's report. The cooperation of the entente powers was still regarded as crucial, as Sazonov had persistently indicated in his messages to Grey and Poincaré. The conference participants decided that if entente support was not forthcoming, Russia would have to be satisfied with measures entailing no risk of war.[138]

In the event, these measures proved unnecessary. In early January 1914, the German government found the face-saving solution of raising Liman's rank to that of honorary marshal, thus eliminating the possibility of his active command over Turkish troops. Predictably, Kokovtsev was overjoyed at this news, and Nicholas expressed satisfaction to the German ambassador that a way had been found to satisfy Russian wishes in the Liman matter.[139] Sazonov was also grateful but much more reserved in expression than either Kokovtsev or the emperor.

The Liman affair's significance lay less in its substance than in its role in precipitating an important change in Russian views of policy options, which now took a definite turn toward greater assertiveness. This new outlook departed markedly from that espoused by Kokovtsev, which had been the cornerstone of Russian diplomacy since the revolutions of 1905–1907. Henceforth the risk of war would not automatically exclude the possibility of action in defense of Russian interests. Moreover, Sazonov and the military representatives had cast Russia's lot entirely with the Triple

Entente. As Sazonov had noted on 23 December, a policy of peace at any price had seen Russia humiliated repeatedly, first in 1909 and then during the two Balkan wars. Now Germany was showing a cavalier disregard for the central area of Russian interests. Sazonov's frustration, already evident during the discussions of the Serbian port question, finally gave way to a rejection of the automatic equation of war abroad and revolution at home.

There was, in fact, a new evaluation of the domestic component in Sazonov's view. The press had seized upon the Liman crisis as yet another failure of Russian diplomacy, which it accused of continuing to labor under the delusion that Germany could be Russia's friend.[140] Anti-German opinion had been growing since the Bosnian crisis and had been exacerbated by Russo-German negotiations for the renewal of a trade treaty signed under extremely unfavorable circumstances for Russia in 1904. Minister of Agriculture A. V. Krivoshein, who was emerging as a redoubtable adversary to Kokovtsev in the council, had voiced such views in late 1912.[141] The Liman incident seemed to exemplify the weakness of Russian diplomacy and the extent of German arrogance. Public opinion demanded action and found in the state's inactivity a pretext for criticizing in foreign policy the same bureaucratism that it was attacking in domestic politics.

Seven days after the special conference on the Liman question, Naval Minister Grigorovich wrote to Sazonov and Kokovtsev asking for their support in his efforts to increase the Black Sea fleet as a response to the anticipated growth in the Turkish Black Sea squadron, which he felt would preempt any possible favorable resolution of the Straits Question in the future.[142] In his arguments, he referred to the international political aspects of the problem and then brought up "domestic policy considerations." He feared the "moral impression of our fleet's defeat, inflicted upon us, it would seem, by a long shattered Turkey."

Grigorovich's was one of the first statements in defense of a more active foreign policy grounded in the demands of public opinion. It reflected both a sympathy with society's goals and probably a vulnerability to demands which were more effective than previously, given the disintegration of unity in government and the rupture of all but the crudest links between "state" and "society." On the part of Sazonov and Grigorovich, this responsiveness to the demands of public opinion grew out of an outlook on the domestic roots of foreign policy that had been expressed in different ways both by Kuropatkin in 1903 and Stolypin in advocating a cooperative relationship with the nation as represented in the Duma.

Both Sazonov and Grigorovich seemed to accept the nation as a legitimate force in the consideration of Russian policy. The definition of this force seemed to vary with circumstances; Sazonov often identified Russian views with those of public opinion, while Krivoshein had a quasi-Slavophile or pan-Slav vision of the strength and loyalty of the Russian people. Both represented a full inversion of the position taken by Stolypin and other statesmen after 1905. Now, it was argued, there was a threat in *not* taking proper action to uphold Russia's international stature; or, from Krivoshein's point of view, the state misperceived its own capacities by underestimating the strength of the *narod* as a resource. Given, too, the inevitable associations with the late 1870s evoked by issues in the Near East, and Russia's "historic mission" there, the unity of tsar and nation was assured in any measures the state might undertake.

These connections became for Sazonov an impetus toward a more active policy during the demonstrations arising from the Balkan situation in the spring of 1913. With the Liman crisis, his own views of Russia's position and capabilities were reinforced by those he encountered in the press. By July, this consideration became paramount. If Sazonov had moderated in any way his demands for quick and decisive measures against the German activity in Constantinople, it had been due to the restraining influence of Kokovtsev. The chairman had continued to entertain the post-1905 associations between war and revolution, which were made clearer to him, as minister of finances, by the sensitivity of the stock market and Russian bonds to the prospects of war. The restraint he exercised over Russian policy disappeared when Nicholas dismissed him as council chairman and minister of finances at the end of January 1914.[143]

Kokovtsev's dismissal, like Stolypin's assassination, took place after his actual political demise. All observers agreed on the reasons for his dismissal.[144] Unity in the council had begun to unravel shortly after his appointment as chairman. Other ministers had long resented his insistence on fiscal restraint and cabinet unity. The immediate cause for his downfall was a campaign in late 1913, involving several ministers and conservative members of the State Council, including Witte, who blamed Kokovtsev's resistance to a bill for the abolition of the state monopoly on the sale of alcohol for all the ills besetting rural Russia. Meshcherskii's *Grazhdanin* revived the charges that the council chairman had become a Grand Vizier.[145] These and other causes seem to have given Nicholas sufficient pretext to part with Kokovtsev.

Equally significant was the ultimate fate of the offices Kokovtsev had vacated. Nicholas intentionally divided the duties of council chairman from any other portfolios. As Kokovtsev's successor in finance, Nicholas appointed the undistinguished P. A. Bark, whose merits seemed to be the favor of Meshcherskii and Krivoshein, who had masterminded the cabal against Kokovtsev.[146]

As chairman, Nicholas reappointed the second man to serve in that capacity in 1906, I. L. Goremykin. In a rescript to his new chairman, Nicholas wrote, "Your state experience, your calm firmness and tried and tested loyalty to OUR Throne will serve for a true unification of MY Government under Your wise guidance."[147] The appointment was universally seen as the placing of a figurehead at the helm of a moribund United Government. Sazonov called him "an old man who had long since lost not only the ability to be interested in any matter except for his personal tranquillity and well-being, but even simply to reckon with the surrounding reality."[148]

Like his predecessors, Kokovtsev had ultimately come up against the problem of Nicholas's confidence as the critical element in his ability to act. However, his career as council chairman had been undermined from the very outset by Nicholas's resolve not to place a strong actor between himself and his other ministers. At the same time, Kokovtsev was forced to act without the authority Stolypin had enjoyed, in a situation that amounted to the unraveling of the 3 June system. As the "ministerial strike" of 1913 had demonstrated, there were those in government who questioned cooperating with the elective instance. For their part, a significant number of Duma deputies had long since abandoned any hopes they may have entertained about the good will of the government. Yet other observers in both the Duma and the government felt that Russia had changed, and that Kokovtsev's fiscal conservatism and hidebound adherence to a policy of foreign restraint, if not inertia, were no longer necessary under the new conditions.[149]

Most paradoxical in Kokovtsev's ministry was the fact that he sought to promote the principle of United Government by legal means. This characterized his approach to his role as council chairman and attests to the fact that United Government had acquired an ideative life of its own. Like his predecessors, however, he foundered on the emphasis placed by the ministerial reform on the relationship between emperor and chairman as the critical moment in the functioning of the reformed government. Nowhere was this paradox more sharply limned than in his provisions for the formal incorporation of foreign policy discussion into the council and his inability to maintain unity on any of the issues facing the council. Like Witte and Stolypin, but through a more protracted and painful process, Kokovtsev was forced to confront the fact that the entire system required Nicholas's assent for its sustenance.

# · 9 ·

# The Decision to Go to War

Kokovtsev's dismissal was widely interpreted as a signal that Nicholas was now going to rule as the autocrat conservatives wished him to be.[1] Inevitably, this interpretation affected thinking on Russia's foreign policy, provoking rumors that Sazonov would soon follow his colleague into retirement. It is not accidental that two weeks after Kokovtsev's removal, the elder conservative statesman P. N. Durnovo "presented" to Nicholas, and distributed to the ministers, a long memorandum on Russia's foreign relations.[2]

This famous memorandum echoed the Germanophile thinking that had first surfaced in statements by Lamzdorf and Shvanebakh in 1906. Looking at the same world as Sazonov and Grigorovich, the state councillor drew sharply different conclusions. He noted that Russia's international relations had undergone a *volte-face* since the war with Japan. Where once there had existed a pragmatic, defensive alliance with France and good, dynastic-based relations with Germany, Russia was now on England's side in its confrontation with Germany, the central conflict in European affairs. This realignment had not served Russian interests as recent Balkan and Turkish events had clearly demonstrated.

According to Durnovo, the entente would end by pitting Russia against Germany in a war that would inevitably arise from the Balkan or colonial conflicts between members of the two groups.[3] The possibility of this war was equally the fault of dilettantes in "our young legislative institutions" and the Ministry of Foreign Affairs. Russia was in no way prepared for such a war, which did not serve Russian interests. Indeed, there was no real conflict of interests between Russia and Germany: Russia had no maritime aspirations; both had an interest in keeping Poland calm; and Russia had nothing to gain from the acquisition of the fractious provinces of Poland,

Prussia, or Galicia. Even in the Straits, the chief obstacle to Russian success was not Germany but England.[4] Further, Russian economic interests were closely tied to Germany; the solution to conflicts between the two in this matter would better be solved through improved relations, not confrontation.

Despite the economic and strategic ills resulting from Russia's present ties, "they retreat to the second level before the political consequences of this . . . unnatural alliance."[5] Russia and Germany were representatives "of the conservative principle in the civilized world" against democratic England and France. The impending war was fraught with disaster for both Russia and Germany. Defeat would give rise in the vanquished state to a revolution that would soon spread to the victor. Russia, 'where the popular masses undoubtedly preach the principles of an unconscious socialism," would provide particularly fertile ground for such an upheaval. Any but a socialist revolution would be impossible, since the opposition had no support among the *narod,* which in its simple desire for land, not rights, refused to distinguish between the intelligentsia and the bureaucracy.[6]

War with Germany presented a special threat, since Russia's unpreparedness would lead to inevitable setbacks at first. "Given the exceptional nervousness of our society, an exaggerated significance will be attributed to these circumstances, and given the oppositionism of this society, everything will be put to the government's blame."[7] Durnovo was extrapolating from the same circumstances that had driven Sazonov to advocate a more assertive Russian policy. Durnovo predicted that the government could well make concessions to society, which would only weaken the state by driving a broad gulf between the new coalition and the people as a whole. "[T]he peasant will sooner trust a landless state functionary than a landlord Octobrist."

Russia might win a war with only minor social disturbances when the soldiers demanded land and wages fell after demobilization. But it was more likely that, given Germany as the enemy, Russia would lose, and defeat would give rise to "a social revolution in its most extreme manifestation."[8] This process would begin with military setbacks and criticism of the government from the legislative tribune. Soon there would be rural disturbances, which would quickly solidify around slogans like "black repartition." With the return of the peasant army, a full collapse of law and order would quickly follow, and society would be incapable of restraining the wave it had called into being. From Russia, revolution would soon spread to Germany.

Thus, Durnovo concluded, Russia's ties with England were "deeply mistaken."[9] Germany and England had inevitably to resolve their differences, but it was not Russia's fight. Echoing a motif in conservative rhetoric, Durnovo wrote: "The Triple Entente is an artificial combination, which does not have any common interests behind it, and the future belongs not to it," but to a Continental Bloc comprised of Russia, Germany, France, and Japan.[10] This bloc would guarantee a long peace and "would give no grounds for the anti-German agitation . . . of our constitutional liberal parties, who by their very nature are forced to adhere not to a conservative-German, but to a liberal-English orientation."

The Durnovo memorandum was a classic statement of the post-1905 conservative view of the links between Russia's orientation abroad and the state's ability to govern at home. But most significant was its timing, hard upon Kokovtsev's departure, which had been seen as a conservative triumph. Nicholas was now being asked to complete in Russia's foreign policy what he was seen to have begun in Russia—a return to a course dictated by the monarchical principle.

Durnovo was not alone in seeing opportunity in Nicholas's dismissal of Kokovtsev. During the spring of 1914 there was a flurry of efforts by separate groups of officials to persuade Nicholas to bring Russia closer to Germany and to replace the Anglophile Sazonov at the head of the foreign ministry.[11] Former ministry councillor Taube and several of his colleagues saw Kokovtsev's removal as eliminating the last vote for peace in Russian government; "Sazonov's reckless Anglophilism could lead us to a conflict with Germany, of which they had long dreamed in London."[12] Their choice to replace Sazonov was P. S. Botkin, the Russian envoy to Morocco, who was both anti-English and well-connected at court.[13] Witte publicized his goal of a Continental Bloc, apparently encouraged by Wilhelm; his ideas were said to find sympathy at court.[14]

By mid-March the drive for a pro-German policy and the removal of Sazonov had reached the foreign ministry. The Russian ambassador in Constantinople, N. N. Girs, had a long talk about this issue with his German counterpart, Hans von Wangenheim.[15] Girs had just returned from leave in St. Petersburg and was said to be very excited about his chances for replacing Sazonov. At dinner in the German embassy, Girs talked at length about Russo-German relations: "[i]n Russia, there is a large and strong party to which he belongs, which sees the pivot of Russian policy in the relationship with Germany."[16] Although they were bound by separate alliances, neither state wanted to be brought into a war by its allies. Here, Girs disavowed any Russian interest in the ultimate disposition of Alsace-Lorraine. Girs noted that events in the Balkans had shown that the

Triple Alliance was now led by Vienna, whose designs in the Balkans could be the only source of a Russo-German conflict. Since the chief threats to peace were French revanchism and Austrian designs in the Balkans, Girs suggested a Russo-German agreement in which each side would pledge to allow the other to mediate in any conflict that might arise between Russia and Germany and their respective allies.[17]

All of these attempts to reorient Russian policy are interesting for revealing the paradoxes they tried to confront. Witte's Continental Bloc foundered, as it had in 1905, on the question of Franco-German relations. By the same token, Girs and Taube felt it was possible to separate Germany and Austria-Hungary. Needing peace with Germany, either for its own sake or for purposes connected with the preservation of the monarchical principle, partisans of reorientation still wanted to be able to maintain Russia's aspirations in the Balkans. But the most ironic aspect of these attempts to inspire Nicholas to change direction was the implicit assumption that Nicholas wished to. The Germanophiles thought that in having dispensed with Kokovtsev and his program, Nicholas was reasserting his autocratic authority against the post-1905 settlement in defense of the monarchical principle at home and abroad—an assumption that indicated the ironclad connections they drew between foreign affairs and domestic politics. They were mistaken, however. Nicholas had also been deeply impressed by the Liman affair. In an audience with the French ambassador in mid-January, he said that the crisis had "made manifest the German threat to Russia's essential interests"; "we will not allow our feet to be trodden upon, and *this time,* it will not be as it was in the Far East war, national sentiment will support us."[18]

In mid-March, the emperor discussed the possibility of rapprochement with Germany:[19]

> It was . . . commonly supposed that there was nothing to keep Germany and Russia apart. This was, however, not the case . . . He had reason to believe that Germany was aiming at acquiring such a position at Constantinople as would enable her to shut in Russia altogether in the Black Sea. Should she attempt to carry out this policy He would have to resist it with all His power, even should war be the only alternative.

As ever, Nicholas's behavior confounded conservatives who wished him to take matters back into his own hands.

In the envenomed atmosphere following the Liman von Sanders crisis, the prospect of war with Germany seemed to assume the same air of inevitability as conflict with Austria-Hungary. During the spring, at the same time as Taube, Witte, Orlov, and Girs were all promoting alignment with Germany, a bitter polemic was taking place in the Russian and German press over Russia's ability to fight.

In March, the French *chargé* remarked on the "surprising rapidity" with which Russo-German antagonisms had increased in the preceding two years,[20] citing "a veritable transformation in the feelings of official Russia with regard to Germany." He attributed the change to the Balkan wars, in which German strength had decided matters in Austria's favor. Remarks by the German chancellor about the inevitable clash between Germanism and Slavism also dismayed official observers who were already being carried by the nationalist fervor set loose by the Balkan wars. It was felt that the Near East, over which Russo-German amity had first been damaged at the Congress of Berlin, would be the cause of the future conflict, as Russia was confronted there only by Germany. "The Sanders mission appeared as the symbol of the new state of things: hence the enormous impression that it produced in this country."

In the wake of Kokovtsev's departure, Sazonov had relative freedom of action. His policy was shaped largely by the impressions he had derived from the Liman incident, and he strengthened the line he had developed in December. Writing to Izvolskii in March, Sazonov stated, "the further strengthening and development of the so-called 'Triple Entente' and its conversion (so far as is possible) into a new alliance, presents itself to me as an urgent task."[21] Shortly thereafter, Nicholas spoke to British Ambassador Sir George Buchanan about the benefits of an Anglo-Russian alliance.[22] Talks soon began for a naval convention between the two countries.[23]

Indeed, during the months before World War I, contrary to conservatives' expectations and confirming their worst fears, not Nicholas, but Sazonov directed foreign policy. In conservative circles, there was growing disappointment at Nicholas's failure to follow through on his assertion of power in January. "Certainly, in high society, one does not hesitate to criticize the person of the Emperor. One reproaches him with living too removed in his palace at Tsarskoie [*sic*] Selo."[24] The impression of Nicholas's passivity is further confirmed by Sazonov's account of the ruler's visit to Romania in June 1914. With the second Balkan war, Romania had emerged as an important force in the Balkans and one that might be open to an agreement with Russia. "In order ultimately to propel the . . . improvement in our relations with Romania, it was necessary to crown the efforts of Russian diplomacy in this direction with a voyage by the Sovereign to Romania."[25] This voyage took place at Sazonov's instigation, to use Nicholas in aid of a policy Sazonov had devised.

Ironically, given Nicholas's weakening of the council under Kokovtsev, when the crisis following the assassination of Franz Ferdinand reached its peak with the Austro-Hungarian ultimatum to Serbia, the Council of Ministers was the body that met to discuss Russian policy.[26] From the outset of the July crisis, war was virtually a foregone conclusion.[27] Since its earliest days, the alliance with France had presumed a war against Germany. Twenty-odd years of talks between the allied General Staffs had focused on the logistics of this war; French funds had been poured into the construction of railways leading to Russia's western frontier. As early as 1903 Kuropatkin had assigned priority to the western frontier in Russia's defense, a view reflected among senior officers.[28] Furthermore, the frictions that had arisen in Austro-Russian relations after the Bosnian crisis, and especially after November 1912, distinguished the Dual Monarchy as the chief adversary, while also leading to the realization that Germany would firmly support its ally.

At a Council of Ministers meeting on 11 July 1914,[29] Sazonov outlined the political situation in terms he had first used during the Liman affair. He accused Germany of seeking hegemony in Europe through aggression. Since the war with Japan, Russia had had to concede to Germany at every step, yet Germany had only become more aggressive. "The moment had come when Russia, faced with the annihilation of Serbia, would lose all her authority if she did not declare herself the defender of a Slavonic nation threatened by powerful neighbors."[30] Russia had fought to liberate the Slavic Balkans in 1876–1878 at immense cost; its subsequent policy had been to defend the Slavs. "If Russia failed to fulfill her historic mission she would be considered a decadent State and would henceforth have to take second place among the powers."

In January 1908, Izvolskii had made similar arguments, only to be rebuffed with the threat posed to the internal stability of the empire by the possibility of complications. Now Krivoshein recalled the domestic effects of Japanese defeat.[31] The revolution had been beaten, and there had been a period of convalescence during which the government's efforts had been directed toward the reorganization of national life. Most of this program had been completed. Since 1906 there had been a constitution, Duma, and State Council organized on a democratic basis; the country's finances were secure. He admitted that Russia's military preparations were not on the same level as Germany's or Austria's, but other conditions in Russia had improved greatly.

Here, Krivoshein added, "public and parliamentary opinion would fail to understand why, at this critical moment involving Russia's vital interests, the Imperial Government was reluctant to act boldly." While war was undesirable, for its potential domestic effects, Russia could no longer remain passive, it had to use stronger language than hitherto. Krivoshein's remarks "made a profound impression on the Cabinet."[32] This impression was probably strengthened by the widespread authority enjoyed by Krivoshein; rumored to be Kokovtsev's successor in January, he had been unable to take the council chairmanship because of ill health.[33] With his return to the capital, and given Goremykin's own attitude to council matters, Krivoshein had emerged as the *de facto* leader in council deliberations.

Sazonov's and Krivoshein's remarks reflected the inversion of Russian official thinking since 1909. Hitherto, war had been avoided precisely because of the fear of domestic upheaval. There had always been two coexisting components in conceptions of such unrest. On one hand, there was society, whose influence had grown with international tensions in the Balkans.[34] On the other hand, there was that elemental source of upheaval, the *narod*. Durnovo had identified this group simply as the peasantry, but as the ministers met, there were occurring in St. Petersburg the largest strikes since 1905. Both Sazonov and Krivoshein chose to emphasize the attitude of society in their calculations. This was due in part to the fact that the demands of society for action, and the terms in which these demands were argued, coincided with their own views.

Since 1907, the Council of Ministers had participated in foreign policy making on the basis of the links perceived between Russia's position abroad and peace at home. The role of the council chairmen had been largely dictated by the domestic concerns of their own ministries and the political outlooks and personal foibles of their colleagues in the MID. Thus, both Kokovtsev and Stolypin had acted as a brake on their foreign ministers, forcing them to discuss their policy under council auspices in order to exercise the needed degree of restraint. They sought by these means to assure consistency in all areas of Russian state activity at home and abroad.

This restraint had disappeared with Kokovtsev. It had been barely exercised during the first Balkan war, in face of the abortive mobilization, when the thinking had been that any war would lead to revolution. However, as Krivoshein argued in support of Sazonov's call for a forceful response to the Austrian ultimatum to Serbia, the situation had changed—Russia had largely been rebuilt. He may well have overestimated the degree to which this was indeed true, but that he wished to believe this was important in itself.

Thus, the traditional formula connecting war and revolution had been completely inverted by the summer of 1914. Not only was there no spokesman for restraint in the council, but because of the empire's diplomatic career since 1908, statesmen felt a threat from the prospect of society's response to inaction. This feeling can only have been intensified under the circumstances of the July crisis. To capitulate yet again could damage the state's own authority at home while casting into doubt its international claims to Great Power status.

These were the arguments Sazonov made to Nicholas on 30 July 1914, in persuading him to approve an already delayed Russian mobilization as a demonstration of support for Serbia's protests against the more categorical points in the Austro-Hungarian ultimatum. Nicholas temporized, referring to a telegram from Wilhelm threatening the withdrawal of his services as a mediator with Austria-Hungary should Russia mobilize. Wilhelm, knowing Nicholas, had told him that all responsibility for war and peace would be on the tsar's shoulders. Nicholas recognized the impossibility of further delay but resisted a final decision.

Sazonov argued for mobilization; he felt that Vienna had already decided on war against Serbia.[35] "[I]n Berlin, where one might have expected words of reason, they do not want to say them." Instead, they demanded "from us a capitulation to the Central Powers, for which Russia would never forgive the Sovereign, and which would cover the good name of the Russian people in shame."[36] Sazonov's statement alluded to the events within and outside Russia that had taken place since 1905: each successive crisis in the Near East—the Bosnian annexation, the Balkan wars, and the Liman affair—had seen the Russian government forced into a conciliatory posture by its sense of internal weakness following defeat in Asia and revolution at home. Public opinion had alluded to the same period as a demonstration of the state's continued incompetence with references to each episode as a "Tsushima" for Russian diplomacy. The same frustration had been felt in different ways within the Ministry of Foreign Affairs under Izvolskii and Sazonov, in turn.

Now Sazonov had several powerful sources of support for his view. Krivoshein backed Sazonov's estimate of society's attitude to Russia's obligations to the Slavic states in the Balkans. Krivoshein also echoed a broadly held view that Russia had successfully rebuilt itself after the revolution. To use Stolypin's image from 1908 (later repeated by Izvolskii and Guchkov), Russia was now in the view of many able to "speak with its former language." In this view, the Russia confronted by Austria in its ultimatum to Serbia was not the shaken power of 1908. Its military strength had been largely restored, and it had strong and encouraging relations with its partners in the entente. Sazonov may have overestimated the strength of

Russia's support in London, but it appears to have been a real factor in his calculations.[37]

Moreover, Russia's very authority as a Great Power, and its self-appointed role as protector of the lesser Slavic states, were seen by statesmen and the public alike as hanging in the balance. Added to these considerations was the general climate of growing estrangement between the government and an increasingly self-assertive fourth Duma at a time of tensions engendered by the strike wave sweeping St. Petersburg in July 1914. Thus, when Sazonov said to Nicholas that Russia would not "forgive" Nicholas for capitulating in this instance, he was not indulging in mere rhetorical flourishes.

For his part, Nicholas arrived at a new and much more encouraging idea of the "Russia" invoked by Sazonov. This was not the Russia of the Duma tribune or of newspaper campaigns. Rather, this was more likely the Russia he had seen during the tercentenary celebrations in 1913—a loyal *narod* gathered around its tsar in defense of autocracy and orthodoxy. Indeed, as diplomatic and governmental negotiations proceeded, crowds gathered in front of the Winter Palace, "carrying portraits of the tsar and national flags, with the singing of the hymn, 'Lord, save Your people.' "[38] As his statements in the waning days of the Liman affair indicate, Nicholas was confident of popular support for any war in defense of Russia's position in the Near East, in tacit contrast with the attitude shown in the war with Japan. Thus, for Nicholas, the prospect of war was daunting, but only in terms of the prospect of sending so many good subjects to their deaths;[39] in this case, war brought with it none of the fears of revolution that Durnovo had invoked as recently as February.

Nicholas approved the mobilization order. Again, as in 1876, Russian society greeted the national war in an effort that brought state and society together, at least temporarily. The Council of Ministers, united in its agreement on the domestic political necessity of resisting an Austro-Hungarian attack on Slavic Serbia, reached its decisions on the basis of arguments that could be read in the capital's press. Having so long resisted war for fear of social repercussions, the Russian government now entered it for the same reasons. Placed atop this union was Nicholas, who took the country to war, confident in the role of Russian tsar to which he had aspired all his life.

# Conclusion

The surge of patriotism greeting the outbreak of war was short-lived. Defeats at the front mirrored the breakdown of order within Russia as the economy and the state structure proved incapable of meeting even the most basic requirements of the war effort. As Durnovo predicted, and as had been the case in 1904–1905, systemic breakdown contributed to revolutionary ferment in Russia; the component parts of the empire—peasants, workers, national minorities, and regions broke away from the state in search of their own real or perceived needs, whether "land and freedom" or "responsible government." The pressure of war did not undo the empire but showed instead how little had been achieved by the attempt to restore it after 1905.

Particularly among those parts of society that had embraced the cause of a national war, confidence in the state's ability to prosecute Russia's needs and interests effectively was already wavering before 1914. This was evident not only among the centrist and center-left Duma fractions but also on the right, where doubts about the legitimacy of any but the most personal autocracy were expressed with increasing frequency. Such views were also shared in official circles, ranging from Maklakov's Ministry of Internal Affairs to court, at the center of which stood an emperor who was seeking to restore the autocracy as he imagined it had existed either before 1905 or under his father.

From this point of view, the outbreak of war may actually have bought the autocracy a little time in its efforts to cope with the array of crises confronting it after 1905. Gains had been minor and extremely hard-won in every area the government had sought to address during the years of the constitutional experiment. The effects of the Stolypin land reform were as yet unclear; reforms in education, religious legislation, and local self-administration had emerged as half-measures from bruising conflicts within government and in the legislative institutions. They satisfied no one, and the accompanying debates demonstrated the profound disagreements among statesmen and "public men" *(obshchestvennye deiateli)* alike over the meaning of 1905 for Russia and for autocracy. If certain sectors of the intelligentsia turned from politics to introspection, others cleaved more closely to interpretations of Marx as received in Russia, helping in the resurgence of a workers' movement that had by 1914 begun to assume the proportions of 1905.[1]

Facing all of these chronic problems—the legacy not only of 1905, but of the entire sixty-odd years since the Great Reforms, was a government which had itself been critically riven by its experience since 1905. If Durnovo's memorandum stands out for its eerie accuracy in foretelling the downfall of the *ancien régime* in Russia, Kryzhanovskii's call for a cabinet in 1905 helps explain the means by which the order unraveled from above in its failure to confront the burgeoning foreign and domestic challenges that beset it with increasing insistence after the spring of 1912. At the center of this process was the figure of Nicholas II.

Reflecting on these years, Taube called Nicholas a "constitutional autocrat";[2] when faced with difficult situations he tried to stay within the law. He did not watch closely enough over the activity of his ministers, and nobody ever thought to make Nicholas chairman. This critique was itself an unwitting echo of Vonliarliarskii's lament that his tsar was a "legalist" who showed an unwonted respect for the dictates of procedure rather than ruling "autocratically." Taube's expression captures the deep ambiguities assailing autocracy before and after 1905, as well as Nicholas's own ambivalence toward his government.

Barely a month after dismissing Kokovtsev, Nicholas presided at a meeting of the Council of Ministers where he "administered a little lecture to his Ministers, impressing on them the necessity of working together as a united government" in its relations with the Duma and the State Council.[3] This vignette provides some insight into the ironies underlying Nicholas's behavior after Stolypin's fall from grace in the spring of 1911: in defense of his power he conducted a *fronde* against his own government, but in so doing he observed the forms and procedures by which that government operated.

Just as he had dealt with the triumvirate in 1903, Nicholas once again broke up a united faction in his government that he found confining upon his prerogatives. By dismissing Kokovtsev, he was not signifying a change of course in his policy—although he was admittedly dissatisfied with the fourth Duma and growing unrest in the cities—he was rather stating his disapproval of United Government as propounded by Stolypin and Kokovtsev. The clearest testimony to this attitude was his appointment of Goremykin in Kokovtsev's stead. During his first sojourn as chairman, Goremykin had elicited the complaints of both Stolypin and Izvolskii for his disinclination to enforce unity within the fractious council in his charge.

In letting Kokovtsev go, Nicholas was also ridding himself of the last, if the least effective, spokesman for a unified council headed by an authoritative chairman, as first proposed by Witte and embodied by Stolypin. In this light, such criticisms as that in the 1909 anonymous memorandum against the office of chairman, or the intermittent complaints of a vizierate, had probably found their mark. However, having asserted his sovereign power and encouraged fracture in Kokovtsev's council, Nicholas still did not go the distance demanded by conservatives and reestablish full and direct control of Russian government.

Again, as with his undermining of the triumvirate, Nicholas contented himself with the fact of that achievement. Russian government retained the necessary minimum of unity demanded by its dealings with the legislative bodies but lost the solidarity that had characterized it under Stolypin and to which Kokovtsev had aspired in his bureaucrat's fashion.

It has been argued elsewhere that Nicholas failed properly to internalize his role as autocrat.[4] Certainly, he never seems to have formed a concrete appreciation of his power as an instrument, rather than a belonging of not always unalloyed benefit. It can be stated that he saw his government as something external to himself as ruler, and as a threat to his power. This conception is implicit in the image of the vizierate, so ardently set forth by conservative commentators whose views he shared in so many other areas. Stolypin and Kokovtsev also came to similar conclusions about Nicholas's attitude: the former at the height of the Western *zemstvo* imbroglio, the latter during the celebrations for the tercentenary of the Romanov dynasty.

Taking together Nicholas's procedural formalism and his jealousy of his power, a certain pattern emerges in his behavior toward the united Council of Ministers forced on him in 1905. In looking at the successive premiers, particularly Stolypin, Kokovtsev, and Goremykin, one sees that each in turn embodied what Nicholas felt his government ought to be. Thus, Stolypin was appointed chairman to restore order to Russia; however, when he proved too successful, he was dismissed. Kokovtsev, was made chairman, to judge from the remarks of Alexandra Fedorovna and others, because he was *not* Stolypin but rather the quintessential St. Petersburg *chinovnik*. When Kokovtsev proved overly devoted to Stolypin's view of

United Government and the chairman's role therein, he too was replaced by Goremykin, who seemed to understand Nicholas's demands that the form of cabinet rule be respected but within very limited boundaries. In this light, United Government may have succeeded too well, to the extent that it gave concrete expression to Nicholas's suspicions of his government.

Of course, these problems, and Nicholas's ability to exploit and exacerbate them, were built into the very fabric of the reform that had given rise to the united Council of Ministers. Russian statesmen were themselves caught in a set of ironies and paradoxes which they were conceptually unequipped to appreciate. As a result of processes of professionalization, institutional development, and routinization, many Russian officials had come to entertain certain assumptions of how the empire ought to be governed. These assumptions centered on a *Rechtstaat,* in which the administrative apparatus, from its vantage point atop a multinational and socially particularistic empire, could use its professional skills and understanding of rational law to mobilize resources in pursuit of interests defined by criteria they themselves conceived as governors. This vision had roots extending to the Petrine reforms, and its rhetoric suffused intragovernmental discussion throughout the nineteenth century.[5] They harbored at the same time a belief in an unlimited autocrat—the arbitrary nature *(proizvol)* of whose power was fully incorporated in bureaucratic politics in a never ending struggle for the emperor's confidence or favor. To use Witte's imagery, confidence had been integrated into the workings of autocracy as the lever through which motion was imparted to the machine.

One of the strongest factors aiding the tacit confirmation and rooting of such assumptions was the fact that since the reign of Alexander II, if not of his father, Russian tsars had ruled through the bureaucratic machine at their disposal. The Bezobrazovshchina, and similar manifestations of Nicholas's idea of autocratic power, had confronted many officials with a challenge to these assumptions, but this challenge was unassailable because it issued from the source of their own authority. At the same time, under the pressure of this challenge, many officials came increasingly to separate the person of Nicholas from his function as sovereign emperor.

The reform of the Council of Ministers in 1905 represented a bureaucratic attempt to square this circle. It sought both to protect the legitimacy of state power and authority against encroachment from the Duma, and also to regulate closely the actions of the autocrat; in brief, it was an attempt to protect autocracy from a willful and immature population and from Nicholas himself. Kryzhanovskii's memorandum, with its talk of distancing autocratic power from the details of daily rule and of raising it above people and government alike so as to preserve its legitimacy, was in fact a veiled argument for limiting the autocrat's power and obliging him to rule exclusively through his bureaucracy. Conservative defenders of autocracy accurately saw this attempt, and sought to thwart it, first in the council reform discussions and later in the revision of the Fundamental Laws. Witte pursued Kryzhanovskii's line in his efforts to assure the authority of the council chairman to rein in ministers who flouted cabinet discipline, but also to control relations between the sovereign and his advisers. Both Kryzhanovskii's recommendations and Witte's aspirations owed their thrust to their respective experience in Russian government before 1904.

The career of United Government illustrated trenchantly the problem underlying its creation: it worked only when Nicholas respected it. Nicholas's confidence remained an essential attribute in Russian government, as Witte, Stolypin, and Kokovtsev each learned in turn. Indeed, one could argue, along with Kokovtsev, that United Government was undone by its own success. It was one thing to discuss, even allusively, the necessity for limiting the autocrat's power when the entire order was under direct threat of revolutionary overthrow in 1905. Matters looked different to critics, and to Nicholas, when order was restored and the new regime began to take on a routine of its own.

Yet, the new institutions atop the government provided only a gradually evolving structure within which order could be established and consolidated. As turmoil gave way to seeming stability, older memories asserted themselves; figures at court or in government, including Nicholas, began to look back beyond 1905 as an ideal period. Meanwhile, those in the Duma, from the Octobrists leftward, looked forward to the more or less distant future when the existing order would be replaced by a constitutional monarchy or republic, and contended with the representatives of autocracy in order to bring that day closer.

The growing tendency to criticize the new order from all quarters—and particularly from court and conservative circles—is itself testimony to how fragile its existence was. Council chairmen, with the exception of Goremykin, had to contend with charges that they were seeking to erect a wall around Nicholas—arguments that Nicholas found persuasive, to judge from the testimony of Stolypin and Kokovtsev. At the same time, they had to defend before an increasingly intractable Duma policies for which they were statutorily responsible. Moreover, under Kokovtsev, ministers began to resort to the type of intrigues and institutional evasions that had characterized bureaucratic politics before 1905. This was a function of several circumstances: long-entrenched patterns of bureaucratic politics; lack of personal respect for Kokovtsev among many ministers; and, most important, Nicholas's own increasingly evident discontent with the constraints of the new order.

The consequences of all these developments were manifold and foreseen by Kryzhanovskii, when he made his original argument for council reform and the removal of the Supreme Power from day-to-day political activity. Worsening relations with the Duma after the spring of 1911 were exacerbated by the split within the council, as ministers who dissented with policies advocated by Kokovtsev often simply ignored his views with the tacit or explicit connivance of Nicholas; this pattern had been anticipated with his undermining of Stolypin during the Western *zemstvo* crisis. Increasing disarray, as Kryzhanovskii had predicted, also diminished what little authority the government had enjoyed in the Duma under Stolypin.

There was another consequence of the increasing disunity in the council, which, although not as immediately apparent, was also of great significance for the career of autocracy after 1905. In warning Nicholas of the need to separate autocratic power from the minutiae of politics, Kryzhanovskii had contended that for the Supreme Power to do otherwise would lend it a partisan air and thus undermine the legitimacy of power in the eyes of the population. In looking at the history of the Council of Ministers before World War I, one sees signs that this same problem may have been emerging as well in officials' attitudes toward Nicholas.

Throughout Nicholas's reign, there is discernible among his highest servitors an advancing lack of respect for the ruler, or at least a change in the contours of their relationship with him, in response to Nicholas's behavior. Rather than stating his dissatisfaction with one or another of his ministers, as Alexander III was known to do, Nicholas would intrigue against the object of his disapproval. Pleve had defended this behavior to Kuropatkin in 1903 as a necessary concomitant of autocratic rule, but this view was contested by many of his contemporaries. Much of the explicit contempt for Nicholas in Witte's memoirs is rooted in his reaction to this type of conduct by the ruler. During Kokovtsev's tenure, Nicholas abetted actively and passively the efforts of Sukhomlinov, Krivoshein, and others in undermining the authority of the council chairman.

It is in the activities of Kokovtsev's opponents, and even in those of Sazonov, that one sees the diminution of Nicholas's elevation above politics that Kryzhanovskii had identified as crucial to the maintenance of his authority. If Nicholas had customarily sought to protect his power by manipulating the political and institutional relationships revolving around him, participants in these relationships made increasing use of the emperor in their battles. Nicholas became the ultimate instrument with which to undermine one's adversary.

Thus, Krivoshein and his allies in the State Council and the press had used Nicholas to get rid of the meddlesome Kokovtsev; Sukhomlinov had done the same in the mobilization crisis of November 1912. The same attitude was apparent in different circumstances, when Sazonov dispatched Nicholas to Romania in June 1914, to cement ties with the Balkan state. The roots of this shrinking distance between Nicholas and his official servants, and the consequent decline in their respect for him as ruler, extended to the earliest days of his rule. Here, one can point to Pleve's intrigues against Witte; Lamzdorf's reaction to Björkö; or Izvolskii's views of Nicholas before and during the Bosnian crisis.

Indeed, recollections by tsarist officials about this period reflect a dawning lack of confidence in autocracy as it was defined by Nicholas on the eve of war and revolution. As the war continued, Nicholas seemed to demonstrate his view of government by appointing as ministers such nullities as the reactionary B. V. Shturmer; such moves found a response in the growing disillusionment of many officials with autocracy. Witte resigned himself to the necessity of constitutional rule. Charykov connected Kokovtsev's dismissal with the beginnings of his own waning confidence in the autocracy.[6]

For many officials and members of society, the most compelling illustration of the decline of Nicholas's and the autocracy's authority was the rise to preeminence of Rasputin, which saw in the sphere of public opinion a diminishing of Nicholas's stature parallel to that which occurred in government. Rasputin's intervention in intrigue had made him another player in bureaucratic politics—admittedly more powerful than the others—but his influence over the imperial family ultimately demystified the Romanovs in the eyes of the public, to the point where they became the object of more or less open ridicule. Indeed, Rasputin became a powerful lightning rod for all who were dissatisfied with the state of autocracy before and during World War I. It is not accidental that the cabal that ultimately assassinated him was composed of figures as politically diverse as the reactionary V. M. Purishkevich and Duma Chairman M. V. Rodzianko.

Reflecting on all of the foregoing, then, it is clear that the crisis besetting autocracy at the end of its career was much more complex and grievous than that set forth in the traditional interpretation of the irreconcilability of state and society, the chief historiographical legacy of the prerevolutionary intelligentsia. As a result of the events leading into and out of the war with Japan, and the effort to set Russia aright after the revolution, the very relationship binding the emperor or tsar to his government came under increasingly close and critical scrutiny, the long-term result of which was to lead many officials to question the bases of the system they served.

The personality and views of Nicholas forced officials to address long inchoate conflicts in their own worldviews about their roles as servants and defenders of the autocracy. They had sought to resolve these conflicts in 1905. In those revolutionary times, however, they could not renounce the autocrat's sovereignty without surrendering power to society. The best solution they could come up with in the circumstances, and given their understanding of order, was to regulate as closely as possible Nicholas's intervention in their administrative world. In doing so, they were unable to confront or regulate Nicholas's confidence as the key factor in the post-revolutionary order. The narrower sphere of foreign policy making, which has been the focus of this book, reflected many of these problems and the degree to which officials succeeded in harnessing the sovereign power of the emperor to the needs of the empire as defined by these officials.

In his efforts to subordinate foreign policy to domestic tasks, Stolypin was setting forth his view of political priorities. For autocracy to survive, and for Russia to be rebuilt, Russia's foreign policy had to be directly and consciously subjected to the Council of Ministers. In arguing this claim, Stolypin noted that disunity atop the government had led to the war with Japan, which, as had become a commonplace in official and unofficial circles after 1905, had led in turn to the revolution. Of course, in pursuing this claim Stolypin was also encroaching on the prerogatives of the emperor, as Izvolskii and many conservatives complained.

Stolypin's success over Izvolskii showed how dissipated or undefined political power in Russian government had become as a result of the revolution and the reforms it engendered. Nicholas's retreat from active and constant participation in policy making after 1905 had created a vacuum in the state, which was only partially filled by the confidence he showed in his chairman at certain critical instances. Armed with this confidence, Stolypin was able at critical junctures to assert his own view of how policy ought to be made. In the meantime, officials were forced to work out among themselves the allocation of responsibilities and means for assessing and making policy under the new conditions. This took place informally, in the construction of the governmental consensus in favor of the agreement with Great Britain, and the arrangement gave rise to expectations on the part of Stolypin and Kokovtsev that they would be consulted on all such questions.

Equally important as an indicator of the reconfiguration of power and political relationships within the government was the fact that both Stolypin and Kokovtsev grounded their claims for council participation in such discussion by appealing to the statutes governing the relationship of the council to the Ministry of Foreign Affairs. Izvolskii abetted the subordination of foreign policy to United Government through his own adaptation to this new situation, conditioned by his sympathies for the modernity or liberalism of cabinet rule and his personal regard for Stolypin and the policies he represented within Russia, at least until 1910.

The degree to which Stolypin's vision of cabinet rule had become entrenched was demonstrated by the career of his successor, Kokovtsev. After having opposed the unification of government and the creation of a strong chairman throughout 1905, Kokovtsev in 1911 was arguing for the legal recognition of the regime Stolypin had introduced into foreign policy making. In seeking formally to consolidate the procedures that had evolved during preceding years, Kokovtsev was showing both his own bureaucrat's faith in the routinization of procedures and how quickly the improvisations of Stolypin's years had assumed concrete and legal form for many high officials. It was this conflation of legalism and routine that made Kokovtsev so vulnerable to the campaign mounted against him at the end of 1913 and so unequipped to deal with Nicholas's withdrawal of confidence. Nicholas's withdrawal from active participation had allowed the entrenchment of the routines Kokovtsev and others had come to accept as fact, without ever raising the question of confidence. This is what had also caught Stolypin, and to a lesser degree Witte, unawares at the end of their respective careers as chairman.

At the same time, Nicholas's own behavior after 1911 shows the degree to which the principles of United Government had acquired at least formal acceptability. Thus, he assented to Kokovtsev's request for the explicit inclusion of foreign policy discussion in the council; the council remained in most cases the forum for the discussion of such issues, as seen in July 1914, when the council discussed Russia's response to the Austro-Hungarian measures against Serbia. Nicholas's acceptance of the united council was also apparent in a negative light in his admonition to his ministers after appointing Goremykin to succeed Kokovtsev in February 1914. Given his treatment of Kokovtsev over the preceding half year, these remarks had a hollow ring and indicated his own inability, or lack of desire, to recognize the incompatibility of United Government as originally conceived with his own aspirations to rule as an autocrat. By contributing to the undermining of Kokovtsev, Nicholas had helped to discredit cabinet rule in all but name, leading to many of the consequences Kryzhanovskii had warned of in 1905.

Of course, the question inevitably arises of United Government's role in the decision to mobilize in 1914, with the full awareness that such an action could lead to war. Since 1908, the Council of Ministers had served as the forum within which foreign and domestic policies interacted directly and consciously. The effort to integrate foreign policy in the council's area of responsibility, as has been argued here, was based on the simple yet compelling link seen by virtually all interested parties between war abroad and disorder at home. Stolypin and Kokovtsev in turn manipulated the legislation governing the council's activity to argue successfully that since foreign affairs affected the interests and activities of ministries in charge of domestic affairs, the latter had the right to a role in the determination of foreign policy.

United Government was victimized by its own success on many levels. It was hampered in its initial role as a restraint on efforts to frame an assertive Russian policy by its ability to create the impression of stability in Russia. Stolypin had always argued that the active diplomacy advocated by Izvolskii was inappropriate for a Russia just emerging from revolution; but he had added that the time would come when Russia "could speak in its previous language." He and a chastened Izvolskii had used such arguments to win over Duma figures like Guchkov. However, this view could prevail only as long as it was felt that order had not been restored. As Kokovtsev noted, Stolypin owed his downfall to the feeling that normality had been reimposed so successfully that Nicholas and others could question the extent of his authority. In foreign affairs, the same feeling led to an increasing official and unofficial impatience with Russian restraint in the face of successive challenges to its position in the Balkans. By the time of the first Balkan war, many observers, including Sazonov, Duma deputies, and journalists, felt that the time had come when Russia could take up once more its "traditional" role as the defender of Slavic interests in the Balkans.[7] Indeed, Kokovtsev's successful efforts to restrain Sukhomlinov and Sazonov in the name of the policy first propounded by Stolypin may well have increased the pressures for a more assertive policy as instability in the Balkans persisted.

Kokovtsev's restraint came to be viewed by Krivoshein and Sukhomlinov as being of a piece with the pusillanimity and narrow-mindedness they associated with him as minister of finance. Certainly, Krivoshein felt that Kokovtsev underestimated the loyalty of the Russian population and the success of the reform process undertaken after 1905. For his own reasons, Nicholas shared this view. Kokovtsev's reluctance to back a strong Russian foreign policy thus became one of the accusations against him in 1913. The feeling that Russia could count on popular support for a more assertive stance in the Balkans particularly can only have been enhanced by the fervor of the demonstrations on behalf of the Slavic "little brothers" in the spring of 1913. Another pressure acting against the policy of restraint was the fact that Russia had had to back down from positions it had taken on behalf of the Balkan states in successive instances from the Bosnian crisis through the two Balkan wars. Sazonov was sensitive to the public outrage on these occasions as he demonstrated in his conduct during the Liman affair, which surprised his counterparts in Paris and London for its ardor.

In addition, advancing disarray within the council attenuated Kokovtsev's ability to restrain his more restive colleagues. After Kokovtsev's dismissal, Sazonov, who had chafed increasingly at the former's restraint, could no longer rely on the chairman's support when having to make unpopular decisions. Even if he had wanted to continue Stolypin's and Kokovtsev's course, he was isolated within the council against Krivoshein and Sukhomlinov, whose views the public and many within his own ministry supported. Kokovtsev's departure in fact saw the emergence of a significant faction within the council that favored a strong policy in support of Russia's Balkan allies.

In light of all of these considerations, it is difficult to conceive of any Russian government that could have held back from action in support of Serbia in July 1914. Its domestic authority already severely compromised by deteriorating relations with the Duma, advancing social unrest, and disarray within its own ranks, in refusing to aid Serbia the Russian government would have severed its last link with civil society. Sazonov recognized this fact in telling Nicholas that Russia would never forgive its sovereign were Russia not to come to Serbia's aid. Perhaps most ironically, it was a United Government, at least in form, that took the decision which Stolypin most feared and which had led to his efforts to control foreign policy in the first place. Within three years both he and his enemy Durnovo were proven right in their forebodings.

Notes

Bibliographical Essay

Index

# Abbreviations

BAR       Bakhmeteff Archive, Columbia University, New York.

BDOW      G. P. Gooch and H. N. Temperley, eds., *British Documents on the Origins of the War* (London: H. M. Stationery Office, 1927–1938).

DDF       Ministère des Affaires Etrangères, *Documents Diplomatiques Françaises* (Paris: Imprimerie Nationale, 1929–1936). Followed by series, volume, and page numbers.

FO        Public Record Office, Foreign Office records, London. Followed by department and file numbers.

GP        A. M. Bartholdy et al., eds., *Die Grosse Politik der Europäischen Kabinetten, 1871–1914: Sammlung der diplomatischen akten des Auswärtigen amtes* (Berlin: Deutsche Verlagsgesellschaft für Politik und Geschichte, 1922–1927). Followed by volume number.

HHSA, PA  Haus- Hof- und Staatsarkhiv (Vienna, Foreign Ministry archive) Politisches Archiv. Followed by department and carton numbers.

KA        *Krasnyi Arkhiv.* Followed by volume and page numbers.

MAE       Ministère des Affaires Etrangères (Paris); NS: Nouvelle Série; R: Russie. Followed by dossier number.

Ö-U A     *Österreich-Ungarns Aussenpolitik, von der Bosnischer Krise 1908 bis zum Kriegsausbruch 1914* (Vienna: österreicher Bundesverlag, 1930–1936).

TsGIA     Tsentral'nyi Gosudarstvennyi Istoricheskii Arkhiv, Leningrad. Followed by fund (*fond,* f.), register (*opis',* op.), and file (*delo,* d.) numbers.

TsGAOR    Tsentral'nyi Gosudarstvennyi Arkhiv Oktiabr'skoi Revoliutsii, Moscow. Followed by fund, register, and file numbers.

# Notes

## Introduction

1. See, for example, D. C. B. Lieven, *Russia and the Origins of the First World War* (New York: St. Martin's Press, 1983). On civil-military and strategic issues, William Fuller, *Civil-Military Conflict in Imperial Russia, 1881–1914* (Princeton: Princeton University Press, 1985); and K. F. Shatsillo, *Rossiia pered pervoi mirovoi voiny: Vooruzhennye sily tsarizma v 1905–1914 gg.* (Moscow: Nauka, 1974); on economic factors, Dietrich Geyer, *Der russische Imperialismus: Studien über den Zusammenhang von innerer und auswärtiger Politik, 1860–1914* (Göttingen: Vandenhoeck und Ruprecht, 1977), and René Girault, *Emprunts russes et investissements français en Russie, 1887–1914: Recherches sur l'investissement international* (Paris: A. Colin, 1973).
2. For good examples of such work in English, see the many works of Barbara Jelavich and George Kennan; Andrew Rossos, *Russia and the Balkans, 1908–1914* (Toronto: University of Toronto Press, 1981); Edward Thaden, *Russia and the Balkan Alliance of 1912* (State College, Penn.: Pennsylvania State University Press, 1965).
3. I. V. Bestuzhev, *Bor'ba po voprosam vneshnei politiki v Rossii, 1906–1910* (Moscow: Nauka, 1961). This is the most fully realized of his many studies. I. I. Astaf'ev, *Russko-germanskie diplomaticheskie otnosheniia, 1905–1911* (Moscow: Izdatel'stvo Moskovskogo Universiteta, 1972). This work undertakes an incisive critique of several methodological and documentary lapses in Bestuzhev's studies. At present, A. V. Georgiev is studying decision making within the Ministry of Foreign Affairs, including aspects of its relationship with the Council of Ministers during 1907–1914. See his article "Tsarizm i rossiiskaia diplomatiia nakanune pervoi mirovoi voiny," *Voprosy Istorii*, 3 (1988), 58–73.
4. Two German historians have adapted many of Bestuzhev's findings and sources, and added research of their own, to the analytical framework developed by Fritz Fischer. The result is a perplexing mixture of impressive sourcework and a Russia that looks curiously like the Kaiserreich, complete with the same mechanisms to absorb or divert the energies of newly modernized and urbanized Russian society, despite the relative peculiarities of pace and intensity in Russian industrialization. Another unexplained difference is the fact that social transformation compelled

tsarist policymakers after 1905 to renounce, rather than pursue, a course of imperial expansion. Dietrich Geyer, *Der russische Imperialismus;* and Caspar Ferenczi, *Aussenpolitik und öffentlichkeit in Russland, 1906–1912* (Husum: Matthiesen, 1982).

5. Although a very rich term in Russian political language, "society" *(obshchestvo)* usually meant educated urban and landowning noble society, rather than the broader group conveyed by the modern English use of the term. Thus, "public opinion" *(obshchestvennoe mnenie)* and "public men" *(obshchestvennye deiateli),* reflect the same restrictive sense of "society" as used in Russia. The term described those members of the population who, by virtue of education, wealth, or public service (in the press, the *zemstvo,* or other autonomous institutions), had an implied right to participate in politics but were thwarted by the state— portrayed as unitary, arbitrary, and external in intelligentsia and historical literature—at least until the advent of the post-1905 order. In this sense, "society" was notionally opposed to the state, on the one hand, and the as yet unconscious *narod*—peasants and workers—on the other.

 As is evident, all of these terminological juxtapositions of the components of imperial political and social life reflected an intellectual heritage rooted in the intelligentsia's embrace of Hegelian philosophy read *à la russe.* The larger dialectical *cum* metaphysical attributes of this definition were never far beneath the surface of this term, as seen in the title of V. A. Maklakov's memoir of the Duma period, *Vlast' i obshchestvennost' na zakate staroi Rossii* (Paris, 1930).

6. B. Anan'ich et al., *Krizis samoderzhaviia v Rossii, 1895–1917* (Leningrad: Nauka, 1984); L. G. Zakharova, "Krizis samoderzhaviia nakanune revoliutsii 1905 goda," *Voprosy Istorii,* 8 (1972), 119–141; Andrew Verner, *The Crisis of Russian Autocracy: Nicholas II and the 1905 Revolution* (Princeton: Princeton University Press, 1990); R. T. Manning, *The Crisis of the Old Order in Russia: Gentry and Government* (Princeton: Princeton University Press, 1982).

7. "Pis'ma S. Iu. Vitte k D. S. Sipiaginu," KA 18, 31–32.

8. See the treatments of the so-called Kakhanov Commission and the origins of the "Counter-Reforms" in P. A. Zaionchkovskii, *Krizis samoderzhaviia na rubezhe 1870–1880 godov* (Moscow: Mysl', 1964); and Francis William Wcislo, *Reforming Rural Russia: State, Local Society, and National Politics, 1855–1914* (Princeton: Princeton University Press, 1990), chaps. 2, 3.

9. The role of Nicholas's personality is the subject of Verner's recent study, *The Crisis of Russian Autocracy.*

10. See Wcislo, *Reforming Rural Russia,* introduction.

11. There is a large and still growing literature on the development of these views in imperial officialdom. Among the better works in English are: George Yaney, *The Systematization of Russian Government* (Champaign-Urbana, Ill.: University of Illinois Press, 1973); Walter Pintner and Don Rowney, eds., *Russian Officialdom: The Bureaucratization of Russian Society from the Seventeenth to the Twentieth Century* (Chapel Hill: University of North Carolina Press, 1980); Daniel Orlovsky, *The Limits of Reform: The Ministry of Internal Affairs in Imperial Russia, 1802–1881* (Cambridge, Mass.: Harvard University Press, 1981); Richard Wortman, *The Development of a Russian Legal Consciousness* (Chicago: University of Chicago Press, 1976); W. B. Lincoln, *In the Vanguard of Reform: Russia's*

*Enlightened Bureaucrats, 1825–1861* (De Kalb, Ill.: Northern Illinois University Press, 1982); Wcislo, *Reforming Rural Russia*.
12. Wcislo, *Reforming Rural Russia*, pp. 197–202.
13. A similar sort of argument is made in Verner's political biography of Nicholas II. My argument approaches the same relationship from the point of view of imperial officials, giving a correspondingly different view of Nicholas's ability and willingness to act.
14. TsGIA, f. 1544, op. 1, d. 5, 3–9.

## 1. The Witte Kingdom in the Far East

1. S. Iu. Vitte, *Vospominaniia* (Moscow: Sotsekgiz, 1960), II, 290–291.
2. General A. N. Kuropatkin, *The Russian Army and the Japanese War* (London, 1909), p. 185.
3. Ibid., p. 186. See also, "Perepiska S. Iu. Witte i A. N. Kuropatkina v 1904–1905gg.," KA 19, 68.
4. See "Nakanune russko-iaponskoi voiny," KA 63, 3–55.
5. A. M. de Besobrasow, "Les premières causes de l'effondrement de la Russie: Le conflit russo-japonais," *Le Correspondant,* 291 (1923), 577–615; Kuropatkin, *The Russian Army;* [V. M. Vonliarliarskii], "Why Russia Went to War with Japan: The Story of the Yalu Concession," *Fortnightly Review,* 87, n.s. (1910), 816–831, 1030–1043; B. B. Glinskii, *Prolog russko-iaponskoi voiny: Materialy iz arkhiva grafa S. Iu. Vitte* (Petrograd: Brockgauz-Efron, 1916). The themes touched on in these works have been elaborated in the histories of these events, e.g., J. A. White, *The Diplomacy of the Russo-Japanese War* (Princeton: Princeton University Press, 1964); still the best work on the origins of the war in English is the Andrew Malozemoff's posthumously published *Russian Far Eastern Policy, 1881–1904* (Berkeley: University of California Press, 1958). The newest interpretation is given in Dietrich Geyer, *Der russische Imperialismus, Kritische Studien zur Geschichtswissenschaft* (Göttingen: Vandenhoeck und Ruprecht, 1977). A more traditional definition of imperialism and its dynamic is found in B. A. Romanov's definitive *Rossiia v Manchzhurii (1892–1906)* (Leningrad: Izdatel'stvo Instituta Dal'nego Vostoka, 1928). From its initial publication the work was the subject of controversy. An introduction appended by the publisher criticizes Romanov for overrating the role of personalities while neglecting the underpinnings of Russian imperialism. In 1947, Romanov published an eviscerated version of his masterwork, entitled *Ocherki diplomaticheskoi istorii russko-iaponskoi voiny, 1895–1907* (Moscow and Leningrad: Nauka, 1947), which was reissued in the late 1950s, with a slight pruning of the frequent references to Stalin in the first edition.
6. Two exceptions are Romanov, *Rossiia v Manchzhurii,* and L. G. Zakharova, "Krizis samoderzhaviia nakanune revoliutsii 1905 goda," *Voprosy Istorii,* 8 (1972), 119–141. For published primary sources giving these perspectives, see the diaries of General A. N. Kuropatkin, published in KA 2, 5–112, and KA 5, 82–99; and State Council member A. A. Polovtsev, in KA 3, 75–172, and KA 4, 64–128.
7. "Pis'ma S. Iu. Vitte k D. S. Sipiaginu," KA 18, 31–32.

8. For an interesting discussion of the mixed nature of autocratic power, see Andrew Verner, *The Crisis of Russian Autocracy: Nicholas II and the 1905 Revolution* (Princeton: Princeton University Press, 1990), chap. 3.
9. A. F. Koni, *Sobranie sochinenii* (Moscow: Iuridicheskaia Literatura, 1968), V, 252.
10. "Dnevnik A. N. Kuropatkina," KA 2, 11.
11. *Dnevnik A. N. Kuropatkina* (Nizhnii Novgorod: Nizhpoligraf, 1924), pp. 11–12.
12. Romanov, *Rossiia v Manchzhurii*, p. 111, n. 2. Construction of single lines for most of the route in Russia and all of the Chinese track was completed in late 1901. Glinskii, *Prolog*, p. 62.
13. Glinskii, *Prolog*, pp. 61–62.
14. See, for example, BDOW, I, 6–8, II, 39–40.
15. Vitte, *Vospominaniia*, I, 212.
16. A. P. Iswolsky, *Recollections of a Foreign Minister* (Toronto: Doubleday, 1921), p. 128.
17. Romanov, *Rossiia v Manchzhurii*, p. 121. These payments were treated in CER accounts as a construction expense. See also Witte's copy of a MF report dated 20 November 1902, "On the secret fund for the affairs of the Chinese Eastern Railway," BAR, Witte Collection. It gives an account of expenditures "in accordance with SUPREME instructions given out to Chinese *sanovniki*." According to the report, Li Hun-chan received in excess of 1.6 million rubles, with other Chinese and Mongolian officials being paid considerably less.
18. Text in Romanov, *Rossiia v Manchzhurii*, p. 44.
19. Iswolsky, *Recollections*, p. 121.
20. V. I. Gurko, *Features and Figures of the Past* (Stanford: Stanford University Press, 1939), p. 259.
21. See also E. J. Dillon, *The Eclipse of Russia* (New York, George H. Doran Co., 1918), p. 255.
22. Kuropatkin, *The Russian Army*, pp. 139–140.
23. Iswolsky, *Recollections*, p. 113.
24. Article attributed to Vonliarliarskii, "Why Russia Went to War with Japan," p. 820.
25. Ibid.; Gurko, *Features*, p. 32; Iswolsky, *Recollections*, pp. 112–113.
26. For biographical information on Witte see his *Vospominaniia*, vol. 1, and T. von Laue, *Sergei Witte and the Industrialization of Russia* (New York: Atheneum, 1969).
27. Von Laue, *Sergei Witte*, p. 48; Vitte, *Vospominaniia*, I, 203.
28. Von Laue, *Sergei Witte*, p. 47.
29. Vitte, *Vospominaniia*, I, 207.
30. Text in Romanov, *Rossiia v Manchzhurii*, pp. 56–59. See also Glinskii, *Prolog*, pp. 9–13.
31. Vitte, *Vospominaniia*, I, 434. Earlier attempts to build the railway had been thwarted by the resistance of Witte's predecessor, I. A. Vyshnegradskii.
32. Ibid., p. 434. Witte claimed Alexander was skeptical about Nicholas's ability to chair this committee.
33. According to Malozemoff, Nicholas's interest in Siberia and neighboring East Asia was due to the influence of Prince Enver Enverovich Ukhtomskii, who had

served as the tsarevich's tutor during the Asian voyage. Ukhtomskii was tied to a school of thought known as the Easterners *(Vostochniki)*, who felt that Russia's historical destiny lay in the East. Malozemoff, *Russian Far Eastern Policy*, pp. 42–43.

34. See Romanov, *Rossiia v Manchzhurii*, p. 111, n. 2; Vitte, *Vospominaniia*, II, 50–52.

35. Gurko, *Features*, p. 32.

36. On Nicholas see, among many other works, Verner, *The Crisis of Russian Autocracy;* Alexander, Grand Duke of Russia, *Once a Grand Duke* (New York: Farrar and Rinehart, 1932); Jacques Grand-Carteret, *Nicolas ange de la paix, empereur du knout, devant l'objectif caricatural* (Paris: J. Michaud, 1906); Constantine de Grunwald, *Le Tsar Nicolas II* (Paris: Editions Berger-Leviault, 1965); V. I. Gurko, *Tsar' i tsaritsa* (Paris: Vozrozhdenie, 1927); A. A. Mosolov, *At the Court of the Last Tsar* (London, 1935); S. S. Ol'denburg, *Tsarstvovanie Imperatora Nikolaia II* (Munich, 1949), 2 vols.

37. Alexander Mikhailovich, *Once a Grand Duke*, p. 1.

38. Vitte, *Vospominaniia*, I, 435.

39. His sometime tutor K. P. Pobedonostsev was scathing in discussing the new emperor. In conversation with a fellow official, the procurator remarked that "he grasps what he hears, but grasps only the meaning of the isolated fact, without relation to the rest, without connection to the totality of other factors, events, currents, phenomenon . . . For him there exists no broad, general view worked out through the exchange of ideas, argument, debate." Cited in P. A. Zaionchkovskii, *Pravitel'stvennyi apparat samoderzhavnoi Rossii v XIX v.* (Moscow: Mysl', 1978), p. 195.

40. Verner in *The Crisis of Russian Autocracy*, gives a particularly good account of these tensions, pp. 14–20.

41. See ibid., pp. 34–44.

42. Alexander III has been a strangely neglected figure in Russian historical biography. See P. A. Zaionchkovskii, *Rossiiskoe samoderzhavie v kontse XIX stoletiia* (Moscow: Izdatel'stvo Moskovskogo Universiteta, 1970), chap. 1; Vitte, *Vospominaniia*, I, chap. 18.

43. This "distance" between Nicholas as ruler and in other capacities is evident throughout his reign. It is reflected in his laconic diary, TsGAOR, f. 601, op. 1, dd. 217–276, and in his correspondence, both of which largely ignore the momentous events of his reign in favor of details about the weather or family life. See Verner, *Crisis of Russian Autocracy*, p. 43.

44. A. V. Bogdanovich, *Tri poslednikh samoderzhtsa: Dnevnik A. V. Bogdanovich* (Moscow and Leningrad, 1924), p. 252.

45. Cited in Verner, *Crisis of Russian Autocracy*, pp. 35–36.

46. See Nicholas's remarks at Tsarskoe Selo in April 1906, during the revision of the Fundamental Laws. The protocols of these conferences are given in "Tsarskosel'skie soveshchaniia," *Byloe*, 4 (1917), 283–345.

47. See, for example, Witte's essay *Autocracy and the Zemstvo*, of which there is an excellent discussion in Francis William Wcislo, *Reforming Rural Russia: State, Local Society, and National Politics, 1855–1914* (Princeton: Princeton University Press, 1990), pp. 131–134.

48. Romanov, *Rossiia v Manchzhurii,* pp. 98–99; A. Popov, "Pervye shagi russkogo imperializma na Dal'nem Vostoke (1888–1903gg.)," KA vol. 52 (for "Pervye shagi"), pp. 83–91 (for MID objections to the Manchurian route and Witte's response).
49. On the MID's attitude to the Far East, see Vitte, *Vospominaniia,* I, 44.
50. Romanov, *Rossiia v Manchzhurii,* pp. 186–190; Vitte, *Vospominaniia,* II, chap. 27. The events associated with the Port Arthur annexation are also given in great detail in *Istoricheskaia spravka o vazhneishikh dlia Rossii sobytiiakh na Dal'nem Vostoke v trekhletie 1898–1900* (St. Petersburg: Izdatel'stvo Ministerstva Finansov, 1902).
51. Vitte, *Vospominaniia,* II, 111–113; and a letter from Muravev to Witte, 17 January 1898, in response to a letter in which Witte criticized Muravev's policy. Muravev answered, "I have the honor to inform your dear sir [*Milostivyi Gosudar'*] that Russia's general policy is directed exclusively by the Autocratic will of the SOVEREIGN EMPEROR," which was fulfilled by the Ministry of Foreign Affairs. TsGIA, f. 1622, op. 1, d. 130. Others shared Witte's attitude. See, e.g., "Dnevnik A. A. Polovtseva," KA 3, 109; Gurko, *Features,* p. 255.
52. Vitte, *Vospominaniia,* II, 140–141.
53. Glinskii, *Prolog,* pp. 53–54.
54. Ibid., p. 54.
55. BDOW, I, 16.
56. Vitte, *Vospominaniia,* II, 141. Witte's acceptance was forced in a meeting with Nicholas, who told him that the decision on Port Arthur had been made for better or worse "but in any case, this matter was finished and he would not change it; therefore the sovereign asked me to offer him co-operation, so that this matter be executed as favorably as possible."
57. TsGIA, f. 560, op. 22, d. 209. This *delo* from the MF chancellery is entitled "On payments from the special fund in connection with the conclusion of the Port Arthur convention." The convention cost the Russian government 1.4 million rubles (p. 49).
58. Vitte, *Vospominaniia,* II, 142.
59. The emperor found the news "[s]o good that it is even hard to believe." Ibid.
60. Ibid.
61. Text in Glinskii, *Prolog,* p. 61.
62. BDOW, I, 40–41. The accord was signed on 16/28 April.
63. BDOW, I, 39.
64. Romanov, *Rossiia v Manchzhurii,* p. 237.
65. See Kuropatkin's letter to Witte, text in ibid., p. 226.
66. "Bokserskoe vosstanie," KA 4, 13.
67. Ibid., pp. 14–15.
68. Vitte, *Vospominaniia,* II, 175–176.
69. On Lamzdorf, see Iswolsky, *Recollections,* pp. 136–140; Dillon, *Eclipse,* pp. 253–254; Vitte, *Vospominaniia,* II, 177.
70. Vitte, *Vospominaniia,* II, 177–179; "Pis'ma k Sipiaginu," KA 18, 36.
71. Dillon, *Eclipse,* p. 254.
72. Iswolsky, *Recollections,* pp. 137–138.
73. "Bokserskoe vosstanie," p. 16; Glinskii, *Prolog,* pp. 112–113.

74. Glinskii, *Prolog*, pp. 111–112.
75. Ibid., p. 115.
76. "Bokserskoe vosstanie," pp. 17–19.
77. Ibid., p. 33.
78. Ibid., p. 37.
79. Gurko, *Features*, p. 51.
80. "Pis'ma k Sipiaginu," KA 18, 36.
81. Glinskii, *Prolog*, p. 109.
82. For a detailed account of these operations, see ibid., pp. 110–117.
83. Ibid., pp. 116–117.
84. "Pis'ma k Sipiaginu," KA 18, 39.
85. Ibid., p. 40.
86. Glinskii, *Prolog*, p. 106.
87. One biographer suggests that the only happy and comfortable time of Nicholas's life was his service as a colonel in the Preobrazhenskii Guards in the early 1890s. Grunwald, *Nicolas II*, pp. 6–7.
88. Text in Glinskii, *Prolog*, pp. 121–122.
89. Romanov, *Rossiia v Manchzhurii*, pp. 259–260.
90. Ibid., p. 266.
91. Ibid., pp. 267–268.
92. Ibid., p. 267.
93. Glinskii, *Prolog*, pp. 118–119.
94. See, for example, the conference journal from 31 October 1900, cited at length in Romanov, *Rossiia v Manchzhurii*, pp. 269–270; Kuropatkin's letter to Lamsdorf, 3 December 1900, "Bokserskoe vosstanie," p. 41.
95. See, for example, the journal of a special conference held in June 1901 on this issue in Glinskii, *Prolog*, pp. 173–175.
96. He later complained of the ensuing "duality of authority" in Manchuria, contrasting the CER administration's "peaceloving policy" with Kuropatkin's annexationist urges. Vitte, *Vospominaniia*, II, 180.
97. Romanov, *Rossiia v Manchzhurii*, pp. 284–290.
98. Glinskii, *Prolog*, pp. 141–145.
99. Text in Romanov, *Rossiia v Manchzhurii*, pp. 296–301.
100. "Dnevnik Polovtseva," KA 3, 87.
101. Romanov, *Ocherki*, pp. 37–38.
102. "Dnevnik Polovtseva," KA 3, 94.
103. See, for example, BDOW, II, 39–40; "Nakanune russko-iaponskoi voiny," KA 63 (1934), 16.
104. BDOW, II, 50.
105. "Nakanune russko-iaponskoi voiny," pp. 23–24.
106. Ibid., pp. 3–55; BDOW, II, 34.
107. "Nakanune russlo-iaponskoi voiny," p. 28; Romanov, *Ocherki*, pp. 136–137.
108. "Nakanune russko-iaponskoi voiny," pp. 32–35.
109. BDOW, II, 130–131.
110. A good summary of Russia's Korean policy is given by Lamzdorf in a letter from 1901, published in "Nakanune russko-iaponskoi voiny," pp. 42–43.
111. Glinskii, *Prolog*, pp. 173–175.

112. Text in "Nakanune russko-iaponskoi voiny," p. 46; Lamzdorf's comments to Nicholas and Izvol'skii are given in ibid., pp. 44, 47.
113. Gurko, *Features*, p. 271. On Izvolskii's discussions in Tokyo, see "Nakanune russko-iaponskoi voiny," pp. 38–41.
114. Nicholas in particular had come to oppose Russia's previous official position on Korea. In October, he told a visitor, "I do not want to seize Korea—but under no circumstances can I allow the Japanese to become firmly established there. That would be a *casus belli*." Quoted in Oldenburg, *Tsarstvovanie*, II, 55 and in Romanov, *Ocherki*, p. 163. The war minister warned that agreement with Japan "should not be bought at too dear a price," "Nakanune russko-iaponskoi voiny," p. 49.
115. Text in "Nakanune russko-iaponskoi voiny," p. 51.
116. Glinskii, *Prolog*, pp. 188–189.
117. In addition, deployment of Chinese troops would depend only on Russian approval while Russian soldiers remained in Manchuria; thereafter, China would merely inform the Russian government of troop movements without seeking preliminary approval. Glinskii, *Prolog*, p. 179.
118. Romanov, *Rossiia v Manchzhurii*, p. 354.
119. Text in Glinskii, *Prolog*, pp. 180–183.
120. In a letter informing Witte of the treaty's signing, Lamzdorf wrote, "Hurrah! or only Oof!" TsGIA, f. 1622, op. 1, d. 339, p. 1.
121. The word used by Alekseev was *ustupchivost'*. "Dnevnik Polovtseva," KA 3, 134–135, entry for 11 April 1902. See the letter written to Nicholas from Manchuria by I. P. Balashev, cited in M. N. Pokrovskii, ed., *Russko-iaponskaia voina: Iz dnevnikov A. N. Kuropatkina i N. P. Linevicha* (Leningrad: Tsentrarkhiv, 1925), pp. 133–135.
122. Vitte, *Vospominaniia*, II, 225.
123. Romanov, *Rossiia v Manchzhurii*, pp. 360–362.
124. Witte muted the much harsher tone of his original draft. This report is cited almost in its entirety in Glinskii, *Prolog*, pp. 190–241. TsGIA, f. 560, op. 22, d. 767, contains Witte's original draft and a corrected final version.
125. Glinskii, *Prolog*, p. 194.
126. Ibid., pp. 218–221.
127. Ibid., p. 204.
128. Ibid., pp. 204–205.
129. Ibid., p. 214.
130. Ibid., p. 215.
131. Ibid., p. 216.
132. Ibid., p. 243.
133. "Dnevnik Kuropatkina," KA 2, 12.
134. Glinskii, *Prolog*, p. 368; Romanov, *Rossiia v Manchzhurii*, p. 415.
135. Glinskii, *Prolog*, p. 369.
136. "Dnevnik Kuropatkina," KA 2, 20.
137. Text in Popov, "Pervye shagi," pp. 110–123.
138. Ibid., pp. 117–120.
139. Ibid., pp. 120–122.
140. Ibid., p. 122.

141. Ibid., p. 123.
142. Ibid., p. 111.
143. Ibid., pp. 114–115.
144. His report on Russian security in 1900 had noted that "our western frontier has never in the whole history of Russia been exposed to such danger in the event of a European war as it is now." Kuropatkin, *The Russian Army,* p. 77.

## 2. The All-Out Bezobrazovshchina

1. "Pis'ma S. Iu. Vitte k D. S. Sipiaginu," KA 18, 44. The expression "all-out Bezobrazovshchina" is the title given by Witte to the file in his personal papers that treats these events. BAR, Witte Collection, file 23.
2. "Pis'ma k Sipiaginu," p. 45.
3. M. N. Pokrovskii, ed., *Russko-iaponskaia voina: Iz dnevnikov A. N. Kuropatkina i N. P. Linevicha* (Leningrad: Tsentrarkhiv, 1926). This compilation contains excerpts from the diaries referred to in the title, as well as correspondence among the members of the Bezobrazov group, Nicholas, and the three ministers.
4. On Bezobrazov, see J. A. White, *The Diplomacy of the Russo-Japanese War* (Princeton: Princeton University Press, 1964), pp. 35–36; B. A. Romanov, *Ocherki diplomaticheskoi istorii russko-iaponskoi voiny* (Moscow and Leningrad: Nauka, 1947), p. 77.
5. S. Iu. Vitte, *Vospominaniia,* (Moscow: Sotsekgiz, 1960), II, 182.
6. V. M. Vonliarliarskii, *Moi vospominaniia* (Berlin: Russkoe Natsional'noe Izdatel'stvo, 1939), pp. 104–105.
7. See R. Manning, *The Crisis of the Old Order in Russia: Gentry and Government* (Princeton: Princeton University Press, 1982); B. Veselovskii, "Dvizhenie zemlevladel'tsev," in L. Martov, P. Maslov, and A. Potresov, eds., *Obshchestvennoe dvizhenie v Rossii v nachale XX-go veka* (St. Petersburg: Obshchestvennaia Pol'za, 1909), I, 291–312.
8. Vonliarliarskii, *Vospominaniia,* pp. 115–117.
9. Clothworkers had struck the factory. Witte summoned the affected factory owners and blamed them for the strikes, ordering them to concede to many of the strikers' demands. Ibid., pp. 122–123.
10. Ibid., p. 139.
11. [Vonliarliarskii], "Why Russia Went to War with Japan: The Story of the Yalu Concession," *Fortnightly Review,* 87, n.s. (1910), 822–824. The article is unsigned but attributed to Vonliarliarskii by the editors in an introductory section.
12. Ibid., p. 824.
13. A. M. de Besobrasow, "Les premières causes de l'effondrement de la Russie: Le conflit russo-japonais," *Le Correspondant,* 291 (1923), 578.
14. Vonliarliarskii, *Vospominaniia,* pp. 150–151.
15. B. B. Glinskii, *Prolog russko-iaponskoi voiny: Materialy iz arkhiva grafa S. Iu. Vitte* (Petrograd: Brokgauz-Efron, 1916), p. 250.
16. [Vonliarliarskii], "Why Russia Went to War," 1056.
17. Ibid., p. 1032; Vonliarliarskii, *Vospominaniia,* p. 132.
18. Vonliarliarskii, *Vospominaniia,* p. 134.

19. B. A. Romanov, *Rossiia v Manchzhurii* (Leningrad: Izdatel'stvo Instituta Dal'nego Vostoka, 1926), pp. 388–389.
20. Besobrasow, "Les premières causes," pp. 586–587.
21. Text in Romanov, *Rossiia v Manchzhurii*, pp. 393–394.
22. Text in Vonliarliarskii, *Vospominaniia*, pp. 139–143, and Besobrasow, "Les premières causes," pp. 587–588.
23. Vonliarliarskii, *Vospominaniia*, p. 120.
24. Text in Romanov, *Rossiia v Manchzhurii*, p. 395.
25. Text in A. Popov, "Pervye shagi russkogo imperializma na Dal'nem Vostoke (1888–1903gg.)," KA 52, 108–109. The minister of finances was now to be informed of all available Manchurian concessions and could order the bank to acquire them. Such concessions would be entrusted to companies or individuals to be named by the minister. Witte further shored up his position by including the statement that the bank was "obliged generally to act according to the instructions of the Minister of Finances in all questions connected with the . . . agreements between the bank and the Chinese government."
26. Besobrasow, "Les premières causes," p. 590.
27. Romanov, *Rossiia v Manchzhurii*, pp. 399–400.
28. Cited in ibid., p. 400.
29. *Dnevnik A. N. Kuropatkina*, (Nizhnii Novgorod: Nizhpoligraf, 1923), pp. 11–12.
30. For a good discussion of Witte's and Pleve's differences in this regard, see Francis William Wcislo, *Reforming Rural Russia: State, Local Society, and National Politics, 1855–1914* (Princeton: Princeton University Press, 1990), pp. 120–151.
31. V. I. Gurko, *Features and Figures of the Past: Government and Opinion in the Reign of Nicholas* (Stanford: Stanford University Press, 1939), pp. 108–110.
32. Ibid., p. 272.
33. "Dnevnik A. A. Polovtseva," KA 3, 99–100.
34. Ibid., pp. 164–165. This contrast was also drawn by Kuropatkin, who observed that "[t]hese days have passed in the celebration of the centennial of the Corps de Pages. They have inflated these holidays not a little. It is as if nobody in Russia did anything anywhere except for the pages." *Dnevnik A. N. Kuropatkina*, p. 15.
35. Gurko, *Features*, p. 33.
36. "Dnevnik A. N. Kuropatkina," KA 2, 11.
37. For Witte's account of these events, see his *Vospominaniia*, II, 228–237.
38. "Dnevnik Polovtseva," KA 3, 150.
39. "Dnevnik Kuropatkina," KA 2, 11–12. The Yalu enterprise also cropped up in a conversation between Kuropatkin and Russia's man in Seoul, Pavlov, on the eve of the 11 January 1903 conference. Pavlov was concerned about the motives and goals of the owners of the concession. *Dnevnik A. N. Kuropatkina*, p. 23.
40. Romanov, *Rossiia v Manchzhurii*, p. 405.
41. *Dnevnik A. N. Kuropatkina*, p. 7.
42. Ibid., p. 29.
43. TsGIA, f. 1622, op. 1, dd. 185–209; and B. A. Romanov, "Vitte nakanune russko-iaponskoi voiny," *Rossiia i Zapad*, 1 (1923), 240, 242, 247.
44. TsGIA, f. 1622, op. 1, d. 186.
45. Ibid., d. 191.

46. Text in Vonliarliarskii, *Vospominaniia,* pp. 148–149.

47. TsGIA, f. 1622, op. 1, dd. 188, 192.

48. Ibid., d. 192.

49. "Dnevnik Kuropatkina," KA 2, 30.

50. Ibid., p. 31.

51. Ibid.

52. Ibid., pp. 31–32.

53. TsGIA, f. 1622, op. 1, d. 192.

54. Romanov, "Vitte nakanune," p. 255.

55. TsGIA, f. 1622, op. 1, d. 194.

56. "Dnevnik Kuropatkina," KA 2, 37.

57. Ibid., p. 33.

58. Ibid., p. 34.

59. An abridged text of this report, "Rastsenka polozheniia," is given in Glinskii, *Prolog,* pp. 314ff.

60. "Dnevnik Kuropatkina," KA 2, 34.

61. Ibid., p. 38; *imperatorskaia* and *bezobrazovskaia.*

62. Romanov,"Vitte nakanune," pp. 160–161; Glinskii, *Prolog,* p. 257.

63. Glinskii, *Prolog,* p. 257. The security force was made up of local toughs *(khunkhuzy)* who had been recruited after Kuropatkin's objections to the proposed use of Russian troops. *Dnevnik A. N. Kuropatkina,* p. 44. Kuropatkin learned of this measure from Abaza, who added that it represented a favorable outcome to the problem. Kuropatkin called this information *dikovinnaia novost'*.

64. Telegram, Pokotilov to the MF, 10 March 1903, TsGIA, f. 1622, op. 1, d. 199, p. 1ob.

65. Text in Besobrasow, "Les premières causes," pp. 596–597.

66. Ibid., p. 597.

67. "Dnevnik Kuropatkina," KA 2, 40. There is no complete published primary account of this conference. Romanov, Glinskii, and Bezobrazov all give truncated reports, each of which includes lengthy citations from the protocols. A copy of the conference journal can be found in BAR, Witte Collection, file 23.

68. BAR, Witte Collection, file 23; Glinskii, *Prolog,* p. 277; Romanov, "Vitte nakanune," p. 262.

69. Romanov, "Vitte nakanune," p. 263.

70. Glinskii, *Prolog,* p. 277.

71. Romanov, "Vitte nakanune," p. 264.

72. Glinskii, *Prolog,* p. 278.

73. Ibid.

74. "Kopiia zhurnala soveshchaniia 28 marta 1903 g.," BAR, Witte Collection, file 23; Romanov, "Vitte nakanune," p. 264.

75. "Kopiia zhurnala"; Glinskii, *Prolog,* pp. 278–281; Romanov, "Vitte nakanune," p. 264; Besobrasow, "Les premières causes," pp. 598–599.

76. "Kopiia zhurnala."

77. Witte had received a telegram from Shanghai about press reports on the possibility of a Russo-Japanese war over the Yalu concession. He gave it to Nicholas on the eve of the conference. Romanov, "Vitte nakanune," p. 262.

78. Romanov, "Vitte nakanune," pp. 259–261.

79. TsGIA, f. 1622, op. 1, dd. 202, 203.
80. Ibid., d. 206.
81. "Dnevnik Kuropatkina," KA 2, 41.
82. *Dnevnik A. N. Kuropatkina*, p. 49.
83. Ibid., p. 43.
84. A. P. Iswolsky, *Recollections of a Foreign Minister* (Toronto: Doubleday, 1921), p. 123.
85. Cited in Glinskii, *Prolog*, p. 262.
86. Text in Besobrasow, "Les premières causes," pp. 592–596.
87. Text in Glinskii, *Prolog*, pp. 260–268.
88. Ibid., p. 593.
89. Ibid., p. 595.
90. Glinskii, *Prolog*, p. 262.
91. Ibid., p. 263; emphasis in original.
92. Ibid.
93. Glinskii, *Prolog*, pp. 263–264; see also Besobrasow, "Les premières causes," pp. 612–613. The tortuous language in these reports is not solely the responsibility of the translator. Ironically, as Bezobrazov rose in Nicholas's favor, he began to affect a grandiloquent sort of what he must have imagined as "bureaucratese" in his written language. This tendency became especially noticeable after 7 May.
94. In addition to the forestry operation, Bezobrazov claimed to control concessions for coal mines, steamship lines, and electrical lighting in Mukden and Girin, "Les premières causes," pp. 612–613.
95. Ibid., p. 261.
96. TsGAOR, f. 601, d. 245, p. 178.
97. Cited in Romanov, *Rossiia v Manchzhurii*, p. 409; also Besobrasow, "Les premières causes," p. 613.
98. Romanov, *Ocherki*, p. 209; L. G. Zakharova, "Krizis samoderzhaviia nakanune revoliutsii 1905 goda," *Voprosy Istorii*, 8 (1972), 129; Vitte, *Vospominaniia*, II, 239.
99. Pokrovskii, *Russko-iaponskaia voina*, p. 135.
100. Besobrasow, "Les premières causes," p. 605.
101. Pokrovskii, *Russko-iaponskaia voina*, p. 135. Interestingly, this letter was dated 7 May.
102. Both reports are given in Pokrovskii, *Russko-iaponskaia voina;* Vogak memo, pp. 12–16; Abaza, pp. 18–20. See also Glinskii, *Prolog*, p. 285, on the Vogak memo; and Besobrasow, "Les premières causes," p. 604. These last two sources note that Abaza's memorandum was submitted after the conference.
103. BAR, Witte Collection, file 23, "Zhurnal Osobogo Soveshchaniia, 7-go maia, 1903"; Pokrovskii, *Russko-iaponskaia voina*, p. 21.
104. Pokrovskii, *Russko-iaponskaia voina*, p. 21.
105. Ibid., p. 23.
106. Ibid.
107. Ibid.
108. Ibid., pp. 21–22.
109. Ibid., p. 22.
110. Kuropatkin clearly shared this view. He described the conference as merely the

occasion on which to inform the participants of the new decisions; it was not meant to discuss them, ibid., pp. 24–25.

111. Ibid., p. 23.
112. Ibid., pp. 12–15.; precis given in BAR, Witte Collection, file 23, "Zhurnal Osobogo Soveschaniia."
113. Cited in Besobrasow, "Les premières causes," p. 606; see also Glinskii, *Prolog*, p. 286, on Pleve's support for the Bezobrazov group; and Vonliarliarskii, *Vospominaniia*, p. 152.
114. Glinskii, *Prolog*, pp. 281, 285–286.
115. Pokrovskii, *Russko-iaponskaia voina*, p. 24.
116. Ibid.; Besobrasow, "Les premières causes," p. 606.
117. Pokrovskii, *Russko-iaponskaia voina*, p. 9.
118. Vonliarliarskii, *Vospominaniia*, p. 152.
119. Pokrovskii, *Russko-iaponskai voina*, p. 9.
120. Ibid., p. 136.
121. Text of letter in ibid., pp. 137–138.
122. Ibid., pp. 141–142.
123. See his letter to Witte, dated 30 May 1903, in BAR, Witte Collection, file 23.
124. Letter from Bezobrazov to Nicholas, 29 May, in Pokrovskii, *Russko-iaponskaia voina*, pp. 142–143.
125. Ibid., p. 139, They also visited Witte and Sakharov, pp. 139–140.
126. Romanov, "Vitte nakanune," p. 439.
127. Pokrovskii, *Russko-iaponskaia voina*, p. 11.
128. Glinskii, *Prolog*, p. 289, including the text of the charter, which is also in BAR, Witte Collection, file 23.

## 3. The Defeat of the Triumvirate and the Coming of War

1. B. A. Romanov, *Rossiia v Manchzhurii* (Leningrad: Izdatel'stvo Instituta Dal'nego Vostoka, 1926), pp. 430–431.
2. Ibid.
3. M. N. Pokrovskii, ed., *Russko-iaponskaia voina: Iz dnevnikov A. N. Kuropatkina i N. P. Linevicha* (Leningrad: Tsentrarkhiv, 1926), p. 8.
4. Ibid.
5. Of these developments, Lamzdorf wrote to Witte, "the information gathered by War Minister Kuropatkin will hardly have any meaning. The once ruined Military Agent, and now genial Major General of the Suite Vogak will correct and add to this information!" TsGIA, f. 1622, op. 1, d. 210, 19 May 1903.
6. Pokrovskii, *Russko-iaponskaia voina*, pp. 26–30.
7. The Russian envoy Rosen supported this impression. He noted popular feelings that Japan had already been slighted by Russia in 1895. Pokrovskii, *Russko-iaponskaia voina*, p. 26. See also J. A. White, *The Diplomacy of the Russo-Japanese War* (Princeton: Princeton University Press, 1964), pp. 66–69.
8. Pokrovskii, *Russko-iaponskaia voina*, p. 8.
9. Ibid., p. 143. The words are from a letter written by Bezobrazov on 3 June.
10. Text in *Dnevnik A. N. Kuropatkina* (Nizhnii Novgorod: Nizhpoligraf, 1923), pp. 73–74.
11. Text in *Dokumenty po peregovoram s Iaponiei 1903–1904gg., khraniashchiesya*

    *v Kantseliarii Osobogo Komiteta Dal'nego Vostoka* (St. Petersburg, 1905), pp. 13–14, and Pokrovskii, *Russko-iaponskaia voina,* p. 29.

12. This is also how Kuropatkin understood it, Pokrovskii, *Russko-iaponskaia voina,* p. 26.

13. Ibid., p. 29.

14. There are several published accounts of the conferences: B. B. Glinskii, *Prolog russko-iaponskoi voiny: Materialy iz arkhiva grafa S. Iu. Vitte* (Petrograd: Brokgauz-Efron, 1916), pp. 293–309; Pokrovskii, *Russko-iaponskaia voina,* pp. 29–32; A. M. de Besobrasow, "Les premières causes de l'effondrement de la Russie: Le conflit russo-japonais," *Le Correspondant,* 291 (1923), 608–610; Romanov, *Rossiia v Manchzhurii,* pp. 437–439.

15. Pokrovskii, *Russko-iaponskaia voina,* p. 30; Glinskii, *Prolog,* p. 295.

16. Glinskii, *Prolog,* p. 297.

17. Pokrovskii, *Russko-iaponskaia voina,* p. 32.

18. Glinskii, *Prolog,* pp. 304–305.

19. Ibid., p. 305; journal cited in Pokrovskii, *Russko-iaponskaia voina,* pp. 31–32.

20. Pokrovskii, *Russko-iaponskaia voina,* p. 32.

21. Glinskii, *Prolog,* p. 309.

22. Besobrasow, "Les premières causes," 609.

23. TsGIA, f. 1622, op. 1, d. 224.

24. Pokrovskii, *Russko-iaponskaia voina,* p. 158: letter from Bezobrazov to Nicholas. "I could not cope with the coalition alone."

25. Romanov, *Rossiia v Manchzhurii,* p. 439; Besobrasow, "Les premières causes," p. 611.

26. "Dnevnik A. N. Kuropatkina," KA 2, 44.

27. Ibid. The editor of the diary, B. A. Romanov, suggests this interpretation.

28. Glinskii, *Prolog,* pp. 319–324.

29. Pokrovskii, *Russko-iaponskaia voina,* pp. 152–153.

30. Bezobrazov linked the two—*voenno-politicheskii.* Ibid., p. 152.

31. *Neposredstvennoe rukovodstvo.*

32. Pokrovskii, *Russko-iaponskaia voina,* p. 152.

33. Glinskii, *Prolog,* p. 346; Pokrovskii, *Russko-iaponskaia voina,* p. 34.

34. Glinskii, *Prolog,* p. 346.

35. "Dnevnik Kuropatkina," KA 2, 45; S. Iu. Vitte, *Vospminaniia* (Moscow: Sotsekgiz, 1960), II, 239; Baron R. Rosen, *Forty Years of Diplomacy* (New York: Alfred A. Knopf, 1922), I, 220–223.

36. "Dnevnik Kuropatkina," KA 2, 45.

37. Pokrovskii, *Russko-iaponskaia voina,* p. 33; see also *Dnevnik A. N. Kuropatkina,* p. 62.

38. Pokrovskii, *Russko-iaponskaia voina,* pp. 33–34.

39. Ibid., pp. 154–156.

40. Ibid., p. 157.

41. Ibid., p. 158.

42. *Dnevnik A. N. Kuropatkina,* pp. 62, 63–64.

43. Ibid., p. 65; Vitte, *Vospominaniia,* II, 242–244.

44. Pokrovskii, *Russko-iaponskaia voina,* p. 157.

45. BAR, Kryzhanovskii Collection, box 2, typescript essay on Pleve.

46. "Dnevnik Kuropatkina," KA 2, 59–60.
47. Vitte, *Vospominaniia*, II, 242–247.
48. *Dnevnik A. N. Kuropatkina*, pp. 65–66.
49. Romanov, *Rossiia v Manchzhurii*, is one of the earliest works to discuss this "crisis." See also *Krizis samoderzhaviia 1895–1917* (Leningrad: Nauka, 1984); L. G. Zakharova, "Krizis samoderzhaviia nakanune revoliutsii 1905 goda," *Voprosy Istorii*, 8 (1972), 119–141.
50. L. Martov, P. Maslov, A. Potresov, *Obshchestvennoe dvizhenie v Rossii v nachale XX-go veka* (St. Petersburg: Obshchestvennaia Pol'za, 1910), vol. 1; *Krizis samoderzhaviia v Rossii*, part 1; Francis William Wcislo, *Reforming Rural Russia: State, Local Society, and National Politics, 1855–1914* (Princeton: Princeton University Press, 1990), chap. 6.
51. *Dnevnik A. N. Kuropatkina*, pp. 54–59.
52. Ibid., p. 55.
53. Ibid.
54. Ibid., pp. 56–57.
55. Ibid., pp. 57–58.
56. "Pis'ma S. Iu. Vitte k D. S. Sipiaginu," KA 18, 31–32.
57. Vitte, *Vospominaniia*, I, 250–251.
58. Pokrovskii, *Russko-iaponskaia voina*, p. 34.
59. "Dnevnik Kuropatkina," KA 2, 83.
60. Ibid., p. 53.
61. *Dnevnik A. N. Kuropatkina*, pp. 68–69.
62. Romanov, *Rossiia v Manchzhurii*, p. 461, n. 1.
63. Ibid., p. 428.
64. BDOW, II, 215–216.
65. "Dnevnik Kuropatkina," KA 2, 76, 80.
66. BDOW, II, 218.
67. Ibid., pp. 222–223.
68. "Dnevnik Kuropatkina," KA 2, 80.
69. Pokrovskii, *Russko-iaponskaia voina*, p. 47.
70. *Dokumenty po peregovoram*, p. 28.
71. "Dnevnik Kuropatkina," KA 2, 96.
72. See, e.g., *Dnevnik A. N. Kuropatkina*, pp. 105–107.
73. "Dnevnik Kuropatkina," KA 2, 90. To sugar this pill, he suggested that China also pay reparations of 250 million rubles.
74. General A. N. Kuropatkin, *The Russian Army and the Japanese War* (London, 1909), report from December 1903, cited pp. 188–193; see also "Dnevnik Kuropatkina," KA 2, 90.
75. Kuropatkin, *The Russian Army*, pp. 91–92.
76. "Dnevnik Kuropatkina," KA 2, 92.
77. Ibid., p. 93.
78. Although this phrase has become a cliché through Witte's attribution, there is no other source for it. Kuropatkin recounts a talk with Lamzdorf in which the latter felt that Pleve would support a war as a diversion of the masses' attention from political questions. "Dnevnik Kuropatkina," KA 2, 94.
79. Ibid., p. 84.

80. Romanov, *Rossiia v Manchzhurii*, pp. 447–448.
81. Ibid., p. 458, n. 3. Interestingly the culprit in the retaking of Mukden without Alekseev's permission had acted as an agent for the Yalu concessionaires in their attempt to gain timbering rights on the Manchurian side of the Yalu.
82. "Dnevnik Kuropatkina," KA 2, 80.
83. Ibid., p. 85.
84. *Dnevnik A. N. Kuropatkina*, p. 113; see also "Dnevnik Kuropatkina," KA 2, 92, 94, where Nicholas's sister echoes the emperor's opinion that there would be no war as he did not want one.
85. A. Popov, ed., "V shtabe Adm. E. I. Alekseeva (iz dnevnikov E. A. Plansona)," KA 41–42, 156.
86. "Dnevnik Kuropatkina," KA 2, 100–101.
87. BDOW, II, 236.
88. Pokrovskii, *Russko-iaponskaia voina*, pp. 43, 44, 48, 117; *Dokumenty po peregovoram*, pp. 27–31; "Dnevnik Kuropatkina," KA 2, 103–105.
89. *Dnevnik A. N. Kuropatkina*, pp. 109, 113; Popov, "V shtabe," p. 165.
90. Popov, "V shtabe," pp. 156–157. Planson commented that the warning was "some sort of upstart [*nakhal'naia*] threat"; see also BDOW, II, 233. The Japanese ambassador had told Lord Lansdowne that these were Japan's "final" demands. If a satisfactory answer were not forthcoming in a reasonable amount of time, "the Japanese Government would have to take steps for the protection of their interests."
91. "Dnevnik Kuropatkina," KA 2, 103–105; *Dnevnik A. N. Kuropatkina*, p. 126.
92. Popov, "V shtabe," p. 161. Planson noted that these wires had been sent *ves'ma ekstrenno*.
93. "Dnevnik Kuropatkina," KA 2, 106.
94. Popov, "V shtabe," pp. 161–163.
95. Autograph personal letter, BAR, Urusov Collection, box 1 (unpaginated).
96. Romanov, *Rossiia v Manchzhurii*, pp. 455–458; Pokrovskii, *Russko-iaponskaia voina*, pp. 160–164.
97. "Dnevnik Kuropatkina," KA 2, 86.
98. These fears were so widespread that the British ambassador felt obliged to report them to the Foreign Office. BDOW, II, 227.

## 4. The Lessons of War

1. M. N. Pokrovskii, ed., *Russko-iaponskaia voina: Iz dnevnikov A. N. Kuropatkina i N. P. Linevicha* (Leningrad: Tsentrarkhiv, 1925), p. 101.
2. On the Portsmouth talks, see B. A. Romanov, ed., "Portsmut," KA 6, 3–47, and KA 7, 3–31; S. Iu. Vitte, *Vospominaniia* (Moscow: Sotsekgiz, 1960), II, chap. 45.
3. "Russko-germanskii dogovor 1905 g.," KA 5, 36.
4. "Manifest 17-ogo oktiabria," KA 11, 98.
5. For accounts of the circumstances surrounding the meeting at Björkö, see A. P. Iswolsky, *Recollections of a Foreign Minister* (Toronto: Doubleday, 1921), pp. 40–43, and Vitte, *Vospominaniia*, II, 476–481.
6. "Russko-germanskii dogovor," pp. 5–6.

7. Ibid.
8. Ibid., pp. 6, 14–15, 22.
9. Ibid., p. 21.
10. Text in ibid., p. 25.
11. Vitte, *Vospominaniia*, II, 479–480, and Iswolsky, *Recollections*, p. 47.
12. Iswolsky, *Recollections*, p. 49.
13. "Russko-germanskii dogovor," pp. 35–36.
14. Ibid., p. 24.
15. Ibid.
16. Ibid.
17. Ibid.
18. Ibid.
19. Ibid., p. 33.
20. Ibid., pp. 29–30, 33. Izvolskii wrote of Lamzdorf pursuing a "triple attack" to scuttle the agreement. One of his objectives was to demonstrate the invalidity of the Björkö agreement "on account of its not having been countersigned by the Russian Minister of Foreign Affairs." *Recollections*, p. 35.
21. "Russko-germanskii dogovor," p. 32.
22. Vitte, *Vospominaniia*, 2, 459–460.
23. Ibid., pp. 476–477. Witte called the treaty an "out and out dirty trick [*priamoi podvokh*]."
24. Ibid., p. 477. See also Iswolsky, *Recollections*, p. 35. Izvolskii relays the account of "a Russian journalist" to whom Witte had spoken of the whole incident. In this retelling, one of Witte's first responses to Lamzdorf's revelations was to ask who had countersigned the treaty.
25. "Russko-germanskii dogovor," pp. 37–38.
26. Vitte, *Vospominaniia*, II, 479. The cooperation of the grand duke would also be crucial in securing the consent of a reluctant Nicholas to what became the October Manifesto.
27. "Russko-germanskii dogovor," pp. 38–40.
28. Ibid., p. 34.
29. One can trace these attempts to Peter I's "General'nyi reglament," *Polnoe sobranie zakonov*, no. 3,532. See also Nikita Panin's reform project, in David Ransel, *Nikita Panin and the Politics of Catherinian Russia* (New Haven: Yale University Press, 1975), chap. 4; Alexander I's ministerial and Senate reforms, *Polnoe sobranie zakonov*, no. 20,405 (8 September 1802), "O pravakh Senata"; no. 20,406 (same date), "Ob uchrezhdenii ministerstv"; no. 20,064, "Obrazovanie Gosudarstvennago Soveta"; no. 24,686 (25 June 1811), "Obshchee uchrezhdenie ministerstv." These reforms are discussed in Velikii Kniaz' Nikolai Mikhailovich, *Imperator Aleksandr I* (Petrograd, 1914). M. V. Dovnar-Zapol'skii, "Zarozhdenie ministerstv v Rossii i ukaz o pravakh Senata 8-go sentiabria 1802 goda," in *Iz istorii obshchestvennykh techenii v Rossii* (St. Petersburg, 1905).
30. Walter Pintner and Don Rowney, *Russian Officialdom: The Bureaucratization of Russian Society from the Seventeenth to the Twentieth Century* (Chapel Hill: University of North Carolina Press, 1980); Francis William Wcislo, *Reforming Rural Russia: State, Local Society, and National Politics, 1855–1914* (Princeton:

Princeton University Press, 1990); Richard Wortman, *The Development of a Russian Legal Consciousness* (Chicago: University of Chicago Press, 1976); P. A. Zaionchkovskii, *Pravitel'stvennyi apparat samoderzhavnoi Rossii v XIXv.* (Moscow: Nauka, 1978).

31. There is a revealing anecdote in this regard, from Alexander I's experimentation with ministerial reform. While drafting the *ukaz* on the new Council of Ministers, the emperor argued for the inclusion of ministerial responsibility for laws issued, by making their enactment dependent on the minister's signature as well as the ruler's. Alexander was asked whether an *ukaz* would be considered binding should the minister refuse to countersign it. "Of course," was the reply, "an *ukaz* must be carried out in any case." Nikolai Mikhailovich, *Imperator Aleksandr I,* p. 362. The problem Panin faced in this respect was not dissimilar; Ransel, *Politics,* chaps. 4, 5.

32. V. I. Gurko, *Features and Figures of the Past* (Stanford: Stanford University Press, 1939), pp. 315–316.

33. Ibid.

34. TsGIA, f. 1276, op. 1, d. 1, p. 5.

35. For a good treatment of these discussions, see Andrew Verner, *The Crisis of Russian Autocracy: Nicholas II and the 1905 Revolution* (Princeton: Princeton University Press, 1990), chap. 6.

36. TsGIA, f. 1276, op. 1, d. 1, pp. 5–11.

37. TsGIA, f. 1276, op. 1, d. 1, 51ob.

38. Ibid., pp. 158–163.

39. Ibid., p. 308.

40. S. E. Kryzhanovskii, *Vospominaniia* (Berlin: Petropolis, n. d.), pp. 50–51.

41. TsGIA, f. 1544, op. 1, d. 5, pp. 3–9.

42. Ibid., pp. 3–3ob.

43. Ibid., p. 5.

44. Ibid.

45. Ibid.

46. *Krushenie avtoritet vlasti.*

47. The same concerns were stated in another setting by future Foreign Minister A. P. Izvolskii: "Despotism, i.e. the concentration of so many and such diverse powers in one single hand has produced as elsewhere (the example of Germany) its inevitable fruits, among others: incoherence, if not contradiction in the conduct of affairs which are treated simultaneously by various departments which ignore each other . . . and which obtain from the supreme leader detailed decisions which are irreconcilable in fact: the Russo-Japanese War came from this." MAE, NS, R, 3, p. 109.

48. TsGIA, f. 1544, op. 1, d. 5, p. 6.

49. Ibid.

50. Ibid.

51. Ibid., p. 7ob.

52. Ibid., p. 8.

53. Ibid.

54. Ibid., p. 3.

55. Ibid., p. 1.

56. HHSA, PA X, 126/1, p. 104–105; See also "Dnevnik A. A. Polovtseva," KA 4, 64; and V. N. Kokovtsev, *Iz moego proshlogo: Vospominaniia, 1903–1919 gg.* (Paris: Mouton, reissued 1969), I, 59–66.

57. HHSA, PA X, 126/1, p. 447. This aspect has been the chief focus for most studies of the reform. N. G. Koroleva, *Pervaia rossiiskaia revoliutsiia i tsarizm* (Moscow: 1982); G. S. Doctorow, "The Introduction of Parliamentary Institutions in Russia during the Revolution of 1905–1907" (Ph.D. diss., Columbia University, 1975).

58. He was officially invited to join the conference on 3 September, TsGIA, f. 1544, op. 1, d. 5, p. 12.

59. "Dnevnik Polovtseva," KA 4, 65.

60. See the comparison of their respective draft statutes, dated 10 October 1905, TsGIA, f. 1544, op. 1, d. 5, p. 304.

61. Ibid.

62. See the letter to Witte giving him the particulars of the 1852 legislation, from S. Tatishchev, dated 1 October, TsGIA, f. 1544, op. 1, d. 5, p. 270; and a letter from one of Witte's opponents to Solskii, dated 5 October, ibid., p. 243ob.

63. Ibid., pp. 271–271ob.

64. "Tsarskosel'skie soveshchaniia," *Byloe* 4 (1919), 206. This view was shared by others. See V. I. Gurko, *Tsar' i tsaritsa* (Paris, 1927), pp. 30–39.

65. "Dnevnik Polovtseva," KA 4, 66–67.

66. Here, there was a full-blown clash of views. Ignatev and Stishinskii sought at every turn to diminish the purview and powers of the council and its chairman, while Witte defended the independence of the first minister, since he would be responsible to both the emperor and the country for governmental actions. In the final report of the Solskii conference on this issue, they appended a minority opinion stating their views, TsGIA, f. 1544, op. 1, d. 5, pp. 403ob.–404ob. See also HHSA, PA X, 126/1, pp. 224–226. Aehrenthal was, as always, kept abreast of events by his own dependable contacts, but in this case he also relied a great deal on newspaper reports. The accuracy of these reports, when compared to Polovtsev's diary account or Witte's and Kokovtsev's remembrances is striking and points to rampant "leaking" on the part of conference participants—most probably Witte, who was already beginning to cultivate the support of public opinion. These leaks caused concern in official circles; a particularly well-informed article on the conference, published in *Rus'* on 26 September, was clipped and filed in the conference records, TsGIA, f. 1544, op. 1, d. 5, p. 193.

67. HHSA, PA X, 126/1, pp. 216–218.

68. Ibid., p. 218. See also, TsGIA, f. 1544, op.1, d. 5, pp. 199–207.

69. "Dnevnik Polovtseva," KA 4, 72.

70. Ibid., p. 70.

71. Ibid., p. 72.

72. Ibid., pp. 73, 76. The dissenters were A. P. Ignatev and A. S. Stishinskii.

73. TsGIA, f. 1544, op. 1, d. 5, pp. 404–405.

74. Text in *Svod uchrezhdenii gosudarstvennykh: Kniga vtoraia* (St. Petersburg, 1906), pp. 1–5, "O Sovete ministrov."

75. Ibid., article 1.

76. Ibid., articles 2, 3, 4.

77. Ibid., article 6.
78. Ibid., article 9.
79. Ibid., article 10.
80. Ibid., article 19.
81. Ibid., article 16.
82. Kokovtsev, *Iz moego proshlogo,* I, 101–102.
83. "Dnevnik Polovtseva," KA 4, 74.
84. Vitte, *Vospominaniia,* II, chap. 51, and III, chap. 52. Verner, *The Crisis of Russian Autocracy,* chap. 7.
85. "Tsarskosel'skie soveshchaniia," p. 204.
86. Vitte, *Vospominaniia,* III, 30.
87. E. J. Bing, ed., *The Letters of Tsar Nicholas and Empress Marie* (London, 1937), pp. 186–187.
88. D. S. Abrikosov, *Memoirs,* manuscript in BAR, p. 161.
89. See Vitte, *Vospominaniia,* III, chaps. 58, 63.
90. FO 65/1704, p. 2
91. Kokovtsev, *Iz moego proshlogo,* I, 132.
92. Vitte, *Vospominaniia,* III, 334.
93. Ibid.
94. See also FO 418/30, p. 38.
95. TsGIA, f. 1662, op. 1, d. 107.
96. Vitte, *Vospominaniia,* III, 337–341; TsGAOR, f. 543, op. 1, d. 537, pp. 4–6.
97. See Nicholas's comments on these subjects in Kokovtsev, *Iz moego proshlogo,* I, 169.
98. Vitte, *Vospominaniia,* III, 250.; FO 418/30, p. 74.
99. Vitte, *Vospominaniia,* II, 480.
100. Ibid.
101. "Manifest 17 oktiabria," KA 11–12, 97.
102. Ibid., p. 98.
103. TsGIA, f. 1544, op. 1, d. 5, pp. 404–405.
104. *Svod osnovnykh gosudarstvennykh zakonov* (St. Petersburg, 1906), p. 7.
105. See, e.g., Andrew Rossos, *Russia and the Balkans: Inter-Balkan Rivalry and Russian Foreign Policy, 1908–1914* (Toronto: University of Toronto Press, 1981), introduction; D. C. B. Lieven, *Russia and the Origins of the First World War* (New York: St. Martin's Press, 1983), pp. 51–57.
106. "Tsarskosel'skie soveshchaniia," pp. 216–217; See also Witte's memoir, which further emphasizes this distinction as seen by him, *Vospominaniia,* III, 297–298.
107. This argument is supported by a participant in drafting the final forms of articles 12 and 13 in the Fundamental Laws. The legal councillor M. A. Taube repeats Witte's account of the preliminary discussions between the chairman and Lamzdorf and the military ministers regarding the preliminary draft of these articles. Witte was astonished at the evident lack of concern over the issue voiced by the three ministers involved. Witte had been compelled to explain to them the absolute necessity of placing the sovereign's fundamental rights beyond any "restraining" on the part of the Duma. Taube, *La politique russe d'avant-guerre* (Paris, 1928), pp. 95–96.
108. MAE, NS, R, 38, p. 87.

109. Quoted in ibid., p. 90.
110. Taube, *La politique russe,* p. 89. See also the statement by Benkendorf in London, transmitted by the German chargé, "that he could not and did not want to have anything to do with the Duma." GP 22, pp. 24–25.
111. The news of his appointment was published the morning of 30 April. MAE, NS, R, 3, p. 119.
112. Ibid., pp. 90–92, and E. de Schelking, *Recollections of a Russian Diplomat: the Suicide of Monarchies* (New York: MacMillan, 1918), p. 169.
113. Schelking, *Recollections,* pp. 169–173. Schelking, a one-time servitor in the foreign ministry, was a pseudonymous foreign affairs correspondent for *Novoe Vremia* during Izvolskii's ministry. He knew Izvolskii through several off-the-record meetings, mostly held in the fall of 1908, when the foreign minister seemed to use him both as a conduit to Russian public opinion and as a confidant at a time of great personal distress. Schelking described Izvolskii as "[i]ncontestably very intelligent, with the wide outlook and broad point of view of the real statesman, he had, however, two great faults: a limitless ambition and a snobbishness which amounted to a disease. In order to further his ambitions and his career he would hesitate at nothing" (p. 169). "He also believed that after Bismarck, he was the greatest diplomat in the world!" (p. 171). Izvolskii's co-worker Taube drew the same distinction between the two elements in Izvolskii's personality. Taube, *La politique russe,* pp. 106–108. Hostile observers like Kryzhanovskii (to mention only one), saw in Izvolskii, "a pompous snob, always with a monocle, and never knowing where to put his top-hat"; Kryzhanovskii, *Vospominaniia,* p. 91.
114. On Izvolskii's career see Hélène Izwolsky, ed., *Au service de la Russie* (Paris, 1937), I, introduction; Schelking, *Recollections,* pp. 169–170, and Iswolsky, *Recollections.*
115. An excellent discussion of the lyceé as a formative institution for state officials is given in Lieven, *Origins,* pp. 83–85; N. V. Tcharykow, *Glimpses of High Politics through War and Peace, 1855–1929* (London, 1931), pp. 83–86. See also A. Ia. Iakhontov, *Istoricheskii ocherk Imperatorskogo Aleksandrovskogo (b. Tsarskosel'skogo) Litseia* (Paris, 1936). An appendix lists all the *sanovniki* who were graduates of the lyceé.
116. Iswolsky, *Recollections,* p. 20.
117. See Nicholas's diary, TsGAOR, f. 601, op. 1, d. 249, pp. 63, 68, entries for 20, 27 October 1905; Iswolsky, *Recollections,* p. 16; Taube, *La politique russe,* p. 90, although he misdates the mission.
118. Iswolsky, *Recollections,* p. 11. Also, A. Savinsky, *Recollections of a Russian Diplomat* (London, n.d.), p. 137.
119. Taube, *La politique russe,* pp. 90–91.
120. M. A. Taube, *Vospominaniia,* manuscript in BAR, p. 102.
121. Izvolskii, already aware of his impending promotion, was canvassing the senior Russian ambassadors in Europe for their views on the future direction of Russian foreign policy. Iswolsky, *Recollections,* pp. 70–73.
122. MAE, NS, R, 3, pp. 110–111.
123. Iswolsky, *Recollections,* p. 3.
124. Taube, *Vospominaniia,* p. 102.

125. H. Izwolsky, *Au service*, I, 59.
126. Nicolas Schebeko, *Souvenirs: Essai historique sur les origines de la guerre de 1914* (Paris, 1926), p. 78.
127. See A. V. Georgiev, "Organy vneshnepoliticheskoi propagandy: Puti obrabotki obshchestvennogo mneniia," unpublished manuscript, scheduled to appear in *Mezhdunarodnaia Zhizn'* during 1991, pp. 1–2.
128. Tcharykow, *Glimpses*, pp. 268–269.
129. Ibid.
130. Iswolsky, *Recollections*, p. 13.
131. MAE, NS, R, 3, p. 109. From a private conversation at the Quai d'Orsay in April 1906. Izvolskii's views, with particular regard to foreign policy, were shared in circles with experience in this area. Former diplomat, and later state councillor, P. A. Saburov proposed in the spring of 1905 that the experience of previous wars demonstrated the need for a special committee on foreign affairs to act as an intermediary between the foreign minister and the emperor, on the model of the Committee of Finances. A. V. Ignat'ev, *Vneshniaia politika Rossii v 1905–1907gg.* (Moscow: Nauka, 1986), p. 63.
132. BAR, Urusov Collection, box 1 (unpaginated).
133. The tensions between Izvolskii's and Nicholas's understandings of his position are very evident in a letter he wrote at the height of the July crisis. Remarking on the cabinet changes after Goremykin's dismissal, he wrote, *"hélas,* this change does not affect me, for the Emperor considers me to be outside the Cabinet and I must in spite of myself continue to carry a particularly heavy burden in the present circumstances." H. Izwolsky, *Au service,* II, 59.
134. Iswolsky, *Recollections,* p. 180. He placed part of the blame for this situation on Nicholas (p. 82). This view was corroborated by the British chargé, who had noted in mid-March the rumors of Witte's impending resignation, remarking that "the general belief in Court circles seems to be that with Count Witte's retirement the office of President of the Council will lose its importance and that the old system of independent ministries will again come into force"; FO 418/31, p. 71.
135. H. Izwolsky, *Au service,* I, 324; see also ibid., II, 53, I, 305–306.
136. Kokovtsev, *Iz moego proshlogo,* I, 187–188. See also Kryzhanovskii, who called him a *trafaretnyi diplomat* and *legkovesnyi,* in *Vospominaniia,* p. 91; and Gurko, *Features,* p. 481.
137. H. Izwolsky, *Au service,* I, 53; Iswolsky, *Recollections,* p. 171; Kokovtsev, *Iz moego proshlogo,* I, 187–188.
138. H. Izwolsky, *Au service,* I, 53. One week earlier a concerned Benkendorf had written from London suggesting the formation of a cabinet from the liberal minority in the Duma; ibid., I, 315.
139. Iswolsky, *Recollections,* pp. 183–186, 189–191.
140. H. Izwolsky, *Au service,* I, 314.
141. Iswolsky, *Recollections,* p. 191.
142. An excellent discussion of these events is given in Caspar Ferenczi, *Aussenpolitik und öffentlichkeit in Russland, 1906–1912* (Husum: Matthiesen, 1982), pp. 94–117.
143. BAR, Urusov Collection, box 1. This entente had first been agreed upon in 1898

and was further elaborated in an agreement between Lamzdorf and Austro-Hungarian Foreign Minister Count A. Goluchowski at Mürzsteg in 1903.

144. For biographical details on Stolypin, see A. S. Izgoev, *P. A. Stolypin* (Moscow, 1912), chap. 1; M. P. Bok, *Vospominaniia o moem otse P. A. Stolypine* (New York: Izdatel'stvo imeni Chekhova, 1953); M. S. Conroy, *Peter Arkad'evich Stolypin: Practical Politics in Late Tsarist Russia* (Boulder, Colo.: Westview Press, 1976).

145. E.g., Iswolsky, *Recollections*, pp. 89–92; H. Izwolsky, *Au service*, appendix, letter from Izvolskii to Stolypin from late 1910 or 1911. Izvolskii claimed to have resigned partly in protest of Stolypin's Finland policy, thus preserving to the end Izvolskii's precepts of cabinet solidarity.

146. See Thomas Fallows, "Forging the Zemstvo Movement: Liberalism and Radicalism on the Volga, 1890–1905" (Ph.D. diss., Harvard University, 1981).

147. Kryzhanovskii, *Vospominaniia*, p. 210.

148. Wcislo, *Reforming Rural Russia*, pp. 197–207.

149. The tendency to view Stolypin against Western standards of the time is evident in Conroy, *Stolypin*, pp. 26, 32. Similar standards underlie the discussion of Stolypin as premier in Geoffrey Hosking, *The Russian Constitutional Experiment: Government and Duma, 1907–1914* (London: Cambridge University Press, 1973), pp. 25–26.

150. Bok, *Vospominaniia o moem otse*, p. 137.

151. Conversation cited in Kokovtsev, *Iz moego proshlogo*, I, 203.

152. Bok, *Vospominaniia o moem otse*, p. 168.

153. Iswolsky, *Recollections*, p. 203.

154. Kryzhanovskii, *Vospominaniia*, p. 216. Here, he compares Stolypin to Witte and Sviatopolk-Mirskii for having emphasized the "public" side of the problem to the exclusion of the need for reorganized and strengthened machinery of state.

155. N. G. Koroleva, "Sovet ministrov v Rossii v 1907–1914 gg.," *Istoricheskie Zapiski*, 110 (1984), 118.

156. The council's proceedings contain discussions of myriad topics, from the legal property rights of monasteries in Moldavia, to the amount of funds needed to establish consular health stations in northern Persia; *Osobyi Zhurnal Soveta Ministrov*, issued yearly, 1906–1914. This publication, which was strictly edited in its original form, is due to be republished in its entirety by the Institute of the History of the USSR (Moscow section), of the USSR Academy of Sciences.

157. *Uchrezhdenie Soveta Ministrov* (St. Petersburg, 1906), I, part 2, p. 4, articles 15, 16.

158. M. F. Florinskii, "Sovet ministrov v Rossii v 1907–1914 gg." (diss. synopsis, Leningrad State University, 1978), pp. 11–12; Florinskii, "K istorii obrazovaniia i deiatel'nosti malogo Soveta ministrov, 1906–1914gg.," *Vestnik L.G.U.: Istoriia, Iazyk, i Literatura*, no. 1, issue 2 (1977). As Florinskii notes, this process began as early as May 1906, but there was resistance to the splitting of functions on the part of some ministers until 1909. On the attendance of assistants in lieu of ministers, see the *Osobyi Zhurnal* for signatures of the minutes.

159. Kokovtsev, *Iz moego proshlogo*, I, 235–236; see also Iswolsky, *Recollections*, pp. 241–243.

160. Iswolsky, *Recollections*, pp. 241–242.

161. Ibid., p. 223.
162. Kokovtsev, *Iz moego proshlogo*, I, 232–233.
163. HHSA, PA X, 131, pp. 142–146.
164. Text in *Predsedatel' Soveta Ministrov P. A. Stolypin (sostavleno E. V. po soob-shcheniiam pressy za tri goda)* (St. Petersburg, 1909), pp. 21–23. In English translation, in FO 418/38, pp. 31–32.
165. P. Zverev, ed., "Iz zapisok A. F. Redigera," KA 60, 116.
166. Kokovtsev, *Iz moego proshlogo*, I, 231–232.

## 5. The Building of a Foreign Policy Consensus

1. See especially, I. V. Bestuzhev, *Bor'ba po voprosam vneshnei politiki v Rossii, 1906–1910* (Moscow: Nauka, 1964); Dietrich Geyer, *Der russische Imperialismus: Studien über den Zusammenhang von innerer und auswärtiger Politik, 1860–1914* (Göttingen: Vandenhoeck und Ruprecht, 1977); Caspar Ferenczi, *Aussenpolitik und öffentlichkeit in Russland, 1906–1912* (Husum: Matthiesen, 1982); and Dominic Lieven, "Pro-Germans and Russian Foreign Policy, 1890–1914," *International History Review*, 2, no. 1 (1980), 34–54. The term "orientation," and the casting of the debate as it has subsequently been treated comes from the Durnovo memorandum, first published by E. V. Tarle, "Germanskaia orientatsiia i P. N. Durnovo v 1914g.," *Byloe*, no. 19 (1922), 161–176.
2. On these talks, see BDOW, IV, 183ff.
3. Michel de Taube, *La politique russe d'avant-guerre* (Paris, 1928), p. 74.
4. FO 418/38, p. 28.
5. Ibid. Taube held similar views, *La politique*, pp. 72–74. Readers acquainted with the Durnovo memorandum will recognize the persistence of the dynastic argument in its post-1905 formulation.
6. Kadet, Octobrist, and moderate right fractions based their sympathies on a feeling that the future of the post-1905 system hinged directly on continued partnership with France and a *rapprochement* with Britain. See Bestuzhev, *Bor'ba*, chap. 2; D. C. B. Lieven, *Russia and the Origins of the First World War* (New York: St. Martin's, 1983), pp. 119–140. For more on Shvanebakh and the hopes for a new *Dreikaiserbund*, see Hans Heilbronner, "An Anti-Witte Diplomatic Conspiracy, 1905–1906: The Schwanebach Memorandum," *Jahrbücher für Geschichte Osteuropas*, vol. 14 (1966), 347–361.
7. The phrase is Taube's, *La politique*, p. 34.
8. M. A. Taube, *Vospominaniia*, manuscript in BAR, p. 95. See also *La politique*, which dates the proposal to the time of Björkö. The BAR manuscript dates it specifically 3 January 1906 (pp. 95, 103).
9. A contemporary reaction to the agreement in these terms is given in HHSA, PA VIII, p. 175. The Austrian chargé noted that Izvolskii had been opposed by "influential reactionary members of the Court party," over whom the agreement constituted a personal and political victory.
10. A. S. Suvorin, *Dnevnik A. S. Suvorina* (Moscow and Petrograd, 1923), p. 351. See also excerpts from Lev Tikhomirov, "Iz dnevnika L. Tikhomirova," KA 61, 86–87.
11. MAE, NS, R, 44, p. 164.

12. See, e.g., "Iz dnevnika L. Tikhomirova," pp. 86–87, and an anonymous memorandum submitted to Nicholas in 1909, TsGAOR, f. 543, op. 1, d. 528.
13. HHSA, PA VIII, p. 175; also, letters from the fund of the Princes Orlov, TsGIA, f. 1012, especially d.50.
14. On the views of the various Duma groupings on foreign policy, see H. Jablonowski, "Die Stellungnahme der russischen Parteien zur Aussenpolitik der Regierung von der russisch-englischen Verständigung bis zum ersten Weltkrieg," *Forschungen zur osteuropäischen Geschichte,* vol. 5, 60–93; Bestuzhev, *Bor'ba,* chaps. 1, 2.
15. A. P. Iswolsky, *Recollections of a Foreign Minister* (Toronto: Doubleday, 1921), p. 74.
16. TsGIA, f. 1276, op. 4, d. 10, pp. 1–3.
17. Ibid., p. 1.
18. Ibid., p. 2.
19. Ibid., p. 3.
20. Taube, *La politique,* p. 100; Iswolsky, *Recollections,* pp. 70–73.
21. BDOW, IV, 83ff; S. Pashukanis, ed., "K istorii anglo-russkogo soglasheniia 1907g.," KA 69–70, 6.
22. Cited in A. V. Ignat'ev, *Russko-angliiskie otnosheniia nakanune pervoi mirovoi voiny* (Moscow: Izdatel'stvo Sotsial'no-Ekonomicheskoi Literatury, 1962), p. 63.
23. Ibid., p. 59. As late as April 1906, Palitsyn seems to have anticipated war with England as a real possibility. In a meeting with his French counterpart he asked "categorically" whether France would honor commitments that the allies would support one another in a war with Britain. "He adds that he attaches great importance to a positive response to this question." MAE, NS, R, 38, p. 64.
24. M. I. Grishina, "Chernomorskie prolivy vo vneshnei politike Rossii, 1904–1907gg.," *Istoricheskie Zapiski,* vol. 99 (1977), 156.
25. HHSA, PA VIII, 175, p. 89. Izvolskii wrote disparagingly of these objections to Benkendorf in September 1906: "The General Staff seems to have learned nothing . . . and talks of Seistan, the Persian Gulf, the Indian Ocean, etc., exactly as one spoke before the war with Japan of Manchuria, Korea, the Pacific Ocean"; Hélène Izwolsky, ed., *Au service de la Russie* (Paris, 1937), I, 378.
26. Ignat'ev, *Anglo-russkie otnosheniia,* p. 59.
27. H. Izwolsky, *Au service,* I, 395, 415.
28. Ibid.; Bestuzhev, *Bor'ba,* p. 138.
29. Text in "K istorii anglo-russkogo soglasheniia," KA 69–70, 19–23.
30. Ibid., pp. 19–20.
31. Protocol of special conference on the Afghan question, text in A. Reisner, ed., "Anglo-russkaia konventsiia 1907g. i razdel Afganistana," KA 10, 55.
32. A. A. Polivanov, *Iz dnevnikov i vospominanii po dolzhnosti voennogo ministra i ego pomoshchnika, 1907–1916gg.* (Moscow: Vysshii Voennyi Redaktsionnyi Sovet, 1924), I, 32.
33. Bestuzhev, *Bor'ba,* p. 138.
34. "Anglo-russkaia konventsiia 1907g.," p. 55.
35. Text in "K istorii anglo-russkogo soglasheniia," p. 32.
36. This was the view taken by Russian conservatives. HHSA, PA X, 129, Bericht

39 A-E, Aehrenthal to Goluchowski, 1/14 August 1906; GP 22, pp. 61–65. Schoen felt compelled to defend Izvolskii against charges of anti-Germanism.

37. GP 22, pp. 48, 67.
38. Taube, *La politique*, p. 118.
39. Ibid., p. 115.
40. Taube, *Vospominaniia*, p. 113; See also I. I. Astaf'ev, *Russko-germanskii diplomaticheskie otnosheniia, 1905–1911* (Moscow: Nauka, 1972), p. 185.
41. See Grishina, "Chernomorskie prolivy," pp. 146–152; D. S. Abrikosov, *Memoirs*, manuscript in BAR, p. 169.
42. Grishina, "Chernomorskie prolivy," p. 152.
43. Text in "K istorii anglo-russkogo soglasheniia," pp. 5–18.
44. Ibid., p. 16.
45. Ibid., pp. 16–18.
46. Grishina, "Chernomorskie prolivy," p. 157.
47. Cited in ibid., p. 158.
48. FO 800/338, p. 319.
49. FO 418/38, pp. 79, 91.
50. Ibid., p. 91.
51. FO 418/38, p. 95. See also FO 800/337, p. 162, in which Nicolson writes privately to Grey: "[Izvolskii] is beaming with pleasure over the report . . . of your communication to Ct. Benkendorff in regard to the Bosphorus and the Dardanelles . . . as he expressed it, a great evolution in our relations and an historical event."
52. Polivanov, *Iz dnevnikov*, p. 32.
53. "K istorii anglo-russkogo soglasheniia 1907g.," p. 32.
54. MAE, NS, 38, pp. 289–291.
55. HHSA, PA I, 484/1, pp. 30–31.
56. Bestuzhev, *Bor'ba*, pp. 200–201.
57. HHSA, PA I, 484/1, p. 31.
58. Grishina, "Chernomorskie prolivy," pp. 175–176.
59. M. Nintchitch, *La crise bosniaque 1908–1909 et les Puissances européennes* (Paris, 1937), pp. 125–126.
60. M. N. Pokrovskii, ed., "Tri soveshchaniia," *Vestnik Narodnogo Kommissariata Inostrannykh Del* 1 (1918), 20.
61. Ibid., pp. 19–20.
62. Ibid., pp. 19–22.
63. For an excellent treatment of this complicated question, see A. Rossos, *Russia and the Balkans: Inter-Balkan Rivalries and Russian Foreign Policy, 1908–1914* (Toronto: University of Toronto Press, 1981).
64. Pokrovskii, "Tri soveshchaniia," pp. 21–23.
65. Ibid., pp. 23–24.
66. Ibid., p. 24.
67. Ibid.
68. Ibid.
69. MAE, NS, 3, p. 109.
70. N. G. Koroleva, "Sovet Ministrov v Rossii v 1907–1914gg.," *Istoricheskie Zapiski*, 110 (1984), 121–125 (tables); M. F. Florinskii, "Sovet Ministrov i

Ministerstvo Inostrannykh Del v 1907–1914gg.," *Vestnik L.G.U.: Istoriia, Iazyk, i Literatura*, no. 2, issue 1 (1977).

71. TsGIA, f. 1276, op. 3, d. 601, pp. 8–12. Stolypin's interest in such questions is not surprising given his use, as minister of internal affairs, of the army to reestablish order in Russia.

72. Polivanov, *Iz dnevnikov*, pp. 41–42.

73. H. Izwolsky, *Au service*, I, 134.

74. *Dnevnik A. S. Suvorina*, p. 376.

75. See GP, 25/2, pp. 302–303 and 360–361.

76. HHSA, PA X, 132, Bericht, Berchtold to Aehrenthal 2/15 January 1908. Berchtold notes the rumors in both diplomatic and "higher governmental circles"; MAE, Papiers Georges Louis, 1908, personal letter 25 January 1908 N.S. MAE, NS, 39, p. 6, which remarks on the rumors and the daily attacks "très vives" on Izvolskii in the press "qui lui sont particulièrement sensibles"; GP 25/2, pp. 302–303.

77. V. S. Diakin, *Samoderzhavie, burzhuaziia, i dvorianstvo, 1907–1911gg.* (Leningrad: Nauka, 1975), p. 97.

78. Cited in ibid., p. 98.

79. See FO 800/337, pp. 222–224; GP 25/2, p. 332.

80. On public opinion and foreign policy, see Ferenczi, *Aussenpolitik und öffentlichkeit;* Bestuzhev, *Bor'ba;* Horst Jablonowski, "Die Stellungnahme der russischen Parteien zur Aussenpolitik der Regierung von der russisch-englischen Verständigung bis zum ersten Weltkrieg," *Forschungen zur Osteuropäischen Geschichte,* vol. 5, 60–93.

81. FO 800/337, pp. 222–224.

82. Ibid., p. 189.

83. See, *Dnevnik A. S. Suvorina*, entry for 19 August 1907.

84. Iu. Ia. Solov'ev, *Vospominaniia diplomata, 1893–1922* (Moscow, 1959), p. 175.

85. Ibid., p. 210.

86. P. B. Struve, "Velikaia Rossiia," *Russkaia Mysl'*, 1 (January 1908), 143.

87. Jablonowski, "Die Stellungnahme"; Bestuzhev, *Bor'ba,* p. 68; Kadet support for government policy has allowed Soviet historians to include them in the so-called second majority in their schema of the "Bonapartist" 3 June system.

88. Cited in Bestuzhev, *Bor'ba,* p. 191.

89. *Rech'*, 12 February 1908, clipping in TsGAOR, f. 555, op. 1, d. 650, #160810; and in ibid., #160733, *Birzhevye Vedomosti*, 12 February 1908.

90. The historical problem of pan-Slavism is treated in M. B. Petrovich, *The Emergence of Russian Panslavism, 1856–1870* (New York: Columbia University Press, 1956); on neo-Slavism, see W. Zeil, "Der Neoslawismus," *Jahrbuch für Geschichte sozialistischen Länder Europas,* 19, no. 2 (1975), 29–56; and U. Liszkowski, "Zur Aktualisierung der Stereotype 'Die deutsche Gefahr' im russischen Neoslawismus," in *Russland und Deutschland* (Stuttgart: E. Klett, 1974), pp. 278–294. See also GP 25/2, pp. 531–532, which records a conversation with Izvolskii, who commented, "the old pan-Slav party, with its high-flown plans in regard to foreign policy, is losing ever more meaning and influence; in its place is emerging Neo-panslavism," which was preoccupied with internal questions.

91. P. N. Miliukov, *Vospominaniia* (New York, 1955), I, 67–69; Charykov, *Glimpses,* pp. 90–96.
92. E. N. Trubetskoi, *Vospominaniia* (Sofia: Rossiisko-Bolgarskoe Knigoiz-datel'stvo, 1921), pp. 20–24.
93. Struve, "Velikaia Rossiia," pp. 147–148.
94. *Vostochnyi vopros vo vneshnei politike Rossii, konets XVIII-nachalo XX v.* (Moscow: Nauka, 1978), pp. 305–306.
95. MAE, NS, R, 39, p. 49.
96. *Gosudarstvennyi Duma: Stenograficheskii otchet, 3 sozyv, chast' II, sessiia per-vaia,* cols., 1757–1777.
97. Ibid., col. 1763.
98. Ibid., col. 1764.
99. Ibid., col. 1768.
100. Ibid., col. 1771.
101. Ibid., col. 1776.
102. Ibid., cols. 1757–1763.
103. Cited in Bestuzhev, *Bor'ba,* p. 89; see also H. Izwolsky, *Au service,* II, 138–139.
104. TsGAOR, f. 601, op. 1, d. 755, pp. 17–19.
105. HHSA, PA X, 132, pp. 147–148. Similar concerns were voiced in the State Council's Finance Commission, which discussed the government's draft legislation of the establishment of a Naval General Staff. Polivanov, *Iz dnevnikov,* p. 47.
106. FO 371/517, p. 347.

## 6. The Bosnian Crisis and the Triumph of United Government

1. Ö-U A, I, 187–188.
2. Aehrenthal's views on Izvolskii's political outlook dated from early in the latter's tenure as foreign minister. While still ambassador to Russia in August 1906, Aehrenthal wrote a long report from St. Petersburg, in which he speculated on the outcome of Izvolskii's first foray into European diplomacy. Aehrenthal noted Izvolskii's "preference for the *parliamentarily* governed West," which Aehrenthal saw as going "hand in hand" with a desire to introduce "far-reaching liberal institutions" in Russia. Izvolskii had previously complained about the conservative complexion of Goremykin's cabinet. The ambassador concluded his report with the sarcastic remark that Izvolskii spoke about liberalism and parliament "wie ein Jüngling von seiner Liebe." HHSA, PA X, no. 39 A-E, Aehrenthal to Goluchowski, 1/14 August 1906. On Aehrenthal's conservative contacts, and especially those with Shvanebakh, see the report cited here and HHSA, PA X, 131, personal letter, Berchtold to Aehrenthal, SPb, 30 December 1906/12 January 1907; and HHSA, PA X, 131, "Abschrift eines streng vertraulichen Briefes aus Petersburg ddo. 25/12 Jänner, 1907," which gives the text of a letter from Shvanebakh. See also Hans Heilbronner, "Aehrenthal in Defense of Russian Autocracy," *Jahrbücher für Geschichte Osteuropas,* 17 (1969), 380–396.
3. HHSA, PA I, 485, pp. 587–588.
4. Under the prevailing regime, the passage of Russian warships out of the Black Sea was forbidden by European agreement.
5. HHSA, PA I, 485, p. 588.

6. HHSA, PA X, 132, pp. 214–217. See also, GP 25/2, p. 538.
7. Text of protocol in A. Popov, ed., "Turetskaia revoliutsiia 1908–1909gg.," KA 43, 44–45.
8. Ibid., p. 45. Elsewhere, Stolypin had described the advantages of the Anglo-Russian agreement from a different point of view. Speaking with Sir Arthur Nicolson, Stolypin said that he was watching the Turkish situation "with great interest, as he did not doubt that it would have an echo in the Caucasus, Turkestan and the Tartar provinces of Russia." Given the potential role that might be played by a strong pan-Islamic Turkey, states like Britain and Russian, with their "millions of Mussulman subjects . . . would doubtless feel the effects which the new development would create"; it was fortunate that Britain and Russia were now "in such close amity." FO 371/519, p. 57.
9. Ö-U A, I, 61–62.
10. BAR, Urusov Collection, box 1 (unpaginated); HHSA, PA X, 132, p. 190.
11. I. V. Bestuzhev, "Bor'ba v praviashchikh krugakh vokrug anneksii Bosnii i Gertsegoviny," Istoricheskii Arkhiv, 5 (1964), 116; HHSA, PA I, 483, p. 274.
12. Bestuzhev, "Bor'ba v praviashchikh krugakh," p. 117; personal letter Izvolskii to Urusov, 20 August 1908, BAR, Urusov Collection, box 1.
13. Bestuzhev, "Bor'ba v praviashchikh krugakh," p. 117, and Urusov collection, BAR, box 1. He suggested to Berchtold that a meeting take place on 14 or 15 September, new style, HHSA, PA I, 483, pp. 274, 279.
14. Bestuzhev, "Bor'ba v praviashchikh krugakh," p. 117.
15. Ibid.
16. Bestuzhev, "Bor'ba v praviashchikh krugakh," pp. 118–121.
17. Nicholas told Nicolson of the possibility of a meeting between Izvolskii and Aehrenthal on Balkan matters on 14 August 1908 N.S., FO 371/519, p. 43. See also, N. V. Tcharykow, Glimpses of High Politics through War and Peace, 1855–1929 (London, 1931), p. 269.
18. See, e.g., FO 800/337, pp. 222–224; GP 25/2, p. 360; MAE, Papiers Georges Louis, personal letter, T. Berkheim to Louis, from Berlin, 28 June 1908 N.S.
19. FO 371/519, p. 43.
20. MAE, NS, R, 42bis, p. 129.
21. HHSA, PA I, 485, p. 609.
22. Aehrenthal's version is given in HHSA, PA I, 485, pp. 609–623. Izvolskii wrote two reports, a letter to Charykov, written on 3 September, and a brief telegram sent the following day; the texts of both are given in Bestuzhev, "Bor'ba v praviashchikh krugakh," pp. 121–124.
23. Bestuzhev, "Bor'ba v praviashchikh krugakh," p. 122.
24. HHSA, PA I, 485, p. 611.
25. Ibid., pp. 612–613.
26. Ibid., pp. 615–620.
27. Ibid., p. 614.
28. Ibid.
29. Ibid., pp. 614–615.
30. Bestuzhev, "Bor'ba v praviashchikh krugakh," pp. 121 (telegram), 122 (letter). These included the granting of full independence to Bulgaria and small political compensations to the Balkan states.
31. HHSA, PA I, 485. p. 619.

32. Ibid., p. 620. Izvolskii's version noted the vagueness of the explanation and the approximate date, Bestuzhev, "Bor'ba v praviashchikh krugakh," pp. 121, 122.
33. HHSA, PA I, 485, p. 622.
34. Bestuzhev, "Bor'ba v praviashchikh krugakh," p. 123.
35. Ibid., p. 124.
36. Ibid., pp. 124–125; HHSA, PA X, Bericht 38A-D, 4/17 September, 1908.
37. Bestuzhev, "Bor'ba v praviashchikh krugakh," p. 125.
38. Ibid., pp. 125–128.
39. Ibid., p. 125.
40. Ibid., p. 126.
41. Ibid.
42. Ö-U A, I, 370.
43. Bestuzhev, "Bor'ba v praviashchikh krugakh," pp. 128–129.
44. Ibid., p. 130.
45. Ibid., p. 129.
46. Ibid., p. 128.
47. Hélène Izwolsky, ed., Au service de la Russie (Paris, 1937), I, 178–179.
48. I. I. Astaf'ev, Russko-germanskie diplomaticheskie otnosheniia, 1905–1911gg. (Moscow: Izdatel'stvo Moskovskogo Universiteta, 1972), p. 151.
49. HHSA, PA I, 485, pp. 637–638.
50. FO 371/551, pp. 401–402. See also, Astaf'ev, Russko-germanskie otnosheniia, p. 151.
51. There are several accounts of this moment. N. Tcharykow, "Reminiscences of Nicholas II," Contemporary Review, 134 (1928), 447–449. This rendering is highly inaccurate in its portrayal of the narrator's role and mentions nothing of the fact that he had concealed all knowledge of the Buchlau agreement for over two weeks, revealing it only when instructed to. V. N. Kokovtsev, Iz moego proshlogo (Paris: Mouton, 1969), I, 331–335. This version is more interesting for its record of the immediate impressions produced by Charykov's news. See also, TsGAOR, f. 601, op. 1, d. 755, and Bestuzhev, "Bor'ba v praviashchikh krugakh," p. 137. F. Notovich, "Iz perepiski Nikolaia i Marii Romanovykh," KA 50–51, 154.
52. Bestuzhev, "Bor'ba v praviashchikh krugakh," pp. 131–132.
53. Ibid., p. 133.
54. Astaf'ev, Russko-germanskie otnosheniia, p. 154.
55. Bestuzhev, "Bor'ba v praviashchikh krugakh," p. 133.
56. Ibid.
57. Astaf'ev, Russko-germanskie otnosheniia, p. 155.
58. Eloquent evidence of this shift is the change in the archival provenance of the published documents dealing with these events. Charykov's correspondence with Izvolskii before and immediately after Buchlau was all drawn from the chancellery files of the Ministry of Foreign Affairs. However, documents on events after 19 September, including Charykov's reports to Izvolskii on the 19 September conference, come from the chancellery of the Council of Ministers or from Nicholas's personal papers. Bestuzhev, "Bor'ba v praviashchikh krugakh."
59. Ibid., p. 134.
60. Tcharykow, "Reminiscences," p. 448, Glimpses, p. 270.

61. Bestuzhev, "Bor'ba v praviashchikh krugakh," p. 133.
62. Ibid., p. 134.
63. TsGAOR, f. 601, op. 1, d. 750.
64. Bulgaria declared its independence at the same time as the annexation. This too was a major issue bound up with the Bosnian crisis, but as it was not an important issue for the Council of Ministers, it is not treated here. See Rossos, *Russia and the Balkans: Inter-Balkan Rivalries and Russian Foreign Policy, 1908–1914* (Toronto: University of Toronto Press, 1981).
65. Notovich, "Iz perepiski," p. 184.
66. HHSA, PA I, 485, pp. 674–675.
67. FO 371/550, p. 399; MAE, Papiers de Panafieu, 1907/1908, telegram 169, and MAE, NS, Turquie, 188, p. 150.
68. Ö-U A, I, 187–188.
69. Notovich, "Iz perepiski," p. 168. This assent had been given by Alexander II in 1876, in the Treaty of Reichstadt.
70. FO 371/551, p. 33; HHSA, PA XII, 354/1, p. 57.
71. See MAE, NS, Turquie, 190, pp. 78–83; FO 371/552, p. 227.
72. TsGAOR, f. 601, op. 1, d. 750, p. 26.
73. MAE, NS, Turquie, 179, pp. 161–165; FO 371/552, p. 227.
74. FO 371/552, p. 228.
75. Ibid.
76. HHSA, PA, I, 484, pp. 118–123.
77. HHSA, PA XII, 354/1, pp. 230–233.
78. Ibid., p. 233.
79. HHSA, PA XII, 354/1, p. 323.
80. FO 371/554, pp. 120–123; MAE, NS, Turquie, 191, p. 18; MAE, NS, R, 39, pp. 112–113.
81. Alexander Savinsky, *Recollections of a Russian Diplomat* (London, n.d.), p. 153. See also Bulow's letter to Aehrenthal on discussions with Izvolskii, HHSA, PA I, 484, pp. 118–119.
82. Ö-U A, I, 287; Savinsky, *Recollections,* p. 153; MAE, NS, Turquie, 192, p. 14.
83. Cited in I. V. Bestuzhev, *Bor'ba po voprosam vneshnei politiki v Rossii, 1906–1910* (Moscow: Nauka, 1964), p. 101; see also FO 371/554, p. 337.
84. Bestuzhev, *Bor'ba,* p. 234.
85. FO 371/554, p. 303.
86. Ibid., pp. 305–306; Cf. HHSA, PA I, 485, p. 714.
87. HHSA, PA I, 485, Bericht 44-C, Berchtold to Aehrenthal, 24 October/6 November 1908.
88. Ö-U A, I, 354–355.
89. MAE, Papiers Georges Louis, personal letter, Panafieu to Louis, 30 October 1908 N.S.; M. A. Taube, *Vospominaniia,* manuscript in BAR, p. 129; Kokovtsev, *Iz moego proshlogo,* I, 336.
90. Kokovtsev, *Iz moego proshlogo,* I, 336.
91. TsGAOR, f. 601, op. 1, d. 755, pp. 13–19. Protocols of this meeting are also published in Bestuzhev, "Bor'ba v praviashchikh krugakh," pp. 136–140.
92. TsGAOR, f. 601, op. 1, d. 755, p. 13.
93. Ibid., pp. 13–14.

94. Ibid., pp. 14–15.
95. Apparently he was asked about having declared his intention to appear there, because he told the council that in May 1907 the emperor had endorsed such appearances in principle. Ibid., p. 15.
96. Ibid., pp. 15–16.
97. TsGAOR, f. 601, op. 1, d. 755, "Osobyi zhurnal Soveta Ministrov 25 oktiabria 1908 goda," pp. 1–13. Stolypin's statement, pp. 1–2.
98. Ibid., p. 16.
99. Ibid., p. 17.
100. Ibid.
101. Ibid.
102. B. V. Anan'ich et al., *Krizis samoderzhaviia v Rossii, 1895–1917* (Leningrad: Nauka, 1984), pp. 464–465.
103. TsGAOR, f. 601, op. 1, d. 755, p. 17.
104. Ibid., p. 18.
105. FO 371/729, p. 147.
106. Some of the documents on the German "ultimatum": Ö-U A, II, 72; Notovich, "Iz perepiski," p. 188; FO 371/755, pp. 48, 361; Polivanov, *Iz dnevnikov*, p. 64.
107. GP 26/1, p. 81, n.
108. See, e.g., HHSA, PA I, 485, pp. 859–862. Polivanov, *Iz dnevnikov*, p. 59.
109. FO 371/752, pp. 111–112.
110. See HHSA, Berchtold Nachlass, diary, p. 238.
111. Ö-U A, II, 70; on these differences, see also Ö-U A, I, 604–605.
112. Polivanov, *Iz dnevnikov*, p. 59; Notovich, "Iz perepiski," 188; FO 371/755, p. 48.
113. FO 371/729, p. 164.
114. FO 371/755, p. 382; S. D. Sazonov, *Vospominaniia* (Paris, 1927), p. 21.
115. A. V. Bogdanovich, *Tri poslednikh samoderzhtsa: Dnevnik A. V. Bogdanovich* (Moscow and Leningrad, 1924), pp. 460, 458.
116. Polivanov, *Iz dnevnikov*, pp. 52–53.
117. Bestuzhev, *Bor'ba*, p. 262.
118. Ibid., pp. 262–263.
119. *Gosudarstvennyi Duma: Stenograficheskii otchet, 3 sozyv, chast' I, sessiia vtoraia*, cols. 2616–2630.
120. Ibid., cols. 2625–2626.
121. GP 25/2, p. 352.
122. FO 371/729, p. 165.
123. FO 371/752, p. 118; HHSA, PA XII, 357, p. 292.
124. FO 371/733, p. 253.
125. See, e.g., Michel de Taube, *La politique russe d'avant-guerre* (Paris, 1928), pp. 229–230.
126. MAE, NS, R, 18, p. 6.
127. Ibid., p. 61.
128. Ibid., p. 188; FO 800/337, p. 325.
129. Geoffrey Hosking, *The Russian Constitutional Experiment: Government and Duma, 1907–1914* (London: Cambridge University Press, 1973), p. 93.

## 7. The Apogee of Stolypin's Chairmanship

1. On this issue, see V. S. Diakin, *Samoderzhavie, burzhuaziia, i dvorianstvo, 1907–1911gg.* (Leningrad: Nauka, 1975), pp. 134–136; Geoffrey Hosking, *The Russian Constitutional Experiment: Government and Duma, 1907–1914* (London: Cambridge University Press, 1973), chap. 4.
2. A. V. Bogdanovich, *Tri poslednikh samoderzhtsa: Dnevnik A. V. Bogdanovich* (Moscow and Leningrad, 1924), p. 461.
3. HHSA, PA, X, 132, p. 126.
4. MAE, NS, R, 19bis, p. 55; Ö-U A, II, 254.
5. See FO 371/729, p. 121; FO 800/337, p. 317; HHSA, PA X, 134, p. 98.
6. FO 371/729, p. 130.
7. Ibid., p. 129; FO 800/337, p. 317; HHSA, PA X, 134, pp. 90–95; MAE, Papiers de Panafieu, 1909, dispatches 135, 136.
8. Bogdanovich, *Tri poslednikh samoderzhtsa*, p. 480.
9. "Dnevnik Bobrinskogo," KA 26, 137.
10. TsGAOR, f. 543, op. 1, d. 528.
11. Ibid., p. 6.
12. Ibid., pp. 7–8.
13. Ibid., pp. 2ob.–3.
14. Ibid., p. 9.
15. Bogdanovich, *Tri poslednikh samoderzhtsa*, p. 480.
16. See Hosking, *Constitutional Experiment*, p. 96.
17. See, e.g., GP, 26/2, p. 798; Ö-U A, II, 379; FO 371/733, pp. 23–24.
18. GP 26/2, p. 798.
19. FO 371/730, p. 707.
20. GP 26/2, pp. 823–827, 834–836.
21. FO 371/733, pp. 23–25.
22. Hélène Izwolsky, ed., *Au service de la Russie* (Paris, 1937), II, 225.
23. Ibid.; Michel de Taube, *La politique russe d'avant-guerre* (Paris, 1928), p. 237; FO 371/729, p. 141.
24. See MAE, NS, Allemagne, 62, pp. 54–55, enclosure from the *Lokal Anzeiger*.
25. S. D. Sazonov, *Vospominaniia* (Paris, 1927), p. 23.
26. Ibid., pp. 22–23.
27. HHSA, PA X, 135/2, pp. 101–102.
28. For sketches of Sazonov, see D. I. Abrikosov, *Memoirs*, manusript in BAR, pp. 133–134; GP 26/2, p. 809, second footnote; Taube, *La politique*, pp. 248–251; MAE, NS, R, 19bis, p. 113.
29. HHSA, PA X, 135/2, p. 454; see also MAE, NS, R, 42bis, p. 161; Iu. Ia. Solov'ev, *Vospominaniia diplomata, 1893–1922* (Moscow, 1959), p. 216.
30. Bogdanovich, *Tri poslednikh samoderzhtsa*, p. 480.
31. HHSA, PA X, 137, pp. 149–150; FO 371/1214, p. 346.
32. HHSA, PA X, 137, p. 139.
33. On these talks see GP 27/2, pp. 840–841; MAE, NS, R, 40, pp. 44–45.
34. GP 27/2, pp. 856–857.
35. MAE, NS, R, 40, p. 145; FO 371/1213, pp. 5–6.

36. *Volga,* 1 October 1909.
37. MAE, NS, R, 40, p. 145.
38. H. Izwolsky, *Au service,* II, 304.
39. Sazonov appeared to agree strongly with Stolypin in these matters. Sazonov, *Vospominaniia,* pp. 36–37.
40. HHSA, PA X, 134, p. 356. Here Berchtold recalled that Charykov's activity during the crisis had sought "to paralyze" Izvolskii's *Abenteuerpolitik.*
41. GP 27/1, p. 160.
42. Ibid., pp. 163–164.
43. See, e.g., Bestuzhev, "Bor'ba v Rossii po voprosam vneshnei politiki nakanune pervoi mirovoi voiny (1910–1914 gg.)," *Istoricheskie Zapiski,* vol. 75 (1965), 54–57; A. Rossos, *Russia and the Balkans: Inter-Balkan Rivalries and Russian Foreign Policy, 1908–1914* (Toronto: University of Toronto Press, 1981), chaps. 1, 2; E. C. Helmreich, *The Diplomacy of the Balkan Wars, 1912–1913* (Cambridge, Mass: Harvard University Press, 1938), chaps. 2, 3; Eric Thaden, *Russia and the Balkan Alliance of 1912* (State College, Penn.: Pennsylvania State University Press, 1965), chaps. 3, 4.
44. Rossos, *Russia and the Balkans,* p. 4.
45. FO 371/733, p. 25.
46. See Hosking, *Constitutional Experiment,* chap. 5; Diakin, *Samoderzhavie, burzhuaziia, i dvorianstvo,* chap. 10; and Francis William Wcislo, *Reforming Rural Russia: State, Local Society, and National Politics, 1855–1914* (Princeton: Princeton University Press, 1990), pp. 281–284.
47. Hosking, *Constitutional Experiment,* p. 133; Wcislo, *Reforming Rural Russia,* p. 283.
48. Cited in Wcislo, *Reforming Rural Russia,* p. 283.
49. TsGIA, f. 1662, op. 1, d. 325, p. 1.
50. Ibid.
51. V. N. Kokovtsev, *Iz moego proshlogo* (Paris: Mouton, 1969), I, 458.
52. A. V. Zenkovskii, *Pravda o Stolypine* (New York, 1957), p. 70. Zenkovskii's claim for the authenticity of this report was verified in this volume by Stolypin's daughter and his associate A. F. Meyendorf.
53. Ibid., p. 112.
54. Ibid., pp. 110–111.
55. A. A. Polivanov, *Iz dnevnikov i vospominanii po dozhnosti voennogo ministra i ego pomishchnika* (Moscow, 1924), p. 100.
56. M. A. Taube, *Vospominaniia,* manuscript in BAR, p. 200, and *La politique,* pp. 248–249.
57. Abrikosov, *Memoirs,* pp. 133–134.
58. On Gartvig, see Rossos, *Russia and the Balkans,* pp. 50–51.
59. See especially, *Materialy po istorii franko-russkikh otnoshenii za 1910–1914 gg.* (Moscow, 1922).
60. Taube, *Vospominaniia,* p. 201. On Sazonov, see MAE, NS, R, 19bis, p. 113: "Sazonov makes no mystery of his pan-Slav tendencies and . . . his criticism spares no allied nation when it appears that French policy does not blindly favor Russian intentions"; GP 26/2, p. 809, second footnote, where the German envoy to the Holy See calls Sazonov a *Starkrusse.*

## 8. The Unraveling of United Government

1. FO, 371/2091, pp. 121–122. Sir George Buchanan is citing Sazonov.
2. S. D. Sazonov, *Vospominaniia* (Paris, 1927), p. 246.
3. TsGIA, f. 1662, op. 1, d. 325, p. 2.
4. Kokovtsev's service record, in TsGIA, f. 560, op. 26, d. 911, p. 67.
5. V. A. Krivoshein, *A. V. Krivoshein (1857–1921 gg.): Ego znachenie v istorii Rossii v nachale XX veka* (Paris, n.p., 1973), p. 169.
6. V. N. Kokovtsev, *Iz moego proshlogo* (Paris: Mouton, 1969), II, 7.
7. M. A. Taube, *Vospminaniia,* manuscript in BAR, p. 174.
8. Francis William Wcislo, *Reforming Rural Russia: State, Local Society, and National Politics* (Princeton: Princeton University Press, 1990), p. 285. See also, Geoffrey Hosking, *The Russian Constitutional Experiment: Government and Duma, 1907–1914* (London: Cambridge University Press, 1973), pp. 182–183.
9. V. A. Sukhomlinov, *Vospominaniia* (Berlin: Russkoe Universal'noe Izdatel'stvo, 1924), p. 217; Taube, *Vospominaniia,* p. 172; V. I. Gurko, *Features and Figures of the Past: Government and Public Opinion under Nicholas II* (Stanford: Stanford University Press, 1939), pp. 517–518, 536; Hosking, *Constitutional Experiment,* pp. 197–199; Krivoshein, *A. V. Krivoshein,* pp. 171–172.
10. *Inventarstück,* HHSA, PA X, 137, p. 139.
11. MAE, NS, R, 21, pp. 103–105.
12. I. S. Galkin, "Demarsh Charykova v 1911g. i pozitsiia evropeiskikh derzhav," in V. V. Al'tman, ed., *Iz istorii obshchestvennykh dvizhenii i mezhdunarodnykh otnoshenii* (Moscow: Nauka, 1957), p. 639.
13. *Materialy po istorii franko-russkikh otnoshenii* (Moscow, 1922), pp. 121–122.
14. DDF, 2, XIV, 632.
15. MAE, Papiers de Panafieu, 1911, dispatch 283.
16. DDF, 2, XIV, 647–648, and de Selves's answer of 15 October, in which the latter notes, "Ni ici, ni à Pétersbourg, le Gouvernement russe ne nous a exposé un plan aussi considérable," p. 659.
17. MAE, Papiers de Panafieu, 1911, dispatch 283.
18. TsGAOR, f. 601, op. 1, d. 1267, pp. 20–21.
19. TsGIA, f. 1276, op. 1, d. 29, draft letter, pp. 261–265, and final version, pp. 265–268.
20. Ibid., p. 261.
21. Ibid.
22. Ibid., p. 262.
23. The comments on Lamzdorf and Izvolskii were inserted in pencil in the council chancellery copy, ibid., p. 266.
24. Ibid., pp. 262–263.
25. This sentence occurs in the draft but not in the final copy, which merely states, "The circumstances connected with this event," ibid., p. 266.
26. Ibid., p. 263. In the final version, Kokovtsev noted that Sazonov continued to consult Stolypin "at least on the chief questions of our foreign policy," p. 266ob.
27. Ibid., p. 263.
28. Ibid., p. 264.

29. Ibid., p. 264ob.
30. Ibid.
31. A. A. Polivanov, *Iz dnevnikov i vospominanii po dozhnosti voennogo ministra i ego pomishchnika* (Moscow, 1924), p. 107.
32. TsGAOR, f. 601, op. 1, d. 1267, pp. 20ob.–21.
33. DDF, 3, I, 318, 323; Ö-U A, III, 687; GP 30/1, p. 250.
34. MAE, NS, R, 21, p. 246; HHSA, PA X, 138, pp. 55–56; Bericht 10A-G, Thurn to Berchtold, 1/14 March 1912. All of these reports note Sazonov's displeasure with Charykov.
35. See, e.g., Ö-U A, III, 379.
36. V. I. Gurko, *Features*, p. 536.
37. Polivanov, *Iz dnevnikov*, p. 76.
38. Sukhomlinov, *Vospominaniia*, pp. 217, 220; Kokovtsev, *Iz moego proshlogo*, II, 68–69.
39. Kokovtsev, *Iz moego proshlogo*, II, 61.
40. Ibid., pp. 51, 59–60. In the latter instance, Kokovtsev makes his point through an extended comparison of Sukhomlinov and the more professional Polivanov.
41. Ibid., pp. 68–69.
42. Ibid., p. 109.
43. See FO 371/1468, p. 259; A. Nekludoff, *Diplomatic Reminiscences before and during the World War, 1911–1917* (London: John Murray, 1929), p. 79.
44. A. L. Sidorov, "Interesnaia nakhodka (delo 'Kokovtseva')," *Voprosy Istorii*, vol. 39, no. 2 (1964), 98.
45. Kokovtsev, *Iz moego proshlogo*, II, 83; Sidorov, "Interesnaia nakhodka," p. 98.
46. Kokovtsev, *Iz moego proshlogo*, II, 85.
47. Ibid., p. 31.
48. Ibid., pp. 73–74.
49. Ibid., p. 84.
50. Ibid., p. 88.
51. Taube, *Vospominaniia*, p. 184.
52. A. Popov, ed., "Pervaia balkanskaia voina," KA 15, 3, 14, 19; FO 370/1470, p. 230, "It was only in the Near East that Monsieur Kokovtsoff saw any danger of troubles arising that might lead to international complications, though even here he was inclined to be optimistic," since he felt that Bulgaria would not act without Russian permission; BAR, P. S. Botkin Collection, telegram from Nekliudov, 12 April 1912; HHSA, Berchtold Nachlass, diary MSS, III, 190; GP 31, pp. 439–440.
53. Sazonov, *Vospominaniia*, p. 64; Nekludoff, *Reminiscences*, p. 55; MAE, NS, R, 41, pp. 270–271.
54. On the details of the treaty, see the French source cited in the previous note; Popov, "Pervaia balkanskaia voina," KA 15; and Rossos, *Russia and the Balkans*, appendix.
55. Popov, "Pervaia balkanskaia voina," p. 45; Taube, *La politique*, p. 280.
56. On the making of these treaties, see Rossos, *Russia and the Balkans*, chaps. 1, 2.
57. Popov, "Pervaia balkanskaia voina," KA 15, 13, 14.
58. MAE, NS, R, 41, pp. 270–271; *Materialy po istorii franko-russkikh otnoshenii*, p. 255.

59. FO 371/1504, p. 112.
60. Popov, "Pervaia balkanskaia voina," KA 15, 23; FO 371/1498, telegram, Buchanan to Grey, 17 September 1912 N.S.
61. Cited in E. C. Helmreich, *The Diplomacy of the Balkan Wars, 1912–1913* (Cambridge, Mass: Harvard University Press, 1938), p. 114.
62. FO 371/1500, p. 251.
63. GP 33, p. 190.
64. Hosking, *Constitutional Experiment*, p. 184.
65. By 1910, press reports formed an independent class of diplomatic correspondence, MAE, NS, R, pp. 18–23.
66. Cited in Helmreich, *Diplomacy of the Balkan Wars*, p. 103.
67. HHSA, PA XII, 383, Bericht A-F, Szillasy to Berchtold, 25 September/8 October 1912.
68. "Pervaia balkanskaia voina, prodolzhenie," KA 16, 15.
69. See HHSA, PA XII, 383, Szillasy to Berchtold, 25 September/8 October 1912; HHSA, PA XII, 484, p. 406. Kokovtsev was so concerned that he told Thurn he was going to initiate a countercampaign in the official press; MAE, NS, Turquie, 245, p. 173, and attached clippings from the Moscow press; GP 33, pp. 384–386.
70. MAE, NS, R, 22, p. 108; GP 33, p. 384–385.
71. FO 371/1504, pp. 178, 187–188.
72. Ibid., p. 460; FO 371/1505, p. 294.
73. Ö-U A, IV, 779–780.
74. Ibid., pp. 835–836.
75. MAE, NS, Turquie, 245, p. 95.
76. MAE, NS, Turquie, 244, p. 99; FO 371/1513, text of 10 November 1912 N.S., telegram from Sazonov to Gartvig, forwarded to the Foreign Office by Benkendorf, 18 November 1912 N.S.
77. GP 33, p. 335; FO 371/1513, p. 370.
78. FO 371/1514, pp. 140, 181.
79. Ö-U A, IV, 897.
80. HHSA, PA XII, 382, pp. 431–432.
81. See, e.g., FO 371/1743, "Russia: Annual Report, 1912," pp. 456–457.
82. Ö-U A, IV, 794.
83. D. C. B. Lieven, *Russia and the Origins of the First World War* (New York: St. Martin's, 1983), p. 91.
84. G. N. Trubetskoi, "Nekotorye itogi russkoi vneshnei politiki," in P. Riabushinskii, ed., *Velikaia Rossiia* (St. Petersburg, 1911), II, 323.
85. Kriegsministerium Praesidium, Reserviert 252, pp. 1–3.
86. HHSA, PA XII, 395, pp. 562–567; Kriegsministerium Praesidium, Reserviert 182, Hohenlohe to Kriegsministerium, 16 October 1912 N.S.
87. FO 371/1516, p. 70.
88. FO 371/1515, secret telegram, Bax-Ironside (Sofia) to Grey, 22 November 1912 N.S. This information was attributed to Guchkov.
89. A. V. Ignat'ev, *Russko-angliiskie otnosheniia nakanune pervoi mirovoi voiny* (Moscow: Izdatel'stvo Sotsial'no-Ekonomicheskoi Literatury, 1962), p. 155.
90. Kokovtsev, *Iz moego proshlogo,* II, 128.

91. Ibid., p. 129.
92. Ibid., pp. 122–125.
93. Ibid., p. 125.
94. Taube, *La politique,* p. 281. Taube misdates the incident, but his description corresponds to that given by Kokovtsev.
95. FO 371/1505, p. 551; FO 371/1506, p. 245; MAE, NS, Turquie, 245, p. 67; MAE, NS, Turquie, 146, pp. 100, 102, 181.
96. MAE, NS, Turquie, 245, p. 167; Kriegsministerium Praesidium, Reserviert 252, pp. 1–2.
97. MAE, NS, R, 22, "Revue de la presse," pp. 144–146.
98. HHSA, PA XII, 395, pp. 565–567; Kriegsministerium Praesidium, Reserviert 252, Hohenlohe to Kriegsministerium, 19 November 1912 N.S.
99. Ignat'ev, *Anglo-russkie otnosheniia,* p. 155.
100. *Gosudarstvennyi Duma: Stenograficheskii otchet, 4 sozyv, sessiia vtoraia,* cols. 266ff.; see also, HHSA, PA XII, 396, p. 49; MAE, NS, Turquie, 250, p. 84; FO 371/1774, p. 84.
101. Kokovtsev, *Iz moego proshlogo,* II, 143.
102. Ibid., p. 155.
103. Ibid., pp. 155–156.
104. Ibid., p. 153.
105. Ibid.
106. Krivoshein, *A. V. Krivoshein,* pp. 170–174; Taube, *Vospominaniia,* pp. 171–173.
107. Hosking, *Constitutional Experiment,* chap. 7.
108. Ibid., p. 200; Kokovtsev, *Iz moego proshlogo,* II, 166.
109. MAE, NS, Turquie, 252, pp. 262–263, describing a conversation with A. D. Brianchaninov, a Kadet on a tour of the Balkans.
110. MAE, NS, Turquie, 251, p. 9; FO 371/1518, p. 422. Both reports cite these expressions from *Novoe Vremia* and *Svet.*
111. Kriegsministerium Praesidium, Reserviert 137, Hohenlohe to Kriegsministerium, 10 May 1913 N.S.; HHSA, PA X, 139/1, telegram, Thurn to Ballhausplatz, 6 April 1913 N.S.; MAE, NS, R, 4, pp. 246–247. All of these reports remarked on the participation of uniformed members of the armed forces in these demonstrations.
112. Sazonov, *Vospominaniia,* pp. 87, 92, 104.
113. Ibid., p. 87; HHSA, PA X, 139/1, p. 63–64; FO 371/1811, file 16054, Buchanan to Grey, 5 April 1913 N.S.
114. Sazonov, *Vospominaniia,* p. 93; GP 35, p. 50, n., p. 65.
115. Cited in *Vostochnyi vopros vo vneshnei politike Rossii* (Moscow, 1978), p. 358.
116. Ia. Zakher, "Konstantinopol' i prolivy," KA 7, 38–39.
117. MAE, NS, Turquie, 158, pp. 133–134; GP 38, pp. 208–209.
118. MAE, NS, Turquie, Revue de la presse, pp. 168–169.
119. FO 371/1847, 54365, file 49385, O'Beirne to Grey, 1 December 1913 N.S.
120. BDOW, X/1, p. 365.
121. MAE, NS, Turquie, 158, pp. 136, 138; GP 38, pp. 212–217; Sazonov, *Vospominaniia,* pp. 144ff.; Kokovtsev, *Iz moego proshlogo,* vol. 2, pp. 217ff.
122. "Vsepoddanneishii otchet Predsedatelia Soveta Ministrov, Ministra Finansov

V. N. Kokovtseva o ego poezdke za granitsei," in *Materialy po istorii franko-russkikh otnoshenii,* 609–625.

123. Ibid., p. 610.
124. Ibid.
125. GP 38, p. 215.
126. *Materialy po istorii franko-russkikh otnoshenii,* p. 624; GP 38, pp. 216–217.
127. Kokovtsev, *Iz moego proshlogo,* II, 219–220.
128. On the general course of the crisis and the attendant negotiations, see BDOW X/1 in particular.
129. A copy of this report is in BAR, Sazonoff Collection.
130. Ibid., 1st quarto, 1.
131. Ibid., 2d quarto, 2.
132. Ibid., 3.
133. Ibid., 3d quarto, 1–2.
134. Ibid.
135. Conference journal in Zakher, "Konstantinopol'," KA 7, 46–49.
136. Ibid., p. 47.
137. Ibid., p. 48.
138. Ibid., pp. 48–49.
139. GP 38, pp. 303–304.
140. BDOW, X/1, 397, which conveys a highly detailed description of public response to the crisis.
141. Kokovtsev, *Iz moego proshlogo,* II, 128.
142. Text in Zakher, "Konstantinopol'," pp. 49–50.
143. See Taube's comments, *Vospominaniia,* pp. 208–209.
144. Kokovtsev, *Iz moego proshlogo,* II, 310ff.; FO 371/2091, Buchanan to Grey, 15 February 1914 N.S.; DDF, 3, IX, 446; Hosking, *Constitutional Experiment,* p. 201; Taube, *La politique,* pp. 328–329; Krivoshein, *A. V. Krivoshein,* p. 176; HHSA, PA X, 140/1, p. 87, and Bericht 8 A-F, 31 January/13 February 1914; Nekludoff, *Reminiscences,* pp. 241–244.
145. Kokovtsev, *Iz moego proshlogo,* II, 130.
146. D. Zaslavskii, "Iz perepiski tsarskikh sanovnikov nakanune voiny i revoliutsii," KA 61, 131–132; MAE, NS, R, 53, pp. 245–246.
147. TsGIA, f. 1276, op. 16, d. 60, p. 62ob.
148. Sazonov, *Vospominaniia,* p. 94.
149. Kokovtsev, *Iz moego proshlogo,* II, 128; see also FO 371/1774, p. 84.

## 9. The Decision to Go to War

1. See, e.g., FO 371/2091, pp. 100–103.
2. Copy in BAR, P. L. Bark Collection, box 1, dated 14 February 1914. For an edited translation, see Thomas Riha, *Readings in Russian Civilization,* 3 vols. (Chicago: University of Chicago Press, 1969), II, 465–478.
3. Bark Collection, p. 8.
4. Ibid., pp. 12–15.
5. Ibid., p. 25.
6. Ibid., p. 26.

7. Ibid., p. 27.
8. Ibid., p. 29.
9. Ibid., p. 31.
10. Ibid., p. 32.
11. M. A. Taube, *Vospominaniia,* manuscript in BAR, pp. 208–211. GP 39, p. 547. Prince V. N. Orlov told the German ambassador that he supported the renewal of good ties between Nicholas and Wilhelm; he had seen Germany's cooperation in the Liman von Sanders question as a sign of Germany's desire for the same thing.
12. Taube, *Vospominaniia,* p. 209.
13. See his letters to Orlov, TsGIA, f. 1012, op. 1, d. 50. His distrust of Britain did not rest on arguments of "monarchical solidarity." Instead, as with Gartvig, his outlook seems to have been rooted in the idea that the entente was an English mechanism through which to achieve its traditional aim of blocking Russia's pursuit of goals that remained at crosspurposes with its own.
14. MAE, NS, R, 42, Doulcet to Doumergue, 21 March 1914 N.S.
15. GP 39, pp. 572–577.
16. Ibid., p. 575.
17. Ibid., p. 576.
18. MAE, NS, R, 42, pp. 222–223.
19. BDOW, X/2, 781.
20. MAE, NS, R, 45, p. 145.
21. *Materialy po istorii franko-russkikh otnoshenii* (Moscow, 1924), p. 499.
22. BDOW, X/2, 780–781. See also, DDF, 3, X, 113–114. Paleologue reports on his own audience and on a conversation with Buchanan, who had seen the emperor on the previous day; FO 371/2092, p. 216.
23. BDOW, X/2, 774–821.
24. DDF, 3, X, 113–114.
25. Sazonov, *Vospominaniia,* p. 131.
26. For an excellent account of the July crisis, see D. C. B. Lieven, *Russia and the Origins of the First World War* (New York: St. Martin's Press, 1983), chap. 5. The best collection of relevant primary materials is to be found in "Nachalo voiny 1914 g.: Podennaia zapis' b. ministerstva inostrannykh del," KA 4, 3–62.
27. "Nachalo voiny," KA 4, 7.
28. V. A. Sukhomlinov, *Vospominaniia* (Berlin: Russkoe Universal'noe Izdatel'stvo, 1924), pp. 267–268; Lieven, *Russia and the Origins,* chap 1.
29. P. L. Bark, *Memoirs,* BAR, Bark Collection, chap. 7, p. 7. Lieven, *Russia and the Origins,* pp. 141–144.
30. Bark, *Memoirs,* p. 9.
31. Ibid., pp. 13–15.
32. Ibid.
33. Lieven, *Russia and the Origins,* p. 142.
34. I. V. Bestuzhev, "Osnovnye aspekty vneshnei politiki Rossii nakanune iul'skogo krizisa," in A. L. Sidorov, ed., *Pervaia mirovaia voina* (Moscow: Nauka, 1968), p. 78.
35. Sazonov, *Vospominaniia,* p. 246.
36. Ibid., p. 247.
37. See the English translation of his speech to the Duma in May 1914; BDOW, X/2,

794–795. Nicolson, now in the Foreign Office in London noted on the record that Sazonov may have been too emphatic in his warm comments on increasing cooperation within the Triple Entente.

38. "Nachalo voiny," KA 4, 22.
39. Sazonov, *Vospominaniia*, p. 248.

## Conclusion

1. See Leopold Haimson, "The Problem of Social Stability in Urban Russia," *Slavic Review*, 23 (1964), 619–642, and 24 (1965), 1–22.
2. M. A. Taube, *Vospominaniia*, manuscript in BAR, p. 171.
3. FO 371/2091, pp. 121–122.
4. Andrew Verner, *The Crisis of Russian Autocracy: Nicholas II and the 1905 Revolution* (Princeton: Princeton University Press, 1990).
5. See Marc Raeff, *The Well-Ordered Police-State: Social and Institutional Change through Law in the Germanies and Russia, 1600–1800* (New Haven: Yale University Press, 1983).
6. N. V. Tcharykow, *Glimpses of High Politics through War and Peace, 1855–1921* (London, 1931), p. 253.
7. It has been pointed out to me by Professor Barbara Jelavich that such expressions as Russia's "traditional" interests in the Balkans or its "historic" mission are really shibboleths: examination of the facts of Russian involvement and of the attitudes of Balkan politicians both give the lie to such expressions. However, it must also be recognized that after the Russo-Turkish War, and certainly after the turn of the century, such expressions had become part and parcel of Russian official and unofficial rhetoric on these issues. Whether or not they reflected reality, Russian spokesmen *believed* the phrases did, which is one reason Russians were so sensitive to Austrian action in the area and to Balkan appeals for help.

# Bibliographical Essay

The greatest difficulty for historians of Russian foreign policy has been the chronic inaccessibility of the archives of the Ministry of Foreign Affairs. Only in the late 1980s, and too late for my purposes, was the *Arkhiv vneshnei politiki Rossii* in the Ministry of Foreign Affairs opened to scholars both Soviet and Western. The most important materials here are the personal funds of individual ministers, and the chancellery funds, which are organized year-by-year.

Hence, material for this book was found in the two main Soviet archives known to historians of the imperial period, the Central State Historical Archive in Leningrad (Tsentral'nyi Gosudarstvennyi Istoricheskii Arkhiv: TsGIA), and the Central State Archive of the October Revolution in Moscow (Tsentral'nyi Gosudarstvennyi Arkhiv Oktiabr'skoi Revoliutsii: TsGAOR). The most significant holdings in the latter were funds 543—containing documents gathered at Nicholas's palace in Tsarskoe Selo—and 601, which holds Nicholas's personal papers. The Leningrad archive contains many Russian official documents, including those of the Council of Ministers (fund 1276), the Chancellery of the Ministry of Finances (560, on issues of Far Eastern policy), as well as the personal funds of Witte (1622, which includes much of his correspondence with his deputies in the Far East) and Stolypin (1662, containing little of interest but his notes on his critical audience with Nicholas II in early 1911).

Of great value to this study were the archives of the foreign ministries of the other European Great Powers: the Politisches Archiv in the Haus-, Hof- und Staatsarchiv in Vienna; the Foreign Office records in the Public Record Office in London; and the archives of the Ministère des Affaires Etrangères in Paris. Beyond the most obvious virtue of relaying direct impressions of events as they unfolded, the materials—telegrams, dispatches, personal correspondence, and annual reports—generated by the European embassies, provided other information. Beginning in 1908, the British and French services in particular began to monitor closely the Russian press, both in St. Petersburg and through their consular offices in the provinces. Moreover, each embassy associated with different elite circles in Russian government and society, giving a view of the many currents of opinion in Russian government. With the exception of work by Dominic Lieven (see below), these sources have been inadequately used in examining the domestic context of Russian foreign policy.

One other neglected archival fund is the material available in Columbia University's Bakhmeteff Archive. This archive includes a great many materials of direct interest to the study of Russian foreign policy in the late imperial period. Most important is the S. Iu. Witte Collection, which contains draft stenographic notes of his memoirs—recently published by M. E. Sharpe in a translation by Sidney Harcave—as well as copies of official documents Witte felt to be most germane to the course of Russian policy in the Far East from his appointment as minister of finances to the various postmortem discussions of the war's causes during 1905. Finally, the Witte Collection holds copies of a great deal of his personal correspondence and materials relating to his appointment and tenure as chairman of the Council of Ministers.

In addition to the Witte Collection, the Bakhmeteff archive contains other materials relating to imperial foreign policy. Perhaps most interesting are the various unpublished memoir manuscripts. Most notable among these are the memoirs of M. A. Taube, which differ often significantly from his published version (see below). Also of interest are the memoirs of D. I. Abrikosov—published in edited form by the University of Washington Press in 1964; N. N. Shebeko, Izvolskii's first Duma liaison and later ambassador in Vienna; and S. D. Botkin. Other memoirs of interest for what they have to say about Russian foreign and domestic policy during the years before the Great War are contained in manuscripts by: P. L. Bark, who succeeded Kokovtsev as minister of finances in 1914; I. K. Grigorovich, who served as naval minister under Stolypin; and A. F. Meiendorf, an associate of Stolypin's.

Finally, scattered throughout the personal funds in the Bakhmeteff archive, are documents that shed new light on policy of the time. Much of the fund in L. P. Urusov's name contains important correspondence with Lamzdorf and Izvolskii, dating to Urusov's service as ambassador in Paris and Vienna. P. L. Bark's holdings include some interesting correspondence from the July 1914 crisis and a copy of the Durnovo memorandum.

In the fund of the former assistant minister of internal affairs, and the drafter of the memorandum on the unification of government in 1905, S. E. Kryzhanovskii, is a series of interesting memoir-essays on a variety of issues. In addition, the papers of A. N. Iakhontov, secretary to the Council of Ministers in 1914 and 1915, relate to the decision to go to war in 1914 and to the ministerial crises that confronted the Russian government during the war. Last, the Bakhmeteff archive retains copies of memoranda by S. D. Sazonov, including his reflections on solutions to the Liman crisis in December 1913.

Of course, many important primary materials concerning both the origins of the Great War and the decline of the autocratic order were published in the decades between the two world wars. In the case of the former, various European states sought to exculpate themselves in the "war guilt" debate springing from the peace settlement after World War I. This activity resulted in the publication of multivolume documentary collections by each of the major powers, except the Soviet government: the British government put out G. P. Gooch and H. N. Temperley, eds., *British Documents on the Origins of the War* (London: H. M. Stationery Office, 1927–1938); the Quai d'Orsay published *Documents Diplomatiques Françaises* (Imprimerie Nationale, Paris, 1929–1936); Germany produced *Die Grosse Politik der Europäischen Kabinetten, 1971–1914: Sammlung der diplomatischen akten des Auswärtigen Amtes* (Berlin: Deutsche Veragsgesellschaft für Politik und Geschichte, 1922–1927); and the Austrians printed *Österreich-Ungarns Aussenpolitik, von der Bosnischer Krise 1908 bis zum Kriegsausbruch 1914* (Vienna: Österreicher Bundesverlag, 1930–1936). These collections together convey a remarkably complete picture of the chief developments in European diplomacy from the beginning of the twentieth century until the outbreak of war in 1914.

For its part, the Soviet government was engaged throughout much of the same period in publishing many secret tsarist materials on foreign and domestic policy, so as to discredit further the *ancien régime*. The most common repository for such materials was the journal *Krasnyi Arkhiv*, which was published regularly during the 1920s and 1930s. This journal contains materials ranging from diplomatic correspondence to diaries and personal papers, and is indispensable to any history of late imperial Russia.

Also during this period a great many evocative memoirs were written and published by former tsarist statesmen looking to make sense of the events, foreign and domestic, that had transformed their lives so dramatically. The most useful such sources for my purposes are: S. Iu. Vitte, *Vospominaniia* (Moscow: Sotsekgiz, 1960)—a three-volume work edited officially by A. L. Sidorov; V. N. Kokovtsev, *Iz moego proshlogo* (2d ed., Paris: Mouton, 1969)—a two-volume set that has been translated in abbreviated form into English as *Out of My Past* (Stanford: Stanford University Press, 1935); A. P. Iswolsky, *Recollections of a Foreign Minister* (Toronto: Doubleday, 1921), whose correspondence was selected and edited by his daughter Hélène under the title *Au service de la Russie* (Paris, 1937); S. D. Sazonov, *Vospominaniia* (Paris, 1927); Michel de Taube, *La politique russe d'avant-guerre* (Paris, 1928)—informative due to its author's perspective and his service in the Ministry of Foreign Affairs; N. V. Tcharykow, *Glimpses of High Politics through War and Peace, 1855–1929* (London, 1931); and V. I. Gurko, *Features and Figures of the Past* (Stanford: Stanford University Press, 1939). These are but a few of the very rich memoirs on these topics and this period.

The secondary literatures drawn on in the present study are very broad and continue to grow. Only those works that contributed directly to my own thinking and approach to the problems discussed are cited. Given the persistence of historical and contemporary attitudes about Russian or Soviet "expansionism," there are surprisingly few works on the general history of Russian foreign policy. The most helpful of these is Barbara Jelavich's *St. Petersburg and Moscow: Tsarist and Soviet Foreign Policy, 1814–1974* (Bloomington: Indiana University Press, 1974). There is another older collection of essays on elements of continuity in Russian and Soviet foreign policy, Ivo Lederer, ed., *Russian Foreign Policy: Essays in Historical Perspective* (New Haven: Yale University Press, 1962); although many of the essays are now dated, they are all characterized by a provocative polemical flair that is useful for rethinking the factors behind Russian foreign policy. Finally, George Kennan has written several books on Russian foreign policy during the empire's last quarter-century of existence; the most relevant of these is *The Fateful Alliance: France, Russia, and the Coming of the First World War* (New York: Pantheon Books, 1984). Like Jelavich, he examines Russian policy within the methodological framework of traditional diplomatic history, giving a clear account of the main actors and events in the shaping of Russia's career in Europe.

Recently published are two major works on Russian foreign policy, which deal with larger questions of interpretation and relatively long periods of time. These studies have had marked effects on the discussion of Russian foreign policy during the years before the Great War and have influenced my book strongly, even on points of disagreement. The first of these is Dietrich Geyer's *Der russische Imperialismus: Studien über den Zusammenhang von innerer und auswärtiger Politik, 1860–1914* (Göttingen: Vandenhoeck und Ruprecht, 1977), an English translation of which has been published by Yale University Press under the title *Russian Imperialism: The Interaction of Domestic and Foreign Policy, 1860–1914* (1987). Geyer's is a breathtakingly ambitious attempt to apply the historical techniques first developed by Fritz Fischer and other German historians of the *Kaiserreich* to the policy of imperial Russia at a time of foreign flux and domestic social and economic transformation. The breadth of the sourcework—see the exhaustive bibliography—and the interpretive innovations introduced by Geyer, if not always apposite for the Russian situation, command respect and render his book an absolute requirement for any student of Russian foreign policy. Although shorter in length, Dominic Lieven's *Russia and the Origins of the First World War* (New York: St. Martin's Press, 1983), has probably been the most widely read study in its field since it came out. Lucid, well-researched, and cogently argued, Lieven's study reflects his broader interests in the cultural and institutional milieu of Russian officialdom in the last years of the empire. Lieven's account provides a succinct enumeration and description of the various institutional and social actors involved in shaping Russian foreign policy preceding World War I, although according more weight to Nicholas II and his foreign ministers in the determination of policy than the present study would find warranted.

If there are few general works on Russian foreign policy, this is not the case with examinations of specific aspects of that policy. The origins of the Russo-Japanese War have long been examined from a variety of perspectives. Still the masterwork on the topic is B. A. Romanov's *Rossiia v Manchzhurii (1892–1906)* (Leningrad: Izdatel'stvo Instituta Dal'nego Vostoka, 1928), which draws heavily on relevant archival materials. Interesting for its author's *apologia* for Witte's policies is B. B. Glinskii's *Prolog russko-iaponskoi voiny: Materialy iz arkhiva grafa S. Iu. Vitte* (Petrograd: Brockgauz-Efron, 1916). There are also several English-language works on this subject, including a University of Michigan Press translation of Romanov. Readers should consult Andrew Malozemoff's posthumous *Russian Far Eastern Policy, 1881–1904* (Berkeley: University of California Press, 1958), and J. N. Westwood, *Russia against Japan, 1904–1905 : A New Look at the Russo-Japanese War* (Albany: State University of New York Press, 1986).

Any discussion of the literature on Russian policy after the revolution of 1905 has to begin with the work of I. V. Bestuzhev, and specifically his *Bor'ba po voprosam vneshnei politiki v Rossii, 1906–1910* (Moscow: Nauka, 1961). Despite flaws of interpretation, it is the most influential work among Western and Soviet historians currently researching Russian policy during the Duma monarchy. For more recent Soviet discussions of Russian policy during these years, readers should consult the many works of A. V. Ignat'ev. One older Soviet work that is particularly noteworthy for the quality of its archival work and treatment of its topic is I. I. Astaf'ev, *Russko-germanskie diplomaticheskie otnosheniia, 1905–1911* (Moscow: Izdatel'stvo Moskovskogo Universiteta, 1972). Finally, the young Soviet scholar A. V. Georgiev is undertaking the first serious examination of decision-making structures and procedures within the Ministry of Foreign Affairs during these years. While he has published chiefly articles on his research, a monograph on his research should soon see the light.

In the West, this period of Russian foreign policy has been of particular interest, given the role of Russian interests in the Balkans in helping precipitate the outbreak of war in 1914. While there are many titles treating this topic, readers would be well served to consult, among others: Andrew Rossos, *Russia and the Balkans, 1908–1914* (Toronto: University of Toronto Press, 1981); and Edward Thaden, *Russia and the Balkan Alliance of 1912* (State College, Penn.: Pennsylvania State University Press, 1965). On the Bosnian crisis, Bernadotte Schmitt's *The Annexation of Bosnia, 1908–1909* (New York: MacMillan, 1937) is a standard, as is W. M. Carlgren, *Iswolsky und Aehrenthal vor der bosnischen Annexionskrise, Russische und oesterreichisch-ungarisch Balkanpolitik, 1906–1908* (Uppsala: Almquist, 1955).

Unfortunately, there is little biographical literature on many of the figures discussed in this book. One exception to this rule is Nicholas II, who has been the subject of a great deal of varying types of attention. Of the many works on the last tsar, the two most helpful—from different points of view—are S. S. Ol'denburg, *Tsarstvovanie Imperatora Nikolaia II* (Munich, 1949), 2 vols., and Andrew Verner's new study, *The Crisis of Russian Autocracy: Nicholas II and the 1905 Revolution* (Princeton: Princeton University Press, 1990), which provides interesting psychological background, while differing considerably in emphasis from the perspective I give here. Witte is examined in Theodore von Laue's *Sergei Witte and the Industrialization of Russia* (New York: Atheneum, 1969), while Stolypin is discussed, not entirely satisfyingly, in M. S. Conroy's *Peter Arkad'evich Stolypin: Practical Politics in Late Tsarist Russia* (Boulder, Colo.: Westview Press, 1976). Those readers interested in Stolypin should also look at A. V. Zenkovskii's *Pravda o Stolypine* (New York, 1957); A. S. Izgoev, *P. A. Stolypin* (Moscow, 1912), and M. P. Bok, *Vospominaniia o moem otse P. A. Stolypine* (New York: Izdatel'stvo imeni Chekhova, 1953).

There is a voluminous literature on the development of Russian domestic politics during the Duma period as the informing context of the making of Russian foreign policy. One work directly about this problem is a study by Kaspar Ferenczi, *Aussenpolitik und Öffentlichkeit in Russland, 1906–1912* (Husum: Matthiesen, 1982)—a well-researched and informative account with debts to both Geyer and Bestuzhev. On the domestic politics of this period in general, I drew heavily on many works, of which only a few can be mentioned here. Perhaps most important in shaping my perspectives on "3 June Russia" were: Geoffrey Hosking, *The Russian Constitutional Experiment: Government and Duma, 1907–1914* (London: Cambridge University Press, 1973); B. V. Anan'ich et al., *Krizis samoderzhaviia v Rossii, 1895–1914* (Nauka: Leningrad, 1984); Leopold Haimson, *The Politics of Rural Russia, 1905–1914* (Bloomington: Indiana University Press, 1979); and V. S. Diakin, *Samoderzhavie, burzhuaziia, i dvorianstvo, 1907–1911gg.* (Leningrad: Nauka, 1975).

Of equal importance for this book is the increasingly rich literature on the development of Russian officialdom as a professional, institutional, and social group with its own peculiar and evolving worldview. Many of these works were not cited directly in the preceding discussion, but they are important as background for understanding the views expressed by such critical actors as Witte, Stolypin, and Kokovtsev. The first systematic attempt to examine the emergence of a bureaucratic *mentalité* was George Yaney's *The Systematization of Russian Government* (Champaign-Urbana, Ill.: University of Illinois Press, 1973). Since the publication of that work, the treatment of officialdom has been considerably refined and deepened in such studies as: Walter Pintner and Don Rowney, eds., *Russian Officialdom: The Bureaucratization of Russian Society from the Seventeenth to the Twentieth Century* (Chapel Hill: University of North Carolina Press, 1980); Daniel Orlovsky, *The Limits of Reform: The Ministry of Internal Affairs in Imperial Russia, 1802–1881* (Cambridge, Mass.: Harvard University Press, 1981); Richard Wortman, *The Development of a Russian Legal Consciousness* (Chicago: University of Chicago Press, 1976); W. B. Lincoln, *In the Vanguard of Reform: Russia's Enlightened Bureaucrats, 1825–1861* (De Kalb, Ill.: Northern Illinois University Press, 1982); and Francis William Wcislo, *Reforming Rural Russia: State, Local Society, and National Politics, 1855–1914* (Princeton: Princeton University Press, 1990).

# Index

Abaza, A. M., 31, 42, 44, 45, 46, 52, 55, 56, 57, 58, 59, 68, 72, 73, 82; on Far Eastern policy, 46–47, 54, 70

Aehrenthal, Count Alois, 113, 114, 120, 122, 126, 127, 129, 130, 131–132, 134, 135, 138, 139, 141–142, 144, 147, 151, 160, 248

Alekseev, Admiral E. I., 31, 41, 43, 54, 55, 63, 65, 72, 82: on policy in the Far East, 25, 43, 58, 60, 70; and Bezobrazov, 44, 49, 59; as Viceroy, 61, 64, 68, 69

Alexander I, 11, 32, 82, 86, 238

Alexander III, 10, 13, 15, 16, 17, 32, 33, 67, 213

Alexander Lycée, 33, 170, 231

Alexander Mikhailovich, Grand Duke, 11, 34, 35, 41, 63

Alexandra Fedorovna, 16, 170, 210

Anglo-Russian agreement on China (1899), 18, 23, 25, 108

Anglo-Russian *entente* (1907), 103, 105, 107, 108, 110, 112, 113, 118, 119, 123, 126, 129, 155–156; treaty negotiations, 108–111, 111–114, 215. *See also* Russia: relations with Great Britain

Austria-Hungary, 122, 127, 128, 130, 136, 138, 145, 156, 169, 204. *See also* Russia: relations with Austria-Hungary

Autocratic power, 5–6, 6, 8, 14, 66, 82, 163–165, 208; arbitrariness [*proizvol*], 6, 211; and law, 82, 86, 89

Balkans, 168–169, 171–172; Balkan alliance (1912), 159–160, 169, 179, 180; wars, 169, 179, 181–186, 189, 205, 217–218.

*See also* Bosnian crisis; Bulgaria; Montenegro; Russia: policy in Balkans; Serbia

Benkendorf, Count A. K., 69–70, 112, 189

Berchtold, Count L., 129, 130, 141, 145, 157, 158

Berlin, Treaty of, 127, 130, 131, 132, 133, 134, 136, 138, 141, 147

Bezobrazov, A. M., 31, 33, 34, 35, 37, 41, 56, 59, 61, 68, 71, 74; on Yalu concession as strategic asset, 34, 36, 44–45, 51, 52, 53; and bureaucracy, ministers, 34, 35, 36, 37, 41, 43, 50–51, 58, 59–61, 62, 63; on Nicholas, 35–36, 52; on Russian policy in Far East, 35–36, 41, 42, 44, 50–51, 60–61, 62; on autocratic power, 37, 55, 61; tour of Far East, 38, 41–46, 49–50, 53; plan for troop movements, 44–46, 60; as state secretary, 51–52, 57

"Bezobrazov and Co.," 11, 32, 33, 45, 50–51, 57, 74, 107

Bezobrazovshchina, 30, 44, 62, 82, 94, 211, 229n1

Birilev, Admiral A. A., 78, 79

Björkö agreement, 77, 78–81, 90, 94, 105, 106, 154

Bosnia-Herzegovina, 102, 113, 127, 129, 130, 138; annexation by Austria-Hungary, 131–133, 134, 135, 136

Bosnian crisis, 3, 103, 110, 124, 127–128, 131, 136–151, 154, 155, 156, 160, 169, 172–173, 175, 179, 189, 196, 204; Russian proposal for European conference, 133, 134, 135, 137, 138, 139, 142; German "ultimatum," 145, 146, 148, 156